the GAY
MILITANTS

the GAY MILITANTS

DONN TEAL

STEIN AND DAY/*Publishers*/**New York**

First published in 1971
Copyright © Donn Teal 1971
Library of Congress Catalog Card No. 72-150228
All rights reserved
Published simultaneously in Canada by Saunders of Toronto Ltd.
Designed by Bernard Schleifer
Printed in the United States of America
Stein and Day/*Publishers*/7 East 48 Street, New York, N.Y. 10017
SBN 8128-1373-1

SECOND PRINTING, 1971

*To whom else but the
world's homosexual
millions, my sisters
and brothers*

ACKNOWLEDGMENTS

This is a book by so many gay militants, as well as old-line homophile leaders, that a comprehensive "thanks" will be difficult. Nevertheless:

The author and the women who collaborated on Chapter 9 wish first to express our appreciation to the gay press—especially to GAY, *The Advocate, Come Out!, Gay Power, Gay Flames, Gay Sunshine, Gay Scene,* the *San Francisco Free Press* (succeeded today by the *San Francisco Gay Free Press*), and QQ magazine—as well as to several homophile newsletters and magazines, including *Vector* and *The Ladder: A Lesbian Review.* Gratitude is due also to the many underground newspapers that have carried news of the gay revolution.

The following gays and straights—an incomplete list at best—merit many thanks, their encouragement and aid having made the book possible:

Sidney Abbott	Foster Gunnison, Jr.	Marty Nixon
Breck Ardery	Gerald Hansen	Jack Nichols
Susie Arensberg	John Heys	Charles Pitts
Tom Ashe	Jerry Hoose	Mike Randall
Richy Aunateau	Steve Ihrig	Marty Robinson
Jack Baker	Michael Itkin	Craig Rodwell
Arthur Bell	Don Jackson	Nathalie Rockhill
Lee Brewster	Franklin Kameny	Marc Rubin
Ken Burdick	Arnie Kantrowitz	Don Rundquist
Angus Cameron	Jim Kepner	Craig Schoonmaker
Madolin Cervantes	John Knoebel	Mark Segal
Jim Clifford	Bob Kohler	Jack Stafford
Ann Close	Michael Kotis	Charles Thorp
Louis Crompton	Steve Kuromiya	Kay Tobin
George Desantis	Barbara Love	Gerald Walker
Tom Doerr	Pat Maxwell	Bill Weaver
Angela Douglas (Key)	Gale McGovern	Henry Wiemhoff
Tommy Dutton	George Mendenhall	Sophie Wilkins
Earl Galvin	Dick Michaels	Pete Wilson
Barbara Gittings	Guy Nassberg	Allen Young

The encouragement of my editor, George Caldwell, at Stein and Day has, needless to say, been invaluable.

The most especial thanks must go to the members of Gay Liberation Front New York and Gay Activists Alliance, who brought the book to life . . .

New York, January 1971
                                                        D.T.

CONTENTS

the GAY
MILITANTS

This is the recent story of an oppressed
American people.
It is told in their words . . .

1

Sheridan Square this weekend looked like something from a William Burroughs novel as the sudden specter of "gay power" erected its brazen head and spat out a fairy tale the likes of which the area has never seen.

—Lucian Truscott IV, in the
Village Voice, July 3, 1969

Village Voice reporter Lucian Truscott's alliteration "forces of faggotry" might have stirred up a revolt equal to those of the previous Friday and Saturday nights when his story reached newsstands Wednesday night, July 2. It jolted awake, instead, an only half-remembered outrage against straight society's bigotries in those older, generally conservative "Boys in the Band" who had been out of town on the weekend of the 27th–28th–29th tanning their thighs at Cherry Grove and the Hamptons. And, as a slur, it posed a challenge to and goal for those younger, $90-a-week gays who'd had to make do with Greenwich Village and who'd seen (the) action. It may have created the gay liberation movement.

Homosexuals had never been so news-favored; *Voice*s probably never sold so fast. It seemed that the Village press, nestled in the heart of the nation's largest gay ghetto, had chosen at last to see America's second-largest minority. (Or was it that the riots had been merely a quarter-block away?) There they were, big black letters: GAY POWER COMES TO SHERIDAN SQUARE. Featured news story—top of right-hand column, front page! Moreover, beside it was FULL MOON OVER THE STONEWALL, a "View from Inside" by Howard Smith, who had accompanied Deputy Inspector Seymour Pine,* instigator, so it would seem, of the police raid on the Stonewall Inn. A raid, by the way, which Pine could only have viewed then as routine. Homophile Action League of Philadelphia later reminisced: [1] "When the New York City plainclothes officers entered the Stonewall Inn at 53 Christopher Street in Greenwich Village on Friday night, June 27,** they had no reason to fear this raid would be different from all the others.

---

* Of the First Division of the New York City police department, and over the Public Morals section.
** Friday night's riot started past midnight, so that June 28 has been designated by homosexuals as Christopher Street Liberation Day.

The police claimed that the reason for the raid was that the bar, which operates as a private club, had been selling liquor without a license. The club was closed, the employees arrested, and the patrons ushered out. But, instead of dissolving into the night, grateful for having escaped the scene of someone else's crime anonymous and unscathed——" Truscott's and Smith's *Voice* coverages are more vividly detailed, if capricious. Their stories, unforgettable to American homosexuals, should be made so to American heterosexuals:

[Truscott] . . . as the patrons trapped inside were released one by one, a crowd started to gather on the street . . . initially a festive gathering, composed mostly of Stonewall boys who were waiting around for friends still inside or to see what was going to happen. Cheers would go up as favorites would emerge from the door, strike a pose, and swish by the detective with a "Hello there, fella." The stars were in their element. Wrists were limp, hair was primped, and reactions to the applause were classic. "I gave them the gay power bit, and they loved it, girls. . . ."

Suddenly the paddywagon arrived and the mood of the crowd changed. Three of the more blatant queens—in full drag—were loaded inside, along with the bartender and doorman, to a chorus of catcalls and boos from the crowd. A cry went up to push the paddywagon over, but it drove away before anything could happen. With its exit, the action waned momentarily. The next person to come out was a dyke, and she put up a struggle—from car to door to car again. . . .

[Smith] . . . Pine ordered the three cars and paddywagon to leave with the prisoners before the crowd became more of a mob. "Hurry back," he added, realizing he and his force of eight detectives, two of them women, would be easily overwhelmed if the temper broke. "Just drop them at the Sixth Precinct and hurry back."

[Truscott] . . . It was at that moment that the scene became explosive. Limp wrists were forgotten. . . .

[Smith] . . . "Pigs!" "Faggot cops!" Pennies and dimes flew. I stood against the door. The detectives held at most a 10-foot clearing. Escalate to nickels and quarters. A bottle. Another bottle. Pine says, "Let's get inside. Lock ourselves inside, it's safer." . . .

In goes me. We bolt the heavy door. The front of the Stonewall is mostly brick except for the windows, which are boarded within by plywood. Inside we hear the shattering of windows, followed by what we imagine to be bricks pounding on the door, voices yelling. The floor shudders at each blow. "Aren't you guys scared?" I say.

"No." But they look at least uneasy.

The door crashes open, beer cans and bottles hurtle in. Pine and his troop rush to shut it. At that point the only uniformed cop among them gets hit with something under his eye. He hollers, and his hand comes away scarlet. It looks a lot more serious than it really is. They are all suddenly furious. Three run out in front to see if they can scare the mob from the door. A hail of coins. A beer can glances off Deputy Inspector Smyth's head.

Pine . . . gathers himself, leaps out into the melee, and grabs someone around the waist, pulling him downward and back into the doorway. They fall. Pine regains hold and drags the elected protester inside by the hair. The door slams again. Angry cops converge on the gay, releasing their anger on this sample from the mob. . . .

[Truscott] . . . It was Dave Van Ronk, who had come from the Lion's Head to see what was going on. . . .

[Smith] . . . Pine is saying, "I saw him throwing somethin," and the guy unfortunately is giving some sass, snidely admits to throwing "only a few coins." The cop who was cut is incensed, yells something like, "So you're the one who hit me!" And while the other cops help, he slaps the prisoner five or six times very hard and finishes with a punch to the mouth. They handcuff the guy as he almost passes out. . . .

[Truscott] . . . Three cops [had been] necessary to get Van Ronk away from the crowd and into the Stonewall. The exit left no cops on the street, and almost by signal the crowd erupted into cobblestone and bottle heaving. The reaction was solid: they were pissed. The trashcan I was standing on was nearly yanked out from under me as a kid tried to grab it for use in the window-smashing melee. From nowhere came an uprooted parking meter— used as a battering ram on the Stonewall door. . . .

[Smith] . . . The door is smashed open again. More objects are thrown in. The detectives locate a fire hose, the idea being to ward off the madding crowd until reinforcements arrive. They can't see where to aim it, wedging the hose in a crack in the door. It sends out a weak stream. We all start to slip on water and Pine says to stop.

By now the mind's eye has forgotten the character of the mob; the sound filtering in doesn't suggest dancing faggots any more. It sounds like a powerful rage bent on vendetta. That was why Pine's singling out of the guy . . . was important. The little force of detectives was beginning to feel fear, and Pine's action clinched their morale again.

A door over to the side almost gives. One cop shouts, "Get away from there or I'll shoot!" It stops shaking. The front door is completely open. One of the big plywood windows gives, and it seems inevitable that the mob will pour in. A kind of tribal adrenaline rush bolsters all of us; they all take out and check pistols. . . . I find a big wrench behind the bar, jam it into my belt like a scimitar. Hindsight: my fear on the verge of being trampled by a mob fills the same dimensions as my fear of being clubbed by the TPF.*

Pine places a few men on each side of the corridor leading away from the entrance. They aim unwavering at the door. One detective arms himself in addition with a sawed-off baseball bat he has found. I hear, "We'll shoot the first motherfucker that comes through the door." . . .

I can only see the arm at the window. It squirts liquid into the room, and a flaring match follows. Pine is not more than 10 feet away. He aims his gun at the figures.

He doesn't fire. The sound of sirens coincides with the whoosh of flames where the lighter fluid was thrown. . . . It was that close. . . .

It had lasted 45 minutes. . . .

* The New York City Tactical Patrol Force, sometimes termed the "riot squad."

Exiting the Stonewall as carloads of police reinforcements arrived, Smith finished taking some notes, then went inside again, to find that "all the mirrors, jukeboxes, phones, toilets, and cigarette machines were smashed. Even the sinks were stuffed and running over. And we say the police did it. The courts will say that [they] are innocent."

Truscott summed up the first night's rioting: "By the time the last cop was off the street Saturday morning, a sign was going up announcing that the Stonewall would reopen that night. It did." *

■

As a bright Saturday developed, the Stonewall, just off Sheridan Square, reminded Villagers of a blackened and abandoned Tara. But with graffiti (mainly in chalk): "Insp. Smyth looted our: jukebox, cig. mach, telephones, safe, cash register and the boys tips"; "They invaded our rights"; "Support Gay Power"; "We are open" . . . (and in the next day or two: "How does he [Smyth] like our TV ** that he looted?"; "Drag Power"; etc.). A current of curious passed, sometimes stopped—apprehensively—in front of the club: straights *and* gays, all with an expression not of anger but, rather, of "I didn't think they (we) had it in them (us)!" One Philadelphia gay who witnessed the riot concluded: "It was our Verdun—they shall not pass and all that." 2 The doubtful had it, however, that the riot had been arranged by "the S.D.S., the C.L.U., the Black Panthers, the White Panthers, the Pink Panthers, rival bars, [or] a homosexual police officer whose roommate went dancing at the Stonewall against the officer's wishes." 3 Gay bargoers gossiped about their brothers' unexpected reaction to the raid, but "It was about time!"; Kevan Liscoe, in a letter published by the *Voice* on July 10 and entitled SCARED NO MORE, was to point out that "The Stonewall raid was not the only reason for incidents occurring on that great and glorious weekend. In the last three weeks five gay bars in the Village area that I know of have been hit by police. . . ." *** Gay Liberation Front member Jerry Hoose recalls today how on June 3 he

* In the newsletter of the Mattachine Society of New York (August 1969), an article, "The Stonewall Riots: The Police Story," based on visits by the Chief of the Morals Squad and Deputy Inspectors Smyth and Pine, among others, to its offices, relates: "The police explained that all they can do is make [a] raid, and impound all the liquor stock, cash registers, and other material that can be considered evidence. They arrest the management, who are booked, have bail set, and get themselves released. The next day, they get a new supply of liquor and open as usual. . . . The police cannot force the place to close down, because they, like everyone else, have the right to be presumed innocent until a court finds them guilty. Thus, by hiring smart lawyers, and postponing the case again and again, the bar can stay in operation for years until their case comes to trial and the court closes it."

** The *New York Mattachine Newsletter* (August 1969) reported a police statement that "The television set was reclaimed by a man who said he had loaned it to the Stonewall management [and] showed the police a receipt . . ."

*** The August 1969 Mattachine newsletter mentioned the raids on the Snake Pit and the Sewer and the closing of the Checkerboard, the Tele-Star, and other clubs in weeks just preceding the Stonewall riots.

and a friend had seen about fifteen paddywagons pull up at a homosexual rendezvous near the docks and that "cops were beating people to the ground!" * Members of the Mattachine Society of New York ** were to spend Sunday evening dispensing a leaflet that denounced this renewed harassment of homosexuals by New York City police—a strong "call to action as well as a protest," according to current president Michael Kotis, and "It did fan the flames." Mattachine was, in effect, predicting retribution by the gay community.

But Friday night's action had been retribution. Mattachine, obviously, and indeed thousands of gays in the city hadn't understood who—some painted and in drag ("The so-called 'straight' looking, manly homosexual stood back and watched the police hammer the effeminate boys . . ."), [4] some stoned or high—had "won" that action. Something still only vaguely comprehended had begun Friday night. That something was retribution. And it was to begin again in a few hours.

[Truscott] . . . Friday night's crowd had returned and was being led in "gay power" cheers by a group of gay cheerleaders. "We are the Stonewall girls/We wear our hair in curls/We have no underwear/We show our pubic hairs!" The crowd was gathered across the street from the Stonewall and was growing with additions of onlookers, Eastsiders, and rough street people who saw a chance for a little action. Though dress had changed from Friday night's gayery to Saturday night street clothes, the scene was a command performance for queers. If Friday night had been pick-up night, Saturday was date night. Hand-holding, kissing, and posing accented each of the cheers with a homosexual liberation that had appeared only fleetingly on the street before. One-liners were as practiced as if they had been used for years. "I just want you all to know," quipped a platinum blond with obvious glee, "that sometimes being homosexual is a big pain in the ass." . . . And on and on.

Writers George White's and Gary Alinder's dogged insistence, later, in successive issues of the *San Francisco Free Press,*[5] *** that "Every homosexual is a potential revolutionary," ". . . potential gay militant," is as debatable now, at the height of the gay liberation movement, as it was the night of June 28–9, 1969. Reporter Truscott noticed that

The generation gap existed even here. Older boys had strained looks on their faces and talked in concerned whispers as they watched the up-and-coming generation take being gay and flaunt it before the masses.

* No citation will be given for material taped by the author.
** Under the executive directorship of Dick Leitsch for several years, MSNY had been the most powerful homosexual organization in the city. It is an independent branch of the Mattachine Foundation, established in Los Angeles in 1950, which later became the Mattachine Society, then dissolved its national structure in the early 1960's.
*** The *San Francisco Free Press,* under the editorship of Marcus Overseth, appeared first in September 1969. By its second issue, on October 1, it was about one third gay-oriented. All-gay in succeeding issues—the third headlined HOMOSEXUAL CIVIL WAR—its last was, undated, in April 1970.

As the "gay power" chants on the street rose in frequency and volume, the crowd grew restless. The front of the Stonewall was losing its attraction, despite efforts by the owners to talk the crowd back into the club. . . .

The people on the street were not to be coerced. "Let's go down the street and see what's happening, girls," someone yelled. And down the street went the crowd, smack into the Tactical Patrol Force,* who had been called earlier to dispense the crowd and were walking west on Christopher from Sixth Avenue. Formed in a line, the TPF swept the crowd back to the corner of Waverly Place, where they stopped. A stagnant situation there brought on some gay tomfoolery in the form of a chorus line facing the line of helmeted and club-carrying cops. Just as the line got into a full kick routine, the TPF advanced again and cleared the crowd of screaming gay powerites down Christopher to Seventh Avenue. . . .

Gays who were there have the story differently. Craig Rodwell, owner of the Oscar Wilde Memorial Book Shop, described [6] how the police "chased people away and they would just go around the block [by way of Gay Street, between Sixth and Seventh, off Christopher] and come in another way." How gays "started taking over the street and stopping cars from coming through"—unless driven by homosexuals. Shouts of "Christopher Street belongs to the queens!" "Liberate Christopher Street!" One car of newlyweds was half lifted, then gays relented and the open-mouthed bride and groom were permitted to drive on. (Following rioting the Wednesday night after, a taxi driver whose car had been jumped died of a heart attack.[7])

Lige Clarke and Jack Nichols, co-columnists of *Screw*,** pronounced undaunted that "The police were scared shitless and the massive crowds of angry protesters chased them for blocks screaming 'Catch them! Fuck them!' " [8]

Truscott becomes unprejudiced again:

. . . The crowd finally dispersed around 3:30 a.m. The TPF had come and they had conquered, but Sunday was already there, and it was to be another story.

Sunday night was a time for watching and rapping. Gone were the "gay power" chants of Saturday, but not the new and open brand of exhibitionism. Steps, curbs, and the park provided props for what amounted to the Sunday

* In an article that the New York Gay Liberation Front newspaper *Come Out!* was later to call "cloyingly cute and contemptuous" (November 14, 1969) and which the *Voice* printed July 10 as TOO MUCH, MY DEAR, Walter Troy Spencer noted the "friction this situation may have generated between the Village's Sixth Precinct, the First Division (who made the initial raid without telling the precinct—a standard procedure) and the TPF, who had to be called in when things got out of hand."

** In their popular "Homosexual Citizen" column in straight-oriented *Screw* since late 1968, Clarke and Nichols have been billed as "male lovers who dig life together. They laugh at silly prejudices and laws that make love a crime and look forward to the day when homosexuals and heterosexuals are happily integrated."

fag follies as returning stars from the previous nights' performances stopped by to close the show for the weekend.

It was slow going. Around 1 a.m. a non-helmeted version of the TPF arrived and made a very cool sweep of the area, getting everyone moving and out of the park. That put a damper on posing and primping, and as the last buses were leaving Jerseyward, the crowd grew thin. Allen Ginsberg and Taylor Mead walked by to see what was happening and were filled in on the previous evenings' activities by some gay activists. "Gay power! Isn't that great!" Allen said. "We're one of the largest minorities in the country—10 per cent, you know. It's about time we did something to assert ourselves."

Ginsberg expressed a desire to visit the Stonewall—"You know, I've never been in there"—and ambled on down the street flashing peace signs and helloing the TPF. It was a relief and a kind of joy to see him on the street. He lent an umbrella of serenity to the scene with his laughter and quiet commentary on consciousness, "gay power" as a new movement, and the various implications of what had happened. I followed him into the Stonewall, where rock music blared from speakers all around . . . He was immediately bouncing and dancing wherever he moved.

He left, and I walked east with him. Along the way, he described how things used to be. "You know, the guys there were so beautiful—they've lost that wounded look that fags all had 10 years ago." . . .

The "wounded look" would not return. The New Homosexual was born.

But most Villagers dismissed the Stonewall riots as a *rara avis*. After all, Friday night had been full moon, Judy Garland buried only that afternoon. Even GLFer Bob Kohler recalls that "to me the riot was just like a carnival. . . . I didn't see any massive energy. I just saw a riot. I wasn't able to interpret it any further than that." Kohler remembers, nevertheless, that in the week following "people were running all over the streets with leaflets. 'Insane' people. . . . People talking about saving the Stonewall. (The Stonewall is a dope drop, and should have been bombed three years ago!)" One such flyer was handed about by members of Homophile Youth Movement. It urged:

GET THE MAFIA AND THE COPS OUT OF GAY BARS

The nights of Friday, June 27, 1969 and Saturday, June 28, 1969 will go down in history as the first time that thousands of Homosexual men and women went out into the streets to protest the intolerable situation which has existed in New York City for many years --namely, the Mafia (or syndicate) control of this city's Gay bars in collusion with certain elements in the Police Dept. of the City of New York. The demonstrations were triggered by a Police raid on the Stonewall Inn late Friday night, June 27th. The purported reason for the raid was the Stonewall's lack of a liquor license. Who's kidding whom? Can anybody really believe that an operation as big as the Stonewall could continue for almost 3 years just a few blocks from the 6th Precinct house without having a liquor license? No! The Police have known about the Stonewall operation all along. What has happened is the presence of new "brass" in the 6th Precinct which has vowed to "drive the fags out of the Village."

Many of you have noticed one of the signs which the "management" of the Stonewall has placed outside stating "Legalize Gay bars and lick the problem." This is untrue and they know it. Judge Kenneth Keating (a former U.S. Senator) ruled in January, 1968 that even close dancing between Homosexuals is legal. <u>Since that date there has been nothing illegal, per se, about a Gay bar.</u> What is illegal about New York City's Gay bars today is the Mafia (or syndicate) stranglehold on them. Legitimate Gay businessmen are afraid to open decent Gay bars with a healthy social atmosphere (as opposed to the hell-hole atmosphere of places typified by the Stonewall) because of fear of pressure from the unholy alliance of the Mafia and the elements in the Police Dept. who accept payoffs and protect the Mafia monopoly.

We at the Homophile Youth Movement (HYMN) believe that the only way this monopoly can be broken is through the action of Homosexual men and women themselves. We obviously cannot rely on the various agencies of government who for years have known about this situation but who have refused to do anything about it. Therefore, we urge the following:

1) That Gay businessmen step forward and open Gay bars that will be run legally with competitive pricing and a healthy social atmosphere.

2) That Homosexual men and women boycott places like the Stonewall. The only way, it seems, that we can get criminal elements out of the Gay bars is simply to make it unprofitable for them.

3) That the Homosexual citizens of New York City, and concerned Heterosexuals, write to Mayor Lindsay demanding a thorough investigation and effective action to correct this intolerable situation.

Two Gay Activists Alliance leaders have explained police-syndicate involvement in the harassment of gay bars this way: "The police hit the bars at the prime hours, not so much so that they can give petty fines to the bar owners—it's for the effect of terrorizing the customers and sometimes physically abusing them. This drives the people away, alienates them, and forces the owner to either 'up' the payoff or close down." * Q.—So they will raid places that are already paying off to the police? "Sure. The more successful a place becomes, it's a certain thing that harassment will step up so that they can get more money. Its happened to bars, it's happened to baths, it's happened to restaurants." Q.—And this is whether the place that is paying off is run by the syndicate or not? "Right, because there are individuals who run businesses that are not directly connected with the syndicate. The only reason they have been able to exist is because they've allowed themselves to become corrupted. They've had to go the

* After a raid, gays generally will not patronize the bar until word has got around that the owner "is paying off more."

route of the syndicate and pay off the police. And, then, inevitably, if they are successful they'll probably be taken over by the syndicate."

As if in concerted attack, with HYMN and the Mattachine Society of New York, on New York City police, Lige Clarke and Jack Nichols came out in *Screw* the same week with one of their most sad-funny comments on the oppression of gay people. Admitting that, during the Lindsay administration, enticement and entrapment of gays by members of the "vice squad" had been minimal,* they spoke primarily for gay citizens of other metropolises. Their column [1] contained an imaginary conversation:

Boy: Daddy . . What kind of policeman are you? Why don't you wear a uniform like other policemen?
Dad: I'm a vice-cop, son.
Boy: What do you do all night, Daddy?
Dad: I stand in smelly public rest rooms, son, and play with my diddler.
Boy: But, Daddy, that's what you once gave me a spanking for.
Dad: Yes, son, but you were just having useless fun. I do it for money.
Boy: What else do you do?
Dad: If I see a queer, I wave my diddler at him and show him how big it is.
Boy: Yours isn't as big as my friend Tom's!
Dad: That's beside the point. I use mine to catch nasty queers. I get the queers to follow me.
Boy: What's a queer, Daddy?
Dad: A queer is a guy who likes to play with other men's diddlers. I arrest men like that and put them in jail.
Boy: Why, Daddy? All the boys in our block play with each other's. We all did it in Peter's garage the other day.
Dad: If I ever catch you, you'll be sorry!
Boy: Do you mean that you show a guy your diddler and then arrest him if he likes it?
Dad: Exactly.
Boy: Gosh, I think that's mean . . .

New York police were perhaps still in mild shock over their near-capture/immolation the previous weekend by fairies who didn't fly,** when Tuesday morning's *New York Times* dealt them another blow.

---

* Tom Burke has written ("The New Homosexuality," *Esquire,* December 1969) that "John Lindsay had barely been sworn in before Dick Leitsch, the Mattachine's vociferous director, rose at one of the Mayor's town meetings to denounce the entrapment of homosexuals by police. Even as he spoke, a plainclothesman was entrapping an innocent but effete young man in the back room of Julius Bar, Greenwich Village. An Episcopal minister (who had stopped in the bar for a sandwich) witnessed this, and phoned another minister, who phoned the Mayor and almost everyone else of any importance with a listed number. The result was a meeting in a village café attended by an influential *heterosexual* group that included the Mayor, the police commissioner, the police commissioner's wife, Allen Ginsberg, the Civil Liberties Union, and The Fugs. Entrapment ended the next morning."
** Paraphrase of a statement made to Alex Bennett of the *New York Post* by Dr. Leo Louis Martello, Gay Activist and author of books on witchcraft.

26

Front-page, with a shot of what had been Kew Gardens greenery, David Bird's TREES IN A QUEENS PARK CUT DOWN AS VIGILANTES HARASS HOMO-SEXUALS listed the destruction as fifteen dogwood, eleven London planes, some wild cherry, and other brush. The park had been, recognizedly, a place of assignation for local and non-local homosexuals. According to the *Times,* Myles Tashman, a lawyer and resident of a nearby apartment complex, said that about a month before, a group of men in the building, "concerned for the safety of the women and children," decided to move against the gays. Each night thirty or forty men would go into the park with flashlights and walkie-talkies and tell homosexuals they met to leave. "Admittedly it was against the law," said Tashman, "but we had police consent."

Finally the park was razed. Police stated they did not know who had cut down the trees.[2] On July 2, Bird reported that a Queens resident had twice telephoned the police, after seeing the vigilantes [MSNY was to call them the Kew Gardens KKK] at work with a power saw. Arriving almost an hour after his first call, the officers chatted with the treecutters and then left. The New York City Department of Parks saw the destruction as "a clear case of vandalism"; the Civil Liberties Union urged "that the Police Commissioner and the Mayor make it clear to all members of the police force that homosexuals have just as much right to be in the park as heterosexuals, and are entitled to the same degree of protection by the police."[3] In the meantime, the Mattachine Society and other clubs were starting a fund to replace the foliage. The fund name? Trees for Queens.

Monday and Tuesday nights, following Friday's and Saturday's riots and Sunday's tense watchfulness, were peaceful in Sheridan Square, except for minor outbreaks. Mattachine observers recorded a few:[4]

. . . Some of the police maintained enormous "cool," but others deliberately tried to provoke trouble. "Start something, faggot, just start something," one cop kept telling people. "I'd like to break your ass wide open." After saying that to several dozen people, one man turned and said, "What a Freudian comment, officer!" The cop started swinging . . .

Two cops in a car cruised the streets, yelling obscenities at people, obviously trying to start a fight. Another stood on the corner of Christopher and Waverly, swinging his nightstick . . . and making smart cracks to passersby. A wildly "fem" queen sneaked up behind him, lit a firecracker and dropped it between his feet.

It exploded and he jumped into the air in a leap that Villela would have envied, landing on a part of his anatomy that one queen called a "money-maker." . . . The queen tossed another firecracker under him, and when it went off a melee followed, during which the cop's badge was lifted. The next day, the badge turned up hanging on a tree in Washington Square Park, stuck into a string of pickled pigs' feet.

On Wednesday afternoon, July 2, Truscott's and Smith's *Voice* reportage shocked/delighted, depending on the reader's sympathies. It contributed new courage to homosexuals who'd tried/hadn't tried their strength the previous weekend. In GAY * a year later, John Francis Hunter was to recall that Wednesday was the night "which the young 'old-timers' who participated refer to as the 'worst night.' " [5] Mattachine's newsletter detailed it:

. . . Much of the good humour and high spirits of the weekend had dissipated, and the street people ** were no longer half-serious, half-camping. The cops, who had been caught off-guard and were on the defensive before, had taken the offensive and massive retaliation was their goal.

Some seemed quite ready to depopulate Christopher Street the moment anyone would give them permission to unholster their guns. Failing that, some of them, particularly some of the TPF men, tried to achieve the same objective with their nightsticks.

At one point, 7th Avenue from Christopher to West 10th looked like a battlefield in Vietnam. Young people, many of them queens, were lying on the side walk, bleeding from the head, face, mouth, and even the eyes. Others were nursing bruised and often bleeding arms, legs, backs, and necks.

[But the] composition of the street action had changed. It was no longer gay frustration being vented upon unsuspecting cops by queens who were partly violent but mostly campy. The queens were almost outnumbered by Black Panthers, Yippies, Crazies and young toughs from street gangs all over the city and some from New Jersey. The exploiters had moved in and were using the gay power movement for their own ends. . . .

Looting began Wednesday evening. Obviously, little of it was done by people who live in and frequent Christopher Street and environs, because all the most unlikely places were looted. The first shop to get hit was the "Gingerbread House," a toy shop run by a delightful little lady who is a friend to everyone on Christopher. . . .

. . . Observers in the know doubt if the looting was done by gay people.

A group of gay people did consider burning down the offices of the VILLAGE VOICE.[6] . . .

Evaluating the Stonewall riots and the clashes, verbal and physical, of the following week in its "The Gay View," Mattachine acknowledged the much-improved climate for homosexuals in New York under the John Lindsay administration of the preceding four years. The Society admitted that during the Robert Wagner years

. . . We didn't know what it was like not to be mistreated, expected to be mistreated, and accepted harassment when it came.

Now we've walked in the open and know how pleasant it is to have self-

* GAY, a homosexual biweekly newspaper, first appeared on New York City newsstands in late November 1969.
** "Street people" is a term homosexuals use to describe gays who have no apartment or at best a poor one and who may spend some of their time hustling.

respect and to be treated as citizens and human beings. There's no possible way to make us accept the "old way" again . . .

Should a moralist or a backroom politico succeed John Lindsay, he had better take a lesson from the Stonewall riots and eschew any "clean-ups" of the sort Robert Wagner used to gain headlines and to enforce his brand of morality (or immorality). The homosexual community has tired of the old "We Walk in Shadows" routine. We want to stay in the sunlight from now on. Efforts to force us back into the closet could be disastrous for all concerned.[7]

This quasi-manifesto would not be the last that homosexuals would read in succeeding months. Of greater moment, and an exclusive, was Mattachine's analysis of the riot's origins:

. . . Why the Stonewall, and not the Sewer or the Snake Pit? The answer lies, we believe, in the unique nature of the Stonewall. This club was more than a dance bar, more than just a gay gathering place. It catered largely to a group of people who are not welcome in, or cannot afford, other places of homosexual social gathering.

. . . Apart from the Goldbug and One Two Three, "drags" and "queens" had no place but the Stonewall. . . .

Another group was even more dependent on the Stonewall: the very young homosexuals . . . You've got to be 18 to buy a drink in a bar, and gay life revolved around bars. Where do you go if you are 17 or 16 and gay? The "legitimate" bars won't let you in the place, and gay restaurants and the streets aren't very sociable.

Then, too, there are hundreds of young homosexuals in New York who literally have no home. Most of them are between 16 and 25, and came here from other places without jobs, money or contacts. Many of them are running away from unhappy homes . . .

. . . for $3.00 admission, one could stay inside, out of the winter's cold or the summer's heat, all night long. Not only was the Stonewall better climatically, but it also saved the kids from spending the night in a doorway or from getting arrested as vagrants.

. . . Once the admission price was paid, one could drink or not, as he chose. The Stonewall became "home" to these kids. When it was raided, they fought for it. That, and the fact that they had nothing to lose other than the most tolerant and broadminded gay place in town, explains why [8] . . .

In a later article in GAY, Dick Leitsch, executive director of MSNY, philosophized, "it might be well to look back at the Stonewall . . . It was pretty typical of the sort of places that are still being raided by the cops." He went into detail:

The Stonewall was located in a building that had been a straight bar at one time. The straight place burned out, and the Stonewall management moved in, coated the ruins with black paint, and opened an unlicensed gay place.

There are so many safety hazards, structural faults, and building violations in that building that it has stood empty for almost a year, as nobody wants to dump enough money into it to make it safe for use. Yet, we were crowded in there every night, risking god-knows-what disasters. The building has one exit. Hundreds of people filled the place on Saturday nights. Had there been a fire, hundreds of our brothers and sisters would have been burned alive. . . .

Were the police harassing homosexuals when they put the Stonewall out of business, or were they doing us a favor? Were we . . . justified in giving the cops so much grief over that raid? In the Stonewall incident, at least the police were doing us a favor by putting out of business a group of exploiters who were exposing us to dangers of many kinds, and taking us all for suckers.[9] . . .

■

On Friday morning, July 4, forty-odd gays boarded a HYMN-chartered bus that would take them from New York to Philadelphia and the Annual Reminder, a homosexual picketing demonstration in front of Independence Hall. Sponsored by ERCHO,* the demo was celebrating its fifth birthday. The New Yorkers brought with them more than an Annual determination to prompt changes in American anti-homosexual laws, they carried a week's span of memories that featured an aggravated first strike for liberation—with full *Voice* coverage, however prejudiced; a *New York Times* "rebuke" to straights and police in Queens; and—if they read beyond the July 1 "vigilantes" story—the abolition by Denmark of its last legal barriers against the publishing of pictorial pornography and the showing of blue movies! ** As Dr. Franklin Kameny,*** president and founder of the Mattachine Society of Washington and director of the picketing, was to discover, they also brought an abrasive new self-respect. (A self-respect that even they were to learn later was not mere audacity.) Nineteen-year-old GLF member Bill Weaver remembers that "the New York people were much more militant than anyone else. Two of the lesbians started to hold hands and he [Kameny] went over and slapped their hands. And he said, 'You can't do that! You can't do that!' The New York people sort of caucused and freaked out, and I wrote on my sign—which said something like EQUALITY FOR HOMOSEXUALS—'SMASH SEXUAL FASCISM!' And Craig [Rodwell] was saying 'Right on!' . . . You could *feel* the militancy."

* The Eastern Regional Conference of Homophile Organizations, division of a national association, and which met twice a year.
** Furthermore, precisely one month before, the Connecticut State General Assembly had passed a bill abolishing the penalty for homosexual acts between consenting adults; Illinois had taken the first such step in 1961. The Connecticut law would take effect October 1, 1971.
*** Hans Knight, in the Philadelphia *Sunday Bulletin,* July 19, 1970, described him: "A well-knit, medium-sized man in his 40s, Dr. Kameny, who holds a Ph.D. from Harvard University in astronomy, worked in the maps department of the Pentagon until he was fired in the late 1950's. Reason: The Department had heard that he was a homosexual. Kameny fought the case through court after court. . . . The Supreme Court declined hearing the case and Kameny's dismissal remained in force."

After several hours of circling, many of the picketers now walking hand in hand as couples, the Annual Reminder disbanded, for the last time. It had had a fine history, had been noble; but it had served its purpose. It was to be formally interred at a homosexual conference in November.

The weekend in New York was again to be a signal one. One of the city's biggest legitimate nightclubs, the Electric Circus on St. Mark's Place in the East Village, had extended to gays an invitation: "If you are tired of raids, Mafia control, and checks at the front door," the Circus said, "join us for a beautiful evening on Sunday night, July 6th." [10] Villagers and police may have breathed a sigh of relief: Christopher Street, Sheridan Square, and the Stonewall were on the other side of town!

The Circus was packed with a groovy crowd. . . . There were hip moustaches, long hair, and hundreds of handsome young men [and women]. The acid-rock band blared forth a medley of fast tunes, and the entire audience was lost in a maze of dancing. A few straight couples mixed in with the crowd, seemingly unconcerned with the fact that most of the customers were gay . . . everyone wanted the experiment to work. The officials at the Electric Circus were thrilled by the turnout, and one commented that it seemed to be the best turnout they'd had in a month. For the first time in New York's history, a huge club was experimenting with social integration between heterosexuals and homosexuals.

Shortly after midnight, an elated Randy [Wicker] * prepared to mount the platform and give his speech in support of such ventures. The band stopped playing, and he was introduced by a well-known writer who told of Randy's many accomplishments in years past. . . .

He was only able to say a few words when one rotten apple tried to spoil the barrel. An uncool creep rushed out of the audience and began swinging wildly at everyone within arm's length. "Faggots!" he shrieked, "Goddamn faggots!" For a few moments it looked as though he'd been subdued. Randy resumed his speech, but . . . the violence erupted again, and this time the creep jumped onto the platform. Several Electric Circus big-boys quelled him, however, and he was led from the premises screaming . . .

Next, Dick Leitsch, the Executive Director of the [New York] Mattachine Society, got up and asked for donations from homosexuals to help replant the trees that anti-homosexual vigilantes had uprooted in a public park in Queens. Much of what he said, however, was lost to the crowd, who . . . had had its attention riveted by the lone protester.[11] . . .

GLFer Bill Weaver recalls a conversation with a friend, Michael Brown, just after the Electric Circus benefit. Both were "really depressed. And I said, look what black people have to go through. I think we're going to

---

*Randolfe Wicker was one of New York City's earliest gay activists. A successful businessman, he has worked for homosexual civil rights for over a decade. In 1962, he and seven others spoke *as homosexuals* on a ninety-minute radio program over WBAI. He was the first homosexual to appear as such on New York television, in behalf of homosexuals, when he was a guest on the "Les Crane Show," 1964.

have to die, we're going to have to be beaten up. We're going to have to get ready for things like that."

It was, nevertheless, a start toward open integration.

Three or four days before, something else had started. It was to become known as the Mattachine Action Committee.

Michael Kotis, president of MSNY, tells how "right after the riots, people started to come up to us because of our flyers . . . they wanted to do something . . . they wanted to get involved and overcome the difficulties, the oppression, the injustice." The committee had no elected officers, and met frequently and informally in the library at MSNY. Michael Brown, who composed many of the leaflets distributed by the Society in the days following the riots, and Martha Shelley were acknowledged leaders of the group. The Society left the committee largely to itself, gave them "their independence," states Kotis. Did the committee feel, on the other hand, that Mattachine was in effect dissociating from any radicalisms they might propose? putting them, like boisterous children, alone in a room where they might scrap to their hearts' content? Nineteen-year-old Mark Segal, who helped to establish Gay Youth (see Chapter 10) in 1970, insists that the committee "never had anything to do with Mattachine. We used their paper, machines. They didn't like it because we were gaining power. They started giving us a rough time."

With the committee's aid, and at the suggestion of Dick Leitsch, who saw that the committee represented only a portion of the numbers of homosexuals turned on by the riots, a "community meeting"—the first Gay Power meeting—was announced for Wednesday, July 9. It would take place at Freedom House, monthly site of Mattachine's Town Meetings.

Another leaflet! Kotis remembers that "we mimeographed something different each night . . ." This one shouted:

HOMOSEXUAL
LIBERATION
MEETING

It was to serve "to establish a forum of communication between homosexuals for the first time and to end the apathy which has prevented the homosexual from taking his rightful place in society. Many of us in the community have been heartened by the appearance of a new spirit this past two weeks. . . . We cannot let the homosexual community fall back into a period of indifference and inaction because we have seen that this leads to persecution and explosive bitterness. We at MATTACHINE want you to come to this meeting and express yourselves about what we—all of us—can do to secure rights. Remember—no one is free until everyone is free!"

At this first "community meeting" came a call for a Gay Power demonstration to protest police harassment; the idea would materialize as the

Gay Power Vigil, of July 27. But the Stonewall events, and what had caused the phenomena, were the meeting's focus of discussion, despite Bob Kohler's insistence that the queens and street people—whom the riots had spotlighted to straight and gay public alike—merited its concern. Kohler claims that he "got a quarter from one person, somebody else got up and told me to shut up and sit down and that the queens were irrelevant . . ."

Kohler believes that it was in large part this concern with *people*—people in specific, as well as oppressed people in general—rather than a more protracted goal of law reform that was to sever the first (a second developed) Action Committee from Mattachine in the next week. He insists that "Everybody was on a fantastic ego trip, losing sight of the fact that there were *people* involved in this thing." During one day's leafleting by members of Mattachine and the Action Committee, several Black Panthers were protesting outside the Women's House of Detention, in Greenwich Village: "Free the black sisters!" Hearing the gays' chant of "Power to the people!" they joined in, came over. At a committee meeting later at MSNY, Michael Brown suggested reciprocating the gesture by joining in at a Panther demo. In the words of the Mattachine president, "That was the beginning of the end . . . as far as the first Action Committee was concerned, because it was and still is Mattachine policy only to be involved with issues related to homosexual liberation," and "unless you have a gigantic organization with thousands of dedicated people, you can't take on the cause of human liberation. There are *so many* people who are, to use the overworked word, 'oppressed.'"

The committee and Mattachine seldom saw eye to eye. In one of their leaflets the content was "mattachine," the tone "committee." It asked and demanded:

WHERE DO WE GO
FROM HERE?

. . . we all know that the streets cannot remain an armed camp and that further violence in the streets won't accomplish anything constructive. Therefore, we call upon public officials, particularly the Mayor, the Police Commissioner, and representatives of the state government, to meet with homosexuals to discuss the issues listed below. The Mattachine Society of New York stands ready to arrange a meeting with any responsible public official and to publicize that meeting to the homosexual community.

WHAT HOMOSEXUALS WANT

1) A public commitment from community leaders, political leaders and public officials to full equality for homosexuals.

2) An end to all forms of harassment of homosexuals by police and other public agencies.

3) A full investigation of the terror tactics and vandalism last week in the Queens park, and prosecution of those responsible.

4) Reform of the state sodomy law to eliminate penalties for private sexual behavior between consenting adults.

5) Reform of all laws that discriminate against homosexuals or hold us to a higher standard of conduct than our heterosexual brothers.

6) Amendment of municipal, state and Federal civil and human rights laws to prohibit discrimination against homosexuals.

7) Tax reform to give single taxpayers a break.

8) A thorough investigation and reform of the State Liquor Authority.

9) Leadership to halt discrimination against homosexuals by private employers.

Mattachine and its first Action Committee parted company, definitively, as an outcome of the second "community meeting," held more Village-conveniently in St. John's Episcopal Church on Waverly Place. Flyers had announced that ". . . The positive response to our first Gay Power meeting on July 9 showed that homosexuals are no longer going to sit back and be apathetic pawns for every politician who comes along and trades their rights and privileges for a few votes in Far Rockaway. It is time that the law and order crowd put a halt to the vigilante groups who would destroy the country as well as a park in Queens, to preserve their delusions of virility. Whatever means we use to express our objection to the way this society deprives gay people of the Rights and Liberties guaranteed to all Americans in the Declaration of Independence and Bill of Rights, WE NEED YOUR HELP AND IDEAS TO MAKE GAY POWER A REALITY. . . ."

Michael Kotis remembers that July 16 "was a sweltering night, and in addition . . . there were some people over from England who were filming . . . they had spotlights all over the place . . . And the hall was packed, with standing room only." An early highlight of the meeting was Dr. Leo Louis Martello's admonition to fellow-gays that they must challenge every feeling of worthlessness they may have ever had about themselves. He was to develop his ideas further in the first issue of Gay Liberation Front's Come Out!: * "The passive acceptance of homosexuality as a perversion or emotional illness IN YOUR OWN MIND plays into the hands of your persecutors. This is called THE SANCTION OF THE VICTIM." [12] Tom Burke's Now Generation description of the climax of the meeting, in his Esquire article of December 1969,[13] captured its spirit if not detail:

* The New York GLF paper first appeared in a November 14 issue. Its slogan: "A Newspaper by and for the Gay Community." Come Out! may be obtained by writing to Box 233, Times Square Station, New York, N.Y. 10036.

Dick Leitsch, in a staid brown suit, strides to the front. . . . With professional aplomb, he reopens the meeting. Police brutality and heterosexual indifference must be protested, he asserts; at the same time, the gay world must retain the favor of the Establishment, especially those who make and change the laws. Homosexual acceptance will come slowly, by educating the straight community, with grace and good humor and . . .

A tense boy with leonine hair is suddenly on his feet. "We don't want acceptance, goddamn it! We want respect! Demand it! We're through hiding in dark bars behind Mafia doormen. We're going to go where straights go and do anything with each other they do and if they don't like it, well, *fuck them!* . . . Straights don't have to be ashamed of anything sexy they happen to feel like doing in public, and neither do we! We're through cringing and begging like a lot of nervous old nellies at Cherry Grove!" . . .

"We're going to protest in front of St. Patrick's," another boy calls. "The Catholics have put us down long enough!"

"If every homosexual in New York boycotted Bloomingdale's, they'd be out of business in two weeks!"

"Well, now *I* think," says Mrs. Cervantes [Mattachine assistant], "that what we ought to have is a gay vigil, in a park. Carry candles, perhaps. . . . I think we should be firm, but just as amicable and sweet as . . ."

"Sweet!" The new speaker resembles Billy the Kid. He is James Fouratt, New Left celebrity, seminarian *manqué*, the radical who burned the real money on the floor of the New York Stock Exchange as a war protest.

"Sweet! *Bullshit!* There's the stereotype homo again, man! . . . Bullshit! That's the role society has been forcing these queens to play, and they just sit and accept it. We have got to radicalize, man! Why? Because as long as we accept getting fired from jobs because we are gay, or not being hired at all, or being treated like second-class citizens, we're going to remain neurotic and screwed up. No matter what you do in bed, if you're not a man out of it, you're going to be screwed up. Be proud of what you are, man! And if it takes riots or even guns to show them what we are, well, that's the only language that the pigs understand!"

Wild applause. . . .

Dick Leitsch tries to reply, but Fouratt shouts him down.

"All the oppressed have to unite! The system keeps us all weak by keeping us separate. . . . We've got to work together with *all* the New Left."

A dozen impassioned boys are on their feet, cheering. . . .

Again and again, Dick Leitsch tugs . . . at his clean white tie, shouting for the floor, screaming for order. He is firmly ignored.

A second Mattachine Action Committee succeeded the first, its ideas more in line with MSNY policy of holding to the gay issue. Marty Robinson, as its leader, initiated protest "hangouts," in which a group of homosexuals would congregate at some spot in the Village, declaring who they were and their "right to be there" and refusing to be moved. But young gays' interest in Mattachine-sponsored actions was waning. At a third "community meeting," again in St. John's Episcopal Church, Robinson attempted to interest straight Villagers in the problems of the gay world. Very few, of either kind, even turned out.*

Meanwhile, a terse mimeographed note was thrust, day by day, into Village strollers' hands—hands now not too eager to take "another leaflet." It asked:

DO YOU THINK HOMOSEXUALS ARE REVOLTING?
YOU BET YOUR SWEET ASS WE ARE

```
We're going to make a place for ourselves in the
revolutionary movement.  We challenge the myths
that are screwing up this society.  MEETING:
Thursday, July 24, 6:30 PM, at Alternate U --
69 West 14th Street at Sixth Avenue.**
```

Just another gay leaflet? So it might have appeared to many Villagers, gay and straight alike. And Mattachine, its committee, and the Daughters of Bilitis *** were probably too busy to notice. Sunday, July 27, was to be an important day. Their leaflet announced a rally in Washington Square Park in support of "the rights of homosexuals to openly love whom we please and to an unharassed life style. . . . We refuse to accept the straight person's guilt about sex," it continued. "Help bring about the day when we can walk out in the open as first-class citizens." Marshals would wear lavender sashes: "Wear a lavender armband to show your support."

Two p.m., near the memorial arch. Three hundred, perhaps four hundred gays chanting, parleying, laughing, dishing, grumbling, shouting, narrating, welcoming, or simply standing silent. The first organized demonstration of homosexual unity since the Stonewall rebellion—and its one-month anniversary. Two men had carried a wide rectangular banner, lavender, for all to see. Hoisted, it displayed two linked female sex signs and two linked male.

Mattachine flyers—legal-size, outdoing previous announcements—proclaimed

THE HOMOSEXUAL

REVOLUTION

* At a last Action Committee meeting at MSNY, Robinson was blamed for the "community meeting's" miscarriage and for failure to keep committee members informed; the Society was accused of lack of interest in the group.

** Alternate University described itself, in its catalog, as "an inexpensive evening school free of grades, credit and age restrictions, offering a wide range of courses whose content and approach are not available elsewhere." Classes met once a week for two hours. In September 1970, Friday was designated Gay Night and featured classes, workshops, and activities for and by gay women and men.

*** Founded in San Francisco in 1955, DOB remained, until the recent formation of Radicalesbians (see Chapter 9), the nation's only all-female homosexual organization. In summer 1970, the organization restructured to abolish all its national offices and became a loose federation of autonomous chapters. The name Bilitis is deemed to be that of a sixth-century (B.C.) Greek poetess and lover of Sappho; it was used by poet Pierre Louÿs in his *Chansons de Bilitis* (1894).

and listed

```
WHAT MATTACHINE HAS DONE:

   * As a result of a "sip-in"* by organization members
     several years ago, the State Liquor Authority was
     forced to recognize the legality of "gay" bars,
     which has led to the opening of many such places . . .
```

and so on: many years' work. Then the flyer advised

```
   WHAT MATTACHINE WILL DO -- WITH YOUR HELP: . . .
```

But the list was too long, even too detailed. It spoke to a generation short on patience and distrustful of red tape.

Speeches by Martha Shelley, of the estranged first committee, and by Marty Robinson of the second Action Committee. The Vigil then moved to Sheridan Square, opposite the Stonewall Inn. "People were getting into a great high: they were singing, had their arms around each other. There was a great feeling," Michael Kotis reminisces. Then, brusquely, after conferring with watching police about the dangers of continuing the march to the 6th Precinct house, the Action Committee called out, "Thanks a lot for showing up. Everybody please go home . . ." Abrupt. Too abrupt for protesters who remembered "community meeting" suggestions to demonstrate before the station house. . . . A disgruntled mingling.

All afternoon, they of the terse mimeographed note had circulated a second, even terser. It double-entendred:

HOMOSEXUALS ARE COMING
TOGETHER AT LAST

A second meeting would be held, again at Alternate U., on Thursday, July 31. Announced purposes: "To examine how we are oppressed and how we oppress ourselves. To fight for gay control of gay businesses. To publish our own newspaper. To these and other radical ends . . ." The impatient and the disappointed and the angry grabbed one now.

---

* MSNY's "sip-in" took place at Julius, a Village bar that had—to avoid police pressure—hung a sign saying, IF YOU'RE GAY, STAY AWAY.

37

3

DO YOU THINK HOMOSEXUALS
ARE REVOLTING? YOU BET YOUR
SWEET ASS WE ARE.
 —from the first "GLF" flyer

The heterogeneous alliance of homosexuals that began to meet at Alternate
U. in late July 1969 adopted the name Gay Liberation Front, the suggestion of former members of the Mattachine Action Committee.* An
alternative, Homosexual Liberation Front, might wrongly indicate a male
orientation for the group, women members were quick to point out. The
troika title was based, of course, on National Liberation Front: a name
used by Algerian terrorists who a decade before had sought freedom from
France; and the designation preferred by the Vietcong. Furthermore, by
using "Front," the group saw itself not as an exclusive club but as a
movement that might eventually "involve" all homosexual organizations,
bring all gays under its banner.

Nascent GLF believed, by and large, that it was to be the first organization of homosexual "fighters." If GLFers looked back, at all, on the
twenty-year history of the American homophile movement they saw only
the NAACP-like tactic of the Mattachine Foundation/Society, of the
Daughters of Bilitis, of One, Inc.,** and other groups, that, "If only
society could be convinced that the homosexuals were really good boys
and good girls, not promiscuous, very loving, always law-abiding, forever
the victim and never the victimizer, they would be accepted. They were
loyal, excellent security risks, were no sissies and bull-dykes, and would
make good soldiers and sailors, if only given the opportunity." [1] Barbara
Gittings, who has worked in homophile activities since 1958, was editor

---

* Conscious of the disparity between its tactic and Mattachine's, but nevertheless
valuing the support of the older organization, the first Action Committee had once
suggested working out of Mattachine while bearing the GLF name.

** An organization, established in Los Angeles in 1952, for both female and male
homosexuals and whose primary purpose was publishing. Among its long line of
periodicals and other literature was the monthly ONE magazine (1953 to 1967).

of *The Ladder: A Lesbian Review,* 1963–6, and is currently a member of Homophile Action League (Philadelphia), Gay Activists Alliance, and Mattachine Society of Washington, contrasts the early movement with later homosexual militancy: "During the movement of the 1950's, homosexuals looked inward, focusing on themselves and their problems; and they sought tolerance, understanding. In the 1960's, we looked *outside* ourselves for the roots of the trouble."

Many GLFers considered their organization to be the first significant break with old-line homophile thinking. Yet San Francisco's thriving Society for Individual Rights had its beginnings in 1964 as protest against the sluggishness of the movement. Wanting to involve the city's total gay community, SIR scheduled buffets, outings, dances, and operated its own thrift shop. With revenues from these activities and from gifts, the Society bought its own building, equipped with offices, food facilities, dance floor, stage, and activity rooms—*and* located in downtown San Francisco. California politicos have visited this "community center" on SIR's Candidates' Night before local elections. Nor has the organization been averse to picketing with or lending support to other gay clubs.[2] SIR's program for the homosexual is comprehensive: "Our goal has been and is to help homosexuals in every way we can," declares the Society's *Vector* editor, George Mendenhall. But SIR's militancy—"We are too busy getting things done to stop and make signs to carry"[3]—would have seemed *précieux* in the summer of the Stonewall.

The new GLF would have been little impressed by One, Inc.'s, victory in a postal-censorship case at Supreme Court level that enabled it to send its publications through the mails * fifteen years before. Or by the researched complaint of the Mattachine Society of New York to the city's Human Rights Commission providing case histories of hiring discrimination, to the end that "in January 1967 the city said it had stopped asking job applicants if they were homosexual."[4] Or by the Mattachine Society of Washington's ** scrap with Representative John Dowdy (D, Texas), August 1963. MSW president Franklin Kameny has described it: "We

---

* *The Advocate* (Los Angeles) records, "ONE Magazine became a gay cause celebre in October 1954, when the Post Office held up mailing of that month's issue as obscene, largely because it dealt with homosexuality outside of a clinical context. ONE lost all the way up to the U.S. Supreme Court, which unanimously rejected the government's contentions that the magazine was obscene in a *per curiam* decision— that is, without hearing arguments. Although attorneys for both sides were disappointed by the court's summary action, ONE had made a legal breakthrough. 'That decision has been cited over and over in pornography cases ever since,' Robert Earl, ONE's current president, pointed out." (November 11–24, 1970.)

** MSW "sprang up in 1961 as an independent organization unaffiliated with other societies bearing the name Mattachine. . . . In contrast with many of the organizations, it functions as a small, tight, confrontation-minded group, having a membership more oriented than many toward activism. It eschews social activities, preferring to focus primarily on challenging officialdom and secondarily on dispelling prejudice through an active information-education program." (Foster Gunnison, Jr., in *The Same Sex: An Appraisal of Homosexuality* [Philadelphia, 1969].)

had registered to solicit funds, in accordance with the District's Charitable Solicitations Act; Dowdy objected to a license from the District of Columbia to a 'bunch of perverts.' So he brought a bill against MSW.* We asked for hearings, which his subcommittee (a subcommittee of the House District of Columbia Committee) held. I testified for four and a half hours; our vice president testified for an hour; the ACLU testified for an hour; the DC government testified against the bill. And it didn't pass. We got tremendous publicity in Washington for several days in a row—it really 'made' us as nothing else could have. So at the 1964 East Coast Homophile Organizations conference we gave Dowdy a citation as 'The Public Official Who Has Done the Most for the Homophile Movement in the Year 1964.' "

GLF might well have called tame the homosexual picketing, inaugurated and generally directed by MSW, of the White House, Pentagon, State Department, and Civil Service Commission during the mid-'60's. Leftists of the new gay militant group would not have been eager to remind other GLF members of the "old-liners" who picketed at Hammarskjold Plaza and the White House on April 17 and 18, 1965, protesting Fidel Castro's intended crackdown on Cuban homosexuals: picketers who insisted that CUBA'S GOVERNMENT PERSECUTES HOMOSEXUALS—U.S. GOVERNMENT BEAT THEM TO IT and JEWS TO CONCENTRATION CAMPS UNDER NAZIS; HOMOSEXUALS TO WORK CAMPS UNDER CASTRO—IS THE U.S. MUCH BETTER? [5] But, since today's homosexual militancy is essentially a shedding of shame, *they would undoubtedly have praised* picketers' remarks recorded by *The Ladder: A Lesbian Review* after the first Annual Reminder (1965) at Independence Hall: "Today I lost the last bit of fear"; "Today it was as if a weight dropped off my soul"; "This was the proudest day of my life!" [6]

What some gay militants do not recognize today is that they are, in certain respects, merely the final grassroots development of an awakening that was comparably thrilling when, in 1957, One, Inc., published the words "I'm glad I'm Homosexual" on its magazine cover and many subscribers canceled; or when, on February 11 a decade later, several Angeleno homosexual organizations coordinated the Black Cat demonstration with actions by other oppressed minorities in L.A. Jim Kepner, *Advocate* ** columnist and veteran of seventeen years' homophile activity, remembers that

* *The Ladder: A Lesbian Review* reported (November 1964) that the bill, HR 5990, would have required all organizations raising funds in the District of Columbia to "show to the satisfaction of the District Commissioners" that what was solicited "will benefit or assist in promoting the health, welfare, and morals of the District of Columbia." GAY has noted that Rep. Dowdy was "indicted by a Federal Grand Jury on charges of accepting a $25,000 bribe in 1965" and that he faced "perjury charges on five different counts for lying to the U.S. Attorney at his Grand Jury hearing." (April 27, 1970.)

** Under the editorship of Dick Michaels, this national homosexual newspaper, published in Los Angeles, started in September 1967 as *The Los Angeles Advocate*, an 8½ x 11, two-column monthly publication of PRIDE (Personal Rights in Defense

. . . The owners of Pandora's Box had started the general protest against police brutality and harassment in West Hollywood, mainly on the Sunset Strip. They called for other minorities to join after Sheriff's officers had given the hippies and flower children several bloody weekends. The gay community had just gone through a bloody New Year's Eve, when several bars were raided and there were a large number of arrests and extremely serious beatings at the Black Cat and another bar nearby.

We arranged our demonstration to coincide with the others, but the owner of Pandora's Box made several attempts to have us call off our demonstration when he discovered that the word "homosexual" was going to be mentioned.

Kepner estimates that there were about two hundred in the gay crowd, "with groups of thirty or forty more watching from across the street on each corner, and about forty pickets walking up and down . . . in front of the Black Cat." He quotes from the address he made to the crowd:

"We've come out here tonight to protest arbitrary arrests . . . to protest illegal search and seizures that have taken place in this and other areas of Los Angeles, to protest police perjury in the courts in cases that have arisen in this and other areas of Los Angeles and to protest abuse of our rights and dignity. The other areas of Los Angeles, everyone knows. There is a protest tonight in Watts, and no one has to be told who the victims are who are protesting. Nobody can hide the names of the people who are protesting in Watts. We know who the victims are of police lawlessness in East L.A. [Chicanos]. Nobody needs to hide their name. We know who they are in Pacoima [blacks], and in Venice [blacks and hippies] and on the Sunset Strip [hippies]. Nobody needs to hide the name of those who are protesting on the Sunset Strip. But some of those organizing the demonstration on the Sunset Strip, who fight to defend the victims of police brutality on the Strip, have ordered us to hide our name. They didn't want the public, the press, or maybe the police, to think that they are associating with any of US. . . .

"Look at your neighbor here tonight, at the guy or gal standing next to you now. Do you know who he is? I mean WHAT he or she is? . . . It's unmentionable. . . . And those who bear that name have, like Negroes, Mexicans, juveniles, alcoholics . . . been the constant victims of police lawlessness, and brutality . . . recently here in this neighborhood.

". . . All of us who have borne that name have lived in fear of having it attached to us in public, and we all know how damned little we have gained over the years by keeping it a secret.

". . . the time has come when the love that dared not speak its name will never again be silenced.

". . . We've been copping out to society for centuries, just as a lot of other minorities were doing until very recently. Well, the Negroes aren't copping out anymore—and they're being listened to. The kids aren't copping out anymore

---

and Education), which organized the Black Cat demonstration. Biweekly since May 1970 and in full tabloid size since January 1969, *The Advocate*'s press run was up to nearly 40,000 by late 1970.

—and they're being listened to. And the Ramparts Police have shown us that it doesn't pay to cop out either.* And God help the next one of us who lays down and takes it . . .

"And what is our name? It has been Coward; Furtive; Hidden. . . ." [7]

A local homosexual newsletter which had reported the Black Cat raid noted that "with the homosexual, the police know they have safe game. 'These guys won't fight back.' " Then queried: "We wonder how long they can count on it?" [8]

Kepner continues that, following the demo,

All the [gay] organizations in town became rather militant, and well-attended . . . Both PRIDE [Personal Rights in Defense and Education] and CRH [Council on Religion and the Homophile] made attempts to organize a Citizens' Alert—a police watch patrol, patterned on the then successful one in San Francisco in which gay organizations cooperated with other minorities. PRIDE entertained a good bit of wild talk about ultra-radical and terrorist tactics, and this eventually broke the group up, as most of the members turned to more conservative leadership. [But] we pushed for and finally got a large meeting with the head of Hollywood Vice. We had altercations with police at three of our dances, and won a case ensuing from the last . . . and we organized, Memorial Day 1968, a large GAY IN at Griffith Park to hear a former policeman who was running as Peace-&-Freedom candidate for D.A.[9] **

Radicals in the new GLF, July 1969, were not the first of such in the homophile movement, though they might have liked to think so. Edward Sagarin describes/derides their predecessors in *The Realist:*

. . . a few liberal leftists were active in the first organizations of homosexuals;

* On New Year's Eve, a dozen plainclothes vice officers had "merged into a holiday party at The BLACK CAT, a bar in the Silver Lake area of Los Angeles. . . . At midnight, after the custom . . . there was some kissing among the patrons, whereupon the police took sudden and drastic action. Without identifying themselves, the officers first began to tear down the Christmas decorations, and then began to manhandle patrons and employees alike. Sixteen persons were dragged outside and forced to lie down on the sidewalk until five squad cars arrived to take them away. After stating that they were officers, the police still refused to produce any proper identification, as they are legally required to do, usually replying by hitting the questioner with the butt of their guns, and saying, 'That's all the identification you need.' One bartender was so severely beaten . . . as to suffer two broken ribs and a ruptured spleen, which later had to be removed. Much later, since he was held in jail for 22 hours before being sent finally to County General Hospital for care. The bartender naturally was booked for assaulting an officer (a felony), and others for that or for 'indecent behavior.' " (*Concern* [newsletter of the Southern California Council on Religion and the Homophile, L.A.], January 1967.)
** Kepner viewed the follow-up of the Black Cat demo less favorably in his "Angles on the News" in the June 1969 *Advocate:* "The Bloody Ramparts raids of 1967 stirred the whole homosexual community here, and recruits, ready to battle for their rights, rushed to every local group. The old groups stuck to their tired approaches. The new groups split apart over strategy. The enthusiasm died, burying PRIDE . . . and several bars, and leaving other organizations virtually dead, though not officially buried."

in fact, if anybody remembers the name of Henry Wallace, it was a group of his followers who formed a Bachelors-for-Wallace club when Henry was campaigning for President, and the name was apparently the facade behind which there probably lurked a nice group of left-wing gay guys.

Politics and sexuality notwithstanding, they were respectable people; in fact, from today's vantage point, it was hard to find anybody who didn't fit that sobriquet a generation ago. But when these people, the embarrassing "queer pinkos" as their enemies labeled them, finally awakened to reality on the first Wednesday after the first Monday in November, 1948, they decided to pick up their marbles and save something from the debacle.[10]

The Mattachine *Foundation,* which grew from the Bachelors-for-Wallace prototype, began "When a group of homosexuals met in an apartment in Los Angeles in 1950 to talk about some kind of homosexual organization . . . a daring and fearsome thing. The police might very well have raided the place if they had suspected what was going on," stated an MSNY leader.[11] The first Mattachine was therefore leftish, and was underground-hierarchical in structure. Furthermore, it was committed, beyond a doubt, to cooperation with labor and with other American minorities. Jim Kepner writes [12] that

On most points, Henry Hay's first Mattachine prospectus, dated 7-6-50, and being a revision of the two-years-older prospectus for the Bachelors for Wallace, was quite radical, speaking constantly of the dangers of "encroaching American Fascism," claiming that "the socially censured Androgynous Minority was suborned, blackmailed, cozened and stampeded into serving as hoodlums, stool pigeons, volunteer informers, concentration camp trustees, torturers, and hangmen, before it as a minority was ruthlessly exterminated" (Germany, 1932). The document attacked the government security program's principle of "Guilt by Association," and affirmed that "in order to earn for ourselves any place in the sun, we must with perseverance and self-discipline work collectively on the side of peace, for the program of the four freedoms of the Atlantic Charter, and in the spirit and letter of the United Nations Charter, for the full first-class citizenship participation of Minorities everywhere, including ourselves. We, the Androgynes of the World, have formed this responsible corporate/Body to demonstrate by our efforts that our physical and psychological handicaps need be no deterrent in integrating 10% of the world's population toward the constructive social progress of mankind."

Bits of that last will jar today. It is a measure of how much the issues and definitions have changed—it was very radical then. To suggest the integration of homosexuals into the general community, which now has an establishmentarian ring, was then radical. To suggest that homosexuals constituted a "minority" was almost unthinkable even with the addenda, which now sounds insultingly weepish about our "physical and psychological handicaps." . . . [But] the early movement regarded Albert Ellis as a staunch friend.

After a reorganization in 1953, the group, renamed Mattachine Society, deferred to McCarthyism but continued to have a small radical faction.

The new Gay Liberation Front believed it had found a uniquely unashamed title. The name was a far cry from "Mattachine"—the Italian jester, acrobat, mimic who pleased crowds but kept his truer feelings out of sight. And from "Bilitis"—the quasi-historical lover of more obviously lesbian Sappho. And from "One"—whose ambiguous designation indicated, nonetheless, an organization based on the GLF credo-to-be that female and male homosexuals were "one" in the problems and persecutions they faced. "Homophile," an adjective invented by the movement partly as camouflage but primarily to identify homosexuals' organizations (could a club be homosexual?),* was in special disrepute. It seemed to be saying, We *love* the same sex, not *We have intercourse with* the same sex. Even the term "homosexual" had little real appeal, sounded clinical and antique, though many preferred its honesty to the too censurable "gay" **
—after all, what people could be constantly happy twenty-four hours a day? FREE (see footnote, page 60), a Midwestern club, has argued for the latter that *"Gay,* however, identifies a social relationship . . . but does not indicate that an overt sexual act is involved. Gay people can and do interact in relationships where sex is not involved"! [13]

But GLF New York was not the first gay group to call a spade a spade. The pioneer Council on Religion and the Homosexual, from San Francisco in early 1965, had spread to several American cities under that title. Philadelphia had had its Homosexual Law Reform Society since 1967. Not to mention Los Angeles's Homosexual Information Center (since 1965), New York's Council on Equality for the Homosexual (1967–70), and the short-lived Homosexual League of New York (1962), among others. On April 1, 1969, *Homosexuals Intransigent!* had been chartered at The City College/CUNY.*** Its founder, Craig Schoonmaker, was to explain the club's bold name in its newsletter, *Homosexual Renaissance:* [14]

---

* Homophile Action League, created from a Philadelphia Daughters of Bilitis in 1969, would have preferred "Homosexual . . ." but that was not the kind of action members were in league for!

** In *The Advocate* (March 1970), Reed Severin traced the word's history: "Since about 1930, if not much earlier, the word has been used as slang . . . The term 'gay boy' has been traced to Australia, where it first appeared in print around 1925." He notes that "In the mid-19th century the term 'gay girl' came upon the scene (in print). It meant 'prostitute' or, at least, 'non-aristocratic.' . . . In *The Young Man's Friend,* a book by J. A. James published in 1879, there is this definition of 'gay': 'loving pleasure, especially forbidden pleasure; wanton. . . .'" Severin adds that homosexuals may gain comfort from the fact that the word "is an ambiguous and protean offspring of the old High German word *gahi,* meaning fast, sudden, or impetuous. The Oxford English Dictionary even claims that it may have come from the old High German *wahi*—'pretty, or beautiful, or good.'"

*** GAY announced on February 16, 1970, that *HI!,* "actively engaged in recruitment of members on City College campuses in the Bronx, Queens, and Brooklyn . . . is seeking collaboration with similar NYU and Columbia activist societies in order to promote civil and social rights for homosexuals in academic circles" and that "It also works to instill self-affirming attitudes in students who have recently discovered themselves to be homosexually oriented."

"Homosexuals"—most groups in the homosexual civil-rights movement call themselves "homophile" organizations. We think the word "homophile" is a stupid, cowardly euphemism—and one uses euphemisms only when there is something wrong with the ordinary word. We see nothing at all wrong with the word "homosexual." Besides, "homophile" is intended to give leeway for heterosexuals to participate in the movement. But we think the drive for homosexual self-respect is primarily a homosexual responsibility; indeed, it can only be accomplished by homosexuals. . . .

"Intransigent"—on certain basic points there can be no compromise. Homosexuals must demand their rights undiluted. We must be militant: intransigent.

"!"—we are homosexuals, and we assert that proudly. We are intransigent, and we assert that proudly. The exclamation point tells everybody how we feel about ourselves and about the movement.

Underscoring—Homosexuals Intransigent! is an organization apart, composed of people apart. We want to be set apart, noted as distinct, standing out in any printed matter. So our name is to be underscored or italicized at all times.

And our abbreviation: HI!—welcome to the Homosexual Renaissance, brother!

Nor was the title of California's Committee for Homosexual Freedom euphemistic. And, besides holding indisputable claim to the foundation of the old American homophile movement, the West Coast can with some justification date gay lib from the creation of its CHF, spring 1969, not from the Stonewall riots in June. Jim Kepner enumerates the semi-militant predecessors of the Committee: [15]

Militancy increased considerably on both coasts after 1965, as homosexuals began to demonstrate in public, but with rare exceptions the demonstrations were the polite type already being abandoned by the other "Movement." SIR, the most assertive organization in the movement in 1966, and probably the most effective, became conservative, not so much with aging, as because the issues changed radically. PRIDE, starting as an imitation of SIR, became much more militant, but fell apart after one good demonstration and a few police skirmishes. VANGUARD * had the apolitical tone of the early Hippies —and also didn't survive. The Circle of Loving Companions * and Morris's minions * in the Dow Action Committee not only formed a preview, from 1966 on, of GLF, but they were involved in the formation of GLF-type groups in the Bay Area and here. The CHF, started for the personal ego-trip of Leo Laurence, was the first full-fledged Gay Lib type group.

* VANGUARD, a militant hippie-gay group created in San Francisco in 1966, had a hippie-dropout program for gay street youths.
The Circle of Loving Companions, started in Los Angeles at about the same time, and, according to Kepner, "consisting really of Henry Hay and his companion, John Burnside, came closest before CHF to the new radical outlook and style. Dressed in thoroughly hippie fashion, they rapped with Berkeley radicals and Sunset Boulevard hippies in 1967 about Gay issues, pushed for greater militance in the gay movement, participated prominently in every street action, and also hosted the Traditional Indian Land & Life Committee, a revolutionary Indian group."

Kepner alleges [16] that "Laurence, a tiny, angry man, looks like Abraham Lincoln cut in half. He dresses and trims his beard to keep this comparison obvious." Laurence was

briefly an early member of SIR. After working as a Young Republican organizer for Reagan and for Rafferty (ultra-conservative and anti-gay California Superintendent of Public Instruction, recently defeated) he was in Chicago in August 1968 to cover the Democratic bust for the press. He says this radicalized him.

Laurence soon returned to activity in SIR, which was one of the "out front" organizations in the homophile movement, though its members spanned the political and social-class spectrum. He became editor of SIR's magazine, *Vector,* but his abrasive personality and the changes he made or proposed in the magazine had him out within two months. He made an unsuccessful attempt to take *Vector* with him, and has bitterly denounced SIR ever since. . . .

In mid-March, the *Berkeley Barb,* for which Leo wrote spare time (he was employed at ABC-TV station KGO—which later fired him, leading to a long vendetta), featured a front-page photo showing Leo embracing his lover, Gale Whittington, who was stripped at least to the waist. As a result of the story about their love, Gale, on April 1, 1969, lost his new file-clerk job with States Steamship Lines. On April 9, the newly formed Committee for Homosexual Freedom, made up of hippie-radical young gays, some of them also SIR members, began picketing the steamship company's financial-district headquarters several times a week.

During several weeks' picketing, CHF, co-founded by Laurence and Whittington, leafleted heavily, soon printed newsletters to apprise San Francisco gays of its progress. An early flyer presented CHF's demands: "1) States Lines must immediately rehire Gale Whittington with full pay since his discriminatory dismissal; 2) A public announcement by States Lines that they will give equal employment opportunity to admitted homosexuals, and that persons already in their employ who publicly declare their homosexuality will not be fired for such admissions; and 3) Any employee of States Lines who joins the picket line of the CHF will not be disciplined or dismissed for such acts." Another flyer told how "Whittington was fired even though he had a good work record; had been with States Lines for over a year; had received two pay raises and had never

---

From 1965 on, tells Kepner, "Morris [Kight, a founder of L.A. GLF] had a contingent of identified gays who looked just like Gay Libbers today (many of them have been in GLF–LA from the start) who were out front in every peace action here." Kight with his minions "was chiefly involved in organizing against Dow Chemical and the Peace Action Council, which staged a 6-23-67 donnybrook here at the Century Plaza Hotel when Lyndon was in L.A.—a preview of the streets of Chicago the following summer. Several gays were involved in this and in the aftermath, including Morris's steady band of gay freaks who'd come to dominate many peace activities." (Jim Kepner, memo to the author, November 23, 1970.)

been told his work was other than satisfactory. Attempts to discuss the dismissal with . . . Whittington's boss, were refused, and it became clear that he had been fired solely because of his homosexuality. We assert such discrimination to be as unacceptable as that practiced against any other minority group. A man's performance on his job should be the only criterion for his continued employment; and certainly not his sexual orientation." "WHERE IS FREEDOM? WHERE IS FREEDOM FOR GALE WHITTINGTON?" another leaflet asked. *"Do You Think It's Fair?"* queried another. And another, "WHAT'S ALL THE FUSS ABOUT?" then continued:

People ask us, "Why all the commotion? If you didn't make a lot of noise, and the guy that got fired had been more discreet and not gotten his picture in the <u>Barb,</u> then there wouldn't have been all this trouble." . . .

Well, here's why. Millions of <u>homosexuals live in fear,</u> and all the supposed freedoms in the world don't matter one bit if you're scared. Scared of what?

1) <u>Scared of being fired.</u> Most homosexuals fear that their jobs are in danger if their sexual orientation comes to light. Not only States Lines, but many other private and most public employers, refuse to hire admitted homosexuals and fire people when they "find out."

2) <u>Scared for their safebeing.</u> A number of murders have occurred in recent years alone; the latest was the slaying of Frank Bartley a few weeks ago by a Berkeley policeman who was trying to entrap Frank into a legally compromising situation in a park. Others have been killed or beaten by gangs of kids who feel that it's OK to kill or beat up "queers." These murders and beatings are ignored by the law, and are encouraged by the general atmosphere of scorn, prejudice, and hostility to homosexuals.

3) <u>Scared of being arrested.</u> In most places it's illegal to have sex with someone of your own sex, even in your own apartment. And most gays frustrate their desire to show affection -- even a kiss, or holding hands -- in public for fear of arrest. Many police departments continue to set up entrapments, to lead homosexuals on and then arrest them.

4) <u>Fear of being rejected by family and friends.</u> We've been told in so many ways that our sexuality is bad and wrong, that most of us have been keeping up a "double life" and swallowing this garbage. Any elementary psych textbook will tell you what this fear and self-hatred can do.

BUT WE'RE TIRED OF BEING SCARED. So we're making an issue out of the States Lines' firing . . . .

As the picketing continued and the Committee for Homosexual Freedom grew, Lawrence mused, in a May 13 CHF newsletter, in "An Historic Battle":

Our picket line at States Steamship Company has proven to us that we can "do it" and that the public is ready for homosexual freedom. A straight girl wrote to our CHF headquarters: "Your beautiful love picket line moved me to tears. It was so inspiring to see your courage and unabashed love."

We have proven to States Lines and to San Francisco that we do have the manpower and determination to maintain a spirited picket line EVERY weekday noon hour. It's blown a few minds, but Attorney Terry Hallinan said this week, "I guess homosexual freedom is the next battle for the revolution. I'll help in every way I can."

States Lines received our formal list of demands from Gale Whittington's attorney last week. Every effort should be made THIS WEEK to start DIRECT negotiations. We must be willing to negotiate our demands intelligently, but without sacrificing from our determination to eliminate all vestiges of discrimination against homosexuals at States Lines. If negotiations fail to start, or reach an impasse, we must be ready to take DIRECT ACTION.

The confrontation must be non-violent, but must show the public that we are committed to winning our freedom. We must prove that all homosexuals are not the scared, limp-wristed types typical of the stereotyped homosexuals.

It's tougher than hell to face the realities of a sit-in situation. Thinking about handcuffs, bookings, jail, courtrooms, etc., gives me the jitters. But other militant minorities have gone through it . . . and won. So can we, if it's necessary! We will be forced to muster far greater courage than many of us have ever experienced in life. We are small in number today, but if we continue to show the courage and determination to fight for our rights, I'm convinced the people will join us, that our numbers will multiply.

"Your fight is unique in history," says Max Scheer, editor of *Berkeley Barb*. "Never before have homosexuals dared to be so public, to be so proud, and to fight this way for their freedom."

Unfortunately the negotiations never came about, and CHF's first action failed. As Don Jackson reported later, in a gay lib history for the *Los Angeles Free Press,*[17] "After several weeks of picketing, CHF gave up. It was obvious that States Lines was not going to rehire Gale." But, he continued, "Not discouraged, CHF began picketing Tower Records because they had fired a gay employee."

A May 20 CHF newsletter detailed that Frank Dennaro

was fired this week for alleged homosexual advances to a customer. Frank returned the wink of the customer and a guard reported it to management. The managers then began prying into Frank's sex life, to which he replied, "It has nothing to do with my job." They said, "We don't tolerate that free spirit around here" and fired him!

The picketing was hastily organized at Friday night's regular meeting, and several people worked hard to pull it off, because of the belief that Tower represented such a perfect target. It was a chance to hit a sexually bigoted company with an economic boycott. Tower is a store which hires clerks who look hip, caters to hip customers, and sells hip records. Why? Because they're hip to the Movement? Hell no! They do it only because it's good business. . . .

Unlike States Lines, whose customers never see our line, a boycott was the main weapon at Tower. People were asked not to buy at Tower. . . .

. . . Next Saturday the line will form once again. All those of you who haven't been able to picket at States on weekdays now have the perfect opportunity. Come join in a successful picket line, talk to groovy people. Expose Tower Records for what they are. . . .

A June 5 newsletter headlined V-T DAY, VICTORY SCORED AT TOWER RECORDS: ". . . Frank Dennaro, the fired employee, is now back on the job. An independent arbitrator will soon be appointed to decide on back pay for Frank. The employees' union at Tower has signed a statement in which they affirm that sexual discrimination will be an issue over which their union will act. Finally, those employees who honored the CHF picket line have not been fired. The victory comes just two weeks after CHF members began weekend picketing [and leafleting] of the . . . store. Tower customers were very responsive to our action and many refused to cross our picket line. It was obvious that such economic pressure did much to bring Tower to the bargaining table."

By late spring 1969, therefore, a gay liberation movement seemed to be in the offing—if it had not already begun. In the June *Advocate*—printed before the Stonewall riots—Dick Michaels editorialized that "L.A.'s homosexuals could be a very potent economic and political force, IF UNITED. The time has come for a new leadership to rise from the wreckage of the past. *Here and there are signs of a new movement—dedicated to achieving a place in the sun for all homosexuals, not just for this or that individual egoist.*" (Italics mine.) In the same issue, columnist Jim Kepner sensed that "A new kind of homosexual movement is shaping up, bypassing the corpses . . . Homosexuals are beginning to move freely and surely in their own milieu—and to accept their sexuality (the old ones never did)." Marcus Overseth, in the *San Francisco Free Press,* has judged that the gay liberation movement was inevitable; that three historical strains, wanting but the impetus of an *event,* had prepared its way:

The first ancestor of Gay * liberation was the old homophile movement, which began with the emergence of such groups as the Mattachine society . . . With-

* West Coast gay writers and newspapers have, almost exclusively, preferred to capitalize the word *gay*. The *Los Angeles Free Press* reported, on November 14, 1969, that "The Committee for Homosexual Freedom voted at a recent meeting to request all publications to hereafter capitalize the word 'Gay.' Proponents of the measure argued that 'Gay' is a proper noun and adjective which describes a people." Heterosexual writers and lexicographers were, by lower-casing the word, blamed for psychological oppression of homosexuals.

out the pioneering efforts of such organizations, much of the homosexual ideas and literature which provided the philosophical roots would scarcely have existed.

The second leg of the foundation was the Black civil rights movement and the white radical movement catalyzed by it. Blacks provided the concept of an oppressed minority getting their thing together, threw out notions of cooperation with the oppressors and developed concepts of group consciousness and self-pride.

Yet, Gay liberation was still not inevitable until a third development occurred. That development was the hippie movement and the hip life style. Freedom in dress codes, drugs, long hair and colorful clothing for males, rock music and a generally liberated outlook toward life are elements of the hip movement that have had a deep effect on the development of Gay liberation.[18]

A host of nineteenth- and twentieth-century sociologists and political scientists have concluded that "protests blossom forth when the oppressed social conditions are slightly ameliorated, when they seem to be on the road to improvement, offering hope and promise for change, but creating frustration in those impatient for the change and still suffering under less than tolerable conditions." [19]

■

Early meetings of New York's Gay Liberation Front almost literally shook the walls at Alternate U. They were "mind-bending," says Charles Pitts, an organizer–early member. "There was no agreement about methods or philosophy." At the second meeting, on July 31, "the chairmanship was constantly switched around because there was a rather sharp division in the meeting as to whether the purpose of the group should be self-enlightenment (as a kind of consciousness-raising type thing) or integration immediately with other revolutionary or militant movements.

"*I* felt that we should get our heads together first, then join the rest of the revolution when we knew where we were; that this was the first time we'd communicated and it was too soon to present any kind of united front to other groups. The revolutionary types, including Bob Ketzener, who had attended meetings of SDS in New York and seen that it was interested in organizing other minority groups, wanted the homosexuals immediately to join the SDS-type revolutionaries: the general all-round radicals. We voted on it, and it was a majority slightly in favor—like 52 per cent—of sticking to our own problems. Then there was a lot of shouting, disruption, chaos! People were quite adamant . . . there were a lot of people who had just become radical and who felt very strongly, almost fanatically, that if one is radical about one thing [e.g., homosexuality] then one must be radical about everything—whether one knows about everything or not! So that, even though the majority of the meeting had voted to more or less lay low for about two months and get together before

50

joining the rest of the revolution, the minority people were determined, and they moved off into another room. (A lot of people left, too; said, well, 'This is too much,' and stamped out.) In the other room they held a fairly well-organized meeting—much more than the first meeting had been. A lot of men and women, even though they had voted against joining the SDS-type radicals, went in . . .''

Bill Weaver recalls this '' 'insane' walkout in which no one walked out'' and points out that ''a lot of young people were in GLF who had been in the radical and peace movements for a while''—people who would naturally consider Mattachine and similar organizations ''arch-conservatives.'' But some of the new GLFers who had been in the Movement ''were very upset,'' adds Jerry Hoose, ''because they couldn't be open homosexuals and be in the Movement at the same time.'' By helping to create GLF as a radical front could they now be both?

The combination of the ingredients radicalism *and* homosexuality in GLF created problems unique to the organization. Bob Kohler notes that ''A lot of the problems came, and still come, in GLF from so many of the young people who were radicals first and homosexuals second . . . people with no *homosexual* awareness: you've got people talking about Mafia oppression who've never been in a gay bar.'' Weaver, eighteen years old in the summer of the Stonewall, quips, ''I 'came out' *with* the Gay Liberation Front . . . and went to a Mafia-controlled gay bar *after* I had already been to a GLF dance!'' But Kohler and Weaver spoke of chronology, not preference. Some GLFers' priority, *age and experience notwithstanding,* has been with radicalism *per se,* not with homosexual civil rights. Marcus Overseth was to observe, in the *San Francisco Free Press* at year's end, that the gay liberation movement had slowed down largely because of dissension over priorities:

. . . Anybody involved in Gay liberation is by definition involved most deeply in social or cultural revolution. As such he might be labeled a left Gay. Beyond the left Gays are those caught up in the SDS notions of political revolutionary bullshit. These people—whose emphasis is on left rather than Gay—might be called Gay leftists.

The primary orientation of left Gay social revolutionaries is Gay. Their major interest in Gay liberation is just what the name implies—to end discrimination against homosexuals, to free their brothers and sisters from self-doubt and self-hate and to build the Gay counter culture.

Gay leftists, however, look upon the Gay liberation movement as a means of furthering their peculiar notions about political revolution. They look at Gay liberation through leftist lenses—from a framework of Marxist-Leninist thought. To such persons the most important reason for their involvement is not freedom for Gay brothers and sisters but blood-in-the-streets revolution.[20]

But Overseth oversimplified. Not all GLF members were by any means left gays *or* gay leftists. The call of a liberation movement appealed, in summer 1969 as it still does, to a variety of young or young-minded American homosexuals whose sole common denominator was impatience. They had shed, or were shedding, all vestiges of homosexual shame, wanted to live in the light. They were ready for a confrontation with anybody who might challenge or even delay their right to do so.

Jerry Hoose joined the Front because he "felt that this was a really strong base we had, to work with. . . . I didn't see it as a group of people coming out of their closet. I saw it as a group of people completely out of their closet and ready to get out on the street and fight. I hadn't met people like this before." Bob Kohler appreciated that, in GLF, "you had an age spectrum. Lois [Hart] is not a girl. Lois is into her thirties. Martha [Shelley] is into her thirties. These were not extremely young women. So you were getting an age thing, and you were getting *women* in the organization—which I had never seen before: women being active." Kohler found it equally exciting to be a "public homosexual" in addition to being an "open" one. The very human wrangling, also, that hounded GLF meetings, "that 'insanity,' probably appealed to all of us . . . the very 'insanity' that still exists. . . . This is what's kept it alive and this," Kohler believes, "is why it will always be there." Hoose confesses emphatically, "I ate, slept, and talked nothing but GLF for about six months!"

GLF did not become SDS-type revolutionary. Its public appearances ranged, as did its membership, from support of Movement-sponsored protests to confrontations over American anti-homosexuality, personal, political, and organizational. On Sunday, August 3, the new Front demonstrated, with MSNY members, in a treeless park in Kew Gardens, Queens. A line of female and male homosexuals, sporting lavender armbands left over from the Vigil and bearing signs protesting that HOMOSEXUALS HAVE RIGHTS—AND SO DO TREES, paced for an hour. One gay carried a "Dishonor Roll" of nations that maintained anti-homosexual laws: the United States, Soviet Russia, Cuba, Red China, and South Africa. Speeches—a stirring one by Marty Robinson, soon to leave the Action Committee for GLF—were topped off with a satirical playlet by Martha Shelley. The skit posited three Kew Gardens citizens—a policeman, a real estate salesman, a lawyer—as the kind of inseparable heterosexuals whose "love exceedeth that of David and Jonathan" but never (?) goes beyond that. Did it have the vigilantes in mind? By the Kew Gardens rally, homosexuals intended not merely to let wives and children see what their husbands had protected them from, but "to show that homosexuals intend to go anywhere they choose." [21]

A few days later, fifteen GLFers contributed to the anti-war, anti-draft activities of Hiroshima-Nagasaki Week. Bill Weaver helped unfurl the banner, and "you could hear cameras clicking—hundreds of cameras clicking. Allen Ginsberg came up to us and said, 'Oh, wow, far out!' " Weaver was up on the Central Park bandshell when a fight broke out in front of him. "The GLF banner was on TV that night all over America!" After this first contribution to a non-homosexual protest, the GLFers caucused for what was to become characteristic of the group: "We all, like, had a self-criticism session. We were really relating. And we were really down because we didn't like what had happened: we'd had this horrible 'filth' with two women from Women's Rights for Peace—they were saying, 'Don't you know you're disturbing things?!' We really criticized ourselves, and we said that we probably wouldn't march in anything that was led by straight people. . . ." Weaver is glad today that GLF thought better of this decision.

Relating was to become the goal of goals at GLF. Relating not simply in critiques that followed protest excursions, but relating woman-to-woman, man-to-man, and man-to-woman whenever members got together. Male chauvinism in gay males was shortly to come under attack by GLF women *and* men. Steve Dansky would even suggest, in the Front newspaper a year later, that "we as gay men must relinquish all power in GLF to the women. We must give them final veto power." [22] But in late summer–early autumn 1969 GLFers sought self-discovery, first, in encounter groups.

Encounter-group technique was tough to take. Gay Activist Jim Owles contends that "In GLF there was a great deal of love and understanding at the beginning. And then all of the sudden it got into these encounter groups . . . which were not really meant to further the love and understanding but were used as weapons against political deviates. . . . They would get you into a session where you would tell them what was bothering you, talk about yourself, and this in turn would be used against you." Marty Robinson, another *désaffecté,* continues, ". . . they'd turn on you and say, 'Well, you're kinda pushy, so if you're an honest person, you might examine yourself to see if you're really interested in self-improvement.' Then they'd get you to a point where you were ineffectual and non-aggressive."

But if GLF members disagreed on the value of encounter sessions, they agreed unanimously on communal dinners. A few hours before the meeting, GLF men and women would gather, with more food than they needed, and any gay person—GLFer or not—could eat with them. *Gay Power* * newspaper once advised that "A communal spaghetti dinner will be held at 6 pm this coming Sunday ** (Oct. 5). Members who wish may bring food items . . . by 4 pm on that day. The regular meeting will follow at 8 pm." GP later reported that it was "enjoyed by over 50 people." Bob Kohler admits that "The food at the communal dinners was terrible, but it didn't matter because we loved it and because there was no gay group that had ever said, 'Yes, come on in and bring a piece of fish or a head of lettuce and eat!' "

* *Gay Power,* "New York's First Homosexual Newspaper" and a biweekly, was first published on September 15, 1969. Its editor, until July 1970, was John Heys.

** After several Thusday-night meetings at Alternate U., the Front began to meet on Sunday evenings at 9:00, later 8:00. Because, according to Michael Brown, non-gay radicals came trying to tell them how to run their program, GLFers moved their general meeting from AU to the Washington Square Methodist Church in September. A month or so later, the meeting was moved to the Church of the Holy Apostles.

While GLFers were getting organized/acquainted, a national homosexual conference met in Kansas City, August 24–30. The North American Conference of Homophile Organizations, in its fourth year, was an association of some twenty-four independent gay groups, whose delegates met annually in, alternately, a Western, Midwestern, or Eastern city. Though it had frequently been the scene of disputes between Eastern and less conservative Western representatives over the proper approach to homophile goals, NACHO worked, as Columbia University's Student Homophile League * delegate Bob Martin told *Gay Power* (and later WIN), "much as civil-rights groups worked through the first half of the Sixties: through education, legal action, and voter education, through winning over the straight majority by appealing to their consciences, through building a 'good public image,' through lobbying with Congress and State legislators, through 'respectability.' " [23] In 1969 that "respectability" was to be impugned by a radical caucus that emerged midway through the convention. Following a showing of the film *Seasons Change,* an ACLU documentary on the demos and police tactics at the Chicago 1968 Democratic Convention, the caucus was formed. Supported by the NACHO Youth Committee, the radicals labored through the week, and, on Thursday afternoon, presented: "A RADICAL MANIFESTO—THE HOMOPHILE MOVEMENT MUST BE RADICALIZED!"

1) We see the persecution of homosexuality as part of a general attempt to oppress all minorities and keep them powerless. Our fate is linked with these minorities; if the detention camps are filled tomorrow with blacks, hippies and other radicals, we will not escape that fate, all our attempts to dissociate ourselves from them notwithstanding. A common struggle, however, will bring common triumph.

2) Therefore we declare our support as homosexuals or bisexuals for the struggles of the black, the feminist, the Spanish-American, the Indian, the Hippie, the Young, the Student, and other victims of oppression and prejudice.

3) We call upon these groups to lend us their support and encourage their presence with NACHO and the homophile movement at large.

4) Our enemies, an implacable, repressive governmental system; much of organized religion, business and medicine, will not be moved by appeasement or appeals to reason and justice, but only by power and force.

5) We regard established heterosexual standards of morality as immoral and refuse to condone them by demanding an equality which is merely the common yoke of sexual repression.

6) We declare that homosexuals, as individuals and members of the greater community, must develop homosexual ethics and esthetics independent of, and without reference to, the mores imposed upon heterosexuality.

* The first university-chartered homosexual organization in the United States (April 1967), SHL was founded in October 1966 at Columbia University. Its General Declaration set forth its beliefs in complete equality for homosexuals and that homosexuality in and of itself was not a sickness but an orientation on a par with heterosexuality. For a time in 1969, SHL became a cooperative alliance of independent chapters at Columbia, Cornell University, and New York University.

7) We demand the removal of all restrictions on sex between consenting persons of any sex, of any orientation, of any age, anywhere, whether for money or not, and for the removal of all censorship.

8) We call upon the churches to sanction homosexual liaisons when called upon to do so by the parties concerned.

9) We call upon the homophile movement to be more honestly concerned with youth rather than trying to promote a mythical, non-existent "good public image."

10) The homophile movement must totally reject the insane war in Viet Nam and refuse to encourage complicity in the war and support of the war machine, which may well be turned against us. We oppose any attempts by the movement to obtain security clearances for homosexuals, since these contribute to the war machine.

11) The homophile movement must engage in continuous political struggle on all fronts.

12) We must open the eyes of homosexuals on this continent to the increasingly repressive nature of our society and to the realizations that Chicago may await us tomorrow.[24]

To have their twelve points ratified by the convention, the radicals steamed through three hours of debate. They lost all votes to the conservative competition.

Radical and would-be radical Gay Liberation Front was, itself, a curious competition: a conflict of centrifugal and centripetal forces. It wanted to proclaim itself, unhesitatingly to show American radicals and Establishment that it was around *and* that it was both Movement- and gay-civil-rights-oriented. But whereas it insisted on being part of what was going on—"No revolution without us!" GLFers would soon be shouting—it was pulling inward, too: it wanted gay men and women to come together, to depend on and trust one another, in order to develop an alternative gay culture. Not that gay culture wasn't already "alternative"—it was. For those bold ones who lived it all day long, or for those who could dare live it only after 5:00 p.m. But it was second-best: second-best because it was a limited and limiting role to play, because for many gays it had to be clandestine, and because it was not self-chosen but, rather, was imposed on homosexuals by straight society. The new culture would be divorced from the stereotypical gay life, no matter how much fun that life had seemed to be.* Many though not all GLFers, for example, would come to agree with Westerner Marcus Overseth's insistence that

The barscene is a game. It is a great circus managed by straight and gay capitalists out to make a buck. So they pack them in from all over the

---

* Marty Robinson, of Gay Activists Alliance, told a *New York Times* interviewer in June 1970: "Not that I put down the culture that [gays] have; I enjoy some of the freedoms that homosexuals indulge in very much, and they're very positive things. But sexuality is not the end-all, be-all solution to life's problems . . . life has some problems that matter a little more than getting laid—*any* homosexual can get himself laid and laid well!"

country. The barscene in San Francisco is at once a refuge * and a nirvana for Plasticgays from every crossroads hamlet in Amerika. Used to play the game of the bars, Ghetto-gays soon lose all perspective of reality. They are so busy playing hunter or game that they can perceive no other reality, including the deeper reality of their own existence as Gay people.[25]

Not only the bars, but other fun-institutions of gay life would come under attack. Few gay men, however, would come to accept Steve Dansky's extremist view: "We must begin to make demands on each male GLF member. GLF must demand the complete negation of the use of gay bars, tea rooms,** trucks, baths, streets, and other traditional cruising institutions. These are exploitative institutions designed to keep gay men in the roles given to them by a male heterosexual system. The use of these institutions by GLF men must be seen as copping out to The Man's oppression of homosexuals." [26] Though Dansky's proposals may not be intentionally "anti-sex" they are certainly less appealing to homosexuals than are those, however vague, of Bob Martin, then national chairman of Student Homophile League, in "A Statement of Beliefs." Angered that, even in his "alternative" life-style, the American gay followed—or regretted not following—traditional mores, Martin stated that "the currently established heterosexual standards of sexual morality are in many respects themselves immoral . . . the sexual repression and other undesirable features of heterosexual middle-class value systems . . . I think that those of us who participate in the gay subculture must, both as individuals and as part of the greater community, develop homosexual ethics and homosexual esthetics independent of the mores imposed upon heterosexuality."

In the next months, a young Californian gay militant, Gary Alinder, was to advance that neither the stereotypical gay life nor—à la Martin—the patterns of traditional heterosexual American society were valid for gays. He proposed not an exclusive alternative gay culture but a gay Alternative Culture:

It was Albert Camus who said the ultimate philosophical question is "How do you live your life?"

For us gay brothers and sisters that question is urgent. The plastic two-car suburban married life may possibly still have some meaning for heterosexuals, but for us the traditional roles and patterns can be only an empty sham. If we attempt to copy straight life styles we will only perpetuate the subterfuge, self-hatred and loneliness in which we've wallowed for too long.

We need a thorough housecleaning. We've got to get rid of all the garbage straight society stuffed into our heads. That means questioning every one of the values they've given us, turning them upsidedown—seeing the beauty in

---

* Gale Whittington, co-founder with Leo Laurence of the Committee for Homosexual Freedom, has called gay bars "walk-in closets," where stereotype homosexuals can hide from the world. (Don Jackson, in *Gay Power*, No. 7.)

** Men's public lavatories.

ourselves and building a new life reflecting the health and strength that grows from the transition of self-hatred into self-love.

Beyond self-love, we need love for our brothers and sisters. The butch lesbian, the broken-down old queen, the flower child—they're our brothers and sisters. . . .

Finally we need to get it together in specific ways. For those of us who are hip, radical or just plain fed-up, a real advance in our liberation will come if we pick up the Alternative Culture movement.

Alternative Culture is an outgrowth of the hippie movement. It is based on the realization that straight society is wanting: their minds are repressed, their environment fouled, their food full of chemicals, their values money-oriented and competitive, their culture vapid. None of these insights is new, what is new is the attempt to build ways of doing things better ourselves so we will not have to go begging to straight society.

At the core of Alternative Culture is the need to free ourselves from dependence upon the petty rewards straight society gives us for prostituting ourselves to them. Those rewards are money, possessions and the security which comes from having a little niche in the establishment. Once we realize these are but a crutch to prop up our damaged egos we will go on to really creative work strengthening our community.

Among the garbage to throw out: the belief that money (and lots of it) is necessary for life. It is not. The Capitalist establishment controls money and as long as we are dependent on their cash, we shall be dependent on them. Food, shelter, clothing are real needs, and so long as we live in an urban capitalistic country we probably will need small amounts of cash. Our goal should be to reduce to almost nothing our living expenses. In other words, to reduce to a minimum the energy we must sell them. The more of us who can free ourselves from their "jobs," the stronger will be our community. . . .

Dropping out so decisively is a brave step and we've a lot to learn. Like how to live in communes to reduce rent and get to know each other better. Or like how to get cheap but healthful food. . . . Like making and sharing our clothing. Like organizing more free music, dances; parties, films. Like sponsoring and using free services such as the Free Clinics, Switchboards, crash pads, alternative media. Like forming more communes to provide specialized services to the community. . . . Some people envision an interlocking network of such communes. If this develops, we'll need to give the straight world almost none of our energy.

Power! Power through building our community.[27]

As an outcome of one early meeting, GLF was able to offer New York City gays a beginning to the hoped-for new culture. Jerry Hoose relates that "somebody suggested that we had no plans for fund-raising and no money to do things with—that we couldn't even afford to put out another leaflet. So Susan got up and said, 'Well, other groups hold dances here at AU and why don't you do that?' She told us there was a date available, so we formed a committee to plan the dance. . . . Billy and I wrote the leaflet. We sat down and started thinking about the oppression we faced in the bars that we went to, the things we had to deal with nightly, like the cruising scene, and we decided this dance was going to get us completely away from that." Bill Weaver recalls that members "handed out maybe two thousand leaflets and had five or six hundred people at the dance. You don't ordinarily get a return like that on leaflets!"

At that first—a "Coming Out" dance on August 16—and succeeding GLF dances at Alternate U., a $1.50 donation was asked of every gay woman or man who attended, but no one was turned away whose pockets were empty. Couples were asked to donate $2.50. Beers and sodas were a 25¢ contribution. A strobe light show became standard entertainment— sometimes go-go boys. Lounges, where gays could be humanly affectionate, were available for non-dancers or those who had tired of the frantic rock and acid-rock. *Gay Power* called GLF's fourth dance, on October 18, a "resounding success." Some 450 men and women attended, GP reported, and music was "better than ever. Patrons at the door were welcomed personally by GLF members and made to feel at home. Coat checking, a new addition . . ." [28] In the *Village Voice*, March 19, 1970, Jonathan Black sketched a GLF dance: "On the third floor, in the not-so-dark, several hundred bodies pound to the sound of tape-deck rock and twirling light-show slides, 95 per cent men and boys, smiling, dancing, hugging, kissing, pinching, all as though no one had ever mentioned another sex"! [29] Most significant, gays were hosting gays—not capitalizing on them—and the spirit of the militants infected all non-gay-lib visitors, making the dances real celebrations of life. One gay militant reckoned, "At a dance, the vibrations are certainly a lot better than at a bar."

In April 1970, GLF women sponsored the first of a series of All-Women's Dances. GLFer Ellen Bedoz explained, in *Come Out!,* that "many men voiced strong objections. There were fears that the organization was splitting and fears that the women would usurp GLF's allotted time at Alternate U. for themselves, without regard to men's needs. What actually did happen was that not only did women continue to relate to GLF with a heightened sense of consciousness, but many new women were introduced to GLF through the dances." [30] Steve Dansky has judged why GLF women chose to segregate themselves on these several dance occasions: "At the dances we have used women as pawns, rejoicing in our heterosexual experimentation. We are not proud of the fact that women don't feel like sex objects around gay men. Our omnipresent male flesh and how we throw it around have made women see the necessity of having separate dances. . . . At the dances GLF men have tolerated the presence of straight men who have come with their tongues and cocks dangling, ready to show GLF women that all lesbians need is a good lay." He said that lesbians had not flocked to GLF dances because "they are overwhelmed by our male presence and either leave at the door or are forced to elbow their way through attempting to find other women." [31]

At one of their own dances, GLF women met with unexpected—and uninvited—trouble. Kathy Wakeham reported, for the Front newspaper:

On Friday, April 3, GLF sponsored an all-women's dance which was held at Alternate U. The purpose of the dance was to give our sisters an alternative to the oppressive Mafia-controlled gay bars. In the general locale of the gay community in the Village, only two bars exist predominately for gay women. The GLF dance was held within a four-block radius of these two bars.

Two weeks prior to the dance, six GLF women were threatened by the owner of one of these bars while they were giving small calling cards advertising the dance to other girls in the bar. . . .

At 3:15 a.m., the night of the dance, the first attempt was made to carry out this threat. Three stereotype (big, broad, and mean) mafiosi forcibly pushed their way into the All-Women's Dance. When questioned repeatedly as to their identity, they answered by threatening to arrest the sisters for unlawful assembly. The dance was held in a hall which GLF had legally rented for the evening. They then threatened the GLF women with arrest on the basis of not having a liquor license and rapidly quoted prices that neighboring bars have paid for them. The dance did not require a liquor license because donations and *not* prices were *suggested* for admission and refreshments (beer and soda). After much verbal and physical harassment . . . they showed the women a badge which was later suggested to be phoney by uniformed policemen who appeared twenty minutes after these men left. . . .

The uniformed, legal law-enforcing police were called by the women to verify the identity of these three. The uniformed police stated that no call was made with any precinct to check-out the dance, that the dance was legal, and that these three men showed invalid identification.[32]

Within the twelve months after GLF's August experiment, homosexual students were to sponsor their dances openly in university facilities across the nation. As early as December, gays scheduled dances regularly in the Student Union Building at UC Berkeley.[33] A Philadelphia *Plain Dealer* gay reporter, Basil O'Brien, told how, at "the first gay dance on a campus in Pennsylvania," [34]

some straight heads were blown apart as we filled Temple's student center with the high that you feel when you contact with the rest of the alive world and it's all going your way . . . we'd turned off the bad trip of gay ghetto bars and street cruising and sitting on the wall in Rittenhouse Square . . . this dancefloor full of freed-up people was the beginning of our community, *us*, people who could groove together without power roles and channeled sexual drive.

We were feeling the high energy of the revolution based on love. Dancing together is a sharing thing. It's not the same as toking up, sitting inside earphones. It takes a lot of people . . . It's an interpersonal thing that gay people do because we dig each other. Check out the straights some time as they sit on the benches at the Factory or on the Plateau. No energy. Everybody into their own thing, scared to open up to each other. But we're not scared of each other. We know that sisters dancing with sisters, brothers dancing with brothers, touching, kissing and balling people of the same sex is a far loving out expression of living.

Frequently, gay groups have "integrated" (or "liberated") straight dances on college campuses. F(ight) R(epression of) E(rotic) E(xpression) at the University of Minnesota integrated dances as early as January 1970. Steve Ihrig, FREE * co-founder with Koreen Phelps, remembers that "The straights didn't say anything. But afterwards, we were *the* topic of conversation." One gay sophomore remarked, "These dances are really something—they really release me. I feel just like a straight person who had never danced before. I've been to school dances and things, but now I'm really dancing for the first time." [35] Among signal "integrations" were *HI!*'s first gay mixer for college students and guests, March 14, 1970, at The City College/CUNY; and the "People's Dance" of Gay Students' Union on the UC Berkeley campus, May 22. GSU reported that the dance stood as "perhaps the most significant thing" it had done in its first (school) year. "Not only have we demonstrated the effectiveness of our publicity efforts"—approximately one thousand gays and straights danced to two live bands—"but we have also shown the university that there is an enormous, occasionally cohesive gay community eager to show its face, looking for a chance to celebrate, and beginning at last to make its presence and its needs felt outside the narrow confines of its subcultural 'ghetto.' " [36]

Gay Activists Alliance, which would spring from GLF in December 1969, still talks of liberating that bastion of heterosexuality and citadel of sexism, the Playboy Club!

---

* A "History of FREE," published by the organization, outlines its origins: "April, 1969. 'Free University' (a non-structured university loosely attached to the University of Minnesota) sponsored a course entitled: 'The Homosexual Revolution.' Koreen Phelps and Stephen Ihrig expanded the course into an organization for Gay People. The founders coordinated informal activities thru the spring quarter and into the summer. During 'Welcome Week' (the week before classes began, Sept. 21–25) they and three or four Gay people manned an information booth at the University's 'Activities Fair.' . . . As the students came back to the campus, word of the new organization spread and more students became involved." In August 1970, a FREE newsletter announced a name change to FREE: Gay Liberation of Minnesota.

4

COME OUT FOR FREEDOM! COME
OUT NOW! POWER TO THE PEOPLE!
GAY POWER TO GAY PEOPLE! COME
OUT OF THE CLOSET BEFORE THE
DOOR IS NAILED SHUT!
—from the front page of *Come Out!*,
November 14, 1969

Gay militants couldn't have cared less that on September 3, 1969, a bit
of "history was made in the annals of American scholarly and professional
societies when the annual business meeting of the American Sociological
Association . . . in San Francisco adopted the first resolution on the rights
of Homosexuals and other Sexual Minorities ever adopted by such a
body." ....*another Voice* (newsletter of Central Ohio Mattachine) and
other homophile publications were to detail, thanks to news from One,
Inc., how Western gay activist the Rt. Rev. Michael Itkin * spoke eloquently in behalf of the resolution, which read:

Whereas members of the homosexual minority constitute an oppressed people
in academic as well as non-academic environs, insofar as when their sexual
preferences are discovered by university officials, faculty and students suffer
economic reprisals by the loss of tenure, jobs, scholarship, etc., as well as suffering other reprisals in the form of arrests, blacklisting and other forms of
intimidation; and
Whereas these reprisals constitute direct oppression of this minority group and
violate all rights—professional, academic, and human—and freedoms;
Be it resolved that the American Sociological Association condemns the firing,
taking economic sanctions and other oppressive action against persons for
reasons of sexual preference.[1] **

* Jim Kepner has suggested that "Itkin . . . is a one-man resolutions mill, and next
to Leo Laurence is the stormy petrel of the S.F. gay scene, working hard to be more
militant than anyone else except when questions of violence are raised. More angry
and unrestrained even than Leo, he is adamantly pacifist, and also an exceptional
theoretician." (Memo to the author, November 13, 1970.)

** The American Library Association was to create a Task Force on Gay Liberation
on July 3, 1970. Among its announced goals were "the revision of library classification
schemes to remove homosexuality from the realm of sexual aberration, to encourage

61

Gays wondered, would psychologists follow suit? Not on your pocketbook! Dr. Thomas Szasz, in *The Manufacture of Madness* (New York, 1970), has made it clear that "for a psychopathologist to maintain that homosexuals are not patients and that neither their bodies nor their minds require special efforts at cure would amount to asserting that there is no need for coercive psychiatrists." [2]

GLF was one month old. September would bring, on the heels of one minor failure, the first major victory for the organization. *Gay Power* in its second issue lamented, "Unfortunately the response for the GLF demonstration on Saturday, September 6, 1969 in front of the United Nations wasn't enthusiastic. The demonstration was scheduled to celebrate West Germany's amendment of its Sodomy Laws.* In short: sexual relations between consenting males [female homosexuality had never been proscribed by law] is now legal. Certainly enough of the New York homosexual community can dig that . . . This was not indicated by the sparse turnout of supporters on Saturday." GLF's first coup, a victory for Gay Power, occurred a few days later, Friday, September 12. At the *Village Voice*.

Gays had bristled when Lucian Truscott referred to them as "dykes," "faggots," "queers" in his follow-up of the Stonewall riots; ** had marveled at

the hypocrisy of the "straight liberals," those narrow folk who champion every unpopular cause as long as it's fashionable, love the underdog as long as he doesn't bark, and proclaim their support for sexual freedom as long as you spell that h-e-t-e-r-o. . . .

. . . They deplore the increasing tendency of our society to overlook its

---

all libraries to build objective collections on homosexuality, and to make these collections easily available to all." (ALA release, July 15, 1970.) Meanwhile, universities had begun to offer courses in homophile studies; the University of Nebraska, as one, was to classify its Proseminar in Homophile Studies (fall 1970) as Anthropology 271, English 271, and Sociology 271.

* Effective September 1, 1969. "The law that [had] been in effect until [then] was promulgated in 1931 and carried prison sentences for homosexuals. Hitler used the statute freely: it is estimated that homosexual arrests amounted to 8000 per year between 1933 and 1944. Many were sent to concentration camps, and those who survived the ordeal have not received compensation, as has been the case with members of other persecuted groups." (*Homophile Action League Newsletter* [Philadelphia], August–September 1969.)

** *The Dictionary of American Slang,* comp. & ed. Harold Wentworth and Stuart Flexner (New York, 1967), defines *dyke*: "Any large, masculine woman, whether or not a homosexual. *Prob. from 'hermaphrodite.'* "

In a leaflet, "Fire and Faggot," GLF was to define—combining meanings from *Webster's Third International Dictionary* and the *Oxford English Dictionary*—the term *fagot* or *faggot*: "1. A bundle of sticks or twigs, esp. as used for fuel, a fascine, or as a means of burning heretics alive. 2. With special reference to the practice of burning heretics alive, esp. in phrase *fire and faggot,* and *to fry a faggot,* to be burned alive . . . 3. The embroidered figure of a faggot, which heretics who had recanted were obliged to wear on their sleeve, as an emblem of what they had merited. . . ."

original commitment to equality for all people. And, yet, the Voice is not above publishing in its pages . . . gleaned from the July 10th issue . . .

"I thought it would be a novelty to watch a gay demonstration. It was reassuring to see them mince even under pressure."

And:

"The fag after-hours joint"

And:

"The swishy cheer-leaders"

And . . .

"Maybe the city or state should set aside something like a bird sanctuary for them." . . .

Of the many letters to the Voice which protested its flippant, insulting coverage of gay matters . . . was the following:

Dear Sir:

As Jewish, Spanish-Welsh-Irish, Italian, Black members of the American Homosexual community, we find the use of words like "fag" and "faggot" as offensive as "Kike," "spick," "Mick," "wop," and "nigger."

Leo Skir, Robert Cobizio, Kirk Lindsay, George King, John Lane [3]

GLF members submitted an ad for the Public Notices section of classifieds in the August 7 issue of the *Voice*. It requested articles, art work, and photographs for a GLF newspaper to be named *Come Out!* The ad began, "Gay Power to Gay People" . . . Said *Come Out!:*

. . . Our friendly community monopoly newspaper accepted the ad with payment in full and then before printing simply deleted "Gay Power to Gay People" without the knowledge or consent of GLF.

At the regular Sunday meeting of GLF, general outrage was expressed at the assumed right of the *Voice* to censor classified ads. The feasibility of an action against the *Village Voice* was discussed and dismissed on the basis of insufficient evidence. GLF, however, felt that the *Village Voice* had committed itself to a morally bankrupt policy. Classified ads represent a community service, and are not the newspaper's main income source . . . classifieds should be verbally expressive of individuals who are paying for the service.

We decided at this point to submit another ad using the word "Gay." The opportunity presented itself again in the issue of September 4. GLF then used the *VV* Bulletin Board to advertise a dance for Friday night, September 5th, using the lead-in—Gay Community Dance. Again the ad was accepted when and as presented. Next day the person who placed the ad received a call from *VV* which explained that it was the policy of *VV* to refrain from printing obscure words in classifieds and *VV* thought "Gay" was obscene. When questioned why anyone would consider such a word obscene, the *Voice* said that the staff had decided "Gay" was equatable with "fuck" and other four-letter words, and that either the ad would have to be changed or the ad could not be printed. Since "homosexual" was also not acceptable, and since GLF wanted the ad for the dance placed, we accepted their only possible substitute, "homophile" . . . The *Village Voice* also promised a written explanation of their opposition to the words "Gay" and "homosexual." GLF "deviously" planned to utilize this explanation as the basis for a civil rights suit (Civil Rights Law of 1964: denial of rights of free speech by a public or quasi-public institution). But true to tradition, the *Voice* promised more than it delivered [4] . . .

In an attempt to discuss the *Voice*'s classifieds policy, GLF members delivered a letter to the publisher's home—they had been unable to find him at his office. They were snubbed by him. They felt he had closed the door not only on them, but on further dialogue about the matter. The Sunday-night meeting September 7 was heated and wordy. GLF decided to take picket-line and other streets actions against the *Voice. Come Out!* continued:

The day Gay Power laid itself on the line for the first time started at 9 a.m. on September 12, 1969, with much communal coffee and even more communal confusion. [Publisher] Ed Fancher arrived at 10 a.m., received a proclamation of our grievances, and promptly disappeared through the door into *VV* bureaucracy.

At 4:30 p.m., during the peak of the demonstration, a member of GLF submitted a classified ad saying "The Gay Liberation Front sends love to all Gay men and women in the homosexual community." The picture outside the *Voice* was . . . a chanting picket line, a supply of 5000 leaflets being rapidly exhausted, and large numbers of people signing [a] petition charging the *Voice* with discrimination.

At this point, Howard Smith emerged from the door of the *Village Voice* (to boos from the crowd) and requested three representatives from GLF to "meet with Mr. Fancher." Once inside and upstairs, the representatives encountered a cry of outrage that GLF has chosen the *Village Voice* as a target (sooo liberal we are). The suggestion was made that we negotiate the three points in dispute: 1) changing classified ads without knowledge or consent of purchaser, 2) use of the words "Gay" and "homosexual" in classifieds, and 3) the contemptuous attitude of the *Village Voice* toward the Gay Community. GLF explained that the two issues involving classified ad policy were not negotiable and that the substance of the paper should be of legitimate concern to a responsible publisher. Ed Fancher replied that the *Village Voice* exercised no censorship of its articles, and that if a writer wanted to say derogatory things about faggots, he could not in good conscience stop him. Fancher also said that we had no right to tamper with "freedom of the press."

This GLF accepted with the absolute understanding that Gay Power has the right to return and oppose anything the *Village Voice* staff chooses to include in the paper. On the Classified Ads policy he conceded completely. He said that not only would the *Voice* not alter ads after payment, but that in Classified Ads the words "Gay" and "homosexual" per se were no longer issues. One of the GLF representatives in the upstairs office stepped to the window facing Seventh Avenue and flashed the V for Victory sign to the waiting crowd below. WE HAD WON! [5]

A "Gay Power Victory Dance" on September 27 commemorated the event.

The Front was to commence its greatest battle in the next two weeks. A battle that would be largely abandoned, in a few months, to the GLF *désaffectés* who formed a single-cause, structured organization, Gay Activists Alliance.

Mayoral elections were upcoming, and GLF took to the campaign trail. One warm autumn day, Mario Procaccino, candidate for mayor of New York City, grasped Jim Owles's hand on a street corner in Queens. Owles asked, "Mr. Procaccino, what are you going to do about the oppression of the homosexual?"

Mario is no longer smiling, his look is Christian as he says, "Young man, I can see that you're very interested in this problem." Mario is still holding Jim's hand but is now also patting it in condolence. Continuing: "That is one of the many problems that we must face in New York. It is sick rather than criminal, and we must show understanding and compassion for them." [6]

"Hear that folks—no more jails, just asylums," exclaimed *Come Out!*

Under the chandeliers of the Gotham Young Republican Club, an audience of about 120 listened to State Senator John Marchi, candidate for mayor of New York. Concerned about the urban crises, the Senator seemed, to GLFers, to be promising a democracy which would allow the majority's will to infringe upon the rights of significant minorities, even of the individual.[7] General applause, when he'd finished. A GLFer rose: "Senator Marchi, are you aware of the emerging militancy within the homosexual community, and how does this relate to your views on law and order? Will homosexuals become targets or will you be responsive to their needs?"

Devastating rays of stunned silence reverberated off the crystal chandeliers and clean faces as the room closed in and adrenalin waves caused one's vision to narrow and focus on the Senator . . . For the first time that evening the Senator lost his cool, elegant, articulate style. . . .

. . . he didn't feel it necessary for him to speak on the matter, since it was being considered by some committee and was a topic for the State Legislature.

. . . "Senator, it's not just for the legislature. As Mayor you would have control of the police force. How will this affect the lives of New York's 800,000 homosexuals?" . . . Marchi answered: "I will enforce the laws and prevailing social mores of society." The staccato manner of his delivery seemed devoid of personal moral conscience, as if he were not talking about human beings at all.

"Do you consider homosexuals as an oppressed minority?"

"No," he says . . .

. . . as the Senator exits he is confronted by a GLF member who says: "Evidently you feel no social suffering is involved in the issue (the status of the homosexual). You don't seem to feel obligated to address yourself to it."

"Well, yes," he muttered as he walked away.[8] . . .

Back to Queens on October 1 went thirteen GLF members, to Temple Torah, where the League of Women Voters had brought the mayoral candidates, the media, and about two thousand New Yorkers of both Now and Then generations. After the candidates had responded to selected questions from those submitted by the audience, GLF saw that it would be shunted. Marty Robinson called out, "It's 1776, Mr. Procaccino. The homosexual revolution has begun," and asked him what he was going to do about the homosexual community. GLF rose. "Answer them!" "Let them speak!" from the audience, and "Throw the bum out!"

. . . The cops moved in toward Marty and Jim [Owles], who had signalled the barrage, but the women running the event lined up protectively in front of them. As soon as order was established, and the cops retired, the questions burst forth again. This time Marty and Jim were escorted out gently under the watchful eyes of the women and the cameras of the media. Again the assembly settled down peacefully, only to hear from the remaining gay commandoes, "Why don't you answer our questions?" "Speak to the community," rang out again and again during the now anarchistic proceedings.

The meeting managed to continue. Finally,

When Marchi approached the speaker's podium, the president of the League of Women Voters asked him to respond to the homosexual questions. Marchi: "We have not yet provided room on our platform for them." . . . GLFers started leaving the room, talking with the aroused and interested community as they left; Jerry [Hoose?] and Marty [Stephan] walked casually to the front of the assembly. Jerry handed the leaflet with the GLF demands to the press, while Marty deliberately handed the paper to each of the appalled people on the speaker's platform.[9] . . .

The confrontation made NBC-TV's one o'clock news and the *New York Post*!

But GLF had by no means finished with the candidates. On Tuesday evening, October 7, the Mayor, Marchi, and Procaccino were to visit the Greenwich Village Association.* Proxies, instead, showed up in their place. *Gay Power* reported that "Earlier in the day two GLFers [had] delivered letters to the candidates demanding they address themselves to the homosexual issue as well as other village issues when speaking to residents that evening."[10] GP told that, in the question-and-answer period,

Gay Liberation Front took advantage . . . and posed many questions relating to the homosexual issue. Senator Lerner, representing Sen. John Marchi, was asked whether he believed in the single man's individual rights, taxation

* New York Mattachine representatives Bob Milne and Michael Kotis also visited the Greenwich Village political arena. At an October 27 meeting, they addressed about twenty-five members of the Village Independent Democrats, who told them "to use VID offices in order to get through to the city on any occasion that the city's official doors seemed closed to homosexual complaint." (GAY, January 19, 1970.)

with representation and individuals as property owners. His answer, "Yes." Next question posed was interrupted half-way through by Lerner when the words "800,000 men and women homosexuals in New York City" were mentioned—Lerner laughed and said, "If your figures are right, the country's in trouble!" He suggested that all homosexuals vote for their friend Mayor Lindsay. Lerner also emphasized that if Marchi were elected he would enforce any and all legislation on the books pertaining to homosexuals, including the sodomy laws. . . .

The last question asked that evening was whether Marchi and Procaccino felt homosexuals were sick and depraved. Lerner responded quickly by saying, "Yes!" [Eugene] Connolly for Procaccino replied by whispering and coughing up a "No!" . . . Mario had stated on October 1, 1969 that homosexuals were indeed sick.

Gay Power advised that "Before any . . . homosexual in New York City pulls that lever at his or her polling station, November 4, he'd better know . . ." [11]

Homosexuals did know. Writing for GAY, Dick Leitsch described how, though some few conservative homosexuals did favor Marchi, "there was no perceivable gay vote for Procaccino whatsoever. Never, throughout the long and even tedious campaign, did one see a Procaccino button or poster in a gay place." But "posters and photos of New York's most handsome Mayor covered the walls in many bars around town." [12] On the night of his victory, many gay bars gave free drinks to their customers. Gays had been active in the Mayor's campaign for re-election, manning street-corner tables, working as volunteers at Lindsay headquarters, and canvasing neighborhoods for him.

Gay people are certain they caused him to win. *HI!* president Craig Schoonmaker analyzed, in *Gay Power:*

How do we figure that gay people won the election for Lindsay? Here's how: Take Kinsey's figures as a start: $\frac{1}{6}$ of U.S. men and $\frac{1}{8}$ of U.S. women are predominantly or exclusively homosexual. So in a city of 8 million, $\frac{1}{6}$ of all 4 million men would be 650,000; $\frac{1}{8}$ of the women, 500,000. Together that's 1,150,000. But New York has proportionately more homosexuals than the country in general, because Gotham is a major center of gay in-migration. So add, as a conservative number, another 100,000. Total: 1,250,000 predominantly or exclusively gay people.

However, not all those homosexuals are "out" [have a homosexual sex life] or adults. So chop that figure in half: 625,000. Not all of these homosexuals voted, tho undoubtedly a very substantial percentage did, for homosexual interests were clearly at stake. So perhaps 65 percent voted: about 400,000. Of those, not all voted for Lindsay, although there is every reason to believe that by far the majority did, because Lindsay's administration has been generally very considerate of homosexuals. But even if only 60 percent voted for Lindsay, a *very* conservative figure, that would still mean that some 240,000 homosexuals voted for him. That's between 2 and 3 times as many votes as separated Lindsay from Procaccino. Inescapable conclusion: homosexuals swung this election for Mayor Lindsay.[13]

Advocate editor-in-chief Dick Michaels recalls how gay voting power influenced the fall 1969 City Council election in Los Angeles: "The City Councilman Paul Lamport ran for re-election. And he was very 'bad' on gays. So in the primary we backed an openly gay candidate who did not have much of a chance of getting the nomination—but we wanted to see how many votes he would get. He wound up getting over three thousand. Then, in the election Lamport ran against a man named Stevenson, and we came out openly against Lamport, backing Stevenson. Even though we didn't know a lot about him. Lamport lost by roughly three thousand votes." *

Responding again to the needs of the broader Movement, five GLF members joined participants in the "free the Fort Dix 38" event at the New Jersey army stockade on Sunday, Columbus Day.[14] Three days later, Wednesday, October 15, the Front joined the first moratorium protest against the war in Vietnam, leafleting that "The War is Making America a militaristic society. Militaristic, authoritarian societies are traditionally antagonistic to human freedom, to diversity, to individuality, to non-conformity, to dissent, to difference—and to those who, rightly or wrongly, are unpopular. . . . As long as the war continues, we will at best maintain the status quo, if not retrogress. Progress will be impossible. Homosexuals as homosexuals so often feel themselves at odds with the vast majority of heterosexuals, and this is a deplorable division in our society. Gay Liberation Front therefore welcomes this opportunity to join in common cause with heterosexuals supporting this moratorium, knowing as it does that millions of homosexual men and women have precisely the same anti-war views as millions of heterosexual men and women."

That day, GLF set up a table in Sheridan Square, where it sold armbands, buttons, and distributed its leaflet. Later, members carried the banner to Bryant Park and the anti-war addresses by members of the publishing industry. Pete Hamill, columnist at the *New York Post,* referred to the gays as slim-waisted "freak creeps." Wondering whether the columnist had a weight or a sex problem, GLF sent letters to the *Post* and Hamill. One, Martha Shelley's, got into *Post* print.[15]

* Dick Leitsch details how gays influenced the 1969 election for councilman in the 13th District in Queens: "The Republican-Conservative candidate, Sheldon Farber, made homosexuality an issue in the campaign. His people handed out a circular which called for a stop to 'coddling of homosexuals.' The West Side [homosexual] Discussion Group reprinted the circular and mailed it to their friends and members in that area, which includes parts of Kew Gardens, Flushing and Jamaica, which, in turn, include many gay voters. The leaflet came to the attention of the Mattachine Society the day before the election, and a 'telephone tree' was started. More than 100 phone calls were placed to homosexuals in the 13th Councilmanic District, and residents of the area were requested to call ten friends and tell them about Farber's leaflet and ask them to vote for his opponent, A. J. Katzman. Katzman won by 70,509 votes to Farber's 48,272." (GAY, December 15, 1969.)

During the summer, gay liberation on the West Coast—i.e., CHF—had lain dormant. A few weeks "after the New York GLF started," Jim Kepner notes, "a mild split in the San Francisco group—prompted I think by some of the doctrinaire anarcho-Marxists or Trots—led to setting up a GLF." He states that "the difference between SF–GLF and CHF was slight, hinging on questions of the degree of antagonism considered advisable, as against the 'Gay Establishment' and on involvement with other 'Movement' issues. But membership (to the degree that either had 'membership' as such) was overlapping, and it was unclear from week to week which group was on which side of which issue." [16]

Another GLF was founded in Berkeley. Reese Erlich, writing for the *Los Angeles Free Press*,[17] indicated that "The formation of Gay Liberation has caused a minor tremor in the Berkeley scene: in addition to having theoretical debates on the black revolution and women's liberation, one must now have a position on the homosexual question." Erlich interviewed Konstantin Berlandt, who, a writer for the *Daily Californian,* had just helped establish a third new group, Gay Liberation Theatre. The Theatre's manifesto, by Stevens McClave, explained:

The revolution is in the streets. The continuum of violent and non-violent confrontation becomes for some a way of life, for others life itself. Street theatre, or guerrilla theatre, has evolved as an artistic expression of such a way of life. Theatre is the wrong word for the form of presentation currently developing; theatre is a part of the establishment vocabulary to define an establishment concept, whereas the concept of street theatre annihilates the theatrical. Street theatre is non-theatre and from its inception foresees its own destruction in the fusion of life with art. . . .[18] *

The *Berkeley Barb* recorded how the gay guerrillas performed in Sproul Plaza on October 6 before a crowd of about two thousand, at a CHF-organized rally that was part of the University of California's "disorientation week." [19] GLT was described by the *San Francisco Free Press* [20] as "probably the most militant and activist of all Gay Liberation groups. A together group, the theatre is capable of acting or reacting on very rapid notice to any situation where they feel they are needed."

With a shot of gay liberationist Pat Brown "unhesitatingly burning his SIR card," the *Free Press* told of West Coast inter-gay problems on anti-war day: [21]

The Society for Individual Rights, also known as the Society for Idle Rap, is a goodgrey organization dedicated to total integration within the establishment and to the proposition that, with a little help from a haircut and a suit and tie, all men can look equal. Passing for straight is SIR's ideal, and "Really? You don't look it" the highest compliment it can receive. The Committee for

* Leo Laurence saw GLT, in the *Berkeley Tribe*, as "a sorta 'Mime Troupe' approach to the Gay Revolution movement." (October 10–16, 1969.)

Homosexual Freedom, which, with Gay Liberation Theatre, definitely disrupted and led a walkout of the SIR meeting on October 15th, may be subject to attack for trying to rock the boat. But, as [Putney] Swope says so eloquently in Robert Downey's superlative film, "Rockin' the boat is a drag. You gotta sink the boat."

Wednesday, October 15th, the night of the Vietnam War Moratorium, Gay Liberation Theatre and its company of freaks took over the stage of SIR's former union hall on a cue from folksinger Don Burton. The guerrilla band chaotically shattered the tone of the proceedings of the group which chose not to participate in the Moratorium because the War is "too controversial" and punctured a few holes in the fragile boat wherein its members see homosexual freedom as conformity to the universal dissatisfaction and as safety within the shelter of anonymity and oblivion. The brief and tumultuous presentation of the piece, NO VIETNAMESE EVER CALLED ME A QUEER, received scattered applause from the confused assembly, but the confusion cleared and gave way to a volley between right-wing reactionaries and gay militants when Don resumed the stage and let SIR know that it was coopting and failing to meet the needs of its people. He then invited all those who believed in gay liberation to join him in a walkout, effected with shouts of "All the power to all the people" and "The revolution is in the streets" ringing in the hallowed halls. . . .

Two weeks later, the *Free Press* advised that "For many of us it all changed on Halloween . . . the Gay Liberation movement was rapidly growing from a small hard core into a much larger group. Group identity and consciousness was there. People called each other brothers and sisters. Everybody knew the truth. Everybody felt it but perhaps not as strongly as they might. Then everything snowballed. . . ." [22]

Noon. October 31. A peaceful picket in front of the San Francisco Examiner Building—a day which less than an hour later was to become bloody Friday of the Purple Hand. Larry Clarkson's A FAIRY TALE, one reportage in the *Free Press,* satired:

Once upon a time, in Amerika, there existed a kingdom known as San Francisco. In the kingdom there also existed an evil and not too reputable institution known as the Examiner.

For many years the Examiner had harassed and intimidated the beautiful people of San Francisco by defacing almost every street corner with gaudy little red eye-sores known as vending machines. These machines spewed forth the Examiner's hateful and vindictive propaganda into the minds of the people.

Then on the 22nd day of October a none too competent Examiner muckraker by the name of Robert Patterson dumped another load of Examiner bullshit into the homes of some of the most beautiful people of all, the city's Gay community. He called them such unbecoming names as "semi-males," "drag darlings," and "women who aren't exactly women."

The beautiful people decided that they would make their grievances known by picketing the Examiner.

And so, the legend goes, after a week of high speed leafleting the fateful day known as "Friday of the Purple Hand" arrived.[23] . . .

The gays, from CHF and GLF, held signs of FIRE PATTERSON; GAY BROTHERS AND SISTERS, YOUR SILENCE AIDS OUR OPPRESSORS, COME OUT, COME TOGETHER; CALIFORNIA COPS MURDER HOMOSEXUALS; NO MAN IS FREE UNTIL ALL MEN ARE FREE . . . They chanted, "G–A–Y P–O–W–E–R——Gay Power!" and "Out of your closets and into the streets!" Soon a crowd of spectators, police, and newsmen had collected.

Don Jackson told how the trouble began, in *The Advocate* and in *Gay Power:* [24]

. . . Everyone was good natured up to this time. Suddenly a plastic bag of printers ink was thrown from a second floor Examiner office, soaking the pickets and splattering the walls of the building. Someone wiped his hands off on the wall. In a few seconds, inked hand prints covered the wall and windows. "Fuck the Examiner" was written by a finger dripping with ink. . . .

"Still there was no violence," wrote Marcus Overseth, *Free Press* editor, until a handsome young man wrote "Gay is" on the Examiner wall. He was dragged off by police into a waiting van, kicking and biting at his abductors. Overseth explained, "I was in there with my camera. After taking two shots I called out at the officer and asked him why he was arresting . . . Before I knew what happened porkish hands grabbed my shoulder, someone said I was arrested, and I was dragged to the paddy-wagon. . . . I got my camera going again as brother after brother and then Karen [Harrick] were viciously manhandled and thrown in." [25] Jackson reported how "Karen was jerked from the picket line, thrown to the sidewalk by the masculine officers . . . Karen was [later] charged with obstructing traffic, because she was lying on the sidewalk while she was being clubbed." [26]

. . . The riot police which had been summoned charged into the picket line brandishing riot batons. Persons with cameras were the first to be attacked. . . . Leo Laurence . . . stopped to take a picture of a young guy being clubbed. A riot baton swung at Leo. By the time he was taken to the van, a line was waiting to be tossed in. Quick-minded Leo deftly removed the film from his camera and tossed it to Larry Littlejohn, SIR president, who fled the scene with the film.[27]

Jackson noted that "A transvestite clunked a pig over the head with the picket sign he was carrying. The pole broke and the dazed officer looked shocked as he watched him escape . . . his high heeled shoes clicking . . . as he ran down the sidewalk." [28]

Inside the police van, "The doors closed and there were twelve of us," wrote Overseth. "Michael Cardone was hurt. Darwin [Dias]'s teeth had been knocked out [Jackson told how, "As he was thrown in, a pig standing on the ladder gave him a drop kick in the mouth"] . . . Some of the brothers feared the worst and expected the doors to the van to open at any moment and for the beatings to continue. . . . Michael's injury soon had him lying on the hard metal bench" when the group reached the station house, and "Brotherly hands comforted him as we made repeated calls for a doctor. He was having trouble breathing . . . said his side hurt terribly. . . . We called out again and again for a doctor to see Michael. . . . It was almost an hour until they came to the door and carried him off. They said they were going to take him to a hospital but they never did. He ended up in the felony section." [29] *

Of the remaining picketers—the van was filled to capacity—most had scattered, but Jackson recalled that

52 who stayed in a group marched through the Tenderloin to Glide Methodist Church [a GLF headquarters]. On the march through 8 blocks of the Tenderloin section, they shouted "Pigs!" in unison at cops walking or driving past. At Glide the keyed up Gays were given sanctuary. They rested and discussed strategy for a half hour. At 2 P.M. they left the church still carrying the picket signs.

The angry Gays marched from the church to S.F. City Hall to take their demands for justice to Mayor Alioto, singing and shouting slogans all the way, occasionally interrupted by boos when an Examiner delivery truck would pass and "Pigs!" when patrol cars passed. At the steps of City Hall the group stopped and began making an oblong picket line on the sidewalk at the foot of City Hall steps. A crowd quickly gathered in Civic Center Plaza and on the steps. "We are here to demand justice," shouted CHF co-founder Gale Whittington. "We have been treated like hell for too long. [Then, to the gays:] What are we here for?" The pickets spontaneously and in unison shouted, "Freedom! Stop police brutality" . . .

Gale and 3 others left the picket line and ascended the City Hall steps, under the great granite dome and up the famed marble staircase to the Mayor's Office. "Thirteen of our brothers were savagely beaten and busted," Gale told the Mayor's assistant, Mike McCone. "We demand justice." Mayor Alioto being out of town, McCone stated there was nothing he could do, and suggested they should take their complaint to the police department. The four

* California homosexuals have a history of brutalization by police. On March 9, 1969, three vice officers of the Los Angeles Police Department kicked, beat, and stomped to death J. McCann at the Dover Hotel; a seven-man coroner's jury ruled his death at the hands of police officers "excusable homicide." (*The Advocate,* April and June 1969.) Frank Bartley, an alleged homosexual, died April 22, 1969, after being shot in the head by a Berkeley police officer; a coroner decided that Bartley's death was "accidental." (*The Advocate,* June 1969.) On March 8, 1970, Larry Turner, a twenty-year-old homosexual, was shot fatally by the LAPD; a gay liberationist was cited as saying, "It is hard to understand why the police kill a man just because he wants to suck a dick." (*Gay Power,* No. 13.)

left the office and returned outside. . . . [Then all the gays] went up the stairway into the plush office of Mayor Alioto. The picket signs were leaned against the elegant chairs and richly panelled walls. They sat or lay down on the plush carpet and began to sing in chorus, "Freedom, oh, Freedom, before I'll be a slave I'll lie in my grave, Freedom, oh, Freedom." . . . The sit-in lasted two hours. At 5 P.M. the mayor's assistant came out and said, "The building is now closed. I ask you to leave. In five minutes I will ask the S.F. police department to arrest everyone remaining." The Gays had agreed that each man would do as his conscience directed. Everyone left except for three, who at 5:05 were handcuffed and taken to the waiting van. Jim Connaly, as he was dragged from the Mayor's office, shouted, "Power to the (Gay) People!" On City Hall steps a group of Gay people waited to see their brothers loaded into the patrol car. As the door was closed they shouted together, "Power to our People!" [30] . . .

In New York, Ralph Hall in *Gay Power* asked "anyone concerned for our gay brothers and sisters . . . please send contributions to: Committee for Homosexual Freedom, c/o War Resisters League . . ." [31]

The gay attack on the American press was to spread, if anticlimactically, to Los Angeles on November 5. Homosexual Information Center,* a service organization, brought twenty-five picketers to the offices of the *Los Angeles Times* to protest the paper's refusal to print the word *homosexual* in its ads. The *Los Angeles Free Press* told how "Representatives of the magazine [*Tangents,* published by HIC] sought to place an ad announcing there would be a discussion period dealing with the subject of homosexuality following each performance of the play 'Geese' . . . and they were seeking knowledgeable persons to participate in these discussions." [32]

HIC elucidated:

. . . The *Times* does not go so far as to say it is prejudiced against homosexuals—just the word by which they are designated. For economic reasons, naturally, the *Times* does carry advertisements for products and services that appeal to homosexuals.

The hypocrisy of their position is incredible, and it was carried to the point of absurdity this week when the paper's advertising department refused to accept an ad because the wording included the name of our organization, which happens to be the Homosexual Information Center.

We don't mind the slight for ourselves, but the *Times'* attitude shows that it is cold and indifferent to the efforts of homosexuals to improve their legal and social position in America. Our organization is a part of the over-all homosexual movement taking place in the U.S. today. It is a legally chartered California corporation.[33]

* HIC is the corporation name for Tangents, a Los Angeles organization formed in 1965 under the leadership of Don Slater to provide draft counseling to gays, aid to researchers on homosexuality, and a homosexual speaker's bureau for other interested groups. Its magazine is *Tangents.*

"The news media, however, nearly matched the demonstrators in number," reported *The Advocate*. Four TV and four radio stations were represented, and Don Slater, chairman of the board of HIC, was interviewed. To defend the *Times*'s stance, staff members "read from a lengthy manual a page-long list of terms that are taboo, including the word 'homosexual.'" Despite the fact that *Times* reporters frequently used the word and less complimentary terms when reviewing plays, films, etc., its admen believed they had a protective duty "to purge advertisements that would be suggestive or offensive in a 'family newspaper.'" [34]

The *Free Press* noted, "Without doubt the Times has inadvertently opened the doors to the gay activist in the Los Angeles area." [35]

Meanwhile, Nancy Ross, a feature writer for the *Washington Post*, wrote an appraisal of the increasing militancy among American homosexuals. But, she stated, "As among black leaders, controversy has developed within the ranks of homosexuals as to the best method of achieving their ends." [36] A Western gay militant complained, in IN THE STREETS FOR THE REVOLUTION: [37]

Nothing is so pathetic as a Black who denies his culture and tries to pass for white, becoming more Mr. Charlie than Mr. Charlie in the process, unless it's one of our Gay brothers who denies his Gayness to get along in the straight plastic culture. Both have become less than men and have sunk to the level of imitations. Luckily for the souls of Black folk they have awakened to their beauty and cultural integrity in time. Luckily, also, for the Blacks, racial differences make passing difficult. Unluckily for us passing is the easiest thing in the world. We have only to pretend to be what we are not and show indifference to the suffering of oppressed peoples everywhere—Chicano, Black, Gay, Third World, and others. All too many of our brothers SUCCEED in passing. They become straighter than the straight.

. . . We have been put down by some of our Gay brothers for doing our thing in the streets and pushing revolution. We have had confrontations with all kinds of Auntie Toms who are comfortable living half lives as imitation men and sucking up to the Almighty Dollar to make up for the parts of their lives that are missing. We have seen the effects of years of oppression—poor, tired, sickly imitation men and women who would continue their own oppression and the oppression of their brothers and sisters. We've seen the society in which we live . . .

We will build the new society in the streets, not by giving up on our brothers and sisters who have accepted their oppression, but by continuing to hammer at the chains that bind all of us. The new world will be built by new people who are in the open, free of chains; by proud men and women of all colors . . . by men and women who know love and live it. And it begins in the streets.

Gay Liberation Theatre of San Francisco took to the streets Saturday night, October 25, to picket their gay brothers' annual Halloween Drag

Ball. Leaflets they distributed attacked the ball as a "Gay Establishment circus." [38]

■

Pride in and proclamation of one's homosexuality—violent * and non-violent militancy against oppressors of homosexuals—youth-oriented leftism that advocates overthrow of the capitalist system—alignment with non-homosexual Movement and Movement-type causes. These four became keynotes of Gay Liberation Front thinking and action, these four would build Gay Power. But they were to produce dissension, first, within the homophile movement—which GLF thought wrong, yet sought to join (and reform)—and, second, within the Front itself, to the extent that a split, in New York, yielded Gay Activists Alliance at year's end. GAA would be proud (perhaps prouder) and would proclaim, but its constitution would proscribe violence of any kind except in self-defense, it would work for homosexual civil rights *within* the American political system, and it would forego alliance of its organization with non-homosexual causes.

There were to be many homosexual, as well as heterosexual, critics of Gay Power and what it implied. Dick Leitsch, in GAY, enunciated that " 'Gay Power' raises the spectre of a bunch of people, militantly wearing labels proclaiming, 'I am a homosexual!' and marching to the slogan of 'Power to Homosexuals!' " [39] GLF took no offense: the picture was not unattractive. David McReynolds's "Notes for a More Coherent Article," in WIN magazine, provoked on the other hand a flood of abuse from the blossoming gay militant movement. McReynolds's story, a beautiful and heartfelt confession of his homosexuality and homosexual hang-ups, was both a direct and indirect insult to Gay Power and Pride; the over-30 writer, whose owning-up might have been appreciated five years before, obviously knew not (or was disregarding) the post-Stonewall gay community his "Notes" would reach—a community to whom "Gay Is Good" ** was scripture. Preferring to call himself "queer" and accepting that he was "a walking ton of potential prison terms," he argued that "Gay Power is a Plastic Flower. Gay is *not* good, it is boring. It is sick in a way that queerness is not." But he went on,

I don't even find the gay ghetto particularly repressed or persecuted, and the cry for "Gay Power" is, in a way, an effort to draw on the strength of the blacks, and in a way that is good. Kids who struggle openly to be gay may find in the course of that struggle that their own "masculine" nature has been strengthened. I know faggot eyes too well, tragic cows seated on bar chairs, with smooth, vacant faces. . . . If gay power can give any inner power to those

* Unprovoked personal violence has never been characteristic of Gay Liberation Front.
** Adopted by NACHO in a resolution introduced by Franklin Kameny, the slogan's formulator, at the August 1968 conference in Chicago.

eyes, those desperate eyes that I've seen in the bars of this nation, then okay, I'm for the slogan.[40] . . .

In the same issue of WIN, writer-sociologist Paul Goodman—another self-designated "queer"—launched no broadsides against Gay Power. On the contrary, he maintained that "homosexual acts . . . so far as I have heard, have never done any harm to anybody." [41] But his basically apologetic "Memoirs of an Ancient Activist," which began with the proposition that "In essential ways, homosexual needs have made me a nigger," turned off gay militants. Together with McReynolds's article, it fired up GLFer Marty Stephan to counter, in *Gay Power,* with DELIVER US FROM OUR FRIENDS—PLEASE O LORD. Stephan began, "Homosexual oppression is damn well not limited to the oppression of the homosexual by the heterosexual. We gays also suffer from oppression visited upon us by our fellow gays themselves suffering from homosexual guilt which usually (but not exclusively) manifests itself in the form of 'telling it like it is' . . ." Calling McReynolds "a homosexual neanderthal type," she demolished both his and Goodman's articles, concluding:

The most quoted bit from the article is the "Gay Power is a Plastic Flower" insult. Bullshit. Gay Power means self-love and acceptance, love for other gays, freedom for gays, gay freedom for everyone and ultimately sexual freedom for all. We know you need it, David McReynolds, you are a plastic faggot. Perhaps some day you can make love to a woman for procreation purposes and stop envying Paul Goodman and calling him a crackpot and a misfit. Maybe Paul Goodman will fuck you in the ass while you're making the baby. Wouldn't that be fun? [42]

"Queer" to the gay militant meant a "mistake," a "misfire," a "failure"—"gay" did not. Nor did Gay Power. Its *rightness*—even if not its possible violence, its probable leftism, its inevitable alignments—was enunciated by Bob Martin in "A Statement of Beliefs":

What is Gay Power? It is essentially Pride; it is standing up for one's beliefs; it is saying, "Yes, I love other men (or women) and I don't give a damn what you think of it"; it is refusing to hide by pretending to be that which you are not; it is demanding to be recognized as a powerful minority with just rights which have not been acknowledged; it is an insistence that homosexuality has made its own unique contribution to the building of our civilization and will continue to do so; and it is the realization that homosexuality, while morally and psychologically on a par with heterosexuality, does nonetheless have unique aspects which demand their own standards of evaluation and their own subculture.

Pride, many participants in the old-line homophile movement had. Though few would have thought it necessary to proclaim that pride.

Madolin Cervantes of MSNY has protested that GLFers are "so full of guilt and self-hatred and contempt for themselves that they've got to scream at people, 'I'm gay, you've got to accept me. So, you see, then I can accept myself.'" The Tangents Group (HIC, L.A.) are of the same basic opinion. In the *Los Angeles Free Press,* they asked, "How do you deal with the freak queens who, for personal therapy, pop out of their closets to enact some silly role, thus reinforcing what society is only too eager to believe: that *all* homosexuals are sick and sort of 'queer.'"[43] But, GAY PRIDE, Mattachine placards would exult on June 28, 1970; stickers printed by Philadelphia's Homophile Action League would soon advise, "GAY—Personal Peace, Power, Pride." Two years earlier, "Gay Is Good" had become a slogan for NACHO. In summer 1969, homosexuals bought matches, buttons, bumper stickers, and paper napkins, etc., with that motto or with "Buy Gay," at Craig Rodwell's Oscar Wilde Memorial Book Shop in New York City. Following the Stonewall riots, Rodwell advertised: "GAY & PROUD? Then you're our kind of man or woman. . . ."

By and large, the American homosexual was not—could not have been—proud, certainly not loud if proud, in autumn 1969. In WIN's gay lib issue, Bob Martin explained:

Traditionally, the homosexual has been a social conservative, for traditionally every homosexual who could do so led a double life. He spent half his time building up an image of respectability and perfect straightness to compensate for the dangers of his love life. He "passed," and in so doing sought to pay the utmost homage to a society of whose acceptance he was never sure.

In trying to be more Catholic than the Pope, he denied his unique heritage as a homosexual, the inheritor of a tradition going back to the dawn of recorded history. Moreover, in accepting middle-class heterosexual values of repression, guilt, and inhumanity he was in essential contradiction to his own nature as a sexual non-conformist. Yet here, in coloring himself like a chameleon to the standards around him, he sought safety.[44] . . .

Atypical Randy Wicker has described traditional homosexuals as

. . . sad mattachines, court jesters hiding their true feelings while pandering to the tyrannical intolerance of the heterosexual mass.

They become bankrupt characters, feigning interest in women [or in men], and they may even mouth cliché anti-homosexualisms believing this makes them less suspect to others.

Their lives are split into two worlds. Two distinct personalities emerge. Their "straight" personality cannot be discarded until five o'clock along with "straight" clothes, "straight" friends, "straight" life." At day's end they have only a few fleeting hours to be with others like themselves. They are hypocrites by day and social refugees by night.[45]

Some critics—gay militant, old-line homophile, and gay non-organizational alike—have asked Gay Pride/"Gay Is Good" proponents, "How can one be proud of being gay, and more than one can be proud of being white, or black, or left-handed? One should be proud to be a human being!" Dick Leitsch is adamant, in GAY's HOMOSEXUALS DON'T REALLY EXIST!, that "Only by being *persons,* rather than 'homosexuals,' can we get out of the ghettos and into the mainstream. Only by being *people,* and not 'homosexuals,' can we relate to all possibilities and achieve our personal potentials. Staying in the ghettos, wearing the labels, and limiting our demands to 'gay power' (as opposed to 'people power'), we're perhaps supporting the Homosexual Revolution, but we're sure as hell copping out of the Sexual Revolution." [46]

Thane Hampten, another critic, steams, "I never really liked phrases such as 'Gay Pride' and 'I'm *proud* to be a Homosexual.' " Hampten admits that he distrusts all slogans, "no matter how beneficial they are to believe in. One should not be forced to have pride in one's sexuality. Sexuality *is,* for goshsakes. Imagine how foolish to be put in a position to have to say: 'I am *proud* to drink water!' *Cogito, ergo sum* reduced to 'I urinate; therefore I am.' Big deal." [47] ....*another Voice* newsletter relates how Dr. Fred Goldstein, a well-known psychologist, insisted at a meeting of the National League for Social Understanding in Los Angeles that "Whatever one does with his genitals hardly describes a human being, and the thing I find most aggravating is to talk about the homosexual as someone who is stamped by one aspect of his function." [48] Even GLFer Jim Fouratt confesses, about *gay* or *homosexual,* "I find the word hard to relate to because it puts me in a category which limits my potential. It also prescribes a whole system of behavior to which I'm supposed to conform, which has nothing to do with the reality of my day to day living. . . . What I do with my cock should not determine who or what I am." [49]

Perhaps some critics of Gay Pride were missing the point, a point eminently clearer to younger homosexuals, whose experience with and tolerance of discretion had been near-nullified by today's sexual openness: Gay Pride was (or was soon to be clarified as) "pride *in* being gay," "pride *while* being gay," or, if the reader will, "pride in being a human being who, incidentally, happens to be gay—and this latter consideration *in no way alters that human pride!"* To the New Homosexuals it was inconceivable that one could not have homosexual human pride and that, having it, one should not announce it. But Gay Pride and the proclamation of it was not restricted to the young. Franklin Kameny, whom Bob Martin has depicted as "the only homophile leader to whom the description 'legendary' can be applied," [50] * encouraged gays—in 1968:

---

* Martin had not met Henry May, Morris Kight, and a host of other West Coast figures.

. . it is time to open the closet door and let in the fresh air and the sunshine; it is time to hold up your heads and to look the world squarely in the eye as the homosexuals that you are, confident of your equality, confident in the knowledge that as objects of prejudice and victims of discrimination you are right and they are wrong, and confident of the rightness of what you are and of the goodness of what you do; it is time to live your homosexuality fully, joyously, openly, and proudly, assured that morally, socially, psychologically, emotionally, and in every other way: *Gay is good. It is.*[51] *

Author John LeRoy ** has quipped, "Gay is not merely good. Gay is great!" But he warned that "If enough gay people begin believing that gay is great, might not a lot of not-so-gay people want to try it?" [52]

But full faith in the slogan would not come easy for every gay militant and/or New Homosexual. A year later, a young, "liberated" homosexual wrote, in *Gay Flames*: [53] ***

Gay is good! Gay is proud! Have I really been saying these things, not just saying them but chanting them in the streets? Do I really mean it? I think I can honestly say that I really do mean it, finally, or at the very least I'm beginning to develop a sense of pride in my homosexuality, a sense that gay is good. The very fact that I must go through this awesome process is the essence of gay oppression. While our bodies tell us "yes," the world around us shouts (or whispers), "No, no, no, a thousand times, no."

Spokesman and president of *HI!* Craig Schoonmaker opened the first issue of *Homosexual Renaissance,* November 12, 1969, with an allegation that

Homosexuals can effectively demand respect from others only if we first respect ourselves—*as* homosexuals. That requires that we admit to ourselves that we are homosexual; that we affirm it, understand it, *realize* it in all its implications: I am homosexual. Say it! aloud: "I am homosexual." Shout it, whisper it. Laugh it, cry it. State it, proclaim it, confess it in sobs, but *say* it: "I am homosexual." Say it today, say it tomorrow, say it the day after that. Say it when you wake up, when you go to bed, when you find yourself thinking of someone of your own sex. Say it as often as you need to until you realize that it is true and that the fact that it is true forces you to adjust your attitudes

---

* Leafleting in summer 1970, Louisville Gay Liberation Front urged local gays to join, so that, though "GAY IS GOOD—IT COULD BE BETTER!" Did they intend the self-critical double-entendre?

** Frequent writer for GAY, and co-author with Donald Webster Cory of *The Homosexual and His Society* (New York, 1963).

*** *Gay Flames* first appeared, a small mimeographed weekly, on September 1, 1970. Subtitled "A Bulletin of the Homofire Movement," it was a project of the 17th Street GLF men's commune, New York.

and actions to make the very best of your life as a homosexual. "I am homosexual."

Not "Leonardo da Vinci was homosexual," but "*I* am homosexual." Not "Gore Vidal is homosexual," but "*I* am homosexual." Not "One man of every six, one woman of every eight is homosexual," but "*I* am homosexual." Not even, "Some of the finest, most beautiful, and most talented people in the world are homosexual," but "*I* am homosexual."

Homosexuals Intransigent! requires that its members, in order to gain the right to vote in club decisions, acknowledge their homosexuality to any questioner at any time. In a letter of August 17, 1970, Schoonmaker exhorted, "I personally sometimes think that the world would be a great deal better if every homosexual individual and organization took an ad in the public press and published the names and addresses of every homosexual they know, identifying them as homosexuals; then maybe they'd come the fuck out of their closets and feel forced to fight for their lifestyle." [54]

Allowing that "with the Manhattan apartment shortage being what it is, some people have no other choice than to live in closets," GAY columnist Bob Amsel posited that the so-called closet queen *

will find it much easier to relate to his family *as a homosexual,* to his [straight] friends *as a homosexual,* and to his boss *as a homosexual.* . . . It will take his family a while to accept, but if they love *him* and not a phoney *image* of him, they will continue to love him. . . . If he is scorned by certain members of his family, it will be painful to discover that he was never really loved in the first place. . . . But the pain will pass, and a burden will be lifted; the closet door will start to open.

If he has chosen his friends well, the same will apply. If he has not, he will find out who his friends really are, and ten years from that moment, he will still have those same friends. The closet door will open a little more.

The most difficult part of closet-emerging deals with employment. In certain jobs, discovery would mean instant dismissal. . . . I, for one, have never had any desire to work under discriminatory conditions, but many people have no other choice than to work under such duress. . . . But if one feels that the freedom to live as a human being is worth it, that to walk upright without looking down or back, but ahead, is worth it, then maybe anything is possible.[55]

Covert gays who were still unconvinced by the elation of the New Homosexuals could answer a regular advertisement in *Gay Power:*

* QQ magazine defined *closet queen* (generally referring to males) as "having a basic understanding of their homosexual predilections, perhaps even an occasional gay experience, but finding themselves for whatever reasons too inhibited to acknowledge it or accept it. . . . Some closet queens . . . are so latent they go through life manifesting their fantasies through nothing more than masturbation while looking at physique magazines." The closet queen of course generally shuns gay society. (Alan Henning, "Come Out, Come Out, Wherever You Are," winter 1969–70.)

YOU'VE EVERY RIGHT TO BE A HOMOSEXUAL

Society says homosexuals are sick.
And you agree.
Even though you don't feel you're sick, you agree.
And you forget that you are a man. And that you have
every right to enjoy life.
Once a week, a group of your peers meets
to explore our common problems.
We work at the level of gut feelings. And we work hard.
For guidance, a doctor of psychology from the
University of Paris is at each 3-hour session.
To help you to help yourself to some happiness.

HOMOSEXUAL ENCOUNTER GROUP . . .

Gay Pride had promoted *Gay Power* newspaper, which appeared in September and which thrived—in spite of a charge by GLF that it was (s)exploitative—to become a near-diary of gay militant activities. The highly successful GAY was to begin, as a biweekly, on November 19 (dated December 1), later to develop into "America's 1st Gay Weekly." Its co-editors, Jack Nichols and Lige Clarke, had broken new ground for gays a year before when they became "Homosexual Citizen" columnists in the first and continuing issues of *Screw*, a heterosexual paper. *The Advocate,* before the Stonewall riots predominantly Western in audience, realized sales increases on the East Coast following the events. *Come Out!*, on November 14, was thenceforth to speak a radical voice for Gay Liberation Front. Ten months later, in the initial *Gay Sunshine*, a radical newspaper out of Berkeley—and "(free to all prisoners)"—Nick Benton asked,

What is the value of a gay newspaper?

I mean, is the mere instance of homosexuality enough of a common purpose around which to create a newspaper? If homosexuality is really nothing different than something like lefthandedness. then the creation of a paper for homosexuals makes no more sense than a newspaper for lefthanders.

And where a newspaper for lefthanders would be of special value only to tell its readers where to find the appropriate kind of monkey-wrench, so would a newspaper for gays really be good only to tell where the hottest sex books are sold and where most other gays are getting together.*

Acknowledging, however, that "a gay newspaper would be a powerful tool in the homosexual fight for equal rights, as it would be a catalyst

* Early issues of *Gay Power* and even GAY were criticized because they seemed to aim at such an audience. But, then, gay militant news was not so abundant as it was later to be, nor was there a noticeable gay-news readership in New York until 1970.

that could call forth . . . political potential," he criticized existing gay newspapers for appealing to a limited audience. *Gay Sunshine* would be "a newspaper that will represent those who understand themselves as oppressed—politically oppressed by an oppressor that not only is down on homosexuality, but equally down on all things that are not white, straight, middle class, pro-establishment. . . . It should harken to a greater cause—the cause of human liberation, of which homosexual liberation is just one aspect—and on that level make its stand." [56]

Though homosexuals had for years been well served by a multitude of homophile newsletters, by summer 1970 the gay world had a real gay press: a variety of gay newspapers representing the variety that are gays.

The gay press, however, had not been the first pro-homosexual self-expression to startle and/or please American readers. Angelo d'Arcangelo's *The Homosexual Handbook,* the antithesis of Donald Webster Cory's celebrated apology, *The Homosexual in America* (1951), captured reviews by *Variety,* the *Village Voice,* and the *Saturday Review* * after its publication in January 1969 by Maurice Giorodias's Olympia Press. Gays *and* straights will remember how its final, "Uncle Fudge's Grape-Vine Lineup" chapter prompted a callback of about half of the first, 50,000-copy printing so that the name of one American government official could be deleted—and a few more living homosexuals' names added to d'Arcangelo's list. Publisher Girodias staged a literati cocktailery in New York's Luxor [Turkish] Baths to accentuate its second release. Interviewed at the baths by a *Saturday Review* reporter, d'Arcangelo said, "I think a book like mine is very important . . . don't you see the need? After all, sex education in school is strictly heterosexual." [57] *Variety* [58] explained that "You have to go to one of the 42d St. blue bookstalls to get it . . . the 'hottest' tome making the show biz rounds nowadays . . . Many showbizites who never venture into such stores are reportedly trekking to the 42d St. strip in order to snare a copy." By November 1970, after three printings (another is planned for 1971), *The Homosexual Handbook* had sold nearly 250,000 copies. A German translation has been made.

An elegant, glossy magazine for "Gay Guys Who Have No Hangups" had appeared shortly before the Handbook. *Queen's Quarterly*—as it was called until afterthoughts, and the fact that it was going bimonthly, made the publisher opt for simply **QQ** (or QQ) in 1970—became the first continuingly successful national magazine for homosexual men. It was also to enjoy a wide distribution in Canada, Italy, France, Holland, and Japan. QQ offered a variety of subjects, including health topics and advice for those just coming out sexually, and was written from the gay male's point of view: a reader could feel that, to QQ, "heterosexual life was non-existent." The magazine was "based on the premise that gay life is 100 per cent normal," says publisher George Desantis. A magazine that has

* *The New York Times* nixed an ad for the Handbook in its Sunday Book Review Section, giving "as the reason that its 'medical panel' had ruled the book's contents were not consistent with the purported title." (*Variety,* April 23, 1969.)

always kept the small-town, out-of-touch gay reader in mind, QQ in November 1970 had a circulation of approximately 95,000, of which about 80 per cent was subscription. On newsstands around the nation its sales have averaged a phenomenal 75 per cent.

1969 brought further gay phenomena to New York, such as the appearance of cinemas along 43rd Street and Eighth Avenue that featured solely male-homosexual films—including the nude romances of Pat Rocco Films, Inc., of Los Angeles. Rocco's ten- to thirty-minute color epics had been the rage of California homosexuals since early 1968. *Advocate* columnist Jim Kepner explained why in GAY: [59]

. . . too much homosexual art and writing still carries an overlay of shame and guilt. Rocco's work does not—though some viewers feel naked without a defensive patina of prurience. Rocco can portray, movingly, the toils of a character still trapped in guilt. But he does not, like so many, project shame or hostility *through* his characters to make scapegoats of his audience. Members of his audience are more likely to leave feeling right with themselves. Rocco's beat is definitely up.

His fair young actors approach love as if no one had *ever* labeled male love sick, sinful or seamy. These lyrical fantasies evoke love in a way that makes most gay viewers proud of themselves and glad to be alive.

In his best films, in Kepner's opinion, Rocco had "captured what so many of us have dreamed: seeing young men love one another with that beauty and sensitivity which Hollywood had reserved for heterosexual romance."

In its December 31 issue, GAY printed an ad which blazed, unequivocally,

Let's Not Fuck Around with Semantics—
ZEBEDY COLT IS A
GAY SUPERSTAR.

"The first gay super star on long-playing records," Zebedy was "for those who love bars, turkish baths . . . and just plain MASCULINITY." The ad continued, "At last some guy has the balls to stand up and sing 'The Man I Love' and mean it (with a 50-piece orchestra, yet)." The album, on Ecco Records and available through Libran Prod., Inc., was called "I'll Sing for You." It was recommended, "Not because it's GAY. Because it's GOOD."

Gay Pride may have *profited by* the new homosexual image—or lack of one—in European films in 1969; Gay Pride undoubtedly *prompted* a new homosexual image in American theater, both Broadway and Off-Broadway, 1969.

Late autumn 1968 brought a cinema version of Frank Marcus's

beautiful *The Killing of Sister George,* a poignant tragicomedy of an aging lesbian, victim to "another woman." (1968 had been a banner year for lesbian films, but most had been unpityingly exploitative; in *Gay Women's Liberation,* San Francisco, a comment appeared: "It's a very strange thing to find your existence defined as a part of somebody's pornographic fantasy library—sex episode No. 93." [60]) Spring blew in *If....* from England and *Teorema* from Italy. In the first, a fantasy-epic of bloody insurrection in a boys' school, "an upperclassman gymnast flirts with a younger student and ultimately is seen in bed with him—the sensible British camera glides over the sleeping two one night as unshocked as it does over the rest of the dorm mates," [61] and American spectators were undoubtedly aghast. The second, a tale of a God-like visitor who visits a wealthy Milanese family and sleeps with its members—daughter and son, mother and father—profoundly affecting each, puzzled and annoyed . . . *Teorema*'s director, Pier Paolo Pasolini, had obviously understood something American audiences couldn't: that if the visitor "played God and, as God, gave unreservedly of himself, was there not some message here for Man?" [62] Charles Dyer's *Staircase,* previously an English and American stage success, arrived in New York in late August. Directed by an Anglicized American, the film intensified the bickering of two fiftyish male lovers but pulled no punches about their enduring need for one another. Most gay militants did not appreciate the happy ending—the lovers were too old, their mannerisms too stereotyped.

The Off-Broadway autumn season was ready and waiting, however, with a play that would please the whole gay community: *And Puppy Dog Tails,* by David Gaard. Its way had been paved by Gus Weill's *Geese* (January–November 1969), a duo of one-acts, the first gay-female, the second gay-male, and both ending mildly gay-happy. Homosexuals delighted in a scene in the first play, when the two lesbian lovers "try to bring out old Miss Lucy, the spinster schoolmarm . . . Seems like Miss Lucy did, once upon a time, find Debby rather, mmm, 'fetching.' But, she screams, 'I never touched her.' What do you want, lady, a medal?" asked Bob Martin, who reviewed the San Francisco musical version, then suggested, "She needs a good homosexual rape"! [63] Colin Spencer's *Spitting Image,* over from England in early spring, was too much, too soon, and could manage only a six-weeks run; the first homosexual farce, "As the comedy opened, one of two male lovers was 'expecting'; at its close the other (the 'father') was himself 'pregnant.' " [64] In Neal Weaver's *War Games,* which opened on Off-Broadway April 17, two draft-dodging American homosexuals in Toronto enjoy love until confrontations with Mama, Papa (a general), and a "sweet young thing" convince the younger that he'll make a try at straight life. His lover's heroic exit and his own ambivalence left the gay audience with no doubts about whose side the author was rooting for.

But *And Puppy Dog Tails,* a weak but pleasant play unanimously panned by New York critics, was a confirmation—to gays and straights alike who saw the show—that homosexual lovers need answer to no one but themselves. The plot revolved around the visit of a straight just-ex-Navy man to his old buddie in New York and his ultimate discovery that buddie has a beddie-buddie: ex-Navy exits angrily, beddie-buddies tussle nudiely. But it convinced. And audiences thronged to it. Despite its slim six-weeks sojourn in San Francisco, *The Advocate,* wondering "Why can't we have a play or movie about homosexuals as a lot of them really are—responsible human beings making a worthwhile contribution to society, unashamed and happy in their love affairs?", acknowledged that *Puppy Dog Tails* "seems to be a move in this direction." [65]

New York Times critic Clive Barnes assessed, correctly, that *And Puppy Dog Tails* was primarily "interesting in the area of theater economics and theatrico-social patterns." He discerned that "This is a play that deals with *happy* homosexuals. . . . At least half the members of this four-character cast are perfectly happy and well-adjusted; not only would this be a fair average for a heterosexual play, but the author insists upon their married bliss with almost proselyting zeal." Further, that "While we have had scenes before of homosexual sex and even declarations of homosexual love, this is the first play in my experience to show demonstrations of homosexual affection." But Barnes had to confess that "Incidentally, for the perhaps unimportant record, I found this embarrassing . . ." [66] Gays found it not only unembarrassing but completely natural. So that, determined to "adopt" this self-confirming comedy-drama —in revenge, as it were, on the success (1,002 New York performances) of Mart Crowley's biting satire *The Boys in the Band*—gays bought *Tails* tickets! At its close on January 11, 1970, the play had attracted almost thirty thousand spectators. What's more, GLF was to sloganize a line in the play's final scene: "Up the ass of the ruling class!" *

Gay Pride, for all its need to show off, did not alienate old-liners of the homophile movement, nor uncommitted young and middle-aged gays, nor even old and/or closety homosexuals. But Gay Power—a slogan that always unnerved some—would soon require, according to Gay Liberation Front, more than simply pride: it would require militancy, violent if necessary; it would necessitate overthrow of the capitalist system; and it would obligate alliance with the non-homosexual oppressed, some of whose programs in turn encouraged militancy and revolution. Thus far, the "Homosexual Revolution" had been an enjoyable camp, for all gays. In November, lines were finally to be drawn that would estrange the old-line movement and polarize even the gay militants themselves.

---

* A slogan in disrepute today. GLF, more conscious today of male chauvinism, explains that the statement is essentially sexist—a heterosexual male's punishment of a "queer" or of a recalcitrant female sex object.

5

What I object to are 1) getting involved
in any issues not directly a part of the
homophile cause, and 2) operating or
functioning in an unorganized, non-parlia-
mentarian, non-constitutional, informal or
"consensus-type" manner.

—Foster Gunnison, Jr., in a letter
to the author, August 1970

The first formal regional association of American homosexual groups,
ECHO—for East Coast Homophile Organizations—assembled in 1963.
In early 1966 it gave birth to NACHO, a national structure, and was
itself superseded by the Eastern Regional Conference of Homophile Organizations—ERCHO—which met each spring and fall. (There were Midwestern and Western Regional conferences.) ERCHO, which assembled
in Philadelphia on November 1 and 2, 1969, was to be the scene of the
second—this time premeditated—confrontation between gay militant thinking and the old-liner homophiles.

In his thorough reportage of the event in *Gay Power* and *The Advocate,* Bob Martin asserted that, by adopting a large part of the radicals'
resolutions, "ERCHO became the first association of homophile organizations to take a position *as homosexuals* on *non-homosexual* issues, thus
breaching a wall which the homophile liberals had successfully maintained
since the beginning of inter-organizational cooperation in 1966. With
these resolutions," he insisted, "ERCHO and its members (insofar as
they do not formally dissociate themselves from the resolutions) have
joined the radical movement, even if hesitantly and with reservations." [1]
ERCHO Treasurer Foster Gunnison, Jr.,* protested, in a letter to *Playboy,*[2] that "Martin gives a false picture of the young radical contingent
bulldozing its platform through the Eastern Regional Conference of
Homophile Organizations, leaving the elderly liberals in total defeat. The
fact is that, immediately afterward, E.R.C.H.O. voted to suspend itself

---

* And founder-administrator of the Institute of Social Ethics, Hartford. Created
in 1967, ISE today maintains historical records and archives of the American homophile movement, facilitates communications between homophile organizations, and
handles business for NACHO, ERCHO, and the Christopher Street Liberation Day
Committee (see Chapter 15) through its division Association Management Services.

for one year—a curious move, akin to shooting yourself in the head before the next guy does it for you. In this way, however, we prevented a take-over of our organization by the extremists, and when the dust settles the homophile cause can be resurrected as a sane and rational movement."

GLF New York had not applied for accreditation to the conference, but was reluctantly admitted, as were three separate Student Homophile League delegations, from Columbia, Cornell, and NYU. The Front and other radicals were restive in the meeting place: the "auditorium" of My Sister's Place, a local gay bar. But the "exploited" radicals would do some of their own during the ensuing two-day scene. Martha Shelley, a DOB delegate, staged an attack on *Gay Power,* calling it "basically a salacious newspaper" that was exploiting the gay community to the benefit of its straight publisher, Joel Fabricant. The radicals showed resentment, in addition, that Madolin Cervantes, a heterosexual associate at MSNY, had a vote in the proceedings. Then, climactically, a resolution they produced recommended that ERCHO go on record supporting participation by homosexuals in the November 15 Moratorium. It brought bitter debate. Countering it, old-line delegates maintained that no association of organizations could speak for all homosexuals, who ranged, as did heterosexuals, from arch-reactionary to leftist radical. The resolution defeated, "general agreement was that individual homosexuals who wanted to would probably take part in the demonstration, but . . . ERCHO could not and would not take a formal stand on the question." [3] The radicals had lost round one.

Despite arguments that some parts of the next resolutions which the radicals introduced were extraneous to homosexual goals, ERCHO adopted them, with some amendments:

Resolved, that the Eastern Regional Conference of Homophile Organizations considers these inalienable human rights above and beyond legislation:
1) Dominion over one's own body
   a. through sexual freedom without regard to orientation
   b. through freedom to use birth control and abortion
   c. through freedom to ingest the drugs of one's choice
2) Freedom from society's attempts to define and limit human sexuality, which are inherently manifested in economic, educational, religious, social, personal and legal discrimination
3) Freedom from political and social persecution of all minority groups:
   a. freedom from the institutionalized inequities of the tax structure and the judicial system
   b. freedom and the right of self-determination of all oppressed minority groups in our society
   c. we specifically condemn the systematic and widespread persecution of certain elements of these minorities, including all political prisoners and those accused of crimes without victims [e.g., homosexuals].[4]

Some time after the convention,* Gunnison wrote to Bob Kohler of Gay Liberation Front. Deeply disturbed by the strife at the November ERCHO assembly, Gunnison insisted that he was personally "interested in GLF—no matter how I may disagree with it or rebel against its philosophies . . . a fascinating organization . . . never a dull moment for sure, and I can in some way feel somewhat fond toward it as long as I don't have to get into bed with it." About GLF's participation at the convention, he took issue with three things: "rudeness in personal behavior (not applying to GLF as a whole, but to certain individuals), resentment against authority and structure and systematic administration and procedure (which I believe does apply to much of GLF), and concern with other minority-group and political/social/economic issues (same) . . ." Decrying the GLF assaults on Madolin Cervantes and on the gay-bar site of the conclave, he went on:

. . . To me the manner in which GLF desires to operate, and which to me seems chaotic and disruptive but which I do not condemn in its own right, is based on an anarchic philosophy which I for one . . . do not wish to see introduced into ERCHO or NACHO in the midst of the struggle we have had trying to develop and operate along orderly lines. . . .

Thus it would seem to me befitting neither GLF nor the ERCHO/NACHO to try to mix philosophies here. I would think that each could accomplish more, and with less turmoil, by each going its own way and not trying to foul the other up.

On GLF's desire to align with non-homosexual causes:

. . . I have chosen the homophile cause as the one I wish to devote most of my surplus efforts to. Some of the [other] causes I am on the fence about—uncertain—neither pro nor con. One or two I may be opposed to, or opposed to some aspects of them. But whether I support or oppose a cause, I do not wish to see these dragged into the homophile movement and there are several reasons why. Perhaps I should say dragged into the ERCHO or the NACHO—if GLF and other organizations want to pursue these other causes outside the ERCHO or NACHO in the belief that there is some relevancy here to the homophile movement, or even without any such belief, I say fine! . . .

. . . I don't like being told what causes I am going to support . . . if I do support them I want to choose which ones I am going to support and I want to support them on my own terms and in my own way . . . Nor do I want to waste my or ISE's [see footnote, page 86] time going to conferences and then having to dissociate from half the resolutions that get passed. . . .

Further, I think it would prove divisive in ERCHO or in NACHO to have these what I see as extraneous causes introduced. We have enough trouble getting along on strictly homophile issues ** . . . The one thing that brings us

* Following visits to general meetings of GLF with Franklin Kameny.
** From this purely practical standpoint, the *Advocate* editor-in-chief has argued: "If you make every organization into a broad-spectrum organization dealing with all of the world's problems—if NACHO has to worry about Vietnam and the Panthers and the blacks and the Chicanos, and everything else, then who is going to do *our* work? Certainly not SDS!"

together, and the one thing that we can hope sometime, with much patience and perseverance, to get some modicum of agreement on is the matter of discrimination against homosexuals and the negative valuing of society of homosexuality as a way of life. I see our time as best spent working on these matters and not splitting us all up on items that not only seem to carry a leftist political bias . . . but are not in any way related to the homophile cause other than under the proposition that 5 is related to 11 because they are both numbers.

I know that many in GLF believe that one minority group must support another and that the homosexual is a victim of a general spirit of oppression by the "establishment" and that victory can only be achieved by all minority groups banding together and fighting as a unit for a general overthrow. Fine! You may be right! Far be it from me to argue that this proposition is without merit. . . . No one can prove you wrong and only time will tell.[5]

In its November–December newsletter, Homophile Action League of Philadelphia editorialized: [6] "Alliances with other groups will increase our number and power, will broaden the base of our constituency. But again the issue must be squarely confronted. Should the organized homophile movement go on record supporting the causes and actions of groups who have shown not the least interest in the liberation of the homosexual? We submit that to do so would be to allow ourselves to be used as pawns in someone else's game." Gunnison saw—worse—"a risk to the public image of the movement—i.e., that part of the movement represented by ERCHO and NACHO—by involving us in these other issues. I see for every friend we may gain the loss of one or more other potential friends." [7] In a general bulletin from ISE, July 24, 1970—a month before the 1970 NACHO conference in San Francisco—Gunnison noted, among recent Letters to the Editor, in *The New York Times* (July 12, 1970): ". . . A major flaw in the demonstration concept as it exists today is the inability to demonstrate for a specific cause. On the contrary, recent demonstrations have suffered from what we consider to be a multiplicity of causes. . . From personal experience we have found that the more causes represented, the more people are apt to be alienated. . . ."

Gunnison did not oppose the use of militancy in gay liberation: "I favor virtually across the board all kinds of confrontation tactics, street demonstrations, including violence where called for. I was thrilled with the Christopher Street uprising of 1969 . . ." [8] Franklin Kameny, who judges that the Stonewall riots "pumped an enormous amount of energy and enthusiasm and people into the movement all at once in a very activist and militant kind of way" and rejoices that there is today "for the first time a grassroots, mass, popular homophile movement," approves a qualified militancy: "I don't believe in picketing until you've tried negotiation. On the other hand, if you've tried negotiation and gotten nowhere and then tried picketing and gotten nowhere, then, in terms of meeting for discussing of your demands . . . I'm perfectly willing to go along to the next step—which is probably some sort of confrontation that possibly mildly oversteps the bounds of the law. If that doesn't serve, I'm willing to go further, although I do draw the line at violence."

Many observers of the gay militant scene worried—more than Gunnison and Kameny—that the homophile movement and/or homosexual civil rights cause would not only be hampered by alignment with non-homosexual causes but would be gravely endangered by any militancy—violent or non-violent—and by leftist orientation and/or brotherhood with leftist organizations.

Madolin Cervantes of MSNY has voiced concern that "if we got a piece of legislation introduced into the New York legislature . . . as we hope to, for the repeal of the sodomy laws, and if the GLFers . . . went to Albany or someplace to have a demonstration, that would kill that repeal so dead that God knows when we'd ever be able to get it out again." Jim Kepner, in his *Advocate* "Angles on the News," has observed that "Law reform, [once] a distant hope, now seems an immediate possibility. The courts have begun to listen to homosexual pleas, and 20 years of hard work by homosexual activists seems to be bearing fruit—just as a new generation of Gays comes along to say, 'The hell with all that.' " [9] In IS MILITANCY THE ANSWER?, Mrs. Cervantes stated that, "while one of their demonstrations might gain a small victory at the moment, in the end we will all pay a high price for it. . . . What they might be able to do, unfortunately, is to destroy what some of the minority groups have been able to achieve up to this point, because if they twist the tiger's tail a little too hard, the tiger will not only bite off their heads, but the heads of the rest of us." [10] Kepner has prophesied: "If the police are unleashed . . . Gays will be among the first to be hit. Prosecutor Foran's 'Freaking fag revolutionary' remark * after he finished trying the Chicago Seven made it clear that he considered all hippies, students, and radicals to be homosexuals.** I doubt if it looks any different to other police bosses who are straining at the leash. They see themselves beset by a bunch of queers, and they are ready for the go-ahead signal so they can clean up the lot of us." [11]

In a letter to *Vector,* attorney-at-law K. R. Newell has pleaded eloquently:

* Made before the Loyola Academy Booster Club on February 26, 1970. The U.S. attorney added that one of the seven defendants, "Bobby Seale had more guts and more charisma than any of them and he was the only one I don't think was a fag." James Bradford, president of Mattachine Midwest (Chicago), told newspapermen that Foran "sounds like a dirty-mouthed little boy who has discovered a new swear word. His statement evinces profound contempt for human beings, for dissenters and for the democratic process. His is a totalitarian mentality at work." On March 6, sources had it that the Justice Department had requested the attorney's resignation. (GAY, March 29, 1970.)
** In GAY, June 22, 1970, John LeRoy expanded, "anyone who either enjoys, or demands for himself or others, the freedom which is promised every time the national anthem is sung or the flag is saluted is a 'fag' regardless of sexual preference. Mayor Lindsay is a 'fag,' college professors are 'fags,' U.N. delegates are 'fags,' and hippies must be downright cocksuckers."

Each month, each year, homosexuals are winning their legal rights too—peacefully and with dignity. In Illinois (and soon Connecticut) homosexual acts between consenting adults are no longer crimes. Recently, it was decided in conservative New Jersey that a bar may not be closed down merely because it has a homosexual clientele, following an earlier California case . . . these achievements were accomplished under the rule of law—within our democratic system. More will be accomplished. But not by organizing a club-wielding mob of inarticulate anarchists, a la Berkeley, whose perverted ideas of liberty are to be imposed by *vis et armis*—by force and violence. The voice of militancy will be strangled with repression for all of us—unless we confine our fighting to peaceful modes of struggle. True liberty knows no home without the rule of law.[12]

Newell and other critics of homosexual militancy could not see it as anything but "club-wielding," and condemned it without definition, without further ado. Militancy, capable of broad interpretation, has meant something *less* than violence to the vast majority of gay militants. A leader among California gay liberationists and a "leftist," the Rt. Rev. Michael Itkin echoes Newell's sentiments: "If we are to build a loving and peaceful society, we can only do so by loving and peaceful means. If we meet the violence of the oppressors with violence of our own, then we become the same as them and if our revolution should succeed, we become merely the new masters and oppressors ourselves. . . ." [13] Newell points out that Illinois and Connecticut have no restrictions against homosexual acts between consenting adults in private—he does not point out that Illinois' law went into effect in 1961, Connecticut's will in October 1971. A long wait for homosexuals who have been young and alive—and taxpayers—over those ten years. What's more, Newell does not report that police harassment of homosexuals is considerably worse in the Midwestern state than in some of the forty-nine (forty-eight) whose lawbooks still contain anti-sodomy statutes.

On July 17, 1968, reviewing homosexuals' picketings and other protests in Washington, San Francisco, and New York, the *Wall Street Journal* remarked jovially: "This sounds like a militant minority." [14] Over two years later, from the heart of West Coast gay liberation, and where gay liberation seemed in process of succumbing to gay nationalism (see Chapter 14), the *San Francisco Chronicle*'s "Fearless Spectator," Charles McCabe, warned: "People don't like homosexuals. A bald and boring fact, you say. And unfair. Yet it is a fact which is largely ignored by the Gay Liberation movement. To the peril of the movement, I say." [15] A member of an old-line homophile group might suggest to McCabe, "You mean 'People *think* they don't like homosexuals.' Come and meet us!" A member of a gay militant organization would undoubtedly suggest, "Why don't you change that to 'People don't like *blacks*,' huh, Mr. McCabe? Homosexuals are this nation's second-largest minority—twelve to fifteen million strong—who intend to live as first-class citizens, full-fledged human beings. An immense voting power, or, if you will, another kind of power . . ." Meanwhile, impatient with the snail's pace of American legal processes, many longtime homophile leaders have sympathized with or supported gay militancy. In *The New York Times's* front-page feature, HOMOSEXUALS IN REVOLT, on August 24, 1970, Bob Milne, forty-nine, of the New York Mattachine Society, admitted: "People my own age have been running scared all their lives. The younger people just won't take anything any more." [16] Henry Hay, a founder of the original Mattachine Foundation, has served as chairman of the Gay Liberation Front of Los Angeles. In August 1970, Don Neal, president of the Society of Anubis (Azusa, California), declared: "I myself have always been very conservative but in the last eight months I have found that if I am to live in the homophile community I must help the fight as much as I can." [17]

An early observation that homosexual militants might drift into alignment with leftist groups was made in the May 1969 *Advocate*.[18] "Stop cruising the 'New Left,' " KPFK commentator Randy Darden had advised when he spoke off-the-air at the One Institute lecture series that spring. Darden gave as his objections, that: 1) "the greater part of the gay community has a financial interest in a stable, affluent society. We rely on the patronage of well-heeled, middle-class heteros for our stage shows, beauty parlors, fashion squares, and other services"; 2) "the goals of most homosexuals are opposed to the goals of other minorities repreented in the New Left"—here he explained that homosexuals had been seeking acceptance into the armed forces; 3) "ordinary homosexuals have thus far shown previous little stomach for revolution . . . For Darrel the decorator, the threat of Red China is easily answered by changing the color of the table linen"; 4) "the New Left lies to you when it poses as the friend and ally of homosexuality." In support of objection number 4, Darden recalled how "Allen Ginsberg told of being run out of Cuba and the Soviet Union primarily for his open advocacy of equality for homosexuals." He then struck at the *Los Angeles Free Press* (which had constantly featured gay news and in summer 1970 was to run a gay lib supplement): "In answer to the question, 'What improvements do you plan for the *L.A. Free Press*?' editor Art Kunkin replied in a radio interview, 'I'd like to have so many paid subscriptions that we could do without all the ads for sick sex . . . we seek to be a forum for revolution, not wallpaper for a Greyhound john.' " Darden also cited a cartoon panel called "Fagman" in *The Realist,* ostensibly a New Left journal, in which Pope Paul announces to his cardinals, "We've decided to exonerate the Jews for the crucifixion; we're going to blame it on the queers instead."

More than a year later, *The Advocate* reiterated Darden's fears in Rob Cole's RADICALS' DILEMMA: THE LEFTISTS THEY WOO CALL THEM "FAGGOTS." [19] Cole was, in effect, to denigrate GLF's participation in the summer 1970 World Youth Assembly at the United Nations: ". . . a strange marriage of convenience as awkward as any heterosexual image of a gay union."

Among the participants in the gathering of young revolutionary leaders, New Left activists and dissidents of every color and nationality, were several representatives of New York's Gay Liberation Front.

At first they seemed very much at home. It wasn't long, however, before Ghanaian representative Willie Amarfio took note of their presence by observing that he didn't see how anyone could take the American revolutionary movement seriously as long as it included such "frivolous" groups as homosexuals.

The GLF contingent got up and walked out. No one seemed particularly sorry to see them go. . . .

Some, like Tom Finley, one of the GLFers who walked out . . . take a . . . philosophical view.

"As far as the Movement's relation to homosexuals, what they can do for us is to accept us under their umbrella," Finley explained. "If necessary, we'll go it alone. I'm not begging for acceptance."

Of the incident at the youth assembly, he said, "I cannot continue in a meeting when what I stand for is subject to contempt."

But he said he could sympathize with Amarfio.

"He has his own image problems to cope with.* He is probably only familiar with the stereotype of the homosexual, and in terms of the image he is trying to create for himself, it doesn't fit very well."

Cole continued by pointing out how radicals in GLF were working with the Venceremos Brigade (see Chapter 10), "young volunteers from the U.S. and other countries who cut sugarcane for Castro." "In the meantime," he said, "the Cuban government is putting its own homosexuals in concentration camps." He next poignarded Charles Thorp, twenty-year-old founder of GLF at San Francisco State College, who "quotes from the writings of Chinese Communist leader Mao Tse-tung, whose Red Guards castrated sexual 'degenerates' during the recent 're-newing' of the Communist revolution." And cited spokeswoman Charlene Mitchell of the American Communist Party, who has stated, "homosexuality is part of the problem of a decaying society. In a planned society, you could deal with the problem medically and psychiatrically." Finally Cole insisted that "the Panthers use the word 'faggot' as an insult almost on a par with 'pig.' Malcolm X was quoted as saying that to him 'all white men are blond, blue-eyed faggots.'" Cole had not read Supreme Commander of the Black Panther Party, Newton's A LETTER FROM HUEY TO THE REVOLUTIONARY BROTHERS AND SISTERS ABOUT THE WOMEN'S LIB-

* From Nora Sayre's "New York's Gay-in," in the *New Statesman*, July 17, 1970: "Middle America's myths about dirty commie faggots are going to be bruised by reality: radical homosexuals who will fight for the rights of blacks and others."

ERATION AND GAY LIBERATION MOVEMENTS,* recommending that "The terms 'faggot' and 'punk' should be deleted from our vocabulary . . . Homosexuals are not enemies of the people." An accomplishment for the American homosexual due mainly to GLF's and women's relating to the causes of other, sometimes mocking, oppressed peoples.

In late 1969–early 1970, however, acceptance of GLF by political-revolution-oriented societies or even by mere end-the-war groups was by no means assured. In a February *Los Angeles Free Press,* Douglas Key mentioned that Panther David Hilliard had called fellow-black leader Ron Karenga a "faggot" in *The Black Panther.* (Key asserted that "If Karenga is homosexual, GLF feels he should proclaim this publicly and accord his sexuality the same respect and dignity as he does to his race.") "Hilliard's remarks," wrote Key, "have done much to destroy the efforts of many Gays who have attempted to gain support for the Panthers among those involved in the Gay movement." [20] In mid-December, GAY had reported, "Black playwright, Leroi Jones, has defined the great 'deluge' in 'nakedness' and 'homosexuality' as a white man's weakness, but urges radicals to 'support' 'degenerate' changes in mores to hasten the breakdown of Euro-American culture." [21] In *The New York Times,* November 16,[22] Jones had asked American blacks to beware of the "vague, integrated, plastic, homosexual 'rEVolUTioN.'" GAY's editors enunciated further: [23]

We are tired of the abuse which certain black "leaders" are heaping upon the homosexual community. We should like to ask H. Rap Brown to refrain from calling his enemies "faggots." Would he like homosexuals to call their opponents "niggers"? Does he forget that there are hundreds of thousands of homosexual blacks?

We are weary of Eldridge Cleaver's put-downs of James Baldwin on account of his homosexual leanings.

We are not surprised by the latest anti-homosexual outburst: that by Leroi Jones, who offers backhanded "support" of the homosexual revolution because it weakens the hand that "holds the chain that binds black people." . . .

We do not welcome the support of Leroi Jones, and we are pleased to call him a puritanical bigot. . . .

The Red Butterfly, a Marxist-Leninist "cell" of GLF (see pages 101–03), would protest, too, that "Words like 'faggot' and 'cocksucker' have been used to attack ruling class figures and political tendencies opposed to one's own. Use of the words has been defended as 'street rhetoric.' This is crap. These words are vicious and demeaning, and their use reduces millions of gay people to a less than human status." [24] In the January issue of New York GLF's *Come Out!* [25] Jim Fouratt would ask for understanding of Movement name-callers:

* First printed in *The Black Panther,* August 21, 1970.

Most of my brothers and sisters see red every time Eldridge Cleaver, Abbie Hoffman, the Panthers, or the Yippies are mentioned and are consequently blinded to the more essential issues. It is claimed that these groups are all outspokenly anti-homosexual. And most of it revolves around the word faggot. Cleaver used the word repeatedly in the most pejorative manner in SOUL ON ICE, and it has become a standard part of white and black Panther rhetoric. The problem is that my brothers and sisters don't understand the word faggot as Cleaver and many blacks use it. The word faggot is used to describe any castrated male made impotent by society. The black man has traditionally been castrated by white society by its refusal to allow him the dignity of meaningful work. It has been the black woman who has had to play the black male role in white society; she who can get the jobs; she who can collect welfare; she who holds the family together; rendering the male useless —hence, castrated, hence, faggot. In a similar way, the system renders the homosexual neurotic, hence castrated, hence faggot. The Panthers must be confronted by our community just as all other radical groups must be confronted by the sexual liberation issue, but underlining this confrontation must be an understanding of how our oppressions make us all brothers and sisters. Hoffman, too, must be confronted as a male heterosexual chauvinist and must not be allowed to continue in a rhetoric which only seeks to imitate Cleaver's. But it must also be remembered that Hoffman is quite actively working for an alternative to this society and one would think only needs his awareness heightened.

In his letter to *Playboy,* Foster Gunnison admitted, "It is common knowledge that the Commie-pinko-anarchist fringe tries to take over any minority cause it can latch onto, and for us, it had to come sooner or later." [26] In a letter to William Wynne at NACHO's Kansas City headquarters, expressing an old-liner's revulsion to leftism in the homosexual civil rights movement, he took

an exceedingly dim view of these new radical goings-on in the movement— not insofar as they are directly relevant to homosexuality—I am as militant in the movement as anyone you will find—but rather to the extent that they represent a wholesale attack on the "system," a categorical rejection of the "establishment," of which I am proud to be a member (unilateral as this relationship may sometimes be), a fawning and demeaning effort to suck ass with every other minority cause, an infiltration of some revolutionary elements who could care less about the homosexual than their own bid for personal power and status, and a general embracing of left-wing political and economic views of every sort and in doctrinaire fashion that is alarming in its conformity. Indeed, I have encountered few more rigid examples of conformity—in dress, thought, and action, than are some of these professional non-conformists. . . .

For myself, I am a gung-ho right-winger and damn well proud of it . . . I struggle against heavy odds to keep an open mind.[27] . . .

To no right-winger would a majority of those organizations in America today that can be broadly dubbed "Movement" appeal. For nearly all of them are spearheaded by would-be leftist or leftist-thinking young Americans who have no inherent distrust of either liberalism or radical doctrine and who are out (not to destroy America but) to eliminate Amerika. Each of these organizations may have its "Real Radicals," as GLFer-Radicalesbian * Martha Shelley has called them. But, she protests, "Come on, gang. Known homosexuals, SDS members, Panthers, long hairs—people like us—are light years away from an armed political revolution." She chuckles that these skilled Real Radicals—the dread of right-wing homosexuals like Gunnison—even "prate on, oblivious to the fact that GLF is an open organization, and meetings are attended by police informers, and phones are tapped . . . How in hell can you even conspire to wire your way into a pay toilet when you are practically advertising the whole thing on CBS?" Shelley sees GLF composed, primarily, of "moral individualists"—in contrast to either conservatives or Real Radicals (Communists). "My conservative friends look at these individualists and immediately scream 'Communist dupes!' . . . My Communist friends see a bunch of undisciplined, ragged nuisances and are infuriated because we can't be controlled and formed into a fifth column." [28]

In Philadelphia, Homophile Action League, underlining its faith nevertheless that, "For any minority seeking statutory as well as social equality, the support of the Federal government is crucial," [29] was amused-skeptical about any benefit of leftism to the gay liberation movement:

Two recent articles in WIN magazine, November 15, published by the War Resisters League, help underscore our point. . . . Writing as a homosexual, the noted intellectual and radical social critic Paul Goodman writes, "Frankly, my experience of radical community is that it does not tolerate my freedom." He indicates that it is among the "professional square people" that he has found a greater measure of acceptance than among the radical left which he, nonetheless, exhorts homosexuals to join.

Similarly, Bob Martin, chairman of the NACHO youth committee, writing about the committee's manifesto . . . calls for homosexuals to join with the left and, in a long, parenthetical remark, says:

Revolutionaries are notorious Puritans and so many radicals are uptight about their own sexual orientation. Some of the most prominent movement leaders are gay or bisexual, but they hide it as desperately as the most repressed sergeant.** The straight radicals are often worse . . . rejecting the homosexual's appeal with a bigotry and narrowminded emotionalism which would horrify him if directed against any other minority group.

Messrs. Goodman and Martin make our point well. It would be foolhardy for homosexuals as a group to work for the causes of those who would, if they gain power, reject our own demands. Of the political battle between

* See Chapter 9 for Radicalesbians.
** Does he intend the role Rod Steiger played of a near-psychotic career man in the 1968 film based on Dennis Murphy's *The Sergeant*?

96

radicals and liberals, Martin says: "The game is beginning to get interesting. After all, 15 million people go to the winner." Do this nation's 15 million homosexuals view themselves as a political prize or do they view themselves as a *truly* self-determining minority, which reserves the right to support only those policies and people which guarantee them their freedom? . . .

. . . To change our society, to cause it to accept the homosexual as an equal, demands every tactic, every person, every idea we can command. From street people to college professors, from drag queens to Ivy-Leaguers, from Gold-waterites to Trotskyites—there is room for all under our umbrella. To put all of our eggs in the radical basket would be to deny ourselves many routes to change and, of great importance, it would also serve to alienate the vast majority of those 15 million homosexuals from their own liberation movement.[30]

In its October 31 issue, TIME Magazine alienated New York's gay community by a cover story, "The Homosexual: Newly Visible, Newly Understood." Visible only were photographs available years before and/or chosen to display the "effeminate" side of homosexuality. And ". . . But Still Misunderstood" would have been more apt. The article's "Four Lives in the Gay World" (biographies) ended, calculatedly, with atypical twenty-eight-year-old "Tom Kramer's" conversion: "Women arouse me now. It's a total reversal." [31] GLF was equally aroused. Jerry Hoose recalls: "We went over, for about four hours, the different alternatives. It turned out that we decided we were going to ask for equal space, reparations—figures ranged from half a million dollars up!—but I think we finally agreed on something like $10,000. We agreed that it was going to be a mass demonstration in front of Time and Life. Thousands of people we were going to get out. . . ."

GLF leaflet-billed itself, oddly, as Radical Sexual Coalition. Names such as Mattachine and the Daughters of Bilitis were, without consultation, included as members of "RASCO." GLF leafleted that "In characteristic tight-assed fashion, TIME has attempted to dictate sexual boundaries for the American public and to define what is healthy, moral, fun, and good on the basis of its own narrow, out-dated, warped, perverted, and re-pressed sexual bias." In *J'Accuse* manner they found TIME, on a second leaflet, "GUILTY OF: JOURNALISTIC SLANDER, INNUENDO PRESENTED AS FACT, HOMOSEXUAL-HETEROSEXUAL POLARIZATION, SEXUAL CHAUVINISM, AND EXPLOITATION OF HUMAN SEXUALITY FOR PROFIT!"

On rainy-snowy November 12, the protest turnout in front of the Time and Life Building was slim. Bob Kohler remembers that "we were just a very strange-looking bunch of people, so we started chanting 'Ho ho ho Ho Chi Minh'—we didn't know what else to do. . . . We had our encounter that day with hardhats—about a year before they were even called hardhats. Construction workers were throwing eggs at us from across the street . . . and we were getting hit. I went out in front and said, 'Come on down and fight it out on the sidewalk, if you're so fuckin' smart!' And the pigs came out and said that we would be arrested for inciting a riot." Hoose adds, "We sent two delegations into the offices of TIME. I was in the first delegation, and we never got past the receptionist—three receptionists! . . . [But] I think it raised the consciousness of a lot of people who saw that the few of us there were fair prey, game for anything. We were on television, we were exposed, and that helped other people to come out the next time." Kohler: "I think we had more women at the TIME zap * than men—which was very important."

GLF could not win them all. But, then, the Front had more impressive plans afoot. The entire nation was on the *qui-vive:* the November 15 Moratorium, in Washington, was three days off. GLF would be there!

The Front's *Come Out!* in its second issue (January 10, 1970) presented WASHINGTON MORATORIUM: 3 VIEWS—those of Earl Galvin, Dan Smith, and Mike Brown. Galvin noted how, in this, GLF's second big appearance with Movement Americans, "Most of the [straight] young men smiled slightly, tightened their sphincters, grabbed mom's hand, and gravitated discretely to another area of the street" during the march up Pennsylvania Avenue. But the GLF banner remained aloft.**

Smith allowed that he

wasn't expecting the march to end the war or change the minds of the majorities. I was expecting a gathering of people who knew by whom or how the soldiers were being used. Instead, I saw demonstration marshals tipping their heads and smiling at generals passing in green cars; I heard rostrum speakers praising American business and suggesting that the government try for business's efficiency; and I felt the wall of hatred and disgust that followed the conspiracy people when they walked among the crowd asking for people to come to the Justice Department and demonstrate against the imprisonment of Bobby Seale. . . . They ["over three-fourths of the Moratorium"] were unable to feel the governmental force convincing their leaders that to be as quiet, inoffensive and meek as mother's little children would make their protest valid, a success.

Brown told how,

When we arrived at the Justice Dept., there were strangely few cops. This government still keeps up a pretense of legitimacy and this demonstration had a permit. The building was surrounded with a crowd that had grown to perhaps 50,000. It was very quiet except for the cries of "free Bobby Seale" and "stop the trials." Then from the massed militants in front of the building flew the first rocks and bottles. The door was assaulted with a battering ram. There were no sirens this time, no warnings to disperse and the gas was not tear gas either. As it exploded to my left, I saw the flag of the 28th of June cell of

* A gay zap generally indicates picketing, a sit-in, or other action intended to confront/embarrass anti-homosexual persons or organizations.
** Actually the banner of GLF's first cell, the "28th of June."

Gay Liberation Front begin to move up Constitution Ave. Since the CS (pepper) gas exploded between us and the flag, we ran in the opposite direction and the group was separated. Those of us who were still together left to get above the Government Building along Constitution Avenue. We were driven by huge clouds of gray gas into downtown streets which were filled with people shouting "power to the people." As we moved west onto New York Ave. from 14th Street, it was apparent that a large part of the crowd that had been at Justice earlier intended to take the protest to the White House. We never got there. Just as we reached Penn Ave. and 15th St., the cops and the army drew into ranks to protect the President of the United States from his own people. . . . So they came to Washington over a million strong, not really expecting to change anything but hoping that by being there they would somehow show something as yet undefined. When they left they knew that there are two nations and that the nation of the "silent majority" is afraid to change what must be changed. When they left Washington, they knew that they were an army; what they do with that knowledge will determine the future of America.

Carrying a fifteen-foot banner, HOMOSEXUALS AGAINST WAR, and posters proclaiming BRING THE BEAUTIFUL BOYS HOME and SOLDIERS: MAKE EACH OTHER, NOT WAR, some three hundred San Francisco Bay Area gays representing the Committee for Homosexual Freedom, Gay Liberation Theatre, and Gay Liberation Front gathered at Mission Park at 8:00 a.m., November 15. Marching as a group to the Polo Grounds in Golden Gate Park, they chanted, "Say it clear, say it loud, We're gay and we're proud!" An editorial in the *San Francisco Free Press* threw light on homosexuals' strong anti-war sentiments: "The same oppressive government and society that massacres Vietnamese and victimizes American servicemen conscripted to fight an unjust and imperialistic war oppresses and alienates all of us who fail or refuse to comply with its concept of accepted social behavior. . . . Homosexuals will not fight in a war propagated by a society that fucks us over in all its institutions. We will not fight in an army that discriminates against us . . . that rapes us and gives us less than dishonorable discharges.* We will fight in a truly human revolution that will have as its aim an end to all oppression." [32] Don Jackson, writing for *Gay Power,* hit on perhaps one other important reason why homosexuals are anti-war. He insisted, "I dig beautiful oriental men. Asking me to shoot at them is the same thing as asking heterosexual soldiers to shoot at beautiful young girls that they would like to fuck"! [33]

During their participation in the November 15 events, dissension was

* Edward Sagarin has pointed out that, "While Mattachine and the numerous other groups demand security clearance for homosexuals, GLF denounces security clearances, defense contracts, and working for the war machine. And while Mattachine and its allies fight for equal rights to be drafted, no discrimination in the right to be a soldier or sailor, and to be treated as well (or as badly) as any other young citizen, the GLF denounces the draft, and insists that no one, straight or gay, should be turned into cannon fodder for the purposes of imperialist oppression." (*The Realist,* May–June 1970.)

99

to break out among members of the San Francisco gay liberation groups. At the Polo Grounds rally, Black Panther David Hilliard's speech was jolted when some gay militants joined with other pacifists in shouting "Peace, Now!" Michael Itkin wrote, for gay liberationists, in the *Free Press:*

It is obvious that those of us who hold to the principles of revolutionary nonviolence and the building of a community of love on decentralist lines could not, in any way, support David Hilliard when, under the pretense of speaking for peace he called for violence, when under the pretense of speaking for peace he spoke against the peace movement (like a left-wing Spiro Agnew), when under the pretense of speaking for peace he attempted to have the anthem of his political party (vanguard or not) imposed on us as the anthem of the entire Movement that day. We cannot see that violence, in any man's hand, is any less violence. When a man is murdered, regardless of the polemics surrounding that murder, another human being is dead without consideration of color, class, nation or politics. When a man is helped to become a transformed and liberated human being, he then aids in the revolution. As such, in our consciences we had no choice but to protest his speech as we did. . . .

Itkin, self-described as a "Libertarian Socialist-Anarchist Communitarian," was not by any means speaking for the existing politico-economic system in America. He was speaking against violence as a tool for changing that system and against supporting "such structures as the Black Panther Party and the Weathermen, which we cannot but view as elitist in their insistence that they are the vanguard of the revolution." [34] His views were to be echoed by dissenters to the developing program of GLF New York.

In November 1969, the New York Front was near-victim to a welter of internal issues. A year later, it was a smoother-running, nearly non-sexist organization that served, still, as "soul" of the gay liberation movement. In New York at least, another organization, Gay Activists Alliance, had become the "hand" of the movement, but the founders of GAA had, to a man/woman, been part of GLF.

For Gay Liberation Front welcomed—still welcomes—all gays; it has no "members." *Gay Power* once explained that "you don't really join GLF. Anytime you assemble with GLF at its meetings on Sunday eves, you're an individual . . . with a voice, and a part of the front . . ." [35] Nor any "officers." GP advised that the Front had "no leaders, no followers, just participants." [36] GLF's general-meeting chairmen merely moderated —by 1970 the moderator would be chosen by pulling a name from a hat containing the lots of those who were willing to chair the following four consecutive meetings. Once, late in its second year, GLF "representatives" had to be selected for a radio program. A newcomer to the meeting felt uninformed:

"I don't know who to vote for—"

"—You're not *voting!*"

"I don't know who to choose—"

"—You're not *choosing!*"

And the lots were drawn.

Similarly, when a decision had to be made, voting was unpopular. After sufficient discussion, a "consensus" was arrived at—the membership, undivided, coming to an agreement. Time-consuming often, but solidarity-building.

In early autumn 1969, cells had begun to form. Ralph Hall explained the phenomenon, and questioned it, in *Gay Power*. At a general meeting attended by 110,

Discussion of cellular formation, by some 15 members, met with a little discord and unnecessary accusations were posed. The issue was smoothed out. The cell, branch, chapter or whatever, would function under the GLF banner, but would in fact pursue common interests or actions away from GLF. The cell would in no way be a break-off. . . . The members of the cell believe closer communication and better person-to-person understanding would evolve within GLF if all congregated in cells. . . . Of course, the decision would be left to individuals. A great thought, but one that met with uneasiness and question.[37]

Bob Kohler and Bill Weaver have recalled this uneasiness. Kohler: "Lois Hart, who was very active in pushing cells—and I say that kindly—always saw GLF as an umbrella, the way women's liberation is. How many groups formed under women's lib—like Bitch, and NOW, and Redstockings!" Weaver: "There was a real struggle to establish cells. New York went through this 'cellular' struggle, and now, when Washington GLF or Walla Walla GLF has it, they assume at the very beginning that they're going to have cells. They can start out that way, where it took us almost four or five months of . . . fighting and vilification of one another." Kohler: "A lot of people panicked when the 28th of June cell formed. . . . Jerry [Hoose] and I were responsible for forming the second cell *—which was the Aquarius cell, and which took care of all the dances. . . . The 28th of June cell took the newspaper *Come Out!* That was their purpose: basically to publish."

In November, a cell organized which at first attracted many male GLFers. Of leftist persuasion, it attempted to apply Marxist-Leninist theory to the idea of gay oppression. Self-described, "The Red Butterfly is an association of gay men and women who as revolutionary socialists see their liberation linked to the class struggle."[38] An informational leaflet by the cell announced:

* A year later there were more than fifteen cells, including besides the newspaper cell a leafleting group, a public-speaking cell, etc.

The Red Butterfly recognizes that the United States is fit for many purposes, but not to live in.

The Red Butterfly is a part of the Gay Liberation movement. We are an organization of men and women working towards an end to oppression of homosexuals.

We stand opposed to imperialism, capitalism, racism, sexism-- We advocate a free and democratic socialist society striving for communism.

The Red Butterfly supports the peoples of Southeast Asia, Africa, Latin America--all oppressed people everywhere in their battles against imperialism and for socialism.

We support the Black Panthers; Women's Liberation; the liberation movements of Chicanos, Latins, and native Americans; and **all** oppressed peoples.

We stand prepared to work for and with everyone fighting oppression--everyone engaged in the struggle.

We insist upon an end to oppression of homosexuals. We demand to be treated as equals, as indeed we ARE equal.

The Red Butterfly is also engaged in research and writing projects. We welcome your interest and participation. . . .

In its first year, The Red Butterfly published four multi-page brochures: Carl Wittman's "Gay Manifesto" with RB discussion; "Gay Liberation"; "Gay Oppression: A Radical Analysis"; and a translation of Kurt Hiller's "Appeal" (Copenhagen, 1928) to the Second International Congress for Sexual Reform for the Benefit of an Oppressed Variety of Human Being, with RB discussion. In "Gay Oppression," a comprehensive analysis, RB believed that "The deepest problem faced by gay people in their personal lives is that of positive self-image." A society-induced self-censure "has had bad effects on personal relations. Gay people often have difficulty establishing lasting relationships." The pamphlet saw social oppression of gays as sixfold: physical attack; legal punishment; occupational exclusion; psychological oppression "in the form of harassment, abuse, slander and ridicule"; blackmail; and housing discrimination. The "INSTITUTIONS OF REPRESSION" listed, took in: 1) The family—"The American family is . . . the starting point for anti-gay attitudes. . . . Sexism, discrimination against persons because of sex or sexual activity, begins here"; 2) The educational system, where "Homosexuality receives heavy negative sanctions both directly and by treating it in negative and lurid ways"; 3) Organized religion, by which "religious sanctions are used to infuse attitudes toward homoeroticism with a heavy sense of guilt"; 4) Government—"Anti-gay laws, police harassment, persecution within the military, and nearly universal job discrimination all act to oppress the lives of gay people in very concrete and often painful ways"; 5) Business —"American business enforces conformism and anti-gay prejudices in hiring practices, in unequal opportunities for gays . . . etc."; 6) The mass media, which "extol and reinforce cultural norms"; and 7) Organized crime—"The syndicates exploit our needs for a relatively safe place to meet and socialize with other gay people."

Cells. The Front newspaper announced, in January, that "The many mentalities, dispositions, and persuasions of GLF activists and dissenters are finding expression in small groups structured after the needs, goals and philosophies of the participants." [39] *

As October waned, the New York GLF paper first appeared, bearing the slogan "A Newspaper by and for the Gay Community" and announcing on its face that

COME-OUT, A NEWSPAPER FOR THE HOMOSEXUAL COMMUNITY, dedicates itself to the joy, the humor, and the dignity of the homosexual male and female. COME-OUT has COME OUT to fight for the freedom of the homosexual; to give voice to the rapidly growing militancy within our community; to provide a public forum for the discussion and clarification of methods and actions necessary to end our oppression. COME-OUT has COME OUT indeed for "life, liberty and the pursuit of happiness."

It presented: "Joel Fabricant Perverts Gay Power" **; "The October Rebellion," by the Gay Commandoes; poems by Martha Shelley, Ron

---

* *The Advocate* attested that the Gay Liberation Front in Washington, D.C., coined the word *glonk*. "The word 'committee' was rejected by the group's radicals as being too establishment; the liberals and moderates down-thumbed 'cell' as too revolutionary." (November 11–24, 1970.)

** GLF detailed that Fabricant had "attacked homosexuals by name in print, endorsed mafia-run bars, included borderline pornography, and started a personal column in which people advertised for sex . . ." then proposed that gays could refuse to buy the paper, "tell our local newsstand dealer not to sell it or we won't trade with him any longer," or "boycott those establishments that advertise in 'Gay Power' . . ." (November 14, 1970.)

Ballard, Michael Boyle, and Daniel Smith; "Stepin Fetchit Woman," *
by Martha Shelley; a photoplay centerfold of GLFers; "Christopher Mar-
lowe" (a critique of his "Hero and Leander"); letters to the Front; and
"A Positive Image for the Homosexual," by Leo Martello. On the publication of its second issue, dated January 10, 1970, the slogan had been
doctored. COME OUT was, less pretentiously, "A Liberation Forum of the
Gay Community" (the "of" became "for" in later issues): between its
first two issues the New York gay militant world had split.

A split which was not simply the fault of the 28th of June cell or of
other gay leftist radicals in GLF. The endless haranguing at general meetings, where consensus had to be reached; the lack of elected leadership
and of recent tangible successes; and, particularly, the alignment with
causes that seemed merely to seek their own advantage in a bond with
homosexuals and whose politics included violence if deemed necessary—
these were equally potent ingredients that made GLF tough to swallow
whole. But it was the hell-bent-on-revolution attitude that 28th of June
and other radicals represented which stung. Marcus Overseth maintained,
at the end of 1969: "In both San Francisco and New York inertia has
overcome the Gay Liberation Movement. Some see it as having ground
to a halt." He advanced that "Politicals persisted in laying their trip onto
Gay Liberation. Where many of the members of the San Francisco
[straight] movement had begun to recognize that Gay liberation was part
of the social revolution, they were time and again offset by the red queens
and their tattered theories and dated dogmas. Here lies the real reason
for the current disruption within the Gay Liberation Movement. It has
been coopted by politicos who are still hung up on political revolution." [40]

In New York, GLFer Ralph Hall was to take a long, critical look.
He recognized that "Gay Liberation Front is a very diverse group. . . .
Minds range from moronic at times to super-intelligent. Because of these
wide divergencies . . . discussions do at times have a tendency to get
bogged down, but," he wrote,

certainly a bit of inappropriate rapping should not result in . . . social cyclamates
such as: paranoia, suspicion, power elite, irrationality, fascism, fear, guilt,
egos, innuendos, mistrust, hypocrisy and I could go on and on.

I feel these malignancies have been instilled into GLF by a certain self-
indulgent faction whose actions are aimed at deterioration of the group's structure and purpose. . . .

Weekly, I listen to those politically articulate dogmatists . . . I watch
them shrewdly manipulate and brainwash the membership. Those who do not
fall for their bullshit rhetoric are openly criticized and cleverly attacked when
they express their disapproval. Persons questioning points of view or dissenting
to majority consensus of GLF are openly embarrassed, insulted and/or

* Reprinted in the free press, and as "Notes of a Radical Lesbian" in Robin
Morgan, ed.: *Sisterhood Is Powerful* (New York, 1970).

humiliated. . . . At times one gets the feeling an uncontrollable few on the floor will rise, lasso a victim and proceed to hang him. . . .

Hall pleaded, "Whatever happened to those militant, extraordinary feats in the name of gay liberation we promised would be executed for all our gay brothers and sisters of the establishment and non-establishment communities? Whatever happened to the creative energies we were gathering to confront the heterosexual oppressor? . . . Our continual infighting and bickering proves that homosexuals do oppress one another."

GLF's lack of a recognized membership responsible to the Front made Hall shudder. He suspected it had been a leftist-radical plan "to set GLF up as an unstructured structure,* an umbrella structure with no interconnecting lines, wherein good and bad, violent and non-violent cells could and would evolve, all acting under the GLF banner. One person alone, acting as an individual cell, could bomb the Empire State Building . . . and proclaim he did it under the name of GLF, for the gay liberation cause and humanity as well. All we could do is censure and slap him on the hands and say that was a 'no no.' " [41]

GLFer and member of the 28th of June cell, Lois Hart, elucidated the dissatisfaction that was plaguing the front:

We began attracting large numbers of interested people: some staunch conservatives who came to criticize and disrupt; leftists with preconceptions about change and revolution who came to scorn and repudiate rather than work for the development of GLF; well-meaning establishment types who could not conceive of something democratic that did not involve everyone being controlled by the consensus of a voting membership. For them GLF was the Sunday Night Meeting, not groups of activists for homosexual liberation. They did not realize that we are a movement, not a static organization. [42] . . .

In mid-November GLF hemorrhaged—"There was a whole walkout; we never had a walkout before," remembers Jerry Hoose—when the decision to support the Black Panther Party won majority backing. Memories are still bitter about that night's vote (no consensus could be reached). At the general meeting a week before, the suggestion to support the Panthers had been defeated. That following Sunday, a Panther sympathizer asked for a recount. Bob Kohler recalls that "Marty [Robinson] and Jim [Owles] had, like loaded! And the women hadn't arrived. . . . I went outside. And Lois Hart was arriving with a tremendous contingent of women and I said 'Quick!' (It looked as if I had gone out on street corners and gathered the people.) This threw the whole vote, because all of the women voted to support the Panthers. That was the silver bullet through Jim

---

* Structure for GLF was much debated in late 1970 by young "members" who believed GLFers had learned to relate to one another in a non-sexist manner and could now benefit from some tighter organization.

Owles' heart. We had suddenly overloaded it more than they had loaded it, and they weren't prepared for us to be as dirty as they were—but we hadn't arranged for the women to come, they were just late." Kohler adds that "Jim and Marty freaked out completely. That whole 'John Birch Society' freaked out. And then Jim got up and made this speech about how he was going to resign [as treasurer]. . . . Then he went around and recruited—likely prospects." Jerry Hoose states that, following the rupture, "Jim and Marty came to a couple of meetings. But they were recruiting!"

Owles and Robinson were to become leaders of a new gay militant organization, Gay Activists Alliance. In June 1970, in an interview of GAA leaders by a *New York Times Magazine* editor, Owles detailed why he left GLF: "In its beginnings, GLF, aside from being revolutionary, *was* doing things that were related to the homosexual cause. . . . [But] the majority . . . considered themselves revolutionaries, and they wanted the group to identify and align itself with the other like groups. There was the beginning of a split, very early . . . I personally left the group because I felt that many of these other organizations were viciously anti-homosexual, that many of the leaders they followed had certainly shown no mercy to homosexuals they had taken in. And also because I felt that, in terms of organizing the homosexual community, I was interested in reaching *them* by working to bring about changes, such as the fair employment law; whereas the revolutionaries at GLF said, 'I hope Procaccino gets in, I hope things become so conscious to the gays that they see no alternative but to join up with us and pick up a gun.' They *wanted* the police to shut down the bars so it would completely antagonize and alienate the homosexuals and drive them into the radicals' hands . . . They were really interested in using them, as far as I'm concerned, for fodder—as cannon fodder for the revolution. When they did go out to other actions—let's say a support rally for the Panthers or the Young Lords or the more radical groups—they didn't go as a homosexual group, they went as kind of an auxiliary unit. To me, they were begging for that same kind of acceptance they had accused some of the older homosexuals of wanting. You know, 'Here, I'll put on a suit and tie. Please accept me. I'm one of you.' I felt as if they were going to people like Abbie Hoffman and saying, 'Look, see my hair's the same way as yours. I'm out in the picket line. Please accept me.' *And they were still getting spit at.* The word *faggot* was still being used at them. They were relegated to 'back' roles, and were told, 'Don't come out in front! We don't want our groups to become known as homosexual things.' That happened in other groups: in women's lib the lesbians are told, 'Get in the back. We don't want women's lib to be identified as a lesbian movement.' . . . It was just one put-down, spit-in-the-face thing all the way. And I just couldn't do that. . . ."

Kay Tobin told the *Times* editor, "I was watching what was going on, and knew very well that Marty and Jim were taking a drubbing from people whom I felt were absolutely ruthless in trying to grab hold of power . . . All of us were completely run out by their general meetings

with the personal attacks that went on there. . . . 1 was called a fascist—
I was going around with a Lindsay button at the time." Acknowledging
that Robinson really talked him into it, Owles said he "went back and saw
some of the people I could still talk to in GLF, and said we were starting
a new group: 'We don't even have a name—but if you're interested, come
to my place' . . ."

A few weeks later, a "Gay Liberation Front BULLETIN" called gays
to Sheridan Square to join in the Moratorium III vigil on Christmas Eve:
"Bring candles and posters. Join together for peace, freedom and the
rights of all people." A GLF flyer headed "A TIME FOR MOURNING" met
all comers to the square:

HOMOSEXUAL MEN AND WOMEN HAVE SERVED <u>WILLINGLY</u> IN EVERY ONE
OF AMERICA'S WARS! <u>WE DID NOT HAVE TO</u> -- WE ARE TOLD WE ARE
NOT WORTHY TO -- <u>BUT WE DID SERVE</u>, AND WE FOUGHT AND WE BLED
AND WE DIED BESIDE OUR STRAIGHT BROTHERS AND SISTERS. BUT,
AMERICA, YOUR LAWMAKERS, YOUR CHURCHES, YOUR EDUCATORS, YOUR
MEDICINE MEN, AND YOUR MEDIA HAVE CONTROLLED, MANIPULATED,
AND CORRUPTED US. WE EXIST SOLELY BY SUFFERANCE. YOUR
SYSTEM HAS EXPLOITED US AND ENFORCED INHUMANE AND DESTRUCTIVE
MORALITIES UPON US. WE ARE DENIED OUR BIRTH-RIGHT AND ARE
BRANDED CRIMINALS FOR CLAIMING THE RIGHT TO THE SELF-
DETERMINATION OF OUR OWN BODIES!

THIS IS THE SAME SYSTEM THAT FORCES MILLIONS OF AMERICANS TO
LIVE IN POVERTY, FOSTERS RACISM, SEXISM, AND THE PERSECUTION
OF OTHER MINORITY GROUPS, RAVAGES OUR NATURAL RESOURCES, AND
CHALLENGES ANYONE THAT WOULD OPPOSE ITS IMPERIALISTIC AND
MILITARISTIC AIMS!

<u>JOIN WITH US IN A PROTEST AGAINST WAR PROFITEERS AND THE</u>
<u>COMMERCIALIZATION OF THE HOLIDAY SEASON</u>. <u>THIS YEAR, WE ASK</u>
<u>YOU TO</u>:

      SEND GIFTS TO GI'S IN THE NAME OF THE PEACE
        MOVEMENT.

GIVE A DONATION TO A PEACE OR BLACK-RIGHTS GROUP.

SEND MEDICAL SUPPLIES TO VIETNAMESE VICTIMS OF WAR.

GIVE A DONATION TO A WELFARE-RIGHTS ORGANIZATION.

THIS IS A TIME FOR MOURNING! WEAR A BLACK ARMBAND. PLACE A

LIGHTED CANDLE IN YOUR WINDOW. JOIN OUR CANDLELIGHT VIGIL

IN SHERIDAN SQUARE ON CHRISTMAS EVE.

■

California gay liberation prospered, in spite of Marcus Overseth's prediction that, as 1969 drew to a close, "homophile" types and "bargay socialites" would be able to say, "See, I told you so. I just knew that queens could never 'organize.' " [43] Prospered, and made a temporary rapprochement with old-line groups.

In an anti-Thanksgiving rally, demo, and march, San Francisco gay militants zapped Western and Delta Airlines, the former for allegedly firing stewardesses for lesbian activity and the latter for refusing to sell a plane ticket to a young man wearing a Gay Power button; KFOG radio station for its anti-homosexual editorializing; numerous Tenderloin gay bars that had routinely refused to allow distribution of gay lib materials; the Greyhound bus terminal, where gays had periodically been arrested; and several "sexploitative" cinemas. (Gays' condemnation of cinema sexploitation has been well put by New York GLFer Jim Fouratt, who saw perversion in the films' incompleteness: "People are exploiting our bodies for profit. I am beautiful; my body is beautiful; all our bodies are beautiful; making love is beautiful. If these films do not visualize this, then they are anti-life and must be exposed as such. Why pay 3, 4, or 5 dollars to greedy straights and greedy misguided homosexuals. We must support only those films and film makers who are creating the honest vision. Don't allow them to make you or me ugly by their false projection of what we are." [44]) Gay demonstrators were joined by straight and gay sympathizers from the *Berkeley Tribe* and Sexual Freedom League. At march's end, the group "turned on to a free Thanksgiving dinner by our favorite Auntietoms" [45]: SIR and the Tavern Guild.*

In its pre-Christmas issue, the *San Francisco Free Press* [46] published an interview by RAT with members of New York GLF held several months before. To the question "What is the Gay Liberation Front?" Californians read the Easterners' reply:

We are a revolutionary homosexual group of men and women formed with the realization that complete sexual liberation for all people cannot come about

---

* The Tavern Guild has worked in San Francisco since 1961 for gay control of gay bars, and has exhibited a united front against periodic police pressures.

unless existing social institutions are abolished. We reject society's attempt to impose sexual roles and definitions of our nature. We are stepping outside these roles and simplistic myths. We are going to be who we are. At the same time, we are creating new social forms and relations, that is, relations based upon brotherhood, cooperation, human love, and uninhibited sexuality. Babylon has forced us to commit ourselves to one thing . . . revolution.*

"Why do you identify with the revolution when homosexuals are oppressed in other revolutionary cultures?" asked the interviewer. GLF's response was, "We feel in this respect that previous revolutions have failed, for any revolution that does not deal with the liberation of the total human being is incomplete." Questioned who the enemy was, GLF sounded less than revolutionary: "Certainly the system, but this system does not exist apart from people. Our aggressiveness is in terms of asserting our identity and reaching out to our brothers and sisters. Our program is a program for free love for all, but in a system that denies people that right, we intend to defend ourselves from the violence that is being brought down upon us. . . ."

GLF first organized in Los Angeles on December 21. A few days earlier, a meeting had been held at the Homosexual Information Center in North Hollywood "to develop a unified Gay movement for the Los Angeles area" and at which, wrote Douglas Key for the *Los Angeles Free Press,* "The necessity for an immediate cessation of the present internecine struggle within the Gay community was stressed . . ." [47] Comparing problems in L.A. with those that had split gay-militant New York, Overseth commented:

Believers in the conspiracy theory of history would have had their views reinforced by observing the first meetings of the GLF–Los Angeles. At these meetings two or three Gay leftists, utilizing standard agitprop tactics, thoroughly disrupted the meetings and prevented normal business from being carried out.

Fearful of being diverted from Gay liberation into left deviationism, Los Angeles Gays have decided to take steps to fight the factionalists. There has been no thought of kicking such persons out of GLF. Such tactics are not only unethical but they might tend to destroy the moral position of GLF. [48]

A position that was to be reinforced, seven days later, by a historic first: the West Coast Gay Liberation Conference, December 28, at UC Berkeley. Over 150 homosexuals, primarily from the Bay Area but in-

* This statement of GLF purpose (July 31, 1969) was first published in the August 12–26 issue of RAT. It was to be printed in issues three and four of *Come Out!*, but was superseded in issue five by the following declaration: "Gay Liberation is committed to replacing The American Empire with the sexually liberated community we know is the only one in which all people can be free. Radical Gay women and men are joining other oppressed peoples whenever possible in the struggle to destroy The Empire; we try to understand the unique abuses of their oppressions, their unique dreams of the liberated future, at the same time we try to explain to them why there will be no universal liberation unless we eliminate the ideas of sex which are the basis for psychosexual slavery in every major social system now feeding on the life of the planet."

cluding some from Los Angeles, San Diego, Santa Cruz, San Jose, Sacramento, Santa Barbara, and Bakersfield, and from Portland and Eugene, Oregon, attended—plus a score of young women's liberationists and one member of GLF New York. *The Advocate* marveled, "Fifteen years ago, they wouldn't have gotten homosexuals in the door—certainly not with the large sign out front announcing a five-day 'All-Homosexual Symposium * and Gay Liberation Conference.' " Jim Kepner, who covered the event, remarked that the conference's "tone was narrowly political, and far to the left of any previous homophile conference" and that, "Unlike most [national] conferences, this meeting extended the free style and structure developed at western homophile conferences. The tiresome business of credentials, fees, voting blocs, parliamentary procedures, and endlessly amended resolutions was omitted in exchange for free and vigorous discussion."

Kepner observed that nearly every participant felt gay liberation should join other anti-establishment groups in a general, anti-capitalist revolution. One Berkeley student said that, "Increasingly, black, brown, Women's Lib, peace, and ecology activists are all coming together in one grand movement—a 'rainbow' coalition." Kepner found a near-unanimous view that the homosexual cause was "part of a movement for sexual and ethnic equality and integrity, and for the defense of our plundered planet from corporate exploiters," then detailed some of the give-and-take:

SIR president Larry Littlejohn, an advocate of cooperation with Gay Lib, argued against mixing our cause with other issues, but a member of the original Gay Lib group, Committee for Homosexual Freedom, said, "Police brutality is *one* issue, no matter whose skull is cracked. We get nowhere going-it-alone." . . .

When Leo Laurence said the "pigs" would be "after us" soon after gay power began making itself felt, and predicted that we may soon need to stockpile guns and ammunition, disagreement was overwhelming, but not unanimous.

His co-founder of CHF, Gale Whittington, protested that homosexuals ought to sympathize with the Black Panthers, who are being slaughtered, but not to emulate their suicidal tactics. Leo conceded that "if Gays began to arm, the pigs would wipe us out," but he felt "we'd have to defend ourselves." . . .

Mike (CHF): "Our oppression—centuries of violence against us—is an objective thing. We have to bring that down, even if there's violence—to overturn the system. But let's not get caught in premature efforts. It's foolish to take provocative action without the people behind us."

Jim (GLF–NYC): "This talk of revolution and guns is a lot of masochistic fantasy." . . .

* The symposium was sponsored by a gay magazine, Dunbar Aikens's *Free Particle*, and was "conducted by and for Homosexuals with the purpose of expanding the Homosexual's awareness of his creative potential as a vital element of the free community." Discussions were held 2:00 to 6:00 p.m. and 7:00 to 11:00 p.m., December 26, 27, 29, and 30.

Said Leo: "Gay Liberationists don't believe public officials will *ever* condone homosexuality—so they aren't working for that sort of legal acceptance." * ...

Kepner noticed that there was "much disagreement about integrating the gay community into general society, as opposed to developing a gay culture. . . . When Don Jackson (Bakersfield) proposed that Gays take over an underpopulated but richly subsidized California county [see Chapter 14], the idea was shot down by those who oppose attempts to encourage the gay community to develop its own resources." **

Of this first gay lib conclave, Kepner concluded, "The Gay Lib attitude: 'Be Yourself; Don't be ashamed,' was a contagious thing, not just a bunch of stiffs sitting around discussing some 'social problem.' To those who measure a conference by the number of resolutions, this was a flop. Few who stayed the five days [for the Symposium/Conference] felt that way, but many did who came a long way for one day. Some got into panels monopolized by ego-trippers. Some felt that the political planning was too Berkeley-oriented for a supposed West Coast conference. But the accomplishments will probably be measured by the seeds planted, as new Gay Lib groups spring up on campuses all over the West." [49]

While gay liberationists were in conference and symposium, the California Federation of Teachers convened in Los Angeles, December 27–9. Adopted by CFT was a resolution demanding the development of a "vigorous life and sex education program at all school levels which explains various American life-styles" and "the abolition of all laws or other governmental policy which involves non-victim sexual practices." [50] ***

A final, Christmas gift to gay liberation's first (half) year came in the year-end issue of *San Francisco Free Press:* [51] Carl Wittman's "REFUGEES FROM AMERIKA: A Gay Manifesto." **** It was to be widely reprinted in free presses throughout the country, and has become, in effect, the bible of gay liberation.

The young author of the Manifesto analyzed gay liberation, as well as sexuality, on many levels. In "WHAT HOMOSEXUALITY IS," he declared: "Nature leaves undefined the object of sexual desire. The gender of that object has been imposed socially. Humans originally put a taboo on homosexuality because they needed every bit of energy to produce and raise children—survival of the species was a priority. With overpopulation

---

* Gay Activists Alliance, like other more conservative homophile and gay liberation clubs, would make its primary goal the implementation of homosexual civil rights by changes in the law short of revolution. Nor were all GLFs so adamant, as were those on the East and West Coasts and in Chicago, in their beliefs that legal acceptance was not destined to be worked out.

** An idea that was to develop into gay nationalism, as opposed to gay liberation.

*** The resolution was written and introduced by Morgan Pinney, a delegate-member of San Francisco State College AFT Local #1352 and assistant professor of accounting who had been active in the Committee for Homosexual Freedom in S.F.

**** Copies of the complete manifesto may be obtained from The Council on Religion and the Homosexual, Inc., 330 Ellis St., San Francisco, Cal. 94102.

and technological change, that taboo is absurd and continues only to exploit us and enslave us." He went on:

As kids, we refused to capitulate to demands that we smother our feeling toward each other. Somewhere we found the strength to resist being indoctrinated, and we should count that among our assets. We have to realize that our loving each other is a good thing, not an unfortunate thing, and that we have a lot to teach straights about sex, love, strength, and resistance.

Homosexuality is NOT a lot of things. It is not a makeshift in the absence of the opposite sex; it is not hatred or rejection of the opposite sex . . .

Wittman did not neglect bisexuality or heterosexuality. On the latter, categorically: "Exclusive heterosexuality is fucked up; it is a fear of people of the same sex, it is anti-homosexual, and it is fraught with frustrations. . . . For us to become heterosexuals in the sense that our straight brothers and sisters are is not a cure, it is a disease and a cop out."

In his section "ON WOMEN" he protested, "It's been a male dominated society for too long, and that has warped both men and women. So gay women are going to see things differently from gay men; they are going to feel oppressed as women, too. Their liberation is tied up with both gay liberation and women's liberation [see Chapter 9] . . . it would be arrogant to presume this to be a manifesto for lesbians." Admitting that "All men are infected with male chauvinism," he argued that this was not central to gay men: * "We can junk it much more easily than straight men can. For we understand oppression."

To Wittman, roles—which implied inequality—were a prime target. "Straight . . . thinking sees things always in terms of order and comparison. A is before B, B is after A . . . This idea gets extended to male/female, on top/on bottom . . . Our social institutions cause and reflect this verbal hierarchy. This is Amerika. We have lived in these institutions all our lives, so naturally we mimic the roles. For a long time we mimicked these roles to protect ourselves—a survival mechanism. Now we are becoming free enough to shed these roles which we've picked up from the institutions [that] have imprisoned us." Since "Marriage is a prime example of a straight institution fraught with role playing," he reasoned that "Gay people must stop measuring their self respect by how well they mimic straight marriages." Resenting homosexuals' frequent denigration of flamboyant gay types, in "GAY 'STEREOTYPE' ROLES" he was adamant: "As liberated gays, we must take a clear stand: 1) gays who stand out have been the most courageous among us; they came out and withstood straight disapproval before the rest of us. They are our first martyrs; 2) if they have suffered from being open, it is straight society whom we blame for that suffering." On "CLOSET QUEENS"—and, to Wittman, pre-

* Bob Kohler disagreed, in *Come Out!* (April–May 1970): "I suggest that it is one of our most urgent problems, one that has separated each of us from the other as Male homosexuals and created the greatest single barrier between Male and Female homosexuals."

112

tending to be straight was "probably the most damaging pattern of behavior in the ghetto"—he acknowledged that "1) [they] are our brothers; they are to be defended against attacks by straight people. 2) our fear of coming out is not totally paranoid: the stakes are high . . ." He also contended, about so-called perverted sex—sado-masochism, sex with animals, etc.—that "We've been called perverts enough to be automatically suspicious of this word . . . we shouldn't be apologetic to straights about gay people whose lives we don't understand or share."

Wittman detailed types of gay oppression: "PHYSICAL ATTACKS," "PSYCHOLOGICAL WARFARE" ("right from the beginning we have been subjected to a barrage of straight propaganda"), "SELF OPPRESSION" ("don't rock the boat," "things in SF are ok," "I'm not oppressed"), and "INSTITUTIONAL." Then, in "ON SEX," comparing sexual play and intercourse to music, he saw that "the variety of music is infinite and varied, depending on the capabilities of the players, both as subjects and as objects. Solos, duets, quartets (symphonies, even, if you happen to dig Romantic music!) are possible . . . perhaps what we have called sexual 'orientation' probably just means that we have learned to play certain kinds of music well, and have not yet turned on to other music."

Though Wittman deplored the small percentage of gays who excused their homosexuality by preferring sex with "chicken" and "studs"—unable to relate sexually to their own age-types—he postulated that

kids can take care of themselves, and are sexual beings way earlier than we'd like to admit. Those of us who began cruising in our early teens know this, and we were doing cruising, not being debauched by our elders. Scandals such as that in Boise, Idaho, about homosexuals perverting the youth are a dirty lie: the high school kids were exploiting gay people who were too scared to express the fullness of their homosexuality. And as for child molesting, the overwhelming amount is done by straight guys to little girls: it is not particularly a gay problem, and is a function of an anti-sex puritanism and its resulting frustrations.

For coalition, the writer looked to "WOMEN'S LIBERATION," "BLACK LIBERATION," "CHICANOS," "WHITE RADICALS" (recalling at the same time that "Nobody—capitalist or communist—has treated us as anything other than shit so far"), "HIP AND STREET PEOPLE," and even "HOMOPHILE GROUPS" ("reformist and pokey as they might sometimes be, they are our brothers").

Wittman pointedly described homosexuals in his title:

We are refugees from Amerika. So we came to the ghetto—and as other ghettoes, it has its negative and positive aspects. Refugee camps are better than what preceded them, or people never would have come. But they are still enslaving, inasmuch as we are limited to being ourselves there and only there.

Ghettoes breed self hatred. We stagnate here, accepting the status quo. And the status quo is rotten. We are all warped by our oppression, and in the helplessness of the ghetto we blame ourselves rather than our oppressors. . . .

6

The Snake Pit raid is one more illustration of the ugly games that straights inflict on gays, driving them underground, to be periodically chastised by the city's conscience, driving them into self-conscious, paranoid postures, driving them finally into an up-front struggle for liberation to establish, once and for all, that gay is neither perversion nor sissy nor sick nor faggot nor silly. Gay is good.
—Jonathan Black, in the *Village Voice,* March 19, 1970

VILLAGE VOICE BLACKOUT? headlined GAY newspaper on December 1: "Since the Village Voice was picketed by gay militants who demanded an end to its advertising policy which prohibited the use of the word 'gay,' there has been what seems to be a *Voice* blackout on news which deals with those militants." The Snake Pit raid by New York City police on March 8 turned on the lights. Reporting the raid, its victims, and the victimizer, the *Voice* spelled a biography of gay liberation since the Stonewall—and of the gay press—and took the first steps toward establishing a New Homosexual image in the minds of its readers. Even more noteworthy than the news the raid gathered was the impetus it gave to the fledgling organization that Owles, Robinson & Company had sired from Gay Liberation Front.

The Snake Pit was one of several after-hours homosexual bars in Greenwich Village and much like the Stonewall Inn. It opened at midnight and closed generally at 8:00 a.m., its customers arriving primarily in the mid-wee hours when other gay bars had called it a night. "A small, dark, basement den on West 10th Street," the *Voice* described, "the Snake Pit looks like it would comfortably hold about 50 persons. A week ago Saturday, when Inspector Seymour Pine arrived at 5 a.m. to serve papers for liquor violations more than 200 were squashed between the one-way mirror door and the bar."

Rationales for the raid were that the club did not have—never had had—a liquor license; had no fire inspection; nor a certificate of occupancy from the Buildings Department. "It could easily have become another Coconut Grove," stated Pine. Furthermore, he added, "We've had complaints from all kinds of sources. You could hear the noise half a block

114

away." Pine hauled in a total of 167 men, customers and management. "It looked like an explosive situation," he said. "We didn't want a loud, riotous crowd milling around outside. Our purpose in the arrests was to get them out of there." [1]

"This is not really legal," Dick Leitsch later objected, in THE SNAKE PIT: SOME AFTERTHOUGHTS for GAY, "since it is no crime to be IN a place that is serving liquor illegally; the only crime is to run such a place. There was no grounds for hauling the customers away." [2]

Two customers taken in the raid admitted to GAY that the bar was overcrowded. The night before, police had closed two other after-hours gay clubs, the Zodiac and 17 Barrow Street.* (The Zoo management would be taken a week later.) The interviewees thought the bar had been "relatively quiet inside. . . . A juke box played, but each reported that conditions were such that very little noise escaped from the basement establishment, whose main room is located behind a long narrow corridor." [3] According to Inspector Pine, a "large ventilator" carried out the noise of which residents had complained—the bar itself not being adjacent to the sidewalk. [4] One of the two customers "told GAY that he had walked past there many times and had never heard noises . . . Friends had taken him there that night for the first time. 'As I approached the area, I didn't know there was a bar there,' he said."

GAY related,

Word suddenly went through the crowd that a raid was taking place. There was some disbelief until plainclothesmen from the First Division Morals Squad announced themselves and uniformed police from the 6th precinct entered.

Because of the large crowd, some were kept inside the bar for over an hour, one man said, while paddywagons transported men in small groups to the 6th precinct house. . . .

At the station house, men were not informed at the outset of the charges against them and were not apprised of their rights, including the right to make a telephone call, according to the two men interviewed by GAY. The crowd was herded into one large room in the center of the station house, although some remained in the front entry hall. More were arriving over a period of time. Men milled about. "Things were terribly disorganized," one informant said. . . .

Were the men abused? Were they called names such as "faggot" by the police, as had been rumored? Not according to the two men interviewed by GAY. They claimed the police were very polite, often addressing them as "gentlemen." [5]

Reports of police conduct differed. Gay Activist Arthur Bell (then writing

* Leitsch pointed out how "Those raids were held early in the evening, and the few customers sent home, while the management and employees were taken in for selling liquor without a license, and other violations." (GAY, April 13, 1970.) West Coast gays don't always get off so easily. Jeff Buckley, in the August *Vector*, told how "the visitor must bear in mind that it is police practice to arrest customers first and management second when raiding a gay bar, no matter what the supposed offense . . ."

pseudonymously as Arthur Irving) taped a Snake Pit employee in the grim hours following the raid: [6]

... I tried to ask a guy when they were arresting us "What rights do we have?" and the cop said, "Shut your fucking mouth."

We were treated like animals at the station. We were all herded into one big room. There was a shoeshine machine there. A couple of kids turned on the machine and started shining their shoes with it and the cops started coming over and getting mad. One cop came and called me a faggot. He said, "You're nothing but a prick," and said, "I'm going to tear off both of your fucking feet if you don't get off that machine."

But what was once again to turn on Gay Power was neither the police pejoratives nor the hauling in of the 167 Snake Pit clients. It was Diego Vinales's leap. One of the arrested—and one of those confined longest, waiting to be driven to the station house ("He was very nervous, very frightened," GAY was told [7])—Vinales, a twenty-three-year-old Argentinian national here on a visa, ran up a flight of stairs at the precinct and tried to escape by a second-story window. He could not see the fourteen-inch spikes of the iron picket fence below.

"Suddenly, I heard a sound, like something falling," one of GAY's informants told, "then screams. The police were terribly excited. They couldn't get the lower floor window open to get to the man who fell. Someone screamed, 'Get a doctor!' Then someone else called, 'No, it's too late, get a priest!' " Bell's authority related:

I was at the window right after he landed on the spikes. The remarks the cops made after this happened were unbelievable. One cop said to a fireman, "You don't have to hurry, he's dead, and if he's not, he's not going to live long." I was with three or four kids when one of the kids heard this who happened to be a friend of Diego's. He started crying and screaming out. Then the other kids started crying. They saw what was happening and they were shaken. But the remarks kept coming from the cops. They probably thought they were justified. Diego was a faggot, they said. They used the word faggot so many times, it was unbelievable. . . .

. . . some of the cops that I knew just shook their heads. One of them said, "I'm sorry. I'm just plain sorry."

My head hurts. I still hear Diego crying out in pain and I hear him moaning and screaming. It isn't easy to shake.

GAY's interview continued: "The police had their attention on the fallen man, leaving guards only at station house exits. 'What kept us calm, what kept us from panicking was talking to each other, to keep our spirits up. . . .' So they sang. They sang AMERICA, THE BEAUTIFUL. They sang WE SHALL OVERCOME. And then they chanted: Gay Power, Gay Power, Gay Power."

The GAY informants detailed that, while police and firemen labored outside with Vinales, telephone calls were made, including one to Gay Activists Alliance. *The New York Times* and *New York Post* "were pretty cool about the whole thing and didn't seem really interested," but the *Daily News* came running. In the office where the calls were made were "all sorts of record books lying around . . ." the two ended. "So we kind of snuck them out and dumped them outside into a shaftway."

Rescue Company No. 1 of the city fire department had, meanwhile, been called to assist police—Vinales could not be moved to a hospital without an accompanying area of the fence. On Monday, the *News* published a gruesome five-photo exposé of the victim as its centerfold. In IMPALED, SAVED BY FIRE "DOCS," reporter Philip McCarthy outlined: "An unusual operation was performed in St. Vincent's Hospital yesterday when city firemen were called in, with an electric saw, to assist surgeons in freeing a young man who had impaled himself on an iron picket fence. . . . They were ordered to scrub and don surgical garments and sterile masks . . . cut away a crossbar and managed to ease out the prongs." * Detailing further that "about 500 [the *Times* estimated 200] men and women demonstrated that night in Sheridan Square and then in front of the Charles St. station house," the *News* nowhere mentioned, to its presumably puzzled readers, that the arrested as well as the protesters were homosexuals.

Summonses for disorderly conduct were given the 166 men before they were released from the station house. One source had it that the gays were told "you don't have to show up if you don't want to." [8] The *Voice* recorded that, "According to those arrested, cops at the precinct laughed and told them to tear up the summonses. No one checked identification at the precinct." [9] **

■

* Vinales, listed as critical for more than a week, underwent several major operations and remained at St. Vincent's for more than three months. During much of this time two policemen were on guard outside the victim's door; visitors were told he was a prisoner and were generally referred to the 6th Precinct. In a visit Arthur Bell reported in *Gay Power* (No. 15), he said that Vinales did not talk "about the scars and wounds he'll be carrying with him for life. He was grateful for the help and support he's had from various groups. . . . His family is in Argentina and Alfredo [Diego] suspects that they may now know of the Snake Pit incident. He has not heard from them."

** By a curious and macabre coincidence, "In the early morning of March 8 . . . a Los Angeles officer fatally shot Larry Turner, aged 20, admitted homosexual and black," who, in drag, flagged down an unmarked police car, "got in and allegedly offered to do oral copulation," reported *The Advocate* (April 29–May 12, 1970). Turner would have been taken in, but pulled a .22-caliber pistol from his waist, according to police reports. One of the officers shot him in the chest, though several witnesses told that "Turner was running away when he was shot." The same day, a service was held by several homosexual groups at the Dover Hotel in downtown L.A. to memorialize the death of J. McCann (Howard Efland), who registered there a year before, was seized a short time after by three plainclothes officers who entered the hotel, and beaten to death in front of witnesses.

Arthur Bell told *Gay Power* how he woke up at 10:00 a.m. on Sunday, March 8, "turned on the faucet and the radio, and got the news. WCBS did not indicate the name of the bar, or if the bar was Gay. Just the address. And two hundred arrested, one unidentified man seriously hurt, taken to St. Vincent's Hospital. I got [lover] Arthur up. We started phoning." [10]

Bob Kohler of GLF remembers, "I was awakened by my doorbell at about 8:30—I had taken my phone off the hook. It was Bob Smith, a GLF member, who said that he had just come from the police station . . . 167 people had been arrested. It was all very serious . . . we sat down and were having coffee. And, about ten o'clock, my phone rang. It was Arthur Bell. He asked, would GLF want to do an action? I said I thought so, but that I really couldn't speak for GLF." Jerry Hoose recalls, "I had gotten home about 6:00 in the morning. It was about 10:30 when my phone rang. It was Jim Owles. Jim gave me the details of what happened, which he had just heard. He asked me if I thought that GAA and GLF could work together on it."

Kohler, Hoose, and other GLF members worked out of the bookstore where Kohler was employed, ordering "tons of paperboard for posters. And we got hold of the women." At 2:00, about thirty Gay Activists were at Jim Owles's apartment on Jones Street. Leo Martello reported, later, to *The Advocate*: ". . . a phone-in was staged, plans made, circulars written, ideas discussed. The apartment was jam-packed with angry, determined Gays. A recently acquired second-hand mimeographing machine broke down. Fortunately, one of the girls had access to the DOB duplicator." [11] About three thousand copies of the leaflet were run off. It read:

```
Gay  Activists  Alliance -- 691-2748


    "Snakepit" raided, 167 arrested --

One boy near death . . . at St. Vincent's . . .

    either fell or jumped out precinct window,

   landed and was impaled on a metal fence!

      Any way you look at it --

           that boy was PUSHED !!

      We are ALL being pushed.

      _____


   Fighting gays and any of you who

   call yourselves HUMAN BEINGS with guts
```

to stand up to this horror --

Gather at Sheridan Square tonight

March 8 at 9:00 to march on the Sixth Precinct.

Stop the Raids!   Defend *Your* Rights!

There will be a DEATH WATCH VIGIL

at St. Vincent's immediately after protest! . . .

Bell related how the leaflet was circulated: "We covered the East Side, West Side, and all of the Village. Arthur and I pamphleted the West Village bars. Sympathy was with us almost everywhere. Bartenders at Le Bonsoir, the Stud, Julius', let us in, took additional circulars to pass to their later turnover of customers." Kohler tells how GLFers went to Alternate U. to reach a Yippie meeting and that women's liberationists agreed to join the protest. "I had been in the demonstrations the day before," Kohler states, "where women were beaten in front of the House of Detention—and people thought this was the same thing. Like, a field day for the pigs: Saturday afternoon they beat the women down, Sunday morning they raid the gay bars!"

The usual Sunday-night GLF meeting at the Church of the Holy Apostles was canceled—a rare event! But GLFers decided to meet there nevertheless, to make posters. In *Come Out!* [12] Allen Warshawsky described the scene and its effect on him:

I go over to Ellen who is on the floor making a sign. "GAYS ARE GETTING ANGRY," it says. I begin to feel an anger welling up inside of me. The anger of having to pay exorbitant prices for the freedom of dancing with someone of my own sex. The anger of having some pig take me to a precinct house as if I have broken a law because an arrangement he has made with the Mafia has been broken—a pay-off has not been made. An anger at the stinking, rotten, corrupt system that defines, fosters and promotes my "criminal" status. GAYS ARE GETTING ANGRY.

Kohler recalls, "When Father Weeks came in, we told him what was going to happen and asked him to please come down with us in support. He said he would. We had a woman medic and a lawyer giving us legal and medical instructions."

The protesters assembled at Sheridan Square, opposite the former Stonewall Inn: members of women's lib, Yippies, representatives of Homophile Youth Movement and of *Homosexuals Intransigent!*, a crowd of GLFers and Gay Activists, many members of the gay community who were not affiliated with an organization, Village residents straight and gay. Gay marshals had been designated to supervise and keep the marchers on the sidewalk. Warshawsky wrote, "There will be no violence we hope. But the pig with his club and gas, the incidents that his agents provocateurs may provoke—we must rehash the rules of protection—wet handkerchiefs and keep back of head and genitals covered."

On the walk to the 6th Precinct, GAY reported [13] that

Chants rang out. "Gay and proud, Say it loud, Gay and proud, Say it loud!" "Gay, Gay Power to the Gay, Gay People!"

Then at the police barricades spread before the 6th precinct house, the crowd angrily and insistently called for the police captain: "We want Salmieri, We want Salmieri!"

When this individual refused to appear, the chants changed again. "Who gets the pay-off? The police get the pay-off! Who gets the pay-off? The police get the pay-off!" Then, "There's the Mafia in blue, There's the Mafia in blue, There's the Mafia in blue!"

Dozens of police in pale blue helmets were amassed in the street and on the station house steps, behind the barricades. Jim Owles, president of GAA, and Father Weeks approached the officer in charge of their defensive line.

Owles contended that three or four representatives should be allowed to enter the station and to confront verbally Captain Salmieri or whoever was in command at that hour. He argued that the crowd would be mollified, however slightly, and the potential for rioting then and there would be substantially reduced if the police would listen to representatives. The police refused, playing into the hands of extremists in the crowd.

. . . a well-known revolutionary from the Gay Liberation Front then tried to interject his political bias . . . "Don't talk to the pigs, we don't talk to the pigs," he called out. A GAA member shot back . . . "Shut up, you leftist dildo!" Another agitator called out, "Revolution Now!" but found little support.* . . .

Jim Owles turned to the frustrated demonstrators. "Our brother lies near death at St. Vincent's Hospital! We've made our point to the police by our numbers! Now we will march in solemn procession to the hospital."

The crowd cooled and headed for St. Vincent's. Some carried lighted candles. Before the large hospital, and occupying every inch of sidewalk space, the demonstrators halted to hear a prayer offered by Father Weeks for the recovery of the man inside who lay in critical condition in the intensive care unit. They proceeded to march in silence around the block containing the hospital. . . .

Warshawsky told, "We are silent but we are seething. The demonstration cannot end here. We march down Greenwich Avenue past the Women's House of Detention . . . How can we divorce issues any longer? Gay oppression, Black women locked up in that stinkhole, women clubbed on the street demanding their freedom. 'Hey, hey, ho, ho, House of D has got to go,' we scream out. We are cheered from inside and move back into

* One GLFer has insisted, "We were there protesting their actions the night before —I was not into standing there and talking to them as human beings, because I don't think they were acting like human beings. . . . I feel it plays into their hands, and I don't like doing that."

the park." Bob Kohler remembers that he "started telling people to stop at the House of Detention," but that GAA leaders rushed the line around the corner into Christopher Street and "suddenly we were past the House of D and back in Sheridan Square, when I think it was Marty or Jim who addressed the crowd as 'brothers'—I couldn't tell you what *that* brought on from the women!"

GAY finished:

At the close, hoarse from angry shouting and chanting, the demonstrators were scarcely able to handle the singing of "We Shall Overcome," upon their return to Sheridan Square. GAA officers . . . wearily called the demonstration to a close. Jim Owles, nearly unable to speak, announced that blood was needed by the hospital for the critically injured man and urged its donation. He expressed his appreciation for the fact that despite political and ideological differences, members of a variety of homophile groups had been able to join together and work together in what was to be the largest and angriest planned gay demonstration thus far in the history of the homosexual movement in this country. . . .

GLFers and some women's liberationists, disgruntled by the demonstration's failure to relate to Saturday's protest at the Women's House of Detention, marched up Sixth Avenue to Alternate U., which, Warshawsky wrote, "has stayed open all night in case the scene got heavy and we needed a place to regroup. I go with some friends to watch the news on TV. First we hear Channel 7—demonstrations in the Village because a bar was closed. You motherfuckers, that was a Gay bar that was closed and those were Gay demonstrators. Then Channel 4—Some demonstrators chanted 'Gay Power'—How did that ever slip through? . . ."

∎

"I wish I could convince you that I'm not anti-gay. That I'm anti-gay is the furthest from the truth. We're taking non-gay unlicensed places too.* We take more gay places because there are more of them. Unlicensed places are frequented more by gay people than by straight people. Why I don't know. But we are also taking non-gay places," said Deputy Inspector Pine in a telephone interview with GAY. In GAY's words, Pine held "the dubious distinction of being the one who closed the play *Che!* on morals grounds, of being the one who called the raid on the Stonewall last summer . . . that precipitated the first gay riot in history . . ."[14]

Pine explained the mass arrest of customers because it was "impossible to tell" who was making the noise that nearby residents had complained

* Dick Leitsch noted, in "Afterthoughts," that "Of the hundreds of places closed in the past six months, less than one-half of 1% have had gay clientele. To charge that this campaign is directed against the gay community can only be construed to be paranoic or self-serving." (GAY, April 13, 1970.)

about, also in order "to discourage them" from coming to the unlicensed club. John Heys, editor of *Gay Power,* assaulted a third rationale:

"It looked like an explosive situation." Are you serious? You could have gone to El Morocco on that same night and found what you deem an explosive situation or to any other bar in New York for that matter. So bars are bars and they all have to meet specific regulations. If the violations of the Snake Pit were such, why did you take so long to acknowledge them? Why didn't you serve notice of these violations to those responsible? Why victimize more than 100 people? Disorderly conduct? Had it been a straight bar your tactics would have been different.[15] . . .

Pine faulted, for GAY interviewers, "the necessarily lengthy procedures. They are so complex, with so many bureaus involved, he complained. Nevertheless, he said that now there are eviction proceedings under way, that the police have taken action against the landlord to evict the long-standing Snake Pit." The Deputy Inspector also commented that closing gay bars "isn't very important police activity." That, "If GAA puts enough pressure on the Police Commissioner and if there are sufficient complaints about my actions and services [Morals], I would probably be assigned elsewhere, possibly to going after muggers."

He seconded GAA's leafleted contention: "Yes, I agree society pushed that man out the window in an ultimate sense. He reacted to our enforcing society's laws." Then Pine advanced, "Certainly liberalization in the last two years [of laws affecting homosexuals] has not resulted in any disadvantage to the general public." . . . But liberal straights and gays, whose brother's pain was theirs, fumed. *Screw* editorialized [16] that "To some men penalties for being what they are and *must* be are so severe that they can be driven to defenesrate themselves," and queried WHO'S GUILTY? John Heys asked Pine, "Do you know what you've done to Alfredo Vinales?"

About the Snake Pit raid, columnist Nat Hentoff observed, in the *Village Voice:* [17] "But isn't homosexuality, actual or alleged, the real basis for the action against the 167? And if that's true, by what assumption of 'higher' morality do we allow them to be swept up in this kind of dragnet? Certainly 'rehabilitation' isn't the goal. So what is, besides random harassment?"

In its two months' life, Gay Activists Alliance had several times sent visitors to the Village Independent Democrats, one of New York State's powerful political reform clubs. The Human Rights Committee of VID had worked with GAA representatives to help develop a sound civil-libertarian "Position Statement on Rights of Homosexuals," which was adopted by VID on February 19. On Monday night, March 9, Gay Activists visited the club to deliver "a wrathful attack on society's inhuman laws and intolerant attitudes vis-a-vis its homosexual citizens," reported GAY.[18] GAA delegate-at-large Marty Robinson made the indictment, and presented homosexuals' demands. A resolution based on the demands was passed by VID, and resulted in the following letter:

Hon. John V. Lindsay
City Hall, New York

Dear Mayor Lindsay:

At a meeting of its membership held last night the Village Independent Democrats unanimously supported a resolution calling for a moratorium on police raids on bars frequented by homosexuals. The aftermath of Saturday's raid on the "Snake Pit" was the arrest of 166 people, who from the best information available to us, were guilty of nothing more serious than being in a bar after 3 a.m., a young man, driven by shame and fear, lies close to death in St. Vincent's Hospital and a near riot occurred in the Greenwich Village area.

We request this moratorium in order to be free, together with other community groups, to study the facts of this specific incident together with the overall conduct of the police and the State Liquor Authority and to determine whether or not there was a concerted effort underway to harass homosexuals in the Village community. Admittedly reports in the press do indicate that the bar may have been operating in violation of the law, but we are also aware that strict enforcement of laws against a particular group is a classic form of harassment.

As our Village Affairs and Human Rights Committees study in the next few weeks this question, we would also appreciate knowing who in your office would be the appropriate person to be in contact with in order to follow up on any findings those committees may make.

Thank you for your cooperation.

Sincerely,
Robert J. Egan, President

On March 26, United States Representative Edward Koch, D, of the New York 17th Congressional District, released to the press [19] the text of a letter he wrote after speaking with GAA president Jim Owles:

Honorable Howard Leary
Police Commissioner
City of New York

Dear Commissioner:

I have received a number of requests from constituents to inquire into the facts surrounding the arrests of 167 persons on March 8th at the Snake Pit bar for alleged disorderly conduct. I have been told that this incident is one of five in the last 12 months which appears to be part of a crackdown on bars allegedly frequented by homosexuals. The matter was made most tragic as the result of the near death of Diego Vinales who is reported to have thrown himself out of a second floor window in the 6th Precinct Station House and to have been impaled upon spikes as a result of that fall. It is my understanding that the 167 arrested, of which he was one, were taken to the 6th Precinct Station House, held for several hours and then issued summonses and released.

123

What is particularly distressing to me, having practiced law for more than 20 years with some familiarity in representing defendants, including on some occasions those charged with soliciting for the purposes of engaging in sexual deviation, I cannot remember in the course of that more than 20-year period, any comparable arrest of such large numbers in a case of this kind. This is further compounded by the fact that, I am told, several of the defendants have been brought to trial and the cases against them dismissed. Many people in the community are of the opinion that the Police Department has begun again its harassment of homosexuals which had been the practice in the City of New York prior to your being appointed Police Commissioner. I recall a meeting at the Village Gate shortly after your appointment, attended by the Mayor, when you and he made it clear that the various practices which have been engaged in by the Police Department, including entrapment and harassment, would not be tolerated by you.

I would like to know, Commissioner, whether there has been a change in policy. Unless there has been, I cannot understand arresting 167 people in a bar for disorderly conduct. I would appreciate your comments on this particular situation, as well as receiving them covering police incidents taking place within the last 12 months at the Stonewall, Zoo, Zodiac and 17 Barrow St. bars. If there are available separate reports on each of the five places covering police arrests within that period for disorderly conduct including morals offenses, I would very much appreciate your sending them to me.

It should not be required to be said, but evidently must be said—obscene public behavior in violation of the law, homosexual or heterosexual, should not be tolerated, but it is not a violation of the law to be homosexual or heterosexual, and the law should never be used to harass either. I had thought that your public statements in this area of private morals would have the effect of inhibiting the police from engaging in such harassing actions. Without wanting to prejudge the Snake Pit case, but at the same time hearing and seeing what is happening, I do believe that you have permitted your Department to retrogress in this area.

I would appreciate your comments on the entire matter and as soon as possible.

Sincerely,
Edward I. Koch

Jack Nichols and Lige Clarke exulted: "It takes real balls for a politician to stand up for civil rights and liberties of homosexual citizens. In a day when our liberties are threatened on all sides by left-wing and right-wing fanatics, we are in need of conscientious representatives who dare to speak for the rights of ALL citizens. In GAY's last editorial we called for honest politicians to break the deadly silence. Congressman Koch has earned the distinction of being the first to do so." [20] *

The Gay Activists' double coup following the Snake Pit raid came

* Edward Koch was re-elected to the United States House of Representatives in autumn 1970. His district encompasses a great portion of New York City's "gay ghetto."

after a picketing, the week before, of New York's City Hall which secured for three delegates a meeting with Mayor's Counsel Michael Dontzin; a question-and-answer confrontation at the Village Independent Democrats with gubernatorial candidates on January 26; a protest "visit" to the *New York Post* . . . Gay Activists Alliance had met many of its "enemies" and had won a multitude of friends. The club had been busy since its inception in late December.

7

Mayor Lindsay (to Arthur Godfrey): In
many instances it's illegal to blow your
automobile horn . . .
Gay Activist John Kane (from the audience): It's illegal to blow a lotta
things! . . .

—on "With Mayor Lindsay,"
WNEW-TV, April 19, 1970

Preamble.

WE AS LIBERATED HOMOSEXUAL ACTIVISTS demand the freedom for expression of our dignity and value as human beings through confrontation with
and disarmament of all mechanisms which unjustly inhibit us: economic, social,
and political. Before the public conscience, we demand an immediate end to
all oppression of homosexuals and the immediate unconditional recognition of
these basic rights:

The right to our own feelings. This is the right to feel attracted to the
beauty of members of our own sex and to embrace those feelings as truly
our own, free from any question or challenge whatsoever by any other person,
institution, or moral authority.

The right to love. This is the right to express our feelings in action, the
right to make love with anyone, any way, any time, provided only that the
action be freely chosen by all the persons concerned.

The right to our own bodies. This is the right to treat and express our
bodies as we will, to nurture them, to display them, to embellish them, solely
in the manner we ourselves determine independent of any external control
whatsoever.

The right to be persons. This is the right freely to express our own individuality under the governance of laws justly made and executed, and to be
the bearers of social and political rights which are guaranteed by the Constitution of the United States and the Bill of Rights, enjoined upon all legislative bodies and courts, and grounded in the fact of our common humanity.

To secure these rights, we hereby institute the Gay Activists Alliance,
which shall be completely and solely dedicated to their implementation and
maintenance, repudiating at the same time violence (except for the right of
self-defense) as unworthy of social protest, disdaining all ideologies, whether

political or social, and forbearing alliance with any other organization except for those whose concrete actions are likewise so specifically dedicated.*

It is, finally, to the imagination of oppressed homosexuals themselves that we commend the consideration of these rights, upon whose actions alone depends all hope for the prospect of their lasting procurement.

Thus began the constitution of GAA, constructed during several initial meetings of ten to fifteen emigrants from New York Gay Liberation Front and approved on December 21, 1969. It "was very carefully worked over because we were trying to build in all the safeguards, so that we wouldn't be co-opted and wouldn't fall apart—or fall into something different," states Kay Tobin, one of the charter members. Curiously, the strong but often vague preamble resembled a forceful statement introduced by Franklin Kameny and adopted by the summer 1968 NACHO conference: "The homosexual, in our pluralistic society, has the moral right to be a homosexual. Being a homosexual, he has the moral right to live his homosexuality fully, freely, and openly, and to be so and do so free of arrogant and insolent pressures to convert to the prevailing heterosexuality, and free of penalty, disability, or disadvantage of any kind, public or private, official or unofficial, for his nonconformity." [1]

In a brochure the organization soon provided for all newcomers to its crowded meetings, "What Is GAA?" was made clear:

The Gay Activists Alliance is a militant (though nonviolent) homosexual civil rights organization. Membership is open to all persons—male or female, young or old, homosexual or heterosexual—who agree with the purposes of the organization and who are prepared to devote time to their implementation.

GAA is exclusively devoted to the liberation of homosexuals and avoids involvement in any program of action not obviously relevant to homosexuals. Although individual members of GAA are involved in many different social causes, the organization as such is a one-issue organization. GAA adopted this policy in order to win the support of large numbers of homosexuals—regardless of differences in social perspective—and to avoid internal political dispute. This policy is written into the GAA constitution.

GAA is a structured organization. It has officers and committees, but only the membership can decide upon policy. This is done at our weekly general membership meetings.** Meetings are conducted in accordance with parliamentary law. GAA adopted this policy to insure that policy decisions are mutually consistent, arrived at democratically, and carried out efficiently. This policy is also written into the GAA constitution.

* GLF made, of course, no such restrictions. A third viewpoint has been expressed in its constitution by FREE, in Minneapolis: "FREE is willing to support the efforts of any groups fighting against . . . discrimination if said group is in turn willing to defend the rights of Gay People. However, FREE reserves the right not to support any tactics of such groups that it believes harmful to attaining its goals."

** Held at the Church of the Holy Apostles on Thursday evenings. GLF met there on Sunday evenings.

GAA is a political organization. Everything is done with an eye toward political effect. Although dances and other social events are sometimes held, their purpose is to raise the political consciousness of the gay community and to contribute to its sense of social solidarity. GAA adopted this policy because all oppression of homosexuals is based on political oppression and because the liberation of homosexuals can only be effected by means of a powerful political bloc.

GAA uses the tactics of confrontation politics. Politicians and persons of authority in society who contribute to the oppression of homosexuals are publicly exposed through mass demonstrations, disruption of meetings, and sit-ins. GAA adopted this policy because the first necessary stage in homosexual liberation is the development of an open sense of public identity in the gay community and a corresponding sense of fear and embarrassment in the government.

GAA does not endorse any candidate for public office or any political party. The response of politicians to GAA confrontations—whether a favorable or an unfavorable response—is given the widest possible circulation in the straight and gay press, but the organization as such does not commit itself to anyone's political career. GAA adopted this policy to avoid compromising entanglements within the political system. This policy is written into the GAA constitution.

GAA is open to all varieties of homosexual culture.* No member may be discriminated against because of personal appearance, style of behavior, or sexual taste. GAA adopted this policy because prejudice against sub-minorities within the gay community is inconsistent with the struggle for fundamental human rights. . . .

GAA represented a new direction for gay militancy, a sort of "conservative radicalism"—or "middle-of-the-road radicalism" if the old-line homophile movement, gay-civil-rights-oriented too, be considered radical. The trend would spread, in coming months, to Chicago, where Chicago Gay Alliance developed out of Chicago Gay Liberation; to Louisville, where "An abortive attempt was made Sept. 17 to hold a meeting . . . to organize a '2nd Gay Liberation Front' to counter the first group, which has been criticized as too radical . . ." [2] But the trend, which advocated working within the existing political system, would have difficulties in an America whose process had been so anathematized by a majority of its youth. In New York, nevertheless, GAA grew and grew strong. Old-line leaders such as Foster Gunnison were pleased. In a letter to a friend he wrote: "I have also encountered another New York militant group that is not in any way concerned with non-homophile causes, that is wholly dedicated to the homophile cause, that operates in a conventional structured manner, and that manages to accomplish a great deal of good in well-planned confrontation situations." [3] The co-editors of GAY rejoiced that, "While the Mattachine Society works through the courts, the Gay Activists Alliance is engaged in non-violent activism which is meant to equalize the

* GLF has, likewise, championed a variety of homosexual types.

status of the homosexual. Unlike the so-called revolutionary GLF . . . members of the GAA have created a structured organization which does not intend to 'overthrow the system' but to improve life for homosexual men and women." [4]

GAA's more circumscribed goal of, solely, homosexual civil rights— at least as an immediate aim—gave a great degree of unanimity to meetings and of allegiance to the club leaders, who were conscientiously working toward that goal, even gave up full-time jobs to labor, unpaid, for the organization. The Activists have been criticized for this very—and often stifling—consensus and for their devotion to leaders/structure; said one GLFer, "You can't open your mouth at GAA meetings. You interrupt them and—zing! you're stigmatized!"

The founders of GAA were similarly intolerant of GLFers' mind-boggling attempts, at meetings, to relate to one other in a leaderless, structureless way; Leo Martello enunciated, "They take out their hostilities on each other instead of on those they consider their oppressors. They mentally masturbate!" Said Marty Robinson at a June 27 interview with *The New York Times,* "It's an incredible hate session. It isn't, in GAA. We've kept it incredibly *positive."* Believing that, for the pride it developed in its members, GAA was "almost group therapy," Robinson and Kay Tobin and president Jim Owles elaborated, at the *Times* interview: Robinson—"If anything's ever accepted from us [the leaders], it's because members have bought its reasonableness. And if you watch our votes, it's fantastic: our votes are, like, majority to zero. . . . Because it's a very rational, political, common-sense, free-from-rhetoric policy of *going after things.* . . . If we have to sit-in, we will sit-in; if we have to confront, we'll confront; if we have to say 'Fuck you!' we say 'Fuck you!' . . . There is no dogma in GAA. It's a very good way of working, a very, very true-to-Power-to-the-People sort of doctrine without being in that [leftist] kind of light. . . . It really is for homosexuals and we do operate it for homosexuals, and homosexuals get that message very fast: that there's no bullshit about what we're doing. . . . There're no secrets here and there's no fighting. We're all working together." Tobin—"It's really beautiful. It's very Spartan, and everybody leaves his other grievances at the door. When I come in there I don't bring in my women's lib-type grievances. We don't have to sit there and fight about 'Will we support the Black Panthers or won't we?' . . . I was in Philadelphia at a political forum on 'The Homosexual and Politics' the other night, when all these issues intruded themselves: 'What are encounter groups?' 'How 'bout women's lib?' 'Should all oppressed people hang together?' They were discussing everything else except how to get ahead with gay problems in Philadelphia! The GAA representative [at the forum] really turned-on three or four organizations down there who are dying to know all about GAA and why we're so successful. They're floundering around—they realize that there's a big success story in New York and it's right in the political arena and it sticks right to that . . ." Owles—"We have homosexuals in our

organization who are representative of the entire political spectrum. . . .
Now if a John-Bircher can reconcile his John Birch beliefs or if an anarchist
can reconcile his particular beliefs with fighting for homosexual civil rights,
civil liberties, fine! In theory we are open to everyone and no one's politics
is questioned." Owles, asked how he would answer a member who suggested GAA relate to a non-homosexual cause, replied: "If you're particularly anxious to help in another cause, there are already-existing groups. If
you're interested, as a gay, in fighting with the Young Lords, there is
GLF . . ."

GAA meetings have been shaken by its one-minded determination
not to relate to the Movement. At a March meeting, for example, Leo
Skir told *Mademoiselle,*

A girl with a pre-Raphaelite hairstyle speaks. She notes that, after the last vigil
(for the Snake Pit–raid victim), the GAA membership did not go down with
the others . . . to picket the Women's House of Detention, which was nearby
in the Village.

Jim explains that those who came to the demonstration had come to
express one aim, one sentiment—that the Snake Pit arrest was wrong. It was
unfair to ask them, having come to make this one protest, to join another.
The House of Detention protest was not a gay issue.

The girl continued: There *were* lesbians in the Women's House of Detention solely because they were lesbians. . . .

An uncomfortable debate ensued in which the Kent State killings figured.
The girl, and others, left the meeting. Jim Owles faced the remaining:
"We identify with the Kent State students. I'm going to Washington Saturday. I assume most of you are. But we cannot accept policy from another
organization." [5]

Gay Activists Alliance could neither be all things to all people, and
so it came in for another round of criticism in late 1970, this time from a
friendly, non-political organization, the West Side Discussion Group.*
Steve West, in the November *WSDG Newsletter,* attacked GAA's "Everything is done with an eye toward political effect": "GAA almost made
a serious mistake while undergoing its growing pains . . . it almost forgot
about people. *Individual* gay people. It almost forgot that we can't just
march toward a political goal as so many automatons . . . WSDG is
people meeting people. Not gettting together just to go out and confront
the enemy, but getting to know each other."

Maybe the group of twenty-odd Gay Activists in January 1970 thought
they knew each other well enough. Or maybe they just wanted to get to
know someone else: Councilwoman Carol Greitzer. One of their first

* WSDG was created in November 1956 by members of MSNY and other New
York gays to provide a forum for discussion of all aspects of homosexuality; it has
met once a week for discussions followed by socializing.

"actions" was to begin circulating a petition concerning the Council-woman and her failure to serve the needs of her gay constituency. It read:

To Carol Greitzer, of the 2nd Councilmanic District, which includes Greenwich Village, we the undersigned demand the following for immediate consideration and action:

1) That Mrs. Greitzer introduce to the City Council a bill prohibiting public or private employment discrimination on the basis of homosexuality.

2) That Mrs. Greitzer, through the prestige of her office, seek the repeal of existing laws prohibiting the solicitation for and participation in homosexual acts between consenting adults.

3) That Mrs. Greitzer and her colleagues undertake a campaign of eliminating all discriminatory restrictions to the existence of gay businesses.*

. . .

Gays saw Mrs. Greitzer as a longtime foe. Dick Leitsch was to recall in GAY's POLITICIANS MAKE STRANGE BEDFELLOWS!, [6] how *The New York Times* recorded, October 5, 1964, that "Ed Koch and Carol Greitzer (the Village District Leaders) were pushing the Police Commission for more plainclothes cops to control 'perverts' in Washington Square Park and the streets near Village Square," and how, after John Lindsay took office in January 1966, "Koch and Greitzer were after him for support for their spring cleanup." Leitsch remembered that Lindsay's assistant James Marcus "became highly indignant about other people's 'immorality' " and "under-took 'Operation New Broom,' which began as a drive to get rid of cheap theatres, 'porno' shops, muggers, drunks, panhandlers and other 'unde-sirables' in Times Square. . . . Koch (then City Councilman) and Mrs. Greitzer demanded that 'Operation New Broom' be expanded to sweep the Village, too. Entrapment reached an all-time peak." Mattachine took action to end entrapment once and for all (see footnote, page 26).

When Owles and Robinson spoke to Mrs. Greitzer about the fair-

* In Philadelphia, Homophile Action League soon was to petition City Council-man David Cohen with similar suggestions, including one on housing discrimination. In Bethelehem, Pa., Le-Hi-Ho petitioned the Pennsylvania State Human Relations Commission on like points.

131

employment segment of the petition, the GAA president recalls, "she said, 'Well, I'm not sure that it's a problem, fair employment; I'm not sure that it's a proper area for legislation.' . . . It was really all I could do just to keep from hauling off and cracking her one!" He affirms that afterward the Councilwoman spoke to Kay Tobin, insisting snidely, "Well, it's not *my* problem, so I don't quite understand it." Owles: "Here's the same woman, who can—she feels, with quite a bit of knowledge—speak about the problems of blacks and of Puerto Ricans, without being black or Puerto Rican. Yet, when it comes to the problems of her homosexual constituents, it's like a really alien thing!"

After three months of circulation, the petitions were presented to Mrs. Greitzer. She would not accept them, and told Owles that she "didn't relate to the homosexual cause." GAY reported that "She . . . said that she would not be a defender or a spokesman for the homosexual cause in the City Council, and that even if a majority of the City Council sponsored legislation forbidding job discrimination on the basis of homosexuality, she would not join in sponsoring such legislation." Mrs. Greitzer said she wanted to consider such legislation, and would possibly vote for it. But she told Owles she would "not testify in the City Human Rights Commission against job discrimination involving gays." Two days later, May 13, GAA members stormed into a meeting of the Village Independent Democrats to confront her publicly:

. . . Owles said that it was an outrage that homosexuals should not be able to petition their representatives for redress of grievances, and that if she would not accept the petitions, "she's no longer our representative and we'll have to look elsewhere."

Mrs. Greitzer suggested that legislation which she had introduced into the City Council against discrimination on the basis of sex might cover homosexuals and that she would have to check on that angle. A GAA member pointed out that such legislation pertains to gender, not sexual orientation, and is therefore not applicable.

The Councilwoman proceeded to explain that she was not the right politician to accept the petitions, that others could be of more help. She also stated that she had not accepted the petitions from Owles earlier "because she had had many other papers to carry home that day and she couldn't also carry the petitions."

Mrs. Greitzer was put to the test by direct questions from the Activists.

She acceded to each demand saying if discrimination could be shown she would testify at hearings before the City Human Rights Commission when the subject of job discrimination against gays is raised. She also said that she would co-sponsor a bill in the City Council to extend fair employment practices to protect gays. Asked if she would speak out against the sodomy laws, she declared that she had been for years against the sodomy laws. She then accepted the GAA petitions.

. . . A GAA spokesman stressed that no disrespect toward the VID was intended by the action, and apologized for the disruption of their meeting. The Chairman of the VID's Peace Committee told a GAA member, "Thank you for shaking us up. Sometimes we need this." [7]

GAA was not new to meetings of the Village Independent Democrats when it barged in in May. As an action on January 26, Gay Activists attended a VID session addressed by four New York State gubernatorial candidates: Eugene Nickerson, Howard Samuels, William Vanden Heuvel, and Thomas Mackell. Scattered by plan throughout the audience, the gays' queries came unexpectedly during a question-and-answer period. To Samuels, filmed by NBC-TV on the spot: "Mr. Samuels, I'm a homosexual. What would you do if you were elected governor to promote equal opportunities for homosexuals in the state, and what would you do about the stranglehold organized crime seems to have on gay bars as a result of possible collusion between the State Liquor Authority and organized crime?" Samuels returned, "That's the first time I've ever had that question. As to the first part of it, I would respect and support employment rights of homosexuals. As to the second part of it, I would like to study this matter and then I can give you a more specific answer." (Samuels's full statement, a favorable one in the main, came only during the last days of his primaries campaign. Because newspapers did not [would not?] publish it, and the gay press could not do so in time, it reached only the gay militant organizations themselves and a few supporters. The statement, printed in GAY, July 6, promised that "If elected, I will fight to: 1) Reform the state penal code so that the private sexual acts of consenting adults are no longer illegal. 2) Engage the State Human Rights Commission in the fight against discrimination against homosexuals in employment, housing and public accommodations. 3) Reform the Federal, State and City Government view [along with that of private industry] that homosexuals are categorically unfit to hold jobs. The only exception should be those areas where homosexuality in fact makes a person unfit, or a potential risk, on a job.")

In general, the candidates were unversed in the proper replies to gay interrogators. The Gay Activists were nonplused; Jim Owles told a *New York Times* interviewer in June that, thenceforth, "When we've confronted any of these politicians, whether they've been middle-of-the-roaders or liberals, we've stated, 'If you are truly what you say, true to your convictions in terms of your previous stance on fair employment legislation and so forth, *how can you in any way even say that you have to study it!*'" Kay Tobin, covering the event for GAY, related that a prominent Village resident had this to say: "You can bet that after the questioning here tonight, each one of these candidates will go back to his headquarters and do some research so that he will be able to take firm stands in public on these issues." [8]

GAA first sortied for confrontation outside Greenwich Village in mid-January when seven members walked into the *New York Post* offices, direct to the publisher's secretary, and asked for an audience.* The Activists' ire had been roused by ugly gay putdowns in recent weeks in the columns of Pete Hamill, Harriet Van Horne, and Jack Anderson. A conference with an editor in the newsroom—stared at by puzzled *Post* reporters—was the only concession GAA got that day: hammered at by the Activists, the editor agreed that if there were gay news he would print it and received assurances that GAA would provide such news! But more important, a meeting was set up with Editorial Page Editor James Wechsler for three days later. Arthur Bell reported it, in *Gay Power:* [9]

. . . three Gay Activists spent an hour and a half in Wechsler's office talking about the need for positive news coverage of Gays in establishment newspapers. We also talked about . . . our petition to Councilwoman Carol Greitzer, harassment by police, the homosexual's role in society, the possibility of having a Gay run for political office, etc. Wechsler asked good questions and got good answers. . . . He claimed that reporter prejudice comes from a lack of information on current Gay activities. We promised him that that will not be a problem in the future.

Marty Robinson has summed up the value of the *Post* action: "It was important to go after the liberal press because—and this is a peculiar circumstance of the homosexual—homosexuals were fighting their way with the liberals. The press, by keeping homosexuals out of the news, by keeping them something unusual instead of everyday circumstance, had also been guilty of participating in our oppression."

Ron Hollander of the *Post* described GAA's first major in-the-streets action: ** a convergence on City Hall, March 5, by about twenty Activists to seek an appointment with the Mayor.***

Bearing such picket signs as POLICE ON GAY SPREE WHILE MUGGERS GO FREE, the group of generally long-haired men in their 20s was protesting alleged police harassment of bars and baths catering to homosexuals, job discrimination, and existing laws prohibiting solicitation for and participation in homosexual acts.

Jim Owles, president, and Arthur Evans, chairman of the political action committee, [and Joseph Stevens] were prevented from entering the main doors to City Hall by plainclothesmen.

Owles . . . made repeated attempts to push past the police but they shoved him back. "The rest of the public is going in," he shouted.

---

* GAA did not generally confront without previous appeal; letters would be sent or phone calls made, requesting an appointment, unless the organization suspected this would lead nowhere.

** As did *El Diario–La Prensa,* on March 6: "Quince homosexuales, miembros de la Alianza Festiva Militante . . . trataron ayer de 'tomar por asalto' el Ayuntamiento de Nueva York, para presentar sus quejas al alcalde Lindsay, pero fueron rechazados por la Policía. . . ."

*** Gay Liberation Front sent several observers.

"The only people being kept out of City Hall are homosexuals," someone shouted.

After minor scuffling, the group was pushed back by police to Broadway, where they reformed their picket line and solicited signatures on petitions seeking Councilwoman Carol Greitzer's support.

A conservatively dressed businessman signed the petition. . . .

"It's their own life," the man said. "They're entitled to their own lives. I'm not active in this but I think it requires a lot of nerve to march out there."

"Well, they have no morals," a man in a sport jacket and wool cap said.

"What are morals?" the first man said. "Isn't that morals, too, not to discriminate against people?" [10]

A *Gay Power* reporter expanded: [11]

Noon came, and a different kind of people spilled out, the working class of Wall Street with office jobs. They saw us, they heard sweet guitar music, imaginative, quickly improvised songs about love, law, pigs, Lindsay. "This is the best protest I've ever seen and I've been coming to them for years," said one Chase Manhattan employee. . . .

The press felt our vibes, too. The cameras continued shooting as we circled the area outside City Hall, they photographed us and asked us questions, so many questions. How did it get started, what about the Stonewall raid, how do the sodomy laws [oppress] homosexuals, what do our parents know, how would we feel if our parents knew, are we proud of what we're doing, what are we? The sideliners got an education, too. Any concept of namby-pamby homosexuality went by the wayside as they saw and met and witnessed honest-to-God, flesh-and-blood, gorgeous, gorgeous, gorgeous gays. Stereotypes? Did they learn!

Mayor Lindsay was in Buffalo at the time of the City Hall picketing, but within an hour word came that Mayor's Counsel Michael Dontzin would speak with three club representatives. Owles told him that "New York's gay community wanted no back room promises, but insisted that the Mayor take a public stand against police harassment of homosexuals, and in favor of ending all job discrimination, public and private, against homosexuals. Dontzin said the Mayor was sensitive to the problems of the homosexual citizen and that he would present the Gay Activists' demands to the Mayor. He said the group raised valid points." [12] GAY's co-editors commented, "The March 5th demonstration by youthful members of the Gay Activists Alliance on City Hall poses several pertinent questions for the Mayor: can homosexuals rely on him to protect their rights as free citizens, and work meaningfully within the established system? or (as radicals and gay liberationists demand) will the homophile movement fall prey to anti-establishment sentiment? The Mayor must be made aware that most homosexual citizens would prefer to work with him rather than to see their civil liberties organizations drift toward the far left." [13] *Gay Power* concluded, "Shuffle back from Buffalo soon, Mayor Lindsay, and lend an ear. We will persevere. Believe us, Mayor Lindsay, we will persevere."

GAY scourged ABC-TV for its coverage of the event, calling it "an insult to the homosexual community," in particular the remark that "limp wrists stiffened today . . ." The paper reminded its readers of ABC's earlier firing of Leo Laurence, a West Coast editor and co-founder of San Francisco's Committee for Homosexual Freedom.[14]

Gay Activists Alliance leafleted to apprise the gay community of its continuing program:* "Some Past Actions of GAY ACTIVISTS ALLIANCE" and "GAA Action Results" told of the candidate confrontation at VID, the City Hall picketing, the post–Snake Pit raid protest (in combination with GLF), and of a February meeting with Deputy Inspector William Bonacum about harassment of the Continental Baths . . .

QQ magazine featured the Continental in winter 1969–70 in an article by Frank Keating that not only epitomized this cleanest and most well-appointed** of New York City's gay steam meccas but de-stigmatized "sex on the assembly line" (as one *Advocate* reporter dubbed it [15]). Keating began: "God bless America, Mom, hot apple pie—and most of all, the quickie. Scoffed by some, enjoyed by most in this age of speed when daily pressures sap our time, the quickie affords racy excitement and instant relief." Moreover, to gaylyweds: "For those who have found love, discovering that the flames of passion are soon doused by everyday problems, the quickie provides momentary escape without upsetting something of value—a gay marriage." [16]

But somebody was obviously upset: the New York City police force. In February 1969, a first raid had taken place, reported the "Homosexual Citizen" columnists in *Screw:* [17] "Thirty persons who were enticed and entrapped were taken in, booked, and released until their trials in October. At the trial all charges against them were *dismissed* in due process. There was no evidence. In the meantime, the 20th Precinct succeeded in casting a very bad light on a large group of voters, taxpayers and citizens. Some of them had been charged with *sodomy,* which sounds very serious indeed, even if later you're found *not guilty.*" The writers then wrote that

No harassment took place all through 1969 until just recently. The first of the series took place on December 13. Three patrons of the bath were charged with lewd and salacious acts. Three employees were also arrested and booked as "criminal nuisances." On December 16, another patron was arrested for soliciting a police officer. Two nights before Christmas, a patron was taken away for "sexually abusing a policeman."

Let's get serious. A cop who gets sexually abused is asking for it. He's

___

* Flyers almost invariably ended, "The GAA is a militant, rational, nonviolent group of men and women dedicating itself to the homosexual cause exclusively. Open meetings are held every Thursday . . ."

** The Continental Baths, which opened in late summer 1968, by 1970 had a gym, Olympic pool, sauna, dry heat and steam rooms, massage, color TV room, library, restaurant (and frequent buffets), live entertainment, dancing, and a Sunday cinema.

probably digging it too. Only he's got such a big guilt complex, he's got to make an arrest after he's been abused.

Further arrests followed. On January 19, twenty officers entered the Continental to "look for offenses of a homosexual nature." [18] Clarke and Nichols mused, "But, after all, it *is* cold outside and it's much easier to go 'faggot trapping' than to hunt dangerous criminals. A so-called 'criminal' without victims is easier to catch than one of the countless muggers who infest the streets of New York. Such an easy arrest fills up a night's quota. Besides, it gives a cop a chance to frolic." [19]

GAA debated whether to interfere. It was not a political situation. But the gays being punished were brother homosexual citizens. *Screw* identified the raids' instigator: [20] "The man who is primarily responsible for these . . . atrocities is Deputy Inspector Bonacum of the 4th Division. The Continental attorney says that Bonacum admitted the arrests were made at his behest. 'Homosexual activities are going on on the premises,' Bonacum said to the attorney, 'and these must stop.' " GAA sought an interview with the Inspector, also presented the Mayor's Offices with petitions carrying approximately two thousand names (the Continental had collected them) of bath patronizers who protested the police harassment. Meanwhile, it ceased. Gay Activist Arthur Evans asserts that, when GAA representatives met with First Deputy Mayor Richard Aurelio two months later, they were told that Bonacum had been transferred to a precinct in Brooklyn.

As spring developed, so did gay challenges outside New York. GAY told that "Homosexuals dominated a recent hearing held in Boston by a Massachusetts legislative committee. The subject under discussion was proposed reforms in a series of laws affecting the lives of the state's homosexuals. Representatives of HUB (the Homophile Union of Boston), the Daughters of Bilitis, the Boston University Homophile Club and the Harvard University Homophile Club presented testimony." Observers noted that "The legislators were somewhat taken aback . . . at the steady stream of homosexual spokesmen taking the rostrum to speak out for themselves and their fellow gays." [21] Another GAY article detailed how

For the first time gay people in Minnesota will have a role in participation and planning in the programs of the 1971 Minnesota Conference on Human Rights, under terms of a resolution adopted at the 1970 conference April 18.

But the resolution was considered only after an attempt by the chairman to ignore it failed when delegates stomped on the floor to demand it be brought up.

The resolution was introduced in an afternoon session of the conference by Jack Baker of Minneapolis, a law student and member of FREE (Fight Repression of Erotic Expression), a gay group based at the University of Minnesota. All resolutions were postponed until the final session, however, after the evening banquet as the last item on the agenda.

The presiding officer, Donald Lewis, Deputy Commissioner of Human

Rights for the City of St. Paul, completely ignored Baker's resolution and, after other resolutions had been considered, moved toward adjournment.

When some delegates shouted that he had forgotten one resolution, Lewis insisted, "There are no further resolutions to be considered," and called for a priest to offer the benediction.

Foot-stomping and calls of "No! No!" drowned out the chaplain, however, and finally the resolution was read by Cecil Newman. It was then adopted by a 53-to-47 vote, in a show of hands.

There was only one speaker on the motion—Lewis's boss, St. Paul Rights Commissioner Louis H. Ervin, who said Gay People are not covered by any city or state human rights legislation and he urged that the resolution be defeated.

Baker said opponents of the resolution were among those who had shouted for it to be considered. "They wanted a chance to vote on it, too," Baker said.

No reporters were present during consideration of the resolutions and, knowing this, Lewis later told reporters who asked him about the incident that he could not recall terms of any of the resolutions and referred all questions to Newman, who could not be reached. The conference action was confirmed, however, by the body's secretary, Clarence Harris.[22]

In non-gay-militant New York, leaders of the West Side Discussion Group threw out an NBC-TV camera crew on April 1. NBC had requested to film a segment of the gays' Wednesday-night meeting, a discussion on venereal disease. WSDG's leaders "insisted that they be assured that the show contain nothing negative about homosexuals or homosexuality and that they be allowed to see the entire show in advance before approving NBC's use of the segment . . . The producer agreed verbally to these demands, but refused to sign a written agreement to them. Upon this refusal, WSDG leader Steve Adams told him to get his equipment out, explaining that . . . 'We wouldn't want to sit in front of our TV sets and view a negative presentation of homosexuality' . . . there was a tremendous round of applause." [23]

On Monday, April 13, New York City's Metropolitan Museum of Art celebrated its one hundredth anniversary and witnessed the first in a series of GAA zaps of Mayor John Lindsay—zaps that made the peace-fond general gay community shudder and which drew little applause from Gay Activists themselves. Arthur Bell had written, "More than a month has passed since GAA picketed City Hall. . . . We were to hear from Dontzin, but despite innumerable phone calls and letters to him, not a word." [24]

Grace Glueck depicted the gala for *New York Times* readers. It began "at 9:55 A.M. when Mayor Lindsay strode up the new front steps" and "was greeted by Thomas P. F. Hoving, the museum's director, C. Douglas Dillon, its president, and Arthur A. Houghton, Jr., board chairman." The *Times* narrated how "The Mayor's speech was briefly interrupted by a member of the Gay Activists Alliance [Marty Robinson], who attempted to hand him a leaflet protesting job discrimination against homosexuals.

'Why can't a "Gay" be Mayor?' the leaflet asked. The demonstrator was promptly hustled off by two crash-helmeted policemen. Later, members of the group made their way into the museum past the receiving line, and set up a chant of 'Gay Power!' " [25]

In a flyer, "Gays Crack Mayor's Shield," GAA announced the next week that "We Intend To Make Lindsay A Mayor For All The People." The flyer stated that, when confronted during his museum speech, the Mayor "smiled, said nothing and looked on as police removed the questioner," then estimated that "For the next thirty minutes the Mayor was confronted by Alliance members asking: Would he speak out against the anti-homosexual attitudes and practices in this city. Were 'gay' votes important, but the people who cast them too indelicate a topic for' equal representation and protection under the law. When GAA members got to shake the Mayor's hand, they wouldn't let go pending an answer to the questions, but the Mayor would say nothing, maintaining a plastic smile while the police pulled them apart."

The Mayor's aplomb was put to a severer test six days later, at the early-evening taping of his WNEW Sunday-night television show, "With Mayor Lindsay." For *Gay Power*, Arthur Bell related, "At 4 p.m. last Sunday, thirty-seven GAA people showed up at an East Side apartment, close to the television studio. All members had entry tickets to the Lindsay show. The Political Action Committee had prepared a number of questions to ask the Mayor, and, at our rehearsal meeting, we had a run-through—tactics on when to chant, moments to applaud and boo, means of making the most of a situation in which the Mayor might conceivably respond to a few questions, or at least be made aware that we exist. Rehearsals over, we filed out of the apartment in small groups and headed toward the television studio." [26]

Before the program, Mayor's Counsel Michael Dontzin noticed that Gay Activists were present and greeted Publicity Committee chairman Bell. A few minutes later, when questions (to be answered by the Mayor if there were time at the end of the guest interview) were selected from those submitted by the audience, GAA members heard called the names of their spokesmen, who were then herded to the side of the stage to be on hand to query Lindsay. GAA tactics planned that afternoon had been meant for the question-and-answer period, but it now seemed curious that all but one question to be heard were those of Gay Activists . . .

Arthur Godfrey would be the Mayor's guest that night. Together they would discuss plans for the city's Earth Day, April 22, and air their views on pollution. "Ten minutes into the filming, as the Mayor chatted with [his] guest . . . a GAA member rushed up to the Mayor and shouted, 'Homosexuals want an end to job discrimination!' Another GAA member rushed forward shouting, 'Let that man speak!' Bedlam broke out in the studio as security guards grabbed the disrupters . . ." [27] Arthur Evans had been the first to erupt; Kay Tobin now seconded him with, "What good is environmental freedom if we don't have personal freedom?" Gay

Activists, about one-third of the small audience, chanted in unison, "An-swer Ho-mo-sex-u-als!" GAY recorded that "Filming came to a halt. The Mayor smiled but rubbed his hands quite a bit. Godfrey appeared nonplussed as the chant continued."

The *Village Voice* chuckled, and featured LINDSAY & HOMOSEXUALS: AN EDITED ENCOUNTER.[28] Sandra Vaughn reported. She advised that the taping disruption

was blotted out when the program was televised three hours later. WNEW's newscasters failed to mention the disturbance during a news show preceding Lindsay's, but did remind viewers that the Mayor and his guest would discuss ecology on the program to follow.

. . . the most interesting show was left in the studio. For almost 20 minutes after the Evans interruption, GAA members shouted: "What about the laws against sodomy? We want free speech! Lindsay, you need our votes. Homosexuals account for 10 per cent of the vote . . . We want an end to harassment of homosexuals . . . We want the Mayor! We've talked to his aides."

Straight members of the audience joined in: "Answer the question! . . . You can't petition. That's why the kids throw bombs! . . . Lindsay's a phony." . . .

In answer to the almost constant refrain—"What about freedom of speech?"—Sergeant Pat Vecchio of Lindsay's security force announced, "You cannot disrupt a public meeting without being libel [*sic*] to arrest."

After many GAA members were ushered from the studio, Vecchio told the protesters: "I give you one final warning. We're starting the tape [again]. If you aren't quiet you face arrest." . . .

Throughout the incident . . . there were no chinks in the composure of either Lindsay or Godfrey. But the protests continued.

They were single comments—later edited—and after each, the protester who spoke was ushered out or left of his own accord. Among them was Jim Owles, who made a V sign on camera as he left. One Activist countered Lindsay's comment about abandoned cars with "What about abandoning homosexuals?" As the Mayor and Godfrey chatted about the illegality of blowing automobile horns, Gay Activist John Kane yelled, pointedly and clearly, "It's illegal to blow a lotta things!"

Following the filming, GAA members talked with Dontzin, who promised he would meet with some of them the next week if they would call his office. They insisted that Gay Activists still wanted to see the Mayor person-to-person and would continue to press for such a meeting. WNEW-TV news editors sought out GAA officers meanwhile. The following evening, Jim Owles and Marty Robinson told TV newscast listeners that they wanted Lindsay "to take a public stand against the sodomy laws and job discrimination relating to homosexuals," that "homosexuals were a substantial part of the voting constituency in New York and that it was time for politicians to recognize the needs of their gay constituents." [29]

140

Three days later, April 23, Mrs. Eleanor Holmes Norton, newly appointed Chairman of the New York City Commission on Human Rights, sat with members of GAA for more than an hour in a conference initiated by the group. She said she was eager to research the matter of job discrimination and would investigate existing and proposed legislation in that area. "It would be very good if New York led the way in doing something affirmative in areas such as discrimination against homosexuals in employment. Other cities, at least a dozen in the U.S. with large homosexual populations, should also be ready for such action soon." [30] GAY believed that, despite Mrs. Norton's hopes, San Francisco might take the quicker step, told that its Human Rights Commission "recently passed a strong resolution supporting equal and fair employment rights for homosexuals. This Commission took action after receiving a petition from the Society for Individual Rights (SIR) . . . The resolution was passed by a vote of 11 to 1 after a stormy debate that included SIR members. Police had to be called in to maintain order." [31]

Ten days after the television disruption-confrontation, five delegates from GAA met with the city's Deputy Mayor Aurelio. With him were counsel Dontzin and Harry Taylor, Chief of Patrol, representing Police Commissioner Howard Leary. At the outset, Aurelio insisted, "I want you to know that there is an open mind to the questions you have raised, and that we want to hear your grievances and resolve them in as fair a way as possible." GAY reported the conference in full.[32]

The Activists' first demand, verbally and in writing, was for a moratorium on police raids and harassment, to allow time "to work on solutions to the underlying problems of State Liquor Authority and Police Department corruption." One GAA delegate said, "Since the raid on the Stonewall bar and the resulting riots, gays are no longer sitting back and accepting police hanky-panky. One of the reasons we're here is to forewarn the administration of the possibility of spontaneous riots again this summer if police harassment continues. GAA's contention is that riots are good for no one." While all nodded agreement, Chief of Patrol Taylor added that Deputy Inspector Pine, who had called the Stonewall and Snake Pit raids, had been reassigned recently to Brooklyn. Aurelio reiterated that it was "still not the policy of the police department to harass homosexuals *per se*." An Activist argued that harassment that took place with no legal justification whatsoever "must stop immediately. We will not tolerate it."

A GAA spokesman then demanded that a directive go out, similar to those that protect other minorities from pejorative labels and verbal abuse, to curb police insults to homosexuals—which he termed "disgusting." Taylor noted the need for a community relations officer on the police staff, so that colloquy could be held with the gay community. He conveyed a message, too, that Police Commissioner Leary would meet with GAA representatives if they wished.

Aurelio knew of GAA's conference with Mrs. Norton. When Gay Activists underscored the necessity of a public statement from the Mayor on job discrimination against homosexuals, the Deputy Mayor said that "If the problem is proved and the need exists for such legislation, I don't think you will find the Mayor withdrawing from that battle," but insisted that the matter be considered by the Human Rights Commission before the City Council could act. GAA hammered, however, that Lindsay owed a political debt to his gay constituency, that his prior support was imperative. "We don't exist as far as the New York public is concerned. We demand public recognition by the Mayor. It is absolutely essential."

The gay delegation spoke finally for homosexuals in city prisons, told how such prisoners are denied gay visitors or copies of the gay press publications. Even when released on parole, they could not join gay organizations. The Activists thought it "unjustifiable and inhuman to deny prisoners the right to communicate with and to keep informed about the gay community in the larger society that they are expected to rejoin."

All GAA demands submitted to him in writing, Aurelio hoped "that your public confrontations with the Mayor would stop." The homosexuals emphasized that these would be unnecessary if the Mayor spoke publicly on gay issues. A few days later, GAA members conferred with eight of the highest-ranking police officers in Manhattan in a meeting arranged by Chief of Patrol Taylor. Detailing how police had entered bars at prime hours "using gangbuster tactics against customers in order to get shakedowns from managements," GAA declared, "We know the game and the whole community knows the game, and we are prepared to fight it publicly"!

■

Gay Activists Alliance, which knew no homosexual shame, reveled in "fighting publicly." So did GAY newspaper, which in the next few months brought news to its public of those major American corporations that discriminated against them. Even as early as its second issue GAY took aim at New York Telephone, which had declared a young job applicant unacceptable when company examination of his draft records indicated "homosexual tendencies." Dick Leitsch reasoned, "To deny a man employment solely because he has 'homosexual tendencies' subverts his constitutional rights. No one, under the law, is supposed to have access to Selective Service System records." The Federal Civil Service Commission, as well as the New York City Personnel Department, had been reprimanded by Federal courts for such discrimination. "The time has come," said Leitsch, "to go after the private employers as well." [33]

GAY did. Noting PAN AMERICAN'S PERVERSIONS, the paper recalled how Mary Phillips was fired by Pan Am after writing a story about women's liberation in Screw. Several ex-employees of the airline had, in fact, sought employment help from Mattachine during the past year, Dick Leitsch reported.[34] Honeywell, Inc., was next. GAY announced that, to FREE, "the largest employer in the Twin Cities has admitted that it discriminates against gay people in its hiring—and, its board chairman adds, that it considers the matter closed"; FREE would attempt dialogue with executives at Honeywell. But GAY heaped blessings on General Mills, Inc. (home of Betty Crocker and Wheaties), the Pillsbury Company, and Dayton's (biggest Twin Cities department store)—none of which discriminated. The latter stated, "We seek individuals with the professional expertise and creative energies needed to achieve our company objectives. This is our prime and only consideration." [35] From Los Angeles, *The Advocate* hailed the three as well.[36]

In its May 25 issue, GAY scolded mystery novelist Mickey Spillane, who felt bugged and told the *National Tatler* so: "Everywhere I turn, there's some little fruitcake trying to tell me how I should write a book or a scene in a movie. You've got to watch out for them, they'll ruin everything you do." [37] On the other hand, GAY praised Abigail Van Buren, whose "Dear Abby" column answered a reader's query "In your opinion, is homosexuality a disease?" The columnist came back, unequivocally, *"No!* It is the *inability to love at all* which I consider an emotional illness." [38]

If Miss Van Buren startled readers, Hans Knight of the Philadelphia *Sunday Bulletin* staff shocked them further on Sunday, July 19, in a super-article [39] that began,

Homosexuals are sick. Very sick.
They're sick of wearing masks. They're sick of being snickered and sneered at. They're sick of being feared.
They're sick of being called queers, faggots and fairies. They're sick of being punished for being honest, of being labeled criminals by the letter of the law.
They're sick of being barred from federal jobs and the armed forces. They're sick of being insulted on one hand, pitied on the other.
Most of all they're sick of being told they're sick. . . .

But Abby and the *Bulletin* were behind times. Gay militants couldn't have cared less for their belated acknowledgments. For nearly a year—for some, since the beginning of sexual awareness—gay militants had known they weren't sick. The consideration seldom captured their thought; it was straight society's debate. Jim Owles, who had gone to peace demonstrations wearing his "Homosexuals for Peace" button, states: "If I'm with someone I really dig, we hold hands just the same as the heterosexuals who are there. . . . Why should I hassle with my head worrying about their reactions. Their reactions are *their* problems."

A GLFer stopped in a Puerto Rican coffee shop in midtown Manhattan, ordered a sandwich. Two young queens were giggling, and the barman commented to him, "All faggots should be shot!" then asked if he wanted onions on his burger. His answer: "No, my husband doesn't like the smell!" Vito Russo, assistant treasurer of GAA, worked part-time in a restaurant on Greenwich Avenue; one August evening lover Jim Owles finished dinner there, bade him goodbye. Russo responded with a kiss, and the owner told him he'd be fired the next day. "Shove it!" countered Vito, and walked out with Jim.

At GAA's second dance, held in St. Peter's Church, blocks beyond the Village ghetto, incoming gays met a group of pre-teens clustered at the door. One four-footer demanded loudly, "Are you gay?" "Yeah, man!" a homosexual nodded, and smiled. The inquisitor hadn't finished: "Do you *like* doin' it with a man?" "I love it—every minute of it. Why not? It's my thing!" came back. Activists who managed the door that night distributed "Gay Power" balloons to the prepubescents, who withdrew to the windows outside in the hot summer night and quietly watched the phenomenon.

But not everyone would watch quietly. At 2:00 a.m. on May 8, Phil Raia and Morty Manford, both Activists, sat on the stoop of an apartment building on Christopher Street. GAY recorded that "Police took the homosexuals to the 6th Precinct after they had refused to obey the police order to 'move on.' They were charged with disorderly conduct, specifically with 'obstructing vehicular and pedestrian traffic; congregating with others in a public place and refusing to disperse when lawfully ordered to do so by police; and creating a hazardous and physically offensive condition by an act serving no legitimate purpose.' " Told they could take their summonses and leave, pending arraignment, they decided to pass the rest of the night in jail "as a symbolic gesture of their intention to fight the arrest all the way," then called GAA, the New York Civil Liberties Union, and Bella Abzug, primaries contender for the 19th District Congressional seat against incumbent Leonard Farbstein. Mrs. Abzug had received GAA warmly when members visited her headquarters a few days before. On the telephone at 3:30 a.m., she informed police, "Oh, tell them I'm glad to hear from them." In Criminal Court the next morning with a lawyer from Mrs. Abzug, Raia and Manford entered holding hands, then walked forward when called, arms across each other's shoulders—not only "to show solidarity" but "so that the record would clearly show that theirs was a homosexual case." Following a recess, their lawyer apologized that "the defendants meant no disrespect to this Court when they failed to stand at attention for the first time they appeared in Court." The Assistant District Attorney having moved to dismiss the charges because "I don't think we can prove the defendants' guilt beyond the reasonable doubt," the case was dismissed. Raia's only response: "Vote for Bella!" [40]

GAA would—but, by word of its constitution. without endorsement. Mrs. Abzug won the hearts of Gay Activists completely when she entered their May 21 meeting "looking for all the world," wrote Arthur Bell, "like a candidate for the Dolly Levi role in a Rego Park production of you-know-what . . . and it might as well have been Dolly night at Harmonica Gardens. Bella met with a standing ovation. She deserved it. She left with a standing ovation, too, and she deserved it." [41] Mrs. Abzug's visit was a first in Gay Activist history; other politicians would follow suit in the fall campaign. To the rapt attention of two hundred GAA members and visitors, she spoke out against employment discrimination; stated, "I think the question of police harassment is an outrage"; and was convinced that the antiquated laws against sodomy (between consenting adults) should be repealed. She felt also that "all the liberation movements relate to each other, whether it's women's liberation or black liberation or gay liberation. They show people determining to assert their political power and to assert their power over the institutions that are discriminating against them and that are not responding to them." After president Jim Owles's explanation that GAA could not officially endorse a candidate but would leaflet and inform the gay press about candidates' views to help gay voters make up their minds at election time, she concluded, "I am running in the Democratic primary on June 23. Thank you very much— it's really been a pleasure!" [42]

Activist Bell was with Mrs. Abzug on the night, shortly after, when "Sadie, Sadie, married lady, played second fiddle to Bella, Bella the pride of Gay Activists Alliance at a gala gala" to raise funds for her campaign. At Barbra Streisand's, according to Bell, "Bella's approach wasn't much different than when she visited Gay Activists Alliance . . . and talked about homosexual rights. She's a good mama who has her head and heart and politics in the right place . . . Bella *is* the people. Here's hoping she gets the ticket." [43]

Not having heard from gubernatorial candidate Arthur Goldberg where *his* heart lay led fifteen Gay Activists to stage a surprise encounter on Broadway at 86th Street on June 5. It was 5:30 p.m. Mr. Goldberg, with State Assemblyman Al Blumenthal, was on a West Side "walking tour." Eric Thorndale of GAA preserved the scene in *Gay Power:* [44]*

A herald or pursuivant speaks through a megaphone. "Ladies and gentlemen. Your next Governor, Mr. Arthur Goldberg, will be here at any moment to meet you and shake your hands. He will answer any questions you have."

A brass band emits a few notes of exasperation.

Mr. Goldberg arrives. This is the same Mr. Goldberg who, as a Justice of the federal Supreme Court in 1965, very rightly decided that Americans had unenumerated or Ninth Amendment rights of sexual privacy—specifically (in the case of Griswold v. Connecticut) the right to swallow contraceptive pills. Now Mr. Goldberg is on Broadway and 86th Street. He wants votes. He will answer questions. The Questioners (members of the Gay Activists Alliance) converge on him.

Q.: Mr. Goldberg, do the unenumerated or Ninth Amendment rights of sexual privacy apply only to the swallowing of contraceptive pills, or do homosexual citizens have sexual rights too?
Mr. Goldberg: I have more important matters to talk about.

* Breck Ardery's privately produced LP recording *June 28, 1970: Gay and Proud* contains a vivid sequence of this confrontation.

145

Q.: Mr. Goldberg, will you speak out vigorously for total repeal of the New York State sodomy and solicitation laws? Will you campaign for complete separation of sexuality and state?

Mr. Goldberg: I have more important matters to talk about.

Q.: Mr. Goldberg, will you speak out against the numerous legal and extra-legal harassments of homosexual citizens? Will you campaign vigorously to prohibit the use of police to entice and entrap homosexual citizens?

*Mr. Goldberg*s I have more important matters to talk about.

Q.: Mr. Goldberg, if you become governor, will you order an investigation of certain insurance and bonding companies that practice discrimination against homosexual citizens? *

Mr. Goldberg: I have more important matters to talk about.

Q.: Mr. Goldberg, this State is overpopulated. Would you work for a State income tax reform that would permit those who do not beget children to pay less rather than more in the way of taxes?

Mr. Goldberg: I have more important matters to talk about.

Q.: Mr. Goldberg, what *do* you want to talk about?

Mr. Goldberg: [no answer]

Mr. Goldberg re-enters his car. The car leaves.

Before the candidate left, Kay Tobin remembers, "He grabbed my hand. He thought if he shook hands with a woman he'd be safe. I said, 'I'm from GAY newspaper. What do you have to say to the gay press?' . . . So he settled for shaking the hands of children. Finally he scuttled back to his limousine as best he could. We surrounded his limousine and locked it in for about ten minutes. And we chanted, 'Crime of silence! Crime of silence! Shame!' and pointed at him."

Thorndale continued, that the

Questioners are left to confront State Assemblyman Albert A. Blumenthal.

Q.: Mr. Blumenthal,, will you work to revoke the tax-exempt status of those religious cults that defame, disparage or vilify homosexual citizens?

Mr. Blumenthal: You should have the right to say whatever you want to say.

Q.: Mr. Blumenthal, you have not answered the question. Will you, or will you not, work to revoke the tax-exempt status of those cults that defame, disparage or vilify homosexual citizens?

Mr. Blumenthal: They have the right to say what they please, just as you have.

Q.: Mr. Blumenthal, you're evading the question. When I speak against the obscenity of religious cults that corrupt the morals of children—cults that make children feel guilty for natural homosexual inclinations—the law does not exempt me from taxes. Religious cults *are* exempted, however. And if they pay no tax at all, then the rest of us obviously must pay higher taxes to make up for what the churches don't pay. In short, the law permits

---

* This question was first posed by Marty Robinson. Thorndale, who opposes government regulation of private business, was merely reporting.

religious cults to defame, disparage, vilify and corrupt with impunity and with full exemption from taxation—at our expense. Where do you stand?

Mr. Blumenthal: You should be free to express your opinion, but one mustn't deprive others of their right to believe as they wish.

Q.: Mr. Blumenthal, we do not concern ourselves with beliefs. Only with the tax-exempt status of the believers. The question is plain enough. We are sorry you have refused to answer it.

Mr. Blumenthal: I haven't refused to answer it. I've already answered it.

Thorndale subsequently commented on how Blumenthal's responses differed from those of Goldberg: "Although he was unprepared for GAA's line of questioning, Mr. Blumenthal responded in civilized fashion and with recognition that the questioners had rights. Mr. Goldberg, on the other hand, responded as a robot that had not been programmed to answer questions rational men and women answer readily and rightly. Mr. Goldberg rose to greatness when he asserted, in 1965, that no law could deny or disparage. Now he stood on a street corner unable—or unwilling —to understand the righteous wrath of a tenth of the electorate."

Tobin reported to GAY that Blumenthal also stated, "Job discrimination over *anything* that does not concern performance on the job is *wrong*. . . . Job, housing, all discriminatory laws should be changed in this state . . . and I think we're going to succeed." [45]

Gay Activists had at first approached the candidate politely, Jim Owles has emphasized—"the only reason we *weren't* gentlemanly with him is because when we tried that approach, he turned a deaf ear to us. We had to shout in his deaf ear!" On June 27, Owles told an interviewer from *The New York Times:* "Now what Arthur Goldberg has to realize—and any other politician—is that they can't get away with making a statement like 'I don't think that's important enough to discuss.' I'd like to see you go up to Harlem and tell the blacks up there that you've got more important things to talk about than their civil liberties. For him to say something like that was just one big slap in the face."*

In what was GAA's last major confrontation with primaries candidates, Activists sat dispersed through the auditorium of the Greenwich Village Association on June 16. Kay Tobin covered:

The first candidate tackled by GAA members was Paul Rao, Jr., who is running for Democratic nomination to the U.S. House of Representatives. GAA announced that it would not actually question Mr. Rao because of his patently anti-homosexual stand . . . in particular his attacks on homosexual solicitation. GAA said it would urge all homosexuals to vote against Mr. Rao . . .

Gilbert DiLucia, a first-time candidate hoping for the Democratic nomination for State Assembly for the 63rd District . . . was asked what he would

* Goldberg later made a favorable statement in a release to Gay Activists Alliance; see Chapter 12.

do to fight for repeal of the State laws against sodomy. He replied, "I feel that no adult has the right to judge another adult on the question of his private life or sex life. . . . I don't think anybody's had the gumption or guts to face the thing squarely. We're not living in Victorian times." . . . DiLucia was given enthusiastic applause.

Sidney Siller, the incumbent opponent of DiLucia, spoke next. "I think the penalties for homosexuality ought to be stricken from the books by act of the State Legislature and the City Council of the City of New York. . . . I'm in favor of the liberation of the homosexuality problem, period."

Paul O'Dwyer, liberal candidate in the U.S. Senate race, spoke briefly. . . . Asked by GAA if he would speak out on the subject of security clearances and Federal jobs for homosexuals, O'Dwyer said he "would be willing to take a public stand" on the subject. . . .

When Bella Abzug appeared next, she was not questioned by GAA . . . GAA gave her, instead, a standing ovation.

Toward the close of the long political meeting, incumbent State Assemblyman William Passannante spoke. GAA members questioned him extensively and asked that he promise to fight for an investigation of purported collusion between the State Liquor Authority and organized crime, with its reputed stranglehold on gay bars. "I'd be delighted," he contended, "if I could exercise control over the State Liquor Authority. . . . But until you change the Governor that controls the State Liquor Authority, you're not going to get changes! I want to be honest with you. This is a factual matter."

Winding up the evening, a representative for Ted Sorenson, who is running for the Democratic nomination to the U.S. Senate, spoke on his behalf. The representative didn't know Sorenson's views on most gay issues . . . but did offer this view on the matter of deportation of homosexual aliens: "That's absolutely wrong and we'll speak out against it and we'll work against it. I'm now speaking for Ted Sorenson!" [46]

The seven days beginning Monday, June 22, were busy ones for New York's homosexual community; Gay Pride Week they had named it, and it was to be culminated by a Christopher Street Liberation Day march and gay-in in Central Park (see Chapter 15). In addition, GAA's Bella, "the only politician in New York history to openly solicit the gay vote," [47] won in the primaries on Tuesday; Gay Liberation Front members, Franklin Kameny, Jack Nichols of GAY, and Jim Owles were viewed over Channel 13's (WNDT) "Newsfront" program; and GAA members picketed and sat-in at New York Republican State Committee headquarters on East 56th Street.

New York voters—among them an estimated 600,000–800,000 homosexuals—went to the polls Tuesday, June 23. Gays remembered that Leonard Farbstein, fourteen-year veteran of his House seat, had dismissed them with "See me after the primaries." His opponent, Mrs. Abzug, defeated him by a margin of nearly three thousand votes. GAY exclaimed, "We are thrilled by the victory of Mrs. Bella Abzug . . . Her outspoken and courageous approach to pressing social concerns recommends her to thinking people everywhere. Whether addressing herself to ending the Indochinese conflict or to women's rights or gay rights, she brings a direct and heartfelt sincerity to her pledges, which spring from two sources: integrity and ability." [48] Congressional hopeful Paul Rao, recalls Marty Robinson, "came out and attacked [Edward] Koch for criticizing the police who raided the Snake Pit"; Rao had contended that there was an "unwholesome situation" in certain parts of Manhattan, where "Homosexuals loiter in doorways, linger on street corners and follow male pedestrians . . ." [49] Later, in an interview by GAY, his rhetoric was deemed "blatantly antisexual and antihomosexual." Rao was thoroughly trounced by Koch.[50] Thousands of homosexuals were disappointed that Howard Samuels did not win candidacy for the governorship; the *Mattachine Times* groaned, "As of now, it appears that homosexuals really have no one to vote for." [51] GAY observed:

Arthur Goldberg, thus far, has taken no notice of the homosexual community. Since he is a renowned civil libertarian, we can hope he will issue a statement supporting homosexual equality in the near future. Perhaps the Gay Activists Alliance and other well-meaning advisers should help him to see the wisdom of such a statement. . . . Nelson Rockefeller has shown no interest in reforming the State's sodomy laws, and has allowed harassment of homosexuals in Buffalo and other parts of the state to go unchecked.[52]

John LeRoy has written that, "In 1962, when Dr. Frank Kameny, president of Washington Mattachine, made one of his first television appearances, the announcer spent five minutes apologizing to the audience for having as his guest so presumably despicable a creature as a real, live homosexual. Kameny, on that occasion, gave a one-and-a-half-minute talk." [53] * On Wednesday, June 24, 1970, educational station WNDT (Channel 13) introduced seven homosexual leaders on "Newsfront" at 10:00 p.m. in what "was one of the healthiest and most stimulating discussions on the subject ever to come across the boob tube. In spite of sharp disagreements and heated exchanges, nobody blew their cool . . ." Ellen Broidy, of GLF, spoke of her homosexuality as being a type of liberation; as a heterosexual woman she would have felt herself merely a sex object. Lois Hart, also a GLFer, tied in gay lib with the burgeoning women's lib movement. Becky Irons, from Daughters of Bilitis, believed that the lesbian should "maintain a more positive image of herself" and "work within the system for meaningful change." GLFer Jim Fouratt considered his homosexuality "an expression of . . . protest, and as a means whereby he feels he can relate to other oppressed minorities, even if they are antihomosexual." Jack Nichols, in a non-separatist approach

* As late as 1967, CBS did a primarily negative, though hour-long, special on homosexuality. Jack Nichols was one of the few to express not only a positive viewpoint but to allow his full face to be shown. He lost his job as a hotel sales manager the day after the show was televised.

that reflected his many years' work in the older homophile movement, deplored the need for such labels as "homosexual" and "heterosexual." LeRoy suggested that Franklin Kameny best elucidated the needs and hopes of the majority of American homosexuals: "Kameny is to the United States Government with respect to homosexuals what Ralph Nader is to General Motors with respect to automobile safety." Jim Owles, of GAA, waxed autobiographical. LeRoy affirmed that "He and other members of the GAA have become masters of the political confrontation when members of the Establishment ignore legitimate homosexual demands." [54] About the program, however, Owles complained afterward that "The first question was 'Well, how does your family feel about this?' and, I mean, we were told from the beginning that this was to be a discussion of the homosexual movement. I can't imagine any other civil rights group being on there—whether it be Puerto Rican, Indian . . .—and being asked, 'Well, how do your parents feel about your being an Indian?' "

Bearing the Five Demands that had been the heart of Gay Activists Alliance protest since the organization's beginnings in December 1969, five club members arrived at the headquarters of the New York Republican State Committee on Wednesday, June 24.* A flyer proclaimed:

As homosexual citizens, we have been denied representation by our elected officials. We now assert our rights and demand immediate implementation of the following five-point program:

1) Repeal of the New York State sodomy and solicitation laws as they interfere with the private consensual behavior of adults.

2) A law ending the enticement and entrapment of homosexual citizens.

3) A fair employment act to outlaw discrimination on the basis of sexual orientation.

4) An end to the bonding companies' practice of denying bonds to homosexuals.

5) An investigation of any corruption and discrimination in the State Liquor Authority, and an end to the local harassment of gay bars which exists statewide.

Of the Republican State Committee, we demand that the principles and programs represented by these points be made part of the State Party Platform.

Of Governor Rockefeller, we demand his public response within two weeks to our charges of corruption and discrimination in New York State, and to our demands for legislative action.

* The men had first picketed Rockefeller's offices on West 55th Street. Arthur Bell explained, "We hoped there would be some big father figure, someone really high up in Rockefeller's administration there, but there were only lackeys." (Timothy Ferris, in the *New York Post,* June 25, 1970.)

The GAA delegates' visit, requested earlier, and acceptable to the Committee, became a seven-hour sit-in when the Gay Activists were permitted to speak with no person in an official Committee capacity. Soon after they entered the offices,

John Glendinning, Financial Director of the Republican State Committee, said that the person to see was Charles Lanigan, the State Chairman, but that Lanigan was out of town and unable to be reached. He suggested writing a letter to ask for an appointment. The demonstrators announced they were going to sit in the offices until a meeting was arranged.

Although Glendinning insisted there was no one there to whom the demonstrators could address their grievances or talk with about arranging an appointment, it was learned that Wilma Rogalin, vice chairman of the . . . Committee, was in the offices during part of the sit-in. But she did not speak to the demonstrators and her identity was not revealed until after she left the offices. When asked why the Vice Chairman was not asked by Glendinning to speak to the demonstrators, an . . . official of the State Committee replied, "Our moral code hasn't advanced so far that a lady could discuss such matters." [55]

GAA's fourth Demand needs exposition. Gay had noted, on March 15, that "A new ruling of Attorney General Louis Lefkowitz has unwittingly led to a general 'purge' of homosexuals in the world of finance." It went on that, following a

sharp rise in the number (and quantities) of thefts of negotiable bonds and securities in Wall Street firms . . . the Attorney General hoped to weed out potential thieves by running fingerprint checks on all employees in the business.

Through this fingerprint check, many employees who had been arrested for homosexual offenses were found out. Whether they had been convicted or not, they were fired (often with apologies from their employers). Most bonding companies will not insure anyone who has a criminal record, a "sex-offense" record, or simply one who has been arrested. Naturally, companies dealing in money insist employees be bonded, and if the employee cannot qualify for a bond, he cannot keep his job.

Agreeing that Americans generally approved of the fingerprint check, GAY affirmed that the Mattachine Society of New York

has spoken out about the civil liberties issues involved. This homosexual organization has undertaken a campaign to convince bonding companies that homosexuality and larceny are not the same thing . . . The Mattachine Society has also asked the legislature [to make] it a misdemeanor to discriminate against a person simply because he has been arrested. "Anyone," MSNY points out, "can be arrested or accused of a crime. People are arrested every day because of mistaken identity, as harassment against their group, or on false complaints. But if a prosecutor refuses to proceed against them, or a court finds no evidence to convict them, they should not be penalized. The question,

'Have you ever been convicted of a crime?' might be legitimate, but to punish someone simply because he's . . . been arrested is not."

GAY finished, "As the Wall Street firings indicate, this matter is of particular importance to homosexuals, who are often arrested without being convicted. . . . If the legal system [cannot] find any reason to punish these victims of police abuse, why should bonding companies punish them by causing them to lose their jobs?" [56]

The five GAA visitors—sit-ins they had become—relaxed on the floor of the Committee offices, passed out cookies to curious police officers. Tom Doerr and lover Marty Robinson cuddled beneath the standard of an American flag.

Simultaneously, about thirty GAA demonstrators picketed outside in support of their brothers upstairs. Their signs read:

50 GAYS FIRED FROM WALL ST., HALT JOB DISCRIMINATION NOW, GAY IS GOOD, and AMERICA GROW UP. Chants of "2–4–6–8, Gay is just as good as Straight," "3–5–7–9, Lesbians are mighty fine," and "Say it loud, Gay is proud" echoed along East 56th Street and could be heard on the twelfth-floor offices of the Republican State Committee. . . .

Incidents occurred on the picket line as the sit-in continued. One man who tried to assault a demonstrator was restrained by the police. Two middle-aged women spectators quarreled angrily with each other over the issue of civil rights for homosexuals. One deranged man screamed at the demonstrators for fifteen minutes from half a block away. As the hours dragged on, the demonstrators became less formal and walked in couples. And spectators were startled when two male demonstrators spontaneously kissed each other.

At 5:00 p.m., the offices could not be closed because the demonstrators refused to leave. The demonstrators were told that copies of the demands had been sent to the governor's office and to the leaders of the state senate and state assembly. Nothing more could be done, Glendinning insisted, and nothing further could be accomplished by remaining in the offices. The demonstrators would not move. At 6:30 p.m., state committee chairman Lanigan was finally reached by telephone. He had not been driving to Albany all day as the demonstrators had been told. At 6:30 p.m., he was about to board a plane for Albany. He agreed to meet with one representative of GAA for ten minutes at the airport before he left New York but without a member of the press. The demonstrators refused the clandestine, hurriedly arranged meeting and reiterated the demand for an open meeting between the state committee chairman, a representative of GAA, and a representative of the press. That demand was refused by Lanigan, who then hung up and took off for Albany.

Since a meeting to discuss the demands could not even be arranged, the sit-in continued. At 7:00 o'clock Glendinning called the police in to arrest the demonstrators for criminal trespass. A paddywagon arrived, and Tom Doerr, Arthur Evans, Jim Owles, Phil Raia, and Marty Robinson were arrested and led away, thus becoming the first homosexuals ever arrested for a gay sit-in in New York.

The GAA five were taken to the 51st St. precinct station to be booked before being taken to Criminal Court for arraignment. Twenty-five members of GAA were sitting in Night Court during the arraignment. When the accused were called before the judge, the twenty-five members of GAA stood up to show solidarity with the GAA five.[57]

The five themselves—shortly to be christened the "Rockefeller Five"—held hands as they faced the judge.

Timothy Ferris reported, for the *New York Post,* that the five, "Ordered to return to court August 5 on charges of criminal trespass . . . were greeted with hugs and kisses from their colleagues outside the courtroom at 100 Centre Street . . ." and quoted Political Action Committee chairman Marty Robinson: "We are trying to use political power to achieve changes that will benefit homosexuals in the state. We want homosexuals to know who has been responsible for inaction regarding their civil rights . . ." [58]

Robinson, in an afterthought: "It was also strange to realize that the chairman of the Finance Committee of the Republican Party had to appear in court to press charges against five homosexuals who sat-in at Republican State Headquarters. I got a kick out of that!"

8

... I know through reading and through my life experience, my observation, that homosexuals are not given freedom and liberty by anyone in the society. Maybe they might be the most oppressed people in the society.

—Huey Newton, in *The Black Panther,* August 21, 1970

In late summer and autumn 1970, GLF New York was more than ever a "front" rather than an organization.* A year old, it encompassed—besides the Sunday-night general meeting favored generally by only some seventy to eighty GLF "members"—nineteen cells (or action groups, or collectives), twelve consciousness-raising groups, a men's Wednesday-night meeting,** a women's Sunday-night caucus (before the general meeting), three communal-living groups (one female, two male), a Radical Study Group that read and discussed a variety of books, and from time to time marathon groups to debate selected gay lib topics. The groups were self-regulating. GLF has never had either constitution or officers.

A platform for the Front was the purpose of deliberations by about two hundred GLFers in early May. The marathon met, in eight groups, on two successive Sundays at the church, from early evening until 1:30 a.m. GLFer Gerald Hansen has allowed that, "In 1969, GLF did not relate to the gay community. 1970 has been the year of GLF." Out of the May marathon, as an introduction to the "GENERAL PLATFORM" under "Suggestions for Platform and Function," came the statement: "The first focus of GLF's energy and finances is to serve the needs of the Gay community." The "GENERAL PLATFORM" continued:

* "GLF is a process rather than an organization," one member of the 17th Street GLF men's commune has said.
** At the November 22 general meeting a GLF man read a statement: "There will be no more Wednesday-night men's meetings. It has been the consensus of the last three men's meetings that the basis of men's politics in GLF should evolve from the men getting together in consciousness-raising groups to understand our common oppression as Gay men and to determine how best to deal with it." (*Come Out!,* December 1970–January 1971.) Each of the c-r groups would send a representative, on a rotating basis, to the Sunday general meetings. The representatives would constitute a caucus and function collectively.

Each member of GLF is committed to the full development of her- or himself, as an individual human being, and to develop in her- or himself pride as a Gay person in a sexist oriented society, supporting at the same time every other person's right to develop.

GLF is committed to working for increased communication and understanding, wherever possible, between Gays and straights, between women and men, and across racial, class and political divisions, so that all persons may relate to and be responsible to each other as human beings, and every other human being may have the right to love any other human being she or he chooses, openly and without fear.

GLF is committed to liberation to all by way of a social revolution, changing all people's heads and hearts until everyone attains the freedom to stay out of all limiting roles and boxes and function as a Human Being.

Beyond the "GENERAL PLATFORM," the marathon recorded ideas on "issues to which GLF relates." Under "EXPLOITATION," it was suggested that "No Gay articles be published for $$$." The marathon debated the value of gay marriages and the gay clergy (see Chapter 13)—"Gay clergy should identify themselves as Gay." Newly conscious of a need for "INTEGRATION," the marathon affirmed "Gathering in public places and not Gay oriented ones," relating to "making the public world our own," and maintained that there should be "Homosexual education in public schools." "GLF RELATING HUMANLY" categorized a welter of marathon thoughts, that "All adults [gay and straight] help raise children," that human beings should have "Freedom to do to one's body whatever one wants," that GLF should seek release for gays in jail for homosexual acts, and that "Straights must be bi-sexuals."

GLF New York had seldom if ever solicited the attention of the media —and it was acknowledged policy that GLFers would not speak *individually* to the media since no one of them could express the will of the "body." GLF had its own newspaper, *Come Out!,* and was jealous that this medium should reflect the feelings of the Front membership. On Sunday, October 4, an 11:00 a.m.-to-7:00 p.m. marathon of fifteen GLFers debated "OUR RELATIONSHIP TO 'THE MEDIA.'" It made "SUGGESTIONS" which contrasted "their media" with "our media" (in this case, the gay press):

1) Their Media—attitude toward homosexuals
   (a) ignore us—lack of information
   (b) Straight people write, edit, etc., articles
       Our attitude to their media:
       (a) We don't use the media to our advantage
       (b) conflicts about being open for fear of reprisal from sexist society
           (1) reluctance to use names
           (2) reluctance to use photos
       (c) A relationship seems to exist between our attitudes toward openness with parents and openness in the media

Suggestions for using their media effectively:

    (a) Their media should be approached with the question—What do we want from them, and how do we get it?

    (b) Media are repressive to all people. Gay people must take this into consideration when dealing with "their" media

    (c) Gay people should speak for gay people

    (d) understand the audience and the appropriate media

    (e) Gay people do not criticize other gay people in "their" media

    (f) Their media is the only way at this time to reach people outside the city

    (g) Gay "revolutionaries" must as a first step openly affirm their gayness

    (h) Gay presence is in itself terribly important, even if we are not portrayed well

    (i) There are two types of coverage: objective & subjective

2) Our Media

    (a) Media is a fancy word for communication

    (b) re-definition of media to include alternative to the attitude that media is *print*, i.e., dances, demonstrations, coffee house,* leaflets, cruising . . .

    (c) Our media should recognize honestly all aspects of what it is to be gay, including our "bad" aspects, e.g., trucks, cruising, sexual objectification, etc.

    (d) portray the gay life style and culture

Jim Clifford, a participant in the marathon, included a thought at the end of the "MARATHON SUGGESTIONS" as he mimeographed them: "We must begin to recognize that we have a gay media, and we must develop it and break away from 'their' narrow conception of what media is. This will go hand in hand with developing our gay consciousnesses. . . . We want to expand and extend our gay media with 'gay soul' and 'gay pride' . . . This will be revolutionary, this will be our power." Clifford then posed a question: "Do you suppose that the gay bar is gay media?"

In the September–October *Come Out!* Robin de Luis queried whether the words "brothers" and "sisters"—tossed around so conveniently at GLF Sunday-night meetings—"really mean anything to us." She noted that "Familiar faces are no longer here. Are they alive and well, or does it matter? . . . Is Gay Liberation just another quasi-radical, white middle class movement to go the way of all other such movements? Or can it somehow develop what appears to be the potential for the comradeship and sense of unity so needed to bring about the cultural revolution needed in this unloving land?"[1] The casual visitor to the Sunday-night general

---

* Gay coffee houses sprang up in many major cities as informal and non-profit meeting places for gay liberationists who wanted to rap and relax. Hartford's Kalos Society established one, with dancing and food (no liquor), to serve in addition as "an alternative for underage gays and the 'bar rush' crowd" (*The Griffin*, August 1970). Berkeley had its Five-squared, Four-squared; New York gays their night at The People's Coffeegrounds; Philadelphians their gab fests with straights at Hecate's Circle . . .

meeting was nevertheless genuinely impressed with the group consciousness and the interrelating and striving for a non-sexist attitude that characterized GLF in autumn 1970. The meeting might have appeared ploddingly dull— unless he witnessed one of the not-infrequent clashes between GLF women and men—compared to the political dynamics of GAA Thursday nights. But GLF's spectrum was the complete gay.

At one October meeting, which began at 8:15 p.m. and, per custom, with "announcements," GLF found itself nearly insolvent—there had been no fund-raising dances for months, the Front still made no admission charge to meetings, nor dues, and had emptied its treasury of some $1,500 in bail money* following the gay riots of August 28 and 29. Another announcement followed, of a new plan for GLF women to relate one-to-one in consciousness raising; a meeting to organize would be held the next Wednesday night.

A male member then detailed how GY (Gay Youth; see Chapter 10) had given all loose change from its last dance—some $30—to the GLF treasury to be used for bailing out gay rioters who'd been busted. Now, with the treasury nearly gone—"There's *no money coming in!*"—GLF should, by rights, contribute to STAR (Street Transvestite Action Revolutionaries; see Chapter 10), which was planning its first dance.

A group known as Single Parents was seeking two GLFers—a female and a male—to speak the following Thursday; the GLFers would be paid, and the treasury benefit to some extent. A deliberation ensued concerning the purpose the speakers should serve and about their qualifications; now and again the chairman—in his post for the last (the fourth successive) time—avoided interpersonal debate: "Could we please have no cross-dialogue!" When GLF men suggested that the speakers be chosen by lots of those members interested (the usual pattern, even of selecting general-meeting chairmen), an alarm sounded from GLF women: "The women will choose their representative in their own way." At this moment, a male first-timer to the GLF general meeting asked, not too tactfully, why GLF women insisted on such "separation"—he'd thought the Front was "unisexual." Judging that the newcomer could not appreciate the dilemma of the lesbian torn between women's and gay lib movements, a GLF woman clarified: "We have to have our chance *as women* to realize where we are. . . . We're here because we do relate to men's and women's gay liberation, but we must reserve the right to make certain decisions by ourselves." The "unisexual" argument had been used to dominate women before, and though the newcomer might not intend it, his argument signified domination to many women there, she concluded.**

* A few weeks later, the Front set up a Gay Liberation Front Bail Fund for all members of the gay community, leafleting that "checks or money orders should be sent to . . ."
** In an effort to relate more effectively to GLF, the women had abandoned an original Wednesday-night meeting that had become too women's lib–oriented in favor of a Sunday-night caucus that directly preceded the general meeting.

That not all female members of GLF believed in this type of independence within the organization was illustrated by a brief, but unheated exchange between two women present. The male newcomer now challenged again, saying that his ex-wife would soon attend GLF meetings—to which GLF women should she relate? A male GLF member who had all but conquered his male chauvinism intervened: "That is up to *her*. Your wife should make that decision for herself." *

A spokesman-organizer for the New York University demo (a continuation of the Weinstein Hall subcellar sit-in; see Chapter 10) outlined plans for the next day. He asked for volunteers to marshal the demonstration, then specified what to do "in case of a pig attack." When gay demonstrators ultimately left the demo area, he advised, "please leave with sisters and brothers—don't leave alone!" and repeated the telephone number of the National Lawyers Guild. Everyone should have it, in case . . . As he stood there, the young spokesman—wearing lipstick and in full-length woolen sheath and heels—was admired and commented on by some of the meeting's most "masculine"-looking GLFers. "You look good!" said one of the men, and gave him a light kiss.

Worried that the treasury could not stand further pain, a GLFer reminded prospective protesters that, "It's very cute to have an American flag on your ass, but you might get busted and force us to bail you out!" Furthermore, he added, even if GLF had the money for bail—and currently it didn't—"with bail, you're only feeding the pig pocket!"

Attention focused on a trek to Chicago, then Minneapolis, the upcoming weekend for a GLF caucus, then gay lib conference. Jim Clifford —soft-spoken, full-bearded, a twenty-year-old (he had explained an hour earlier that he was in GLF primarily "to find out more about me, to learn who I am and what I am")—now proposed that one Third World person, one woman, and one man should go to the Midwestern meetings; any others who might also go "would be feeding their egos" but would be welcome, too. He'd be willing to contribute so that the three he proposed could attend. Another GLFer observed that the Third World Gay Revolution ** (see also Chapter 10) was now an independent group, and that it had repeatedly asked not to have decisions made for it as if it were a part of GLF. Or had Clifford meant, he wondered, Third World people who attended GLF and not TWGR? A GLF woman interjected, "I think white people should stop talking for Third World people!" She was

---

* GLF men have put forth that male Gay Activists have made no attempt to "get women to relate to GAA," have not tried to eliminate their sexism. Jim Clifford has hinted that "GAA people want themselves accepted by society as they are, and don't realize how much change they need to make in order to be really human."

** TWGR had grown out of GLF in midsummer 1970. "It wasn't trouble with GLF. It was simply that they don't have to go back home following the meetings and face non-white communities. They couldn't help us with that. They would have, if they could have—and they have tried!" stated a TWGR member. Philadelphia GLF, on the other hand, was 50 per cent black in 1970, and had active Third World leadership.

emphatic that since GLF didn't really represent Third World persons (it couldn't: it had too few of them), it should not project to send such a representative even though it might find one.

While the Front continued to discuss how and if to send both a woman and a man, the spokeswoman who had met the newcomer's challenge with understanding now grinned and asked to be recognized. Arms akimbo, shoulders hunched, exuding beneficence, she opined that making provision for a woman was unnecessary: "We women don't *want* to go to Chicago; we're sitting here mumbling to each other, 'Do *you* want to go to Chicago?' 'No, *I* don't want to go to Chicago.' 'Do *you* want to go to Chicago?' 'No, *I* don't want to go to Chicago' . . ." Meanwhile, a GLF male was sharing the recipe of an inexpensive food that could be carried along in containers: a combination of health-food grains, raisins . . . "GLF could make several big jars."

A man brought the meeting's attention to Alternate U., where since September 18 every Friday night had been designated Gay Night. To the classes originally scheduled—Medical, Legal, Demonstration Workshop; Gay Squatters Workshop; Racism (With Participation of Third World Gay People); Gay History and Literature; Sexism (Led by Gay Women); Exploration of Roles and Identity; Marxism and Political Workshop—had been joined Self-Defense and Transvestism. The speaker continued that AU could "not be crashed anymore"—too many street gays, among others, had slept there following the late August riots. AU had been "more than understanding until now," but having had so many . . . A friend of the speaker's mentioned that AU lacked cash to continue its work, and that GLFers as gays must help to provide cash—especially because AU had "done so much for gays. No one [gay or straight] has ever been turned away from printing political leaflets there, whether or not they had the money to pay for the paper."

Because the focus was again on funds, one member suggested that GLF sponsor a dance regularly after each Gay Night's classes adjourned. One young man objected: "It would be too difficult to rap." A GLF woman seconded him: the mood wouldn't be right for dancing. She delineated, further, that Gay Night "must be used by *all* gay organizations —by all gays, organization or non-organization!—not just by GLF."

A GLFer recalled for members the one-and-a-half-hour television spot GLF had been asked to prepare for. Those who would be en route to Chicago/Minneapolis requested that planning await their return. Though GLFers had already expressed interest in working with the project, the chairman made certain, once again: "Are there any *other* people who want to relate to this project? . . ." Clifford, recognized, lost his cool for a moment: "If you want to relate to it, meet in this corner afterward. If you don't want to relate to it, don't meet in this corner—but don't criticize those who *do* relate to it for how they plan the project!"

A final new topic: The chairman reminded the body that "*structure was to be discussed for GLF*," and he wondered when this should be taken up . . . He was answered by a young member, "The matter will be discussed when people in GLF *want* it and not until then." Another, brooding on the fact that many people had left the Front because of its lack of formal organization, thought it "crucial to the survival of the club to have some sort of structure." He hoped to get out some mimeographed information about structure, based on materials and opinions other members had as well as on his own. A less convinced GLFer half-yelled, "Structure is not a panacea for *anything!*" As the meeting ended, the Midwest-bound members hoped that structure would be debated only after their return. It was 11:00 p.m.

The newcomer to the GLF meeting probably would not return. He did not understand the strong and essential part women played in its organization, to him GLF men seemed cowed. Indeed, many male Front members themselves could not accept that women played the "separatist" game on occasion. In *Come Out!,* Ellen Bedoz traced their lack of understanding to GLF men's fear:

Such misdirected fears and the resulting tensions and hostilities they create have always kept people divided from each other in betrayal of their mutual interests. It is exactly this that makes the poor Southern white—who has nothing to gain from racism save false pride, and everything to lose because he is separated from his class interests—into an embittered racist. His fear and rage are skillfully manipulated so they are directed away from the oppressor and onto the oppressed with whom he has everything in common save the illusion of his relative privilege. In GLF this misdirected fear expresses itself through sexism which is just as destructive as racism. Sexism has the potential to keep homosexuals and lesbians divided and to direct gay men's energies away from an analysis that could reveal who the beneficiaries of homosexual sexism are and where our real struggle lies.[2]

The men of GLF's 17th Street commune attempted the analysis Bedoz proposed—and a lot more—in issue three of their publication *Gay Flames.** The lead article asked "Who's on Top?" and confessed,

It's a man's world, brothers. A straight man's, that is. Straight males have made and continue to dictate the laws and institutions of every country in the world. Heterosexual men run the governments, the armies, the big and small businesses, the public services, the factories and mines, the housing, the streets, the farms, the trains, airlines and ships over most of the earth. The culture which walls in your whole life as a gay man is made and enforced by straight men. Break their laws, and you will be arrested by a straight policeman, tried by a straight male judge . . . and jailed by straight guards.

* On September 1, 1970, the commune published the first of its free, 7 x 10, four- and eight-page weeklies "meant to give the gay community news of itself which it can't find in other places. . . . The Gay Flames people are all Gay Liberation Front males, but we do not represent GLF in any way."

Breaking laws aside, should you simply reveal your true nature as a gay man in any institution (church, job, school, home) run by straight men, you are subject at least to abuse and probably to being thrown out. Gay men and lesbians know this like they know that sunlight casts shadows, like night follows day. . . .

The power of straight men everywhere perpetually threatens to cast the lives of gay men and women into the darkness of shame and oblivion. . . .

You are not alone in lacking real power to define your own lives because of your sexual nature. On the basis of sex, half of the world's population—womankind—is denied full equality with the straight men who "make" what passes for history and culture in most of the books, records, pictures, poems and movies.

American gay men must begin to realize that the contempt and oppression which they experience under the straight (white) men who run America is not unique. A large group of straight white American men in fact maintain supremacy over all women, all black and other Third World peoples, and over those other men who work for wages rather than owning stocks and property or businesses and factories.

The word for the way in which men hold supremacy over women is sexism. The expression for the way in which the white men who have power over women also dominate all black and Third World peoples is racism. The word for the way in which these sexist, racist straight white men who own the property of America exploit people who earn wages is capitalism. America is run by these straight men and their values are now shared by a majority of the women and workers and many of the black and Third World peoples whom they oppress. . . .

The oppression of homosexuals is consistent with the absolute supremacy of a whole group of straight white men in America.

Another essay in the same GF issue set forth that,

As gay men, we also feel the oppression of sexism. Not only does it divide us from gay women, who should be our natural allies, but it divides us from ourselves. The divisive butch and fem roles we play out in gay life are actually carry-overs from straight society, where butch is the role that a "real man" is supposed to play towards a fem woman. The roles gay men play, which result in so many of the barriers we feel between us whenever we try to come together, originate in the sexism of a society run by straight white men. . . .

Sexism is part of the society that oppresses. It has no place in a male homosexual publication that is working to end gay oppression. But because we are men who write Gay Flames we share in the sexism of this society, because we are products of the attitudes and institutions of this society. That means that we are going to make mistakes, whether we want to or not, as we struggle to eliminate sexism from our lives.[3]

Publishers-writers of the *Flames,* the men explained in issue one [4] that "We take our name from the words 'flaming faggots.' We are faggots and we are flaming with rage. Rage at those who have put down gay sisters and brothers for too long. . . . Today gay flames do not come from the matches of the church, the state, or the capitalistic businessmen. We are burning from within and our flames will light the path to our liberation."

In Berkeley's September *Gay Sunshine,* California Gary Alinder had preached gays' need for one another: [5]

I need to be together with other Gay men. We have not been together—we've not had enough self respect for that. Isolated sex and then look for another partner. Enough of that, that's where we've been. Let's go somewhere else. Let's go somewhere where we value each other as more than a hunk of meat. We need to recognize one another wherever we are, start talking to each other. We need to say "Hi, Brother" when we see each other on the street. We need consciousness raising groups and communes.

Our Gay souls have nearly been stomped to death in that desert called America. If we are to bloom, we can only do it together.

I need you brother, because brother you are all I have.

The men and women of New York's GLF communes agreed.

The 17th Street commune, out of which the free publication *Gay Flames* was born, breathed variety—the loft featured nine or ten rugs; work tables; a sewing machine and spotless kitchen; a huge planter suspended from the roof light; a World War I helmet; a bulletin board; and posters of Che and Picasso's *Don Quixote* that did not seem incompatible. The commune was, more importantly, a place of learning, where more than a dozen gay men—whom society had programmed to share bodies but seldom souls—discovered mutual and self-respect.

John Knoebel, of a smaller commune on 95th Street, describes how roles and role-playing have been discouraged. "There are no 'mothers' or 'fathers' at the commune. Everyone has to do everything equally. We want to live as equals," he declares. "Roles really fuck people up," Knoebel asserts. "The commune is an attempt to live as a society of the future, where *all* share power." Thursday nights were set aside for communal rapping, and Saturday mornings for consciousness raising.

A critic of GLF communal living has insisted that "They are stifling their individual liberty. If you want to go to a movie, you have to ask the commune." A consensus on either a projected individual or communal action was generally necessary. At the rap session, the subject was broached and "Everyone shares his ideas—no one is ever allowed to remain silent," states Knoebel. If there was a difference of opinion concerning the project, the commune talked it out until a consensus was reached—"until everyone agrees" to accept it or veto it.

Consciousness raising was not restricted to communal collectives, nor by any means to the New York GLF scene. The *Philadelphia Gay Liberation Front–Newsletter* announced, on August 9, 1970, that

GLF consciousness-raising groups have been conducted every Monday night for several weeks and have been making progress in quality and attendance. By breaking into groups of no more than four or five, people have been discussing gay oppression, self-liberation, straight liberation, and the gay movement. Also discussed is how gay people relate to other oppressed peoples. How can we call a woman a "broad" and not expect not to be called a "fag" or "dyke"? It's not lonely hearts club and not organizational shit. Call either . . .

From Kathie Sarachild's "A Program for Feminist 'Consciousness Raising,'" in *Notes from the Second Year: Women's Liberation, Major Writings of the Radical Feminists* (New York, 1970), New York GLF developed/transposed "A PROGRAM FOR HOMOSEXUAL CONSCIOUSNESS RAISING." "Personal recognition and testimony" were a part of each c-r session. Experiences were recalled and shared, similar feelings discovered among the c-r group's members. The "PROGRAM" enunciated the "RESISTANCES TO CONSCIOUSNESS RAISING," among them "Anti-homosexuality," "Glorification of the oppressor," "Excusing the oppressor," "False identification with the oppressor and other socially privileged groups," "Shunning identification with one's own oppressed group and other oppressed groups," "Self-blame," "Rugged individualism," "Ultra-militancy." In "On Our Own: Gay Men in Consciousness-Raising Groups" (an eight-page pamphlet, mimeographed by New York GLF men in November 1970), was a statement of purpose:

. . . We as men are struggling with our eagerness to dominate and ego-trip by being aware of the needs of others in the group, and struggling with our tendency to intellectualize by speaking from our experience. We are also learning what has been forbidden us—to relate to one another with respect and love. CR provides a format in which this potential can develop and operate. We use it to discover our identity as gay men, to recognize our oppression in a straight society, and to seek a collective solution to mutual problems. We as gays must redefine ourselves *in our own terms,* from our own heads and experience, because no political philosophy designed by white heterosexual men can be adequate for us. Thus we use CR to arrive at policy and positions, to plan actions and projects—to evolve a politics out of our experience.

C-r groups often developed when ten to fifteen GLF newcomers wanted to learn to relate to each other and to the gay liberation movement. One experienced group member alleges that "At consciousness-raising groups, everything comes into focus!" Gerald Hansen, coordinator-organizer of many new GLF c-r groups, confesses, however, that sometimes "people get involved with their revolutionary coloring books and the thing goes haywire."

In late 1970 a group of ten men* met, for the second time, in a loft

* Of GLF New York's twelve c-r groups in late 1970, three were mixed-sex. Hansen insists that the women in these three groups will join all-female groups when their sense of woman-identification grows stronger.

apartment whose only hosts seemed to be the seven or eight cats that visited each arrival as he reclined on a mattress-bed or squatted on the floor. Mao beamed from one wall, a poster warning NO LOITERING OR ELECTIONEERING BETWEEN THIS POINT AND THE POLL hung on another. At 9:00 p.m. lights were dimmed and Hansen recommended either of two topics to the newly formed c-r group: "What I dislike about homosexuals" and "Coming out." Almost every man preferred "Coming out"—what better way to level with one another than to tell about the most decisive moment in one's life! Hansen offered, finally, "Does anyone have strong objections to the topic?" and testimonies began, after his explanation that a speaker could be interrupted only by comments such as "When was it that . . . ?" or "I don't understand . . ." and would have no time limit imposed upon him.

"I've come out several times, and I've gone straight several times," said one man who had been married. "Whenever I would masturbate, or when I was having sex with my wife, I'd long to be with a guy." In GLF over the past few months, he had found he could "relate to gay people now, share experiences . . . I really feel very proud to be gay."

Another man had had understandable difficulties in coming out: "I screwed a girl and got clap, then screwed a boy and got clap!"

As testimonies proceeded, two pairs of lovers were caressing, gently massaging each other, resting their chins in one another's hair . . .

Hansen had for a time wanted to be bisexual, he said, in order "to extract the best from both worlds." To him, coming out was more than sexual experience; it was "becoming totally involved with gay people!" Another young man, a Midwesterner, had arrived in the city two weeks before. Though he'd had sexual experience earlier, "The coming out may have happened when I came to New York. . . . And coming out is still very much going on." One handsome gay who called himself bisexual had been active in gay militant organizations for months. But "I don't know at what point I'll really be 'out.' "

One young man had been a loner, had preferred adult company—"I just couldn't get it together with kids my own age." A few weeks before, he had seen a sign above an orientation table at Queens College: GAY STUDENTS. Since then, relating to other gays had made it possible for him to relate not only to his homosexuality but to his sexuality as well.

The June–July *Come Out!* reviewed a formidable list of spring appearances by GLF New York on behalf of homosexuals and in support of the Movement.

A contingent from GLF had joined the April 15, final moratorium, marching under the Front banner from Washington Square to Bryant Park and chanting "Out of the closets and into the streets!", "Say it loud: Gay is proud!" Arrived at the park, the group "confronted the Speaker's platform, along with other radical groups, and demanded to address the rally. For over twenty minutes, during a confrontation between liberals and radicals, the GLF banner completely obscured the Speaker's platform. The area around the platform became a battleground as people pushed, yelled, and fought. In the bedlam, the . . . banner was torn to shreds and the rally abruptly cancelled." Gays' participation in the April 15 events was elucidated in a broad, non-organization statement by Student Homophile Leaguer and Boston GLFer Bruce Gordon that was leafleted, then printed in HUB, newsletter of the Homophile Union of Boston: [6]

There is something rotten in America, not simply in the government, the ghettoes, or the police forces, but in the moral constitution of the community. There is an arrogance in America, that unyielding prejudice of the American dream which gives us the American parent demanding conformity and obedience at home, and the American government spreading democracy abroad. To end the war, to end racism, to end all bigotry, we must confront this arrogance—yes, we must tear down America, shout that this is not heaven on earth, resist the social and moral tyranny of the family, subvert the righteousness on which society is based.

The participation of gay liberation in April 15th is derived from this anti-war movement, the movement rejected by the single-minded obsession of Student Mobe, New Mobe, Moratorium to eliminate one simple *symptom* of the illness rotting society. For this is not an anti-war movement, a black power movement, or a gay liberation movement, but a *Movement* against conformity to arbitrary standards, for an open society in which each of us may choose his own way of life, in which we are not committed to coercing the world or ourselves into assigned roles. Together we may overcome.

It was yet several months until Stephen Gaskin, guru to northern California's hippies, would be quoted by *The New York Times*: "If you're going to do the revolution, here's the criteria: you've got to be nonviolent, you've got to include everybody—can't say some people are expendable—got to be sincerely interested in the welfare of everyone and in truth. And it's got to be motivated out of love." [7] QQ magazine's summer editorialization that "This somewhat logical acceptance of Now Gays by Now Straights has created a more permissive climate for homosexuals and has given our cause impetus" [8] would be only part-truth. And would owe that truth, in part, to Jim Fouratt of GLF New York. When Front members joined May Day supporters of the Panther 21 at Yale University, Fouratt made one of the addresses at the rally:

The proud, strong homosexual brothers and sisters who are in New Haven to show support for the Black Panther Party and its struggle, and to identify with Bobby Seale and all the prisoners that are being held, bring you greetings.

The homosexual sisters and brothers who are in this crowd have a complaint to make. The very oppression that makes us identify with the Black Panther Party and all oppressed people, which makes us revolutionaries, which makes us work for a society and vision which is far beyond what we live in today, we find that oppressiveness pervading this so-called liberated zone. It is that very oppressiveness that is stopping us from organizing our community, which is stopping us from making a revolution, and we call upon every radical here today to Off the word faggot, to Off the sexism which pervades this place and to begin to deal with their own feelings about the homosexual brothers and sisters.

We demand that you treat us as revolutionaries. We demand that you no longer look upon us as sex objects, that you judge us in the total integration of our humanity. We are on the barricades. We are submitting ourselves to the discipline that we see in the vanguard leadership here and there will only be a revolution when all oppressed people work together.

No elitism. No sexism. All power to Gay people. ALL POWER TO THE PEOPLE! 9 *

Gay lib has directly impugned Movement idols. Thus, Step May, of University of Chicago Gay Liberation, in a letter-article, "What's Wrong with Sucking?", originally published in the Madison *Kaleidoscope* and later reprinted in *Gay Flames*'s "Gay Liberation Packet," has charged Jerry Rubin: "Throughout your book, you denigrate the villains of Amerika by suggesting that they are homosexuals. . . . I couldn't be liberated in Yippie society as long as something so central to my life as my sexuality is an object of ridicule. . . . It's ironic that DO IT! places you, the object of Foran's vicious gay-baiting, well at the top on my scale of heterosexual supremacists . . ." 10

Gay Flames, in its seventh issue, was to observe that "Revolutionary Gays have on several occasions in the past several weeks confronted the Communist Party, U.S.A., about their anti-gay beliefs. Street Transvestite Action Revolutionaries [see Chapter 10], Third World Gay Revolution [see Chapter 10], and Gay Liberation Front have been active in support of Angela Davis, a CP member, busted for revolutionary activity in California, but the 'party' hasn't wanted our support. We can march beside them as long as we do not carry our own banners or camp it up too much. Three times, GLF or STAR people have been thrown off the picket lines. So far, we haven't had the numbers to physically resist, but we hope to at the next demo, Nov. 20." With COMMIES FREAK OUT PINKO QUEERS, *Come Out!* in its December 1970–January 1971 issue told how four women and four men were rebuffed by CP members at the Federal Court-house, New York, when they went to lend support to the protest for Angela Davis. When the GLFers eventually forced their way in carrying

* In late 1970, the Seattle Gay Liberation Front went a step further than Fouratt's challenge when it severed relations with the Young Socialist Alliance because the organization excluded homosexuals from membership. In a letter to YSA, GLF Seattle said, "You call yourselves Leninists, yet one of the revolutionary government's first acts . . . was to abolish laws against homosexual acts. Those laws were reinstated under Stalin as a move to reinstate the nuclear family as the social base of Russian society. Thus, YSA carries on the great tradition of counter-revolution." (*The Advocate,* November 25–December 8, 1970.)

the Front banner, "The Communists made a final attempt to control the demonstration—they ran off and got a huge banner reading COMMUNIST PARTY—U.S.A. and marched right in front of the gays, blocking off the gay banner whenever photographers appeared. The march went on for two hours. When the chant of 'Black, black power to the black, black people' was raised, the GLFers inserted 'Gay power' after 'Woman power' . . ." Other groups picked it up. "The Communist Party freaked out every time," said *Come Out!*

In early summer, *Come Out!* noted, "Two Gay Liberation Front representatives walked out of a planning meeting of the New York Strategy Action Conference [a Movement group] after the defeat of a motion to add 'gay liberation' to the list of interest groups participating." [11] Brenda Howard and Tony Diaman reported that the sentence in question stated, "That local Black, White, Brown and Red militants, rank and file labor organizations, peace groups, civil rights movements, students, poverty groups, women's liberation and everyone else must get together on a local basis and seek out the common issues that confront them all and begin the pragmatic steps to deal together with these issues." The Front newspaper detailed how,

Commenting about the unconditional inclusion of the gay liberation movement, Brenda Howard said, "The question here is whether this body will fight against or support the oppression of gay people."

Those who spoke against the motion claimed that homosexuals are not an oppressed minority, that the conference should limit itself to the issues of war and racism, and that the inclusion of gay liberation would alienate other prospective participants in the conference.

Tony Diaman stated that, "If we were invited to participate in this conference of movement groups, then we will participate as equals. Both racism and sexism are important issues. To include us while refusing to mention our participation is mere tokenism."

GLF was to challenge anti-homosexuality in the Movement by other means: in midsummer the Front dipped into its funds to donate $500 to the Committee to Defend the Black Panthers, later bailed two Young Lords out of jail.* Bob Kohler stated, to GAY, that "GLF is not unaware of the sexism and prejudice in the radical movement. As an integral part of this movement, we have made every effort to confront these attitudes and will continue to do so." [12] But GLF preferred to support, rather than confront, as when in early spring the Red Butterfly cell organized and marshaled a contingent of New York gay liberationists at the Central Park rally to Free the Panther 21 and All Political Prisoners. With hun-

---

* Philadelphia GLF members attended a Puerto Rican street festival sponsored by the Young Lords Party on August 8. Members of YLP helped to distribute GLF-dance leaflets during the fun. (*Philadelphia Gay Liberation Front–Newsletter,* August 9, 1970.)

dreds of like-minded New Yorkers they then marched from the 72nd Street mall to the Queensboro Bridge (59th Street) and over to the Queens House of Detention.[13]

Bob Kohler, representing GLF, with two women's liberationists, related to the straight world in an open forum with about fifty high school students at the Washington Square Peace Center one spring day. A GLF cell almost *didn't* relate, one spring evening, to its own gay world:

Members of the *Come Out!* Collective confronted the audience at a meeting of the West Side Discussion Group when all efforts to be included in a symposium on the Gay Press failed. One man had arbitrarily decided that the Gay Press consisted of only two newspapers and GLF decided this ruling should be brought before the people. The Collective members presented themselves and their case to the [WSDG] general membership on Wednesday, April 8, and asked for a vote on the ruling. The vote was overwhelmingly in GLF's favor and *Come Out!* was seated on the panel.[14]

In a not-so-minor action that was duplicated by gay liberationists in Los Angeles and Chicago, three New York GLF women stood outside a Broadway cinema the night of the opening of *The Boys in the Band* to sell *Come Out!* in protest to the movie's denigrating stereotypes. *Gay Power* exulted, "The sight of these three smiling, attractive, and vibrant young women declaring themselves openly blew more minds than any demonstration could have hoped to do. Right on, sisters!" [15] Two GLFers, Martha Shelley and Dan Smith, joined a group of former employees to liberate a Left weekly, the *National Guardian*. The group demanded a restructuring of the paper and a more Movement-responsive policy. The GLF members were given space in the new and renamed *Liberated Guardian*.[16]

On Lindsay-sponsored Earth Day, April 22, in New York, a bold leaflet circulated by the Planned Non-Parenthood cell of GLF praised "all those homosexual women and men through history who in couples and small groups turned for warmth, sex and friendship to members of their own gender, thereby providing the human race with an affirmative and joyous alternative to the problems of population explosion. These fortunate men and women are the vanguard of the revolution—forging life-styles that liberate energies and love for the formation of the NEW HUMANITY and the salvation of PLANET EARTH. HOMOSEXUAL WOMEN AND MEN, WE SALUTE YOU!!!! . . . BE GAY! GIVE EARTH A CHANCE."

But being a GLFer was not all work and no play. Pre-dating the June 28 celebration (see Chapter 15), members held a first gay-in picnic on Sunday, May 10, in Central Park. *Come Out!* observed, however, that the "event was deliberately underplayed by GLF in deference to the murders at Kent State, the Student Strike, and the general feeling of anger that engulfed the Movement that week." [17]

Philadelphia GLFers, more than the New York Front, liked their fun in the sun, and joined straights at music-filled be-ins every Sunday at Belmont Plateau in Fairmount Park. Once they offered one thousand free oranges to the surprised heterosexuals. And once their outing, like the New Yorkers', was less than bright. Basil O'Brien, in the *Plain Dealer,* told why: [18]

We hadn't expected a demonstration of anti-gay sexism on the spot—particularly from the stage. But, towards the end of the music, before the raps and then the rain began, this white male rock group, BOINK, started introducing its last number. The straight boy lead singer was telling the crowd that they were going to play music for dancing, and that he wanted everyone up on their feet, dancing with the person next to them. I smiled at the guy I'd slept with the night before. ". . . and the last one up's a faggot." I was the first one up, chasing to the stage with a brother from GLF.

What's so ironic is that GLF people were the FIRST ones dancing at the previous Sunday's Be-In, beginning a circle that was joined by many straights. We let the straight boy finish his song, then put it to him that he had just laid down some heavy sexism. "No man, it wasn't meant that way, you just took it the wrong way." Oppression exists in the eyes of the oppressed. If I, an oppressed person, feel shat upon, I'm going to act on that feeling and get together with my gay sisters and brothers. We don't go by straight white boys' definitions of oppression. We pointed to the GLF banner and told the straight boy that a lot of gay people felt oppressed by what he'd said, and we wanted all the people on the Plateau to hear if his head was changed any.

He took back the mike, and in a statement laced with condescension, apologized as best he could. GLF isn't into taking much more of this shit from low conscious straights.

Gay Liberationists were not to have end-of-summer blues. Author Kate Millett boosted women's—and indirectly homosexual men's—pride and self-affirmation by her stirring speech in Bryant Park at the August 26 Women's Strike for Equality as well as by her best-selling *Sexual Politics* (New York, 1970). She had written—and by doing so pronounced categorically on what many psychiatrists had long suspected but hesitated to declare—that "Psychosexually there is no differentiation between the sexes at birth. Psychosexual personality is therefore postnatal and learned." [19] In one fell swoop she had equalized women and de-stigmatized male homosexuals! But a greater joy had been occasioned at Gay Liberation Fronts by a statement the weekend before the women's strike. A more GLF-practical statement it was, and one so long worked and hoped for by GLF members throughout the nation. It appeared in *The Black Panther,* August 21, 1970. It was not a capitulation, it was an acknowledgment. It was entitled A LETTER FROM HUEY TO THE REVOLU-

During the past few years, strong movements have developed among women
and among homosexuals seeking their liberation. There has been some uncer-
tainty about how to relate to these movements.

Whatever your personal opinions and your insecurities about homosexuality
and the various liberation movements among homosexuals and women (and I
speak of the homosexuals and women as oppressed groups), we should try to
unite with them in a revolutionary fashion. I say "whatever your insecurities
are" because, as we very well know sometimes our first instinct is to want to
hit a homosexual in the mouth and want a woman to be quiet. We want to
hit the homosexual in the mouth because we're afraid we might be homosexual; and we want to hit the woman or shut her up because we're afraid that
she might castrate us, or take the nuts that we might not have to start with.

We must gain security in ourselves and therefore have respect and feelings
for all oppressed people. We must not use the racist type attitude like the
White racists use against people because they are Black and poor. Many times
the poorest White person is the most racist, because he's afraid that he might
lose something, or discover something that he doesn't have; you're some kind
of threat to him. This kind of psychology is in operation when we view oppressed people and we're angry with them because of their particular kind of
behavior, or their particular kind of deviation from the established norm.

Remember, we haven't established a revolutionary value system; we're
only in the process of establishing it. I don't remember us ever constituting
any value that said that a revolutionary must say offensive things towards homosexuals, or that a revolutionary should make sure that women do not speak
out about their own particular kind of oppression. Matter of fact it's just the
opposite: we say that we recognize the women's right to be free. We haven't
said much about the homosexual at all, and we must relate to the homosexual movement because it's a real thing. And I know through reading and
through my life experience, my observations, that homosexuals are not given
freedom and liberty by anyone in the society. Maybe they might be the most
oppressed people in the society.

And what made them homosexual? Perhaps it's a whole phenomenon that
I don't understand entirely. Some people say that it's the decadence of capitalism. I don't know whether this is the case; I rather doubt it. But whatever
the case is, we know that homosexuality is a fact that exists, and we must
understand it in its purest form: That is, a person should have freedom to use
his body in whatever way he wants to. That's not endorsing things in homosexuality that we wouldn't view as revolutionary. But there's nothing to say
that a homosexual cannot also be a revolutionary. And maybe I'm now in-
jecting some of my prejudice by saying that "even a homosexual can be a
revolutionary." Quite on the contrary, maybe a homosexual could be the most
revolutionary.

When we have revolutionary conferences, rallies and demonstrations there
should be full participation of the gay liberation movement and the women's

liberation movement. Some groups might be more revolutionary than others. We shouldn't use the actions of a few to say that they're all reactionary or counterrevolutionary, because they're not.

We should deal with the factions just as we deal with any other group or party that claims to be revolutionary. We should try to judge somehow, whether they're operating sincerely, in a revolutionary fashion, from a really oppressed situation. (And we'll grant that if they're women, they're probably oppressed.) If they do things that are un-revolutionary or counter-revolutionary, then criticize that action. If we feel that the group in spirit means to be revolutionary in practice, but they make mistakes in interpretation of the revolutionary philosophy, or they don't understand the dialectics of the social forces in operation, we should criticize that and not criticize them because they're women trying to be free. And the same is true for homosexuals. We should never say a whole movement is dishonest, when in fact they're trying to be honest, they're just making honest mistakes. Friends are allowed to make mistakes. The enemy is not allowed to make mistakes because his whole existence is a mistake, and we suffer from it. But the women's liberation front and gay liberation front are our friends, they are potential allies, and we need as many allies as possible.

We should be willing to discuss the insecurities that many people have about homosexuality. When I say "insecurities," I mean the fear that they're some kind of threat to our manhood. I can understand this fear. Because of the long conditioning process which builds insecurity in the American male, homosexuality might produce certain hangups in us. I have hangups myself about male homosexuality. Where, on the other hand, I have no hangup about female homosexuality. And that's phenomena in itself. I think it's probably because male homosexuality is a threat to me, maybe, and the females are no threat.

We should be careful about using those terms that might turn our friends off. The terms "faggot" and "punk" should be deleted from our vocabulary, and especially we should not attach names normally designed for homosexuals to men who are enemies of the people, such as Nixon or Mitchell. Homosexuals are not enemies of the people.

We should try to form a working coalition with the gay liberation and women's liberation groups. We must always handle social forces in the most appropriate manner. And this is really a significant part of the population, both women, and the growing number of homosexuals, that we have to deal with.

ALL POWER TO THE PEOPLE!

> Huey P. Newton,
> SUPREME COMMANDER
> Black Panther Party

Whatever may have been Newton's ulterior motives—if indeed he had any—his statement was the first by a nationally known heterosexual male to recognize the equality of women and of homosexuals, even if as sisters and brothers in arms! No homosexual, violence-approving or Ghandian pacifist, could ignore it.*

Though a number of GLFers, with three Lavender Menaces,** preferred to join New Englanders in Provincetown's homosexual "Solidarity March," on Labor Day weekend many gay—and women's—liberationists experienced a first test of the validity of Newton's statement at the Panther-sponsored Revolutionary People's Constitutional Convention, the plenary session of which was held at Temple University in Philadelphia. A pretest—though it preceded the Newton statement—had been made by Radicalesbian **-GLFer Lois Hart who traveled to Washington in August for a planning meeting preparatory to the convention. Nine members of Third World Gay Revolution (see Chapter 10) and several GLF men accompanied her.

Admittedly "sick and angry at almost everyone except radical Gay sisters, questioning the validity of working with gay men and their infuriating unconscious sexism—ruling out straight men categorically as SUPER PIG," Hart wondered how she would relate to the "brown, muscled, bare-armed, deep-voiced Afro-American" Panthers who had called the meeting. The black leaders were obviously not ready either: "They moved the meeting along tracks of their prearranged program oblivious to everyone unless she or he was in agreement or of use. They insulted us with words of democratic procedure while bulldozing through their agenda. I felt intimidated, angry and defensive. 'I have come here to find out why and if gay people should relate to this convention. Is there receptivity to Women's and Gay Liberation?' 'We'll tolerate that crazy talk about 30 seconds and you'll be asked to leave!' "

Hart then realized she had seemed to be "talking down" to them. She signed up for the agenda committee, which planned workshops on women's rights, sexual self-determination, child oppression, the family, and self-determination for racial minorities. When one of the committee members could not hold back an anti-lesbian barb, a black gay male advised, "Oh no, brother, that just doesn't go anymore." For Hart, "The meeting took off. We were together." Later she met Panther David Hilliard, who spoke of the forthcoming Newton statement. Earlier, in the general meeting, Hilliard had fought with her. Now she understood something of his problems: "As I watched him walk away I felt that I had just talked to a human being . . . The bombastic Panther-in-public gave way to a black man caught in the contradictions of these times. Rising out of his incredible oppression, the assertion of his humanity takes the form of 'Being-A-Man'

---

* Dick Michaels of *The Advocate* editorialized: "So Huey Newton wants to be friends. Sorry, Huey, but somehow this fails to elate us. . . . We see some virtue in evolution. We think it is possible to change the 'system'—to make it what it is supposed to be. In fact, we see much more hope this way than in violence and destruction. Sorry, Huey." (October 14–27, 1970.)

** The Lavender Menace and Radicalesbians are developed in Chapter 9.

and that is what he has become. Now he is being told that this too is oppression and has to go. . . ."[20]

There are two gay versions of the September 5–6–7 weekend in Philadelphia: one is Horatio Alger–like, the other a study in disappointment. The success story was told by the men of *Gay Flames*[21] (who, two issues later, reminded readers to buy *Come Out!* No. 5 for the women's perspective):

About 30 men from New York Gay Liberation Front * went down. Many women, from Radical Lesbians and from GLF, went too. We went by car, bus, and train. We pooled our bread so everyone could go if they wanted to.

When we got there, the women and men each got a place where they could stay together and be with gay people from other cities. Some of the men dressed in drag the first night and rapped to some Panthers who came over; others went to bed early to get ready for the heavy day ahead.

Saturday morning, Panther Michael Tabor of the NY 21—accused of plotting to bomb the tulips at the Bronx Botanical Gardens!—spoke. He's got this really deep, beautiful voice, but doesn't come on like a super-butch at all. He said a lot about how we're all in the same boat when it comes to facing the power of the pigs. He talked about the oppression of gays and women, but it was clear that his understanding of our fight is not yet right on. It appears however that he is moving in the right direction.

That night, we tried to get in to Huey Newton's speech, but only a few of us made it. About 13,000 people came and the hall could hold only 6,500. We went on back to the church. Before we went to sleep, we were treated to the vision of two brothers fucking on top of the church's silk AmeriKKKan flag.

We got up and worked on our statement the next morning. The most important discussion centered around the Third World . . . Gay male statement. They confronted the gay whites on our racism, specifically on our willingness to criticize the sexism of black men but not that of white men. They asked us to recognize Huey Newton's recently stated position in favor of Gay Liberation as being a tremendous advance in the revolution and that the Black Panther Party holds the most out-front position in terms of the struggle to give power to the people. They condemned the middle-class, collegiate viewpoint that is still too often seen in GLF as well as the anti-homosexual attitudes of both Third World and white radicals.

The discussion that followed was deep and involved. In the middle of it, Afeni Shakur of the NY 21 came and took part. She helped to explain a lot about the Black Panthers to all of us. She said that all she wanted was a farm with lots of trees and grass and a place to grow cabbage, but that to get this for herself and her people, it would be necessary to fight. Most of us were convinced by what she had to say.

We therefore decided to include in our statement that gay men at the

* Steve Kuromiya, of Philadelphia GLF, recalls meeting gay conventioneers from Washington, D.C., Chicago, Milwaukee, St. Louis, San Francisco, and Boston as well.

Session recognized the BPP as being presently the vanguard of the people's revolution. By this, we meant that the party is the clearest of all US radical groups in its understanding of the nature of the fight of the peoples of the whole world.

We went on to prepare the following statement and demands, which we read to the people that night. They are meant to become part of the new constitution which we (and you, if you want to) will write in November:

STATEMENT OF THE MALE HOMOSEXUAL WORKSHOP

All power to the people!

The revolution will not be complete until all men are free to express their love for one another sexually. We affirm the sexuality of our love. The social institution which prevents us all from expressing our total revolutionary love we define as sexism. Sexism is a belief or practice that the sex or sexual orientation of human beings gives to some the right to certain privileges, powers, or roles, while denying to others their full potential. Within the context of our society, sexism is primarily manifested through male supremacy and heterosexual chauvinism. Since in the short run sexism benefits certain persons or groups, in the long run it cannot serve all the people, and prevents the forming of complete social consciousness among straight men.

Sexism is irrational, unjust and counter-revolutionary. Sexism prevents the revolutionary solidarity of the people.

We demand that the struggle against sexism be acknowledged as an essential part of the revolutionary struggle. We demand that all revolutionaries deal individually and collectively with their own sexism.

We recognize as a vanguard revolutionary action the Huey P. Newton statement on gay liberation. We recognize the Black Panther Party as being the vanguard of the people's revolution in Amerikkka.

No revolution without us!

An army of lovers cannot lose!

WE DEMAND:

1. The right to be gay, any time, any place.
2. The right to free physiological change and modification of sex upon demand.
3. The right of free dress and adornment.
4. That all modes of human sexual self-expression deserve protection of the law, and social sanction.
5. Every child's right to develop in a non-sexist, non-possessive atmosphere, which is the responsibility of all people to create.
6. That a free educational system present the entire range of human sexuality, without advocating any one form or style; that sex roles and sex-determined skills not be fostered by the schools.
7. That language be modified so that no gender take priority.

174

8. The judicial system be run by the people through people's courts; that all people be tried by members of their peer group.
9. That gays be represented in all governmental and community institutions.
10. That organized religions be condemned for aiding in the genocide of gay people, and enjoined from teaching hatred and superstition.
11. That psychiatry and psychology be enjoined from advocating a preference for any form of sexuality, and the enforcement of that preference by shock treatment, brainwashing, imprisonment, etc.
12. The abolition of the nuclear family because it perpetuates the false categories of homosexuality and heterosexuality.
13. The immediate release of and reparations for gay and other political prisoners from prisons and mental institutions; the support of gay political prisoners by all other political prisoners.
14. That gays determine the destiny of their own communities.
15. That all people share equally the labor and products of society, regardless of sex or sexual orientation.
16. That technology be used to liberate all peoples of the world from drudgery.
17. The full participation of gays in the people's revolutionary army.
18. Finally, the end of domination of one person by another.

Gay power to gay people!
All power to the people!
Seize the time!

At the convention floor, we really made people feel the significance of our presence as they/we the people unified by the same crushing weight on all of our necks by the same pigs for the same design of keeping us *all* down. We chanted Gay Powerful chants. We screamed, shouted, stomped, and clapped. About 60 gay male delegates together with others scattered over the audience screamed together louder than anyone there. "Right Ons" for everything anti-sexist. We just generally turned on everyone to our pride and defiance for our way of life and solidarity with everyone's own goals. It was beautiful, we were beautiful, and we knew it.

Of noticeable absence were our Gay sisters without whom there could be NO true people's constitution. The next day that abuse was at least recognized, if not corrected, by the gay men and the straight women there thru the following statements:

MALE HOMOSEXUALS: The Lesbian Workshop did not address the People's Constitutional Convention as scheduled. Therefore, the Male Homosexual Workshop summons the attention of all participating workshops to the fact that the Plenary Session is incomplete without the inclusion of a position paper from our sisters.

WOMEN: The demands of the gay sisters were not read from the platform last (Sunday) night. The new constitution cannot be complete without these demands. The Radical Lesbians were excluded and ignored at the Workshop on Self-Determination for Women. We feel we have let ourselves and our sisters down.

In the past and here at the conference, the women's movement has not

recognized that the struggle of gay women is our *struggle—*all *women's struggle. All women must be free to love one another.*
Free our sisters, free ourselves. Power to the People.

All but one of the lesbians had returned from Philadelphia to New York on Sunday afternoon "with the clear realization that if women continue to struggle for their liberation within contexts defined by sexist male mentalities, they will never be free."

Having heard most of Tabor's Saturday-afternoon speech, they recalled,

we left early in order to participate in the Lesbian workshop and therefore did not hear that all the workshops were cancelled. Two movement sisters still present, realizing the importance of the workshops and the need for women to talk to each other, asked the Panthers to announce a women's workshop for early the next morning. This request was denied and the women told that any such meeting would be considered a caucus outside the framework of the convention. In the light of the fact that the Panthers then announced a Yippie meeting, the sisters realized that women who dare to identify with their own oppression were felt by the Panthers to be a serious threat.[22]

That afternoon, nevertheless, the gay women sat and produced for the convention a paper on the "DEMANDS OF THE LESBIAN WORKSHOP":

1) Sexual autonomy:
   Prohibit sexual role programming of children.
2) Destruction of the Nuclear Family:
   The nuclear family is a microcosm of the fascist state, where the women and children are owned by, and their fates determined by, the needs of men, in a man's world.
3) Communal care of children:
   Children should be allowed to grow, in a society of their peers, cared for by adults whose aim is not to perpetrate any male-female role programming. It is advised that these adults be under the direction of woman-identified women.
4) Reparations:
   (a) Women are a dispersed minority and we demand that amount of control of all production and industry that would ensure one hundred percent control over our own destinies. This control includes commerce, industry, health facilities, education, transportation, military, etc.
   (b) Because women have been systematically denied information and knowledge and the opportunities for acquiring these, we demand open enrollment of all schools to all women, financial support to any woman who needs it, on the job training with pay for all women attending technical schools and under apprenticeship.
   (c) Women demand the time and support to research, compile and report our history and our identity.
   (d) The power and technology of defense are invested in men. Since these

powers are used to intimidate women, we demand training in self-defense and the use of defense machinery. A Women's Militia would be organized to defend the demands, rights and interests of women struggling towards an unoppressive social system.[23]

Meanwhile, Saturday afternoon a Third World woman speaker with the requisite woman-identification had been found by the agenda committee to share the platform with Huey Newton that night. She was confirmed as a speaker by the Panther leadership but denied access to the building that evening.[24]

As Newton addressed a packed McGonigle Hall, the lesbians listened outside on transistor radios. RAT noted that, though "His speech was very moving and nonrhetorical . . . it was a great disappointment to many that he did not follow up on his earlier statements about Women's Liberation and Gay Liberation. There was no mention of either oppressed group in his speech." [25] His forty-minute address was strictly macho. The New York *Sunday News* recorded the cheer-rousing closing exhortation: "We will have our manhood, even if we have to level the face of the earth!" [26] Newton's speech was followed by that of a "Panther sister whose rap was totally devoid of any awareness of women's oppression and merely an echo of male Panther rhetoric." [27]

According to the lesbians, the Panthers canceled an all-women's meeting that was to have taken place Sunday at 9:00 a.m. and substituted for it the workshop on self-determination for women, one of several contemporaneous workshops. Woman-identified women who joined the self-determination workshop could not lend their strength, therefore, to other convention topics. "Our meeting was presided over by a Panther woman with male Panther guards ringing the room and balconies. Immediately, women began to struggle with the question of the intimidating presence of the men, but lost to the argument that they were there to protect the Panther woman. Meanwhile, across town, the gay men were meeting with another Panther woman who apparently required no such security." The lesbians concluded: "We must, we will, make our women's revolution. No longer will we die alongside men who define our place and keep us there, whose highest flattery for us is our revolutionary wombs. Fuck that. We women of a dispersed nation will build our community, speak in a woman's language born from our woman's oppression, grow strong together and explode in our women's revolution." [28]

As if to second the women, GLF San Francisco was to lodge its complaint against the Panthers and other black nationalists a month later. Members of the Black Cultural Institute, which shared a building with GLF headquarters and several other groups, one of them a gay commune called Children of Paradise, "forcibly evicted commune members the night of Oct. 2, leaving some of them standing in the street half-dressed." *The Advocate* added that "It was not clear whether GLF had been forced out of the building . . . as reported by militant leader Leo Laurence, or had

177

withdrawn in protest after the [blacks] threw out the Children of Paradise . . ." The next day GLFers met with Panther officials and were informed that the issue would be referred to national BPP headquarters. Roger Green, one-time chairman of San Francisco GLF, has described how more than a dozen members had joined a twenty-four-hour vigil in 1969 at the local BPP headquarters when the Panthers were threatened by a police raid. "We put our bodies on the line. Had the pigs come shooting, it might have been our lives. But we didn't take a week to 'investigate' first, as the Panthers are now doing." [29]

*Gay Scene** reported, via the *Plain Dealer,* a late-summer beating of homosexuals by blacks in Philadelphia's Rittenhouse Square. GLFer Joe Covert attempted to come to the aid of a friend who had been struck and was being taunted for being gay. He explained "how gay oppression was linked to the oppression of black people. Gays and blacks must stick together." The assailants "threatened to rip apart the whole gay community—'faggot by faggot.' " [30] Philadelphia GLFers spoke of a Gay Defense League.[31]

Gay liberationists' zealous support of black civil rights and the Black Panther Party would not wane, however. FREE: Gay Liberation of Minnesota gave the party the nod. Jim Cheseboro, a member of the Minneapolis gay organization, qualified, nevertheless, "The resolution to recognize the Panthers does not mean that FREE endorses every strategy and tactic of the Black Panther Party, but only recognizes it as a vanguard** for the elimination of repression for all oppressed people." [32] But some all-women's groups now had second thoughts. Angela Douglas (Key), organizer of Transvestite-transsexual Action Organization (TAO; see Chapter 10), even expressed like doubts in a letter to *The Advocate* announcing the withdrawal of her and her club's support. She presented the lesbian workshop's Demands and averred how, at the rallies for Panther Lonnie McLucas in New Haven, she "felt like a complete fool facing 100 tactical police armed with magnums after hearing a Panther woman read a poem which included derogatory statements about 'white fags.' " [33]

---

* *Gay Scene* (New York) was first published, December 1969–January 1970, as *Gay Ways.* Now a monthly, its editor is Bruce King.
** Don A. Schanche, in his analytical *The Panther Paradox: A Liberal's Dilemma* (New York, 1970), posits that "the so-called 'vanguard party' has only the will to destroy, not to build and certainly not to reform," but confesses that "the Panthers confront us with utterly unacceptable alternatives: if we support the Black Panther Party in any way, we encourage what psychiatrists Grier and Cobbs called 'black rage, apocalyptic and final'; if we condone the unuttered, unwritten national police conspiracy to deprive the Panthers of their constitutional rights, we take the first awful step toward the loss of all liberties for minorities and majority alike." (P. 226.)

Lesbianism is one road to freedom—
freedom from oppression by men.
—Martha Shelley, in
Come Out!, November 14, 1969

*The events and developments of gay liberation/gay militancy that have to do
exclusively with the lesbian, especially those which involve women's liberation, can be most intelligently detailed only by the gay female. The following
chapter is the work of several lesbians who are active in gay and women's
liberation.*

Three hundred women sat in the auditorium of Manhattan's Intermediate
School 70 waiting for the second annual Congress to Unite Women to
come to order. The weekend conference, convening on Friday, May 1,
1970, had brought together from various cities representatives of a broad
spectrum of the women's liberation movement for planning and for workshops. Suddenly, the auditorium lights went out. There were shouts and
sounds of scuffling. In moments the lights went up to reveal walls blossoming with posters: TAKE A LESBIAN TO LUNCH; SUPERDYKE LOVES YOU; THE
WOMEN'S MOVEMENT IS A LESBIAN PLOT . . . Surrounding the astonished
audience were seventeen smiling women in lavender T-shirts emblazoned in
red with "LAVENDER MENACE." At that moment the women's liberation
movement found itself confronted with the fear that had haunted it since
its inception.

A Congress leader objected, GLFer Pat Maxwell detailed for *Gay
Power:* [1] "I realize that the women's movement has problems relating to the
lesbian, but I object to your coming in taking over this meeting. You're
acting like men."

"Lesbians have been brushed aside and ignored by the women's movement," retorted a Menace. "We have tried to work through the planning
sessions. . . . When we said lesbianism is an important issue for women's
liberation, we were ignored or told that it was a dangerous issue which

would divide women. We think that people who believe that are looking for male approval."

"We have come to tell you that we lesbians are being oppressed outside the movement and inside the movement by a sexist attitude. We want to discuss the lesbian issue with you," said another.

Seeing that the panel discussion originally planned for the evening was not to take place, a few women walked out, but, as one GLF woman told *Come Out!*, "There was little opposition due to the lighthearted style of the action." [2] The gay women "went with a smile and rapped from their hearts," said Menace Sidney Abbott.[3] At least for the weekend, reported Maxwell, "the barrier had finally broken down between lesbians and movement women. Heterosexuals and homosexuals of the Women's Congress were discussing lesbianism and its relationship to their lives."

On Sunday, when it appeared that, because the gay workshop had been formed ad-hoc, the lesbians would not be asked for their resolutions at the plenary session, the Menaces struck again, and presented the following:

1) Be it resolved that Women's Liberation is a lesbian plot.
2) Resolved that whenever the label lesbian is used against the movement collectively or against women individually, it is to be affirmed, not denied.
3) In all discussions of birth control, homosexuality must be included as a legitimate method of contraception.
4) All sex education curricula must include lesbianism as a valid, legitimate form of sexual expression and love.[4]

The action taken at the Congress to Unite Women was only one successful skirmish in a battle that has continued since the beginning of the women's liberation movement, in which, "welcome or not, we [lesbians] have been most active . . . from the start," said Rita Laporte, then national president of Daughters of Bilitis, in a letter to *Newsweek* in early 1970. She added, "Though most of us pass as heterosexual, those of us who can afford the risk are working in the movement as known lesbians." [5] Californian Del Martin, a founder of DOB, told the biennial DOB convention in New York City, July 1970: ". . . lesbians are bound up in the women's movement because of their economic concerns for equal pay, equal job opportunities, tax deductions, etc. [though] by life style, they are tied to the gay movement." GAY reporter Kay Tobin related how Martin "admitted that in the feminist movement, lesbians have a dilemma: will they be rejected if known as lesbians?" [6]

Responses from women's lib have varied. Radical groups have tended to welcome lesbians: as women pursuing one of many valid life-styles; as women who have suffered extreme oppression as women; and because they function independently of men and are therefore in a position of natural leadership in the fight for equality. A member of the militant feminist group Redstockings reported in RAT, August 1970, that, "At this point in Women's Liberation, one of the worst things to be accused of is being

'Anti-Lesbian' . . ." She continued, however, that this "has created a wave of verbal support for lesbians and not much more." [7]

In even the most supportive groups, personal hangups had to be faced and overcome. A typical experience (printed in *Gay Women's Liberation*, San Francisco): "One night at my regular women's liberation group meeting, one of the women said, 'You know, the first night you told us you were a lesbian, I sat in terror the rest of the meeting, waiting for you to attack me or something.' " [8]

At the same time they were coming to terms with the open lesbians in their groups, movement women were learning to face the lesbian within themselves. In San Francisco, at the second Bay Area Women's Coalition Conference, February 1970, about two hundred members of women's lib groups heard a panel on lesbianism conducted by gay women active in the movement. Elsa Gidlow reported, for *Women: A Journal of Liberation* (Baltimore), that, concluding her talk, Alice Malloy, of Gay Women's Liberation, announced she had been advised not to do something she'd planned at that point. Sensing audience support, however, she said, "I'll tell you what I had in mind and leave it to you. I was going to ask if every woman in the hall who had ever felt she could be erotically attracted to another woman would care to stand up." A tense moment followed. Gidlow told: "Several women stood. A few more slowly followed. Then, like a dam bursting, practically every woman of the 200 or so in the hall was on her feet." Since, Gidlow noted, most of them had been unquestionably living heterosexual lives, "this could be seen as an expression of acceptance and sisterly solidarity, beautiful in its spontaneity. Perhaps also it was something of a group confession, for the atmosphere of relief was evident, and reflected the frank give-and-take of the platform–audience interchange that followed." [9] "More and more of the sisters I love who I've known in the women's movement in Berkeley are understanding that love for a sister cannot stop short of her body. We are beginning to feel related to our gay sisters . . ." wrote "Laurel" in the feminist paper *It Ain't Me Babe*.[10] * For the same paper, Mary Damon's AN OPEN LETTER TO THE WOMEN'S MOVEMENT [11] noted, "The irony of it all is that I probably would never have discovered my homosexuality without women's liberation. You have helped to create what you despise and fear . . ."

Pressures from outside the women's movement were as effective as gay women within in forcing women to relate to lesbianism: the public had accused movement women of homosexuality regardless of their real sexual

* Such "women's lib lesbians" (women who are exploring the possibilities of a physical relationship with another woman and who are to be distinguished from the "political lesbian" discussed later) are viewed with skepticism by many gay women whose first allegiance has always been to lesbians; they doubt the emotional commitment, if not the sincerity, of the newcomers and accuse them of not being "real" lesbians. That a lifetime of exclusively homosexual experience is not a requirement for "real" lesbianism is indicated by New York DOB president Ruth Simpson's report that one third of the new New York club members have children. Del Martin is herself a grandmother.

orientation. That this was a powerful weapon Martha Shelley has illustrated: [12] "when Women's Liberation picketed the 1968 Miss America pageant, the most terrible epithet heaped on our straight sisters was 'lesbian.' The sisters faced hostile audiences who called them 'commies,' 'tramps,' 'bathless,' etc., and they faced these labels with equanimity; but they broke into tears when they were called lesbians."

In their own analyses, the more radical women's groups have concluded that the same dynamics which make lesbianism such a threat also make it central to the women's movement. A member of the feminist Class Workshop in New York stated it this way, for RAT: [13]

Lesbianism is the supreme insult and threat to the male.

It insults him because it implies that you prefer another woman to him. He is indignant at the fact that you would compare him to a "mere woman," that you would actually consider a woman his equal.

Sexually you are stripping him of his age old prerogative—he is not your only source of love and affection. You have a choice and implicit in that choice is that your needs and pleasure are equal to or have priority over his. This is the reason the "Lesbians" (and let's keep in mind that the word lesbian is a male supremacist distinction which artificially defines love among women as purely sexual) are ridiculed and persecuted in our male supremacist bourgeois society. This is the reason that the oppressor has called the Women's Liberation Movement "a bunch of Lesbians."

All of us must recognize the political significance of what is called by men "Lesbianism." We cannot afford to push aside this issue because of cultural biases or fear. Let's face the truth: the greatest threat to men is solidarity among women and "Lesbianism" epitomizes this solidarity.

Moderates in women's lib, in spite of this, have felt that the movement could not bear the burden of the lesbian, who, in Martha Shelley's words, "faces the most severe contempt and ridicule that society can heap on a woman." [14] Extremely sensitive to criticism that women's lib consisted of "scruffy packs of exhibitionists, lesbians, etc."—as *New York Post* columnist Harriet Van Horne described them, April 1970 [15]—moderates had emphatically dissociated themselves from homosexuality. When the National Organization for Women was said to be run by "lavender menaces" —an allegation that some unspecified NOW officers were lesbian—Betty Friedan, author of *The Feminine Mystique* (New York, 1963) and a founder of the organization, had called lesbianism "a lavender herring." The labels were put to use later, at the Congress to Unite Women.

"Despite the resistance they encountered in women's lib groups, the larger percentage of active lesbians have chosen women's liberation as their primary point of identification and gay liberation second, thus bringing the gay struggle into the heart of the women's movement," a *Washington Monthly* assistant editor, Suzannah Lessard, observed in December.[16] And,

182

in time, more and more lesbians—overt and covert—in the women's movement found it absurd and indefensible that the movement should attempt to exclude them or ignore their existence.

■

Gay women's consciousness as women had been rising steadily, and was creating new closeness and cohesion among the women of the gay liberation movement. In New York a "gay women's movement" can be said to have begun over GLF women's discouragement with the Front's dances, where, inevitably, "the women were lost to each other in a sea of spaced-out men." Planning their All-Women's Dances in spring 1970, when they "had to meet and work together . . . weekly meetings of GLF women became routine. This provided a fine opportunity to work collectively and get to know one another." [17]

Some women from GLF formed a consciousness-raising group with independent lesbians from women's liberation. From their deliberations came the Lavender Menace confrontation and one of the basic documents of gay women's liberation, "The Woman-Identified Woman," which gave clarity to the political meaning of lesbianism, the role of lesbianism in the women's movement, and the reason gay women belonged, *first,* in women's liberation. First published in *Come Out!,* the essay began, "What is a lesbian?" . . .

A lesbian is the rage of all women condensed to the point of explosion. She is the woman who, often beginning at an extremely early age, acts in accordance with her inner compulsion to be a more complete and freer human being than her society . . . cares to allow her. . . . She may not be fully conscious of the political implications of what for her began as personal necessity, but on some level she has not been able to accept the limitations and oppression laid on her by the most basic role of her society—the female role. . . .

. . . Lesbian is the word, the label, the condition that holds women in line. When a woman hears this word tossed her way, she knows she is stepping out of line. She knows that she has crossed the terrible boundary of her sex role. . . . Lesbian is a label invented by the Man to throw at any woman who dares to be his equal, who dares to challenge his prerogatives . . . who dares to assert the primacy of her own needs. . . [In] this sexist society, for a woman to be independent means she *can't* be a *woman,* she must be a *dyke.* That in itself should tell us where women are at. It says as clearly as can be said: woman and person are contradictory terms. . . .

. . . While all women are dehumanized as sex objects, as the objects of men they are given certain compensations . . . Should a woman confront herself by confronting another woman, there are fewer rationalizations, fewer buffers by which to avoid the stark horror of her dehumanized condition. Herein we find the overriding fear of many women towards exploring intimate relationships with other women: the fear of being used as a sexual object by a woman, which not only will bring her no male-connected compensations, but also will reveal the void which is woman's real situation. This dehumanization is expressed when a straight woman learns that a sister is a lesbian; she begins to relate to her lesbian sister as her potential sex object, laying a surrogate male role on the lesbian. This reveals her heterosexual conditioning to make herself into an object when sex is potentially involved in a relationship, and it denies the lesbian her full humanity. . . .

. . . By virtue of having been brought up in a male society, we have internalized the male culture's definition of ourselves. That definition views us as relative beings who exist not for ourselves, but for the servicing, maintenance and comfort of men. That definition consigns us to sexual and family functions and excludes us from defining and shaping the terms of our lives. . . .

The consequence of internalizing this role is an enormous reservoir of self-hate. . . . Women resist relating on all levels to other women who will reflect their own oppression, their own secondary status, their own self-hate. . . .

As the source of self-hate and the lack of real self are rooted in our male-given identity, we must create a new sense of self. . . . Only women can give each other a new sense of self. That identity we have to develop with reference to ourselves, and not in relation to men. . . .

It is the primacy of women relating to women, of women creating a new consciousness of and with each other, which is at the heart of women's liberation, and the basis for the cultural revolution.[18] . . .

Women's desire to work toward this new sense of self was revealed by a turnout of more than fifty women for consciousness-raising groups announced by the Lavender Menace following the Congress to Unite Women. Many of these, reported *Come Out!*, were "straight women who wanted to confront the issue of lesbianism and perhaps the lesbian in themselves. But a very large majority turned out to be active lesbians, latent lesbians, closet lesbians, one-beautiful-experience lesbians, freaked-out lesbians, spaced-out lesbians . . ." The report continued, "After having related for months and years to the broader women's issues at the sacrifice of their own identity, these women were ready now to come out, to use their energies to meet the needs of a lesbian community and to see that the concepts of primary value and commitment between women, developed in the paper 'The Woman-Identified Woman,' were dealt with by the women's liberation movement." [19]

In the next months, a number of these women realized that they had become essentially independent not only from orthodox women's liberation but from GLF, too, and spurred by a desire to affiliate no longer with a male-dominated organization, they broke away entirely from the Front, taking with them the women's share of the GLF fund set up for a "community center"—enough to sponsor their first independent dance. "A movement of radical and revolutionary gay women has organically coalesced," they announced, "not artificially out of rhetorical political necessity, but through the natural flow of our experience and changes in consciousness." [20] The members of the group, who took the name Radicalesbians, represented three points of view: those of women who felt themselves primarily to be a part of the women's liberation movement, struggling against male supremacy; of women who felt that, as gays, they must first fight against sexism in gays and straights—male and female; and of women (many of whom retained membership in GLF) who saw the struggle basically as one of heterosexuals vs. homosexuals. Using techniques typical to women's liberation and to Gay Liberation Front, they now eschewed leaders and organizational hierarchy in order to encourage everyone to participate. Decisions were reached by consensus rather than by majority vote; tasks were often assigned by lot. "We believe that we must live by revolutionary forms while we struggle against sexism, racism, and imperialism; that part of the revolution is our anti-authoritarian life style; that the revolution is process, not goal. Small, action-oriented collectives seems to be the direction in which we are headed," they said in *Come Out!* at the end of 1970.[21]

While Radicalesbians set out to work with women alone, Gay Liberation Front women functioned in late summer 1970 as a powerful and nearly autonomous caucus within the New York Front. They defined themselves for the Front newspaper [22] as

lesbian activists fighting oppression on two fronts: As homosexuals, we work with our gay brothers to fight oppression based on society's exclusion of individuals who love members of the same sex. As women, we work with Women's Liberation to fight the oppression of all women.

Our strongest common denominator and greatest oppression lies with society's injustice against us as homosexuals. We are discriminated against as women, but lesbians who live openly are fired from jobs, expelled from schools, banished from their homes, and even beaten. Lesbians who hide and escape open hostility suffer equal oppression through psychic damage caused by their fear and guilt. With this understanding, we focus on gay liberation, giving priority to gay issues and gay problems. We are part of the revolution of all oppressed people, but we cannot allow the lesbian issue to be an afterthought.

Vowing to "work for a common understanding among all people that lesbianism is the most complete and fulfilling relationship with another woman and a valid life style," the GLF women's statement of purpose defined consciousness raising as a primary goal:

1) So
   that our lesbian sisters understand our oppression and fight against it. . . .
   We denounce the fact that society's rewards and privileges are only given to us when we hide and split our identity. We encourage self-determination and will work for changes in the lesbian self-image, as well as in society, to permit the "coming out" of each gay woman into society as a lesbian. . . .
2) Raising consciousness of people in all movements, so that they become aware of their sexism.
3) Raising the consciousness of our sisters active in Women's Liberation to openly acknowledge and actively support lesbians, with the attitude of soli-

185

darity and not reciprocity. . . . We feel that the core oppression of women is the lesbian's oppression and the ultimate liberation of women is through the liberation of lesbians. Real freedom for lesbians will mean the end of all oppressive relationships based on male dominance and the compulsion women feel to seek male approval and support.

Women's Liberation groups must undertake consciousness-raising on lesbianism. They must accept among their leadership admitted and publicly known lesbians. They must make explicit their acceptance of the lesbian life style now implicit in their analysis.

(a) Feminists speak of rejecting role-playing, but fail to see the pressures in society during children's formative years to love men over women.

(b) They say that women should be free to govern their own bodies, but fail to grant the freedom of sexual preference.

(c) They denounce stereotyped male and female attitudes and characteristics, but fail to accept as natural the so-called masculine female and so-called feminine male.

(d) They talk about being independent of men, but do not see that the lesbian life style is the ultimate form of independence.

(e) They talk of love among women, but do not include physical expression of that love.

4) Education of the public to recognize homosexuals as an oppressed minority and to destroy stereotyped images based on and perpetuated by society's hostility. To fight prejudice with reason and love.[23] . . .

The rising women's consciousness among lesbians took different turns as the gay movement continued to strengthen in 1970. To begin with, consciousness raising, whether organized or spontaneous, was producing startling realizations about women's attitudes toward themselves and about the heterosexually modeled roles many homosexual women play. Del Martin commented during the summer that DOB had always regarded sex roles—"butch" and "femme"—as "arbitrary and culturally imposed," and insisted that lesbians were, more and more, getting away from role playing to accept themselves as individuals.[24] But, clearly, much remained to be done before gay women were rid of the sexist attitudes they deplored in others. In her "Confessions of a Pseudo-Male Chauvinist" in *The Ladder: A Lesbian Review*,[25] Martha Shelley admitted: "I've always admired 'masculine' women . . . However, after I became involved with Women's Liberation, I began to notice something about myself that embarrassed me. I didn't really like women. In bed, yes—but all my friends were men. In rejecting the woman's role, from knitting to cooking to wearing mascara, I had also rejected women—except for women jet pilots, executives and astronauts. . . . I snobbishly (and self-destructively) treated women as sex objects and men as intellectual companions." Shelley realized that she and other "butch" types of her acquaintance had oppressed other gay women in the same way men oppressed straight women. What was more, by identifying with the oppressor class, she had not won significant privileges over other women. In *Gay Sunshine* in October, a woman who signed herself "Pasha" expressed a similar awakening: [26]

A few years ago the idea of meeting with a group of women, gay or straight, would have turned me off. I'd have sneered it off (the typical self-hating superiority syndrome) because immediately the stereotype of a group of tittering gossipy women, alternating between cattiness and sentimentality, would have come to mind. I didn't want to identify with that. Strange to remember now. Strange also to remember that I, a woman, helped perpetuate that stereotype by my acceptance of it. . . .

Strange too that I a lesbian could think that a mixture of men and women would make a more wholesomely balanced group than a group of women alone. I don't recall ever thinking that about a group of men. . . .

The problem of male chauvinism within gay organizations, and the rising insistence that within those groups women receive equal attention and responsibility, were creating conflicts. It was the summer NACHO convention in San Francisco that brought things to a head for Del Martin. Shortly after the conference closed, she published in *The Advocate* a statement headed "IF THAT'S ALL THERE IS . . ." [27] which shocked the West Coast homosexual community by announcing that, "After 15 years of working for the homophile movement—of mediating, counselling, appeasing, of working for coalition and unity—I am facing a very real identity crisis. Like NACHO, I have been torn apart. I am bereft. For I have during this week of struggle between the men and the women, the conservatives and the Gay Liberationists, been forced to the realization that I have no brothers in the homophile movement."

She excoriated the men at NACHO, who "would not address themselves to the underlying reason for the existence of separate women's organizations [e.g., DOB]—that the female homosexual faces sex discrimination not only in the heterosexual world, but within the homophile community. And so," she declared, ". . . I have come to the conclusion that I must say, 'Goodbye to All That.' " She then proceeded to lay out and scathingly denounce the whole range of discriminatory gay groups and institutions:

Goodbye, not just to SIR,* but to all those homophile organizations across the country with an open-door policy for women. It's only window dressing for the public and in the small towns of suburbia, for mutual protection. It doesn't really mean anything and smacks of paternalism. . . .

Goodbye to all the "representative" homophile publications that look more like magazines for male nudist colonies. . . .

Goodbye to the gay bars that discriminate against women. Goodbye to those

---

* Martin had been a regular columnist in SIR's monthly *Vector* magazine and an active member of the Society.

that "allow" them in only if they dress up in skirts, while men slop around in their "queer" costumes. . . .

Goodbye to the Halloween Balls, the drag shows and parties. It was fun, while it lasted. But the humor has gone out of the game. . . .

Goodbye to Gay Liberation, too. They applauded the lesbians who wished to establish common cause with them and the other men at the NACHO meeting. But somehow we are left with the feeling their applause was for the disruption of the meeting, not its purpose. . . .

Goodbye to the male homophile community. "Gay is good," but not good enough—so long as it is limited to white males only. We joined with you in what we mistakenly thought was a common cause. . . .

She then stated her new priorities: ". . . I must go where the action is— where there is still hope, where there is possibility for personal and collective growth. It is a revelation to find acceptance, equality, love, and friendship—everything we sought in the homophile community—not there, but in the women's movement."

Across the nation, from Boston to Los Angeles, gay women were joining forces in independent groups and independent caucuses within co-ed groups. In San Francisco, lesbians from women's lib groups had formed Gay Women's Liberation early in 1970, "partially with the intention of extending roots out into other women's liberation groups, hopefully to start taking the terror out of the word 'lesbian,'" said Judy Grahn in the San Francisco Free Press.[28] GWL also aimed to be influential in gay liberation, and worked on the problem of gay-male chauvinism. A noteworthy development has been the growth of gay women's liberation in the Midwest. At the FREE-sponsored gay lib conference in Minneapolis in October (see Chapter 10), a group of women from the Twin Cities, DeKalb (Ill.), Lawrence (Kan.), Chicago, St. Louis, Milwaukee, and Iowa City caucused separately after deciding they could not participate fully in a preponderantly male meeting. "[Male] homosexual and lesbian experience are very different," the women from the gay cell of Iowa City women's lib pointed out, in Ain't I A Woman?, "especially when lesbian oppression is seen as an integral part of women's oppression." They announced that "A community of midwestern gay women is developing," [29] and laid plans for further meetings and actions. The women's lib paper Ain't I A Woman?, by the Publications Collective of Iowa City Women's Liberation Front, was indicative of the strength of these lesbian spokeswomen. Its motto stated, "We are a collective of 10 women functioning either as a front for a world wide conspiracy of Radical Lesbians or the house cornfield of the Women's Movement." [30] From the heart of the Midwest, the paper presented women's liberation from a consciousness pervaded by a high order of militant lesbianism.

Of an opposite tactic were members of such mixed militant organizations as Philadelphia's Homophile Action League, more than half women, and New York's Gay Activists Alliance, with a small but active group of female members. These women gave first priority to rights for all homosexuals, tacitly or explicitly dissociating themselves from all other movements, including women's lib—at least when within HAL or GAA, to which their allegiance generally belonged. HAL's Barbara Gittings, reported Kay Tobin for GAY, stressed that while gay women have feminist work to do—insisting that men treat them as equals—"if gay men and women don't get together and fight the gay cause, nobody else is going to do it for us." [31] Typical of the prevailing feeling of GAA women was their insistence that it was not vital to send a man *and* a woman as the Alliance's two guests, November 27, to the "Dick Cavett Show" (see Chapter 12); the women's attitude that they would be best represented by GAA's most articulate members, regardless of the fact that those chosen were male, was incomprehensible to many of the city's radical gay women.

The Daughters of Bilitis, oldest and largest all-female homophile organization, came to grips, meanwhile, with two challenging issues: feminism and activism. From its founding in San Francisco in 1955, DOB had engaged in civil rights work. Until 1969–70, however, activism of the sort that included picketing was ordinarily considered too militant for the group. DOB's Statement of Purpose described it as "a woman's organization for the purpose of aiding the Lesbian to discover her place in society, and of educating society to understand and accept her, without prejudice . . ." [32] Its activities included maintaining a library on women and on female homosexuality, acting as a forum for ideas emanating from its members and sometimes for the public, participating in responsible research on homosexuality, and working for legal reforms, in addition to sponsoring gay women's social events.

In 1970, DOB endured the pains of reorganization—problems of maintaining an effective national leadership answerable to widely separated chapters* became insuperable. At the biennial national convention in New York City—unattended by any of DOB's national officers—the New York chapter successfully proposed that the national structure be abolished in favor of a loose federation of virtually autonomous chapters. Replacing the national officers was a board consisting of all chapter presidents, with the power to charter new chapters. DOB severed all ties with the fourteen-year-old *The Ladder,* which had until then been its official publication. *The Ladder* announced immediately that it was "no longer a minority publication. It stands squarely with all women, that majority of human beings that has known oppression longer than anyone." [33] Whether the new chapter autonomy would affect the outlook of DOB, whose incorporated, non-profit tax-exempt status ostensibly precluded taking political stands, was not clear at once. It was plain, however, that a feeling of militancy was growing, brought especially by the younger women who were flocking to join the organization.

* Daughters of Bilitis has had viable chapters in Los Angeles, New Orleans, Cleveland, Boston, Detroit, Chicago, Portland (Ore.), Miami, San Diego, and Denver, as well as in San Francisco and New York.

DOB's New York chapter heard a series of speakers in summer and fall 1970 who brought the issue of feminism to the fore. Kate Millett, who had been a national spokeswoman for the women's liberation movement since her book *Sexual Politics,* made headlines (at first only in the gay press) when she seized her time at DOB to proclaim, "I'm out of the closet!" and told of her early experiences in the gay world—which she described as "hell, every damned moment of it." Following study abroad, and after a number of years of living with a man and subsequently marrying him, she had joined the gay march on June 28, 1970 (see Chapter 15), she said, and "it just blew my mind! . . . Everything was different now. No oppression, no roles!" She continued, "It can be more fun to live this life, more beautiful, than any other life in the world." Love, she said, is "what's so beautiful about the lesbian side of the women's lib movement. This side has parties and dances, and they kiss each other. The rest of women's lib doesn't. I'll tell you a secret—they ought to! For two reasons: they want to, and if they did, they wouldn't yell at each other so much and everybody else!"

Another alliance between women's liberation and lesbian organizations was forged when Ti-Grace Atkinson, former president of New York NOW and founder of the Feminists, joined DOB. Atkinson, a supermilitant with a reputation as one of the top theorists of the women's movement, exemplified a phenomenon known as "political lesbianism." She explained it: "It is this commitment, by choice, full-time, of one woman to others of her class [i.e., the female class] that is called lesbianism. It is this full commitment, against any and all personal considerations if necessary, that constitutes the political significance of lesbianism." [34] Since Atkinson's concept of feminism precluded intimate relationships with men, she eliminated as political lesbians women who had sexual relations with women but who were married to men—in her political analysis, they collaborated with the enemy. Political lesbians did, however, include those "women who have never had sexual relations with other women, but who have made and live a total commitment to this Movement." In various forms, the same attitude was expressed by many radical women's liberation groups.

Invited to keynote ceremonies that opened New York DOB's "center," on January 3, 1971, Atkinson told a receptive audience that "this center is going to be to the government as a declation of war"—feminism was such a threat to the established power structure and the homosexual woman was at the forefront of the struggle. "I'm not interested in who you're sleeping with, I'm interested in who you're going to die with," she declared. "I'm putting women on a war footing. The alternative is to die."

Atkinson's contention that "this place is going to be hit" struck a responsive chord in those of her listeners who had been present Thursday night, October 8, at the regular DOB business meeting in the hall of a private gay club. Two policemen had entered abruptly, asking for DOB's occupancy sign. The organization's November newsletter related how the president, Ruth Simpson, "told [them] that was not our responsibility

190

but that of the Corduroy Club from which we sublet. She repeatedly denied that the policemen had a right to enter our meeting or ask to see anything or anybody. Nobody flapped. Some of us asked what DOB had done and why the police were interested in us." One officer asked for Simpson's "personal identification, and when she refused to show it to him he said, 'Get your coat—we're taking you to the station.' Most of us prepared to go with her." Simpson and the police were at the door, about to leave, when a member came out of the office and announced she had a lawyer on the wire. One of the officers said, "I don't want to break your horns—take your call." On the lawyer's advice, Simpson showed the officers her ID. She was issued a summons to appear in court, at 100 Centre Street, but was not taken from the meeting.[35]

This single event mobilized, perhaps even part-radicalized, New York Daughters of Bilitis. Having decided just minutes before the police arrived that they were not willing to employ picketing as a tool, the women now immediately endorsed a public demonstration for their president's hearing. A shocked gay community interpreted the incident as a clear case of harassment, and members of eight gay organizations supported Simpson by an appearance at 100 Centre Street on October 23.

Their November newsletter explained New York DOB women's new stance:

DOB since its beginnings has been a quiet social and educational organization. It gives a protected first step toward fellowship and self-acceptance. It is a home and family for lesbians. Most of us don't want it to be anything else. We are not marchers and chanters and demanders.

So what are we doing in the streets and courthouses? Why are we issuing demands and allying ourselves with other groups to get the strength to back up our demands?

Because:

• If the police can interrupt our meetings we no longer feel like a safe first step for the shy and hidden.

• If the police can make our officers waste time and thought on legal problems, the quality of our meetings declines.

• If we have to pay legal fees to protect ourselves from whimsical, random charges, our treasury is depleted.

• If our officers have to miss work to go back and back to court, no one will be willing to accept an office.

Our oppressors know all this. Do we know it?

We have . . . voting power, dollar power, and body power.

We must use them concertedly now.[36]

Some DOB members felt, nevertheless, that the new activism threatened the club's effectiveness as a "home" for lesbians. Disturbed by militant and radical speakers who addressed the club, and by "alliances" being formed with other, more radical gay groups and with other causes, they attributed the police harassment to the increasingly political nature of the organization. Espousing this view and resistant to the growing pressure that members, especially officers, should "come out" publicly, more than thirty women (including a former president and several former board members) left DOB at the end of the year to form a new conservative group with strictly apolitical aims.

■

Since Kate Millett's "coming out" at a Daughters of Bilitis meeting, the pressures on women's liberation to acknowledge and work for the lesbian had intensified. A primary focus of this pressure was the moderate National Organization for Women, generally conceded to be politically the most effective. It was national, and the largest women's rights organization in the country, with more than one hundred chapters. At NOW's 1969 national membership council, representatives of New York NOW had tried to amend the organization's Bill of Rights to expand the idea that the individual's right to control over her body—much cited to support abortion reform—include the rights of sexual preference. While chapters from the East and West Coasts supported the amendment, they detected so much opposition from representatives of other parts of the nation that they withdrew the proposal before it could be voted down.

Within the New York chapter itself—considered a key to any national reforms—a difference of opinion existed. NOW founder Betty Friedan was emphatically opposed to forming any kind of alliance with the gay liberation movement. When DOB was visited in November 1970 by members of NOW, one guest, Jacqui Ceballos told the hostesses it was important that an organization like NOW *not* come out fully in relation to the homosexual issue, in order to build as broad a base of women's support as possible. Fear was, she said, that potential members would be alienated by what many considered a controversial issue. Two weeks later, however, NOW sponsored a pro-lesbian symposium on the topic "Is Lesbianism a Feminist Issue?" at which NOW leader Dolores Alexander said she believed that the organization must take a public stand in its Bill of Rights on behalf of every woman's right to control her own sexual life. It should support an end to anti-homosexual laws.

Panelists at the symposium voiced reasons why they thought NOW should come to grips with the issue of lesbianism. Radicalesbian panelist Sidney Abbott noted that gay women were "the natural vanguard of the women's movement" because they had already had to define their own identity independently of men, and had learned to be self-supporting— goals of the entire women's movement. She pleaded with gay women in women's lib to "come out," not merely because being "in the closet" inflicted psychic damage on an individual but because those who remained hidden were the very ones whose influence "could convince even the Midwest" that gay rights were a valid, important issue. Kate Millett reiterated a position she had been stating publicly since the Women's Strike on

August 26—that women's lib should be supporting gay women. She urged that the women's liberation movement work for the repeal of anti-gay laws, and declared that the movement had been "carried on the backs of lesbians for five or six years!" Gay women had worked hard for child-care centers and abortion "while trying not to look like dykes," and now, she said, the movement should reciprocate.

Millett emphasized that it was morally and humanly necessary for women's lib to come to terms with gay liberation. Not only was the gay life-style fraught with legal and psychic oppression—which women's liberation should help fight—but women's liberationists would continue to fear homosexuality until they faced it, she said, and would be insecure until they did. She again called herself bisexual, and spoke of the difficulties of being "open": "I'm going to be dumped on all my life for being gay"— but not for being straight, she reminded them.

Kate Millett's stand served as a rallying point at which lesbians and non-radical women's lib could at last unite publicly. An immediate occasion was the December article in TIME Magazine which warned that Millett's disclosure that she was a bisexual "is bound to discredit her as a spokes-woman for her cause, cast further doubt on her theories, and reinforce the views of those skeptics who routinely dismiss all liberationists as lesbians." [37]

On December 12 at a previously scheduled rally in midtown Man-hattan to demand free abortion and child care, the Women's Strike Coalition handed out leaflets headlined "NO MORE DYKE-BAITING!" Illustrated with cartoons showing a militant feminist brought to her knees when a man called her a dyke, the leaflet began:

```
See how it works?

You discredit a movement by calling a visible member a name
designed to strike fear in the hearts of all respectable
citizens.  Joe McCarthy was an expert at this.  So was Hitler.
So is Time magazine.

Now we're being dyke-baited.  Not too many years ago, Jew-
baiting was equally terrifying.  One man, however, figured out
a way to handle it.  When the Nazis invaded Denmark and
demanded that all Jews wear armbands with the Star of David,
King Christian rode through Copenhagen displaying the armband
on his own sleeve.  Soon every Dane had marked herself or
himself a Jew.  They stood together so the Jews among them
couldn't be singled out and picked off. . . .

On Tuesday, December 8, Time magazine (December 14 issue)
decided to try this time-honored method of intimidation on the
Women's Liberation movement by publicly attacking Kate Millet
for her courageous statement that she is bisexual.  It is not
one woman's sexual preference that is under attack -- it is
the freedom of all women to openly state values that fundamen-
tally challenge the basic structure of patriarchy.  If they
succeed in scaring us with words like "dyke" or "lesbian" or
```

193

"bisexual," they'll have won. AGAIN. They'll have divided us.
AGAIN. Sexism will have triumphed. AGAIN.

But this time we will not be divided. Just as all Danes stood
together so the Jews couldn't be picked off, we stand together
so lesbians can't be picked off. Time magazine wants us to
run scared, disown Kate and all our gay sisters. In essence,
they're asking us to issue lavender armbands. That's why
we're ALL wearing lavender lesbian armbands today -- to show
that we stand together as women, regardless of sexual
preference. They can call us all lesbians until such time as
there is no stigma attached to women loving women.

SISTERHOOD IS POWERFUL!!!

The Women's Strike Coalition told the press: "This action is a historic first. The first time Women's Liberation and Gay Liberation have joined forces. Freedom to control your own body and to live in human dignity and self respect are key issues in both movements. The rationale for free abortion and state provided child-care extends to freedom of sexual preference." [38] Virtually all of the three hundred women who braved a cold rain to demonstrate for the "straight" issues wore a lavender armband and heard Millett proclaim, "They can no longer divide us by calling us queer."

The culmination of the action came at a press conference called by nine movement leaders at Washington Square Methodist Church on December 17 to affirm their "solidarity with the struggle of homosexuals to attain their liberation in a sexist society." Millett read a statement prepared by members of NOW, Radicalesbians, Columbia [University] Women's Liberation, and DOB which contended, "Women's liberation and homosexual liberation are both struggling towards a common goal: A society free from defining and categorizing people by virtue of gender and/or sexual preference." Journalist Gloria Steinem; Ruth Simpson; radical black lawyer Florynce Kennedy; Sally Kempton and Susan Brownmiller, journalists and Radical Feminists; New York NOW president Ivy Bottini; NOW member Dolores Alexander; and radical feminist Ti-Grace Atkinson all appeared in support at the conference, reported Judy Klemesrud for *The New York Times*. They were backed by statements from Congresswoman-Elect Bella Abzug and Caroline Bird, author of *Born Female* (New York, 1968). A powerful indictment from NOW's national president, Aileen Hernandez, called attempts to use lesbianism against the women's movement "sexual McCarthyism." [39] Such broad-based and high-level support uniting gay women's liberation with the women's movement gave new strength to gay women in both causes. An integral part of "the 51 per cent minority," lesbians were able to affirm that, indeed, "Sisterhood *is* Powerful."

10

New York University, which exists in
the world's largest gay ghetto, is not sure
homosexuals are morally desirable.
—from a gay liberation leaflet
during the "Weinstein Affair"

A summer article in the Philadelphia *Plain Dealer* cautioned gays, "the
only time you need worry about raids is around election time when the
D.A. needs a few more points for the record." [1] So might New York gays
have thought in August of election year 1970—if they were regulars at
the Haven, a "private, unisex, membership, nonalcoholic club at 1 Sheridan
Square." [2] Moreover, the Haven had earned the ire of Villagers: a petition
signed by Sheridan Square residents alleged that "sidewalks in front of
our homes are filled with strangers in various stages of intoxication and
stupefaction . . . our streets are strewn with refuse—including glassine
envelopes commonly associated with narcotics—especially around the
Haven's premises; and we are treated to the tragic sight of youngsters
emerging from the premises in a state of advanced disorientation . . ." [3]
GAY detailed how,

On August 15, ten police forced their way into the club charging that liquor
was being sold. They left after finding no liquor on the premises. At 3:30 a.m.
on August 26, fire inspectors and five police entered the Haven to search for
fire violations. One hundred people were ordered from the club and five summonses were given for minor fire regulation violations.

On August 28, police again forced their way into the private club without
a search warrant. Over two hundred people were ejected from the club as
police searched for drugs. Police arrested managers and employees of the
club when some pills and marijuana were found on the floor. The six persons
arrested were taken to the precinct station, held overnight, and released in the
morning when charges against them were dismissed.

On August 29, the TPF were lining up waiting customers outside of the
club and fire inspectors came again to check fire regulations.[4] . . .

Police timing couldn't have been poorer. Two or three hundred GLFers, Gay Activists, and non-organization homosexuals had just returned from Times Square and what had been a peaceful protest against more than usually stepped-up end-of-summer/election-year harassment by New York City police. When the gays reached Sheridan Square what had begun as a mild melee near the Women's House of Detention turned into a full-blown riot in which cars were overturned, a record and jewelry shop looted, and in which, by GAY estimates, over one thousand persons took part.

In early August, the [Randy] "Wicker Basket" in GAY informed that police had "launched a quasilegal crackdown on those cruising Third Avenue between 53rd and 59th Streets. Between three and seventeen people were taken in each night, charged with loitering [the August *Mattachine Times* specified, "The section of the law involved was not 'loitering for a deviate sex act,' but plain 'loitering' " [5]], not released on their own recognizance, and were held overnight. Each morning the D.A. would refuse to prosecute the cases and they were then thrown out of court." [6] Mattachine remarked how harassment "sporadically pops up to remind us of the 'old days.' " [7]*

As arrest totals spiraled—despite warnings by the gay militant organizations that they would not be able to forestall homosexual rioting—GAY published a comprehensive account, which noted threats, harassment, and arrests of over three hundred homosexuals throughout the city in August: [8]

. . . At Christopher's End, three employees were arrested and three customers were charged with sodomy. On Third Avenue, fifteen people were arrested in one night. On Christopher Street, police have told people not to stand and talk to each other on the street.

In Times Square, homosexuals have been threatened and taken into alleys. Five legal observers from Gay Activists Alliance were handcuffed, put into police cars, and driven to the 14th Precinct Police Station, where they were questioned and released. Paddywagons have been used to bus people to the police station. And a transit authority bus filled with police has been seen repeatedly sitting on the corner of 42nd Street and 7th Avenue near the Allied Chemical Building.

On 42nd Street, one policeman took the ID of a homosexual and then told him he would be arrested for not having an ID . . . Two drag queens were in Playland (an arcade) with a straight couple. As soon as they all stepped outside, the drag queens were arrested for loitering.

Police stand on 42nd Street and say to passing homosexuals, "Move out of the way." People are taken into [cinema] lobbies off the street and searched . . . a drag was pulled into a police car, driven into an alley, and told by a

* A Mattachine-connected attorney was to sue the city for false arrest and harassment in three of the cases.

196

cop who held a billy club to his head, "I'm going to beat you to the ground, you obscene punk." . . .

Those homosexuals arrested have been charged with loitering, disorderly conduct, unlawful assembly, or solicitation. They are taken to the 14th Precinct Police Station, where they are booked. In the morning they are filed into court, where the prosecutor routinely says he is not pressing charges and the judge dismisses the cases. An annoyed judge is said to have told a policeman, "You're arresting people on petty charges. I don't want to be bothered." *Even though the cases are dismissed, those arrested will always have a police record on file recording their arrest.* [Italics mine.]

Gay militant clubs debated the problem. One night a young gay who had been arrested simply for "walking in the Times Square area" came to GLF to explain how he'd had to confess to being "guilty"—a night in jail would have cost him his job. This was the straw: GLF called a joint organizational meeting. Together with representatives from GAA and other clubs, a protest march was planned. Young GLFer Paul Aginsky visited a Gay Activists meeting to solicit the group's full endorsement. About the "annual clean-up," he groaned, "Is this America? I keep asking myself . . ." Arthur Evans stood: "*We* are people who have to be cleaned-up! . . . Homosexuals are *not* a forgotten people and are *not* garbage to be cleaned off the streets! The police obviously think that if they treat the people on 42nd Street as garbage nobody will protest!" President Jim Owles added feelingly, "The point is, *our people* are being harassed!"

The march was on. The *Village Voice* advised,[9] "It could be a block-buster, and it's planned for Saturday, August 29, at 8:30 p.m. in midtown's raunchy heartland, 42nd Street and Eighth Avenue."

Two medical stations, one at 42nd and Eighth and one at 42nd and Seventh, were set up; the usual gay marshals were trained to direct and contain the protesters. In mid-evening—when movie crowds were thickest—the throng of homosexuals, many of them uneasy, began to group in double-columns west from Eighth Avenue. Posters read: WHO WILL ARREST THE POLICE?—42ND ST.: SEIZE YOUR COMMUNITY—DESPERTEMOS LOCAS! DEFENDAMOS LO NUESTRO!—LESBIANS UNITE!—BUST POLICE FOR POLICE CORRUPTION. A Zolaesque GAA flyer warned:

WE PUBLICLY ACCUSE

```
POLICE (by order of Police Commissioner Leary):
      of illegal arrests of homosexuals
      of verbal harassment of homosexuals
      of physical brutality against homosexuals


POLITICIANS:
      of official support for police savagery against
         homosexuals
```

of contempt for the social and political rights of
    homosexuals
Councilman Carol Greitzer:
of not protecting the citizens of her district

THE PUBLIC:
    of the crime of silence in the face of government-
        approved, police-enforced persecution against
        the homosexual community

THE PRESS:
    of negligence in not reporting the beatings and
        harassment of homosexuals throughout the city

A Red Butterfly leaflet fumed, "THE POLICE ARE RAIDING EVERY GAY AS-
SEMBLY PLACE IN THE CITY. EVERYWHERE GAYS ARE BEING SHOVED AROUND
BY POLICE." Admitting that "There is more to it than corruption" and that
"A majority of police probably do not take bribes from criminal organiza-
tions," it then went on to trace gay oppression to the capitalistic system:

    Oppressed peoples always regard the police as their
enemy. To understand why this is so, we must examine the role
of the police, and the role of the State.
    A lot of people believe in the liberal view of the State:
an impartial arbiter above selfish class interests, balancing
the claims of various special interest groups. The liberals
claim that a classless State presides over a pure democracy
based upon consent of the people.
    What a laugh! Gays know better than this. They have
seen how impartial police treatment of gays is.
    Police are armed agents of the State. They act in the
same interests that the State acts: the interests of Big
Money. Police; judges; legislators; elected and non-elected
officials; the military; members of the "secret government" of
the CIA, FBI, CID, etc. -- all of these agents of the State
respect the direct interests, values and ideologies of the
capitalist ruling class.
    In the society ruled by monopoly capital, the sacred
value is private ownership of the means of production, which
permits the Big Money class to live in fantastic luxury by
exploiting those who work. Religion is highly valued by the
capitalists because it promotes false consciousness, keeping
people from struggling for freedom and happiness in the real
world. Sex is bad, and sexual repression is used to keep
people in place, fearful and resigned to an unfree life. In
the capitalist society, young men are supposed to prove their
masculinity (heterosexual) by offering themselves as cannon
fodder; the gun becomes the cock; manhood is the ability to
take the lives of unarmed Vietnamese women and children.
    Homosexuality is very bad for the values of capitalism.
It is first of all sex, which is bad. Secondly, it goes
against religion. Third, homosexuality challenges the
mystique of the family, the basic unit of a class domination
society. . . .

"Immediately we need to form gay self-defense groups to defend ourselves from all forms of attack and harassment," the flyer added. Another flyer proposed, "GLF will be organizing classes in self-defense this fall. . . . We are getting to the point where we will be able to offer assistance (physical, legal, medical) to our sisters and brothers who are being attacked."

Gay marshals, assisted by city police, directed the marchers in a long, narrow file that encircled the cinema block between Eighth and Seventh Avenues. Gaped at by curious moviegoers and taunted by an old harridan near the Franklin Savings Bank who shouted, "You're going to hell!" the gays yelled back "We'll see you there!" and continued chanting, "Say it loud: Gay is proud!" . . . Howard Blum, in the *Village Voice*,[10] remembered,

Along the street, people paused to watch the marchers. Someone commented, "It's a better show than the movies." A hard-looking man in a T-shirt and bellbottoms, the nickname "Blue Eyes" tattooed on his forearm, stated, "They have every right. This is a free country and they should be left alone." . . .

Still chanting "Power to the people" or "Hey, hey, try it once the other way," the marchers proceeded to what was to be the end of the demonstration—the 14th Precinct station house. Three rows of police protected their sanctuary as the marchers filed past shouting, "End police harassment." A cop turned and said to a friend, "I'm surprised those fags could accomplish even this. They're fucked up, unnatural." Yet the demonstrators planned to accomplish more. High with the success of what a member of the Gay Liberation Front described as a "beautiful, proud march," a cry of "On to Christopher Street" was met with joyous approval. Spontaneously they were off.

Proceeding down Seventh Avenue toward the Village, the marchers relaxed. The chanting stopped. . . .

Suddenly a bottle crashed into the crowd. Then another, glass splintering the sidewalk. The police flashed their lights on the Penn Garden Hotel. [A gay male] lay with his head cut. Someone started crying. Someone else cursed. Yet the march continued, now moving faster. At 21st Street another marcher was picked off, a rock cutting his skull. One of the police cars following the protesters . . . was stopped to take the bleeding victim to the hospital. The officer refused. Still dazed and bleeding, the demonstrator was forced to wait for a passing cab.

Shaken but having nothing else to do but to proceed to the protection of the bright lights of the Village, the march continued. Reaching Greenwich Avenue, the protesters were greeted by the street queens like soldiers coming home from battle. They shouted at the marchers, "Hiya fellahs" and "Right on." Propelled by a new burst of energy and success, the marchers continued, now joined by the Village's three biggest commodities—the concerned, the curious, and the bored. Almost by accident they bumped into the Women's House of Detention. Now the crowd had a symbol. The building was circled and the night filled with shouts of "Free our sisters, free ourselves." The noise, the soft flashing of the patrol car lights, and the presence of the police signaled that something was up. A Saturday night crowd gathered around the action. Suddenly, from high atop the House of Detention, a shrill plea echoed down to the crowd, "Power to the people." The assemblage cheered and applauded this virtuoso performance. Yet, again inexplicably, they moved on.

Heading toward Sheridan Square, the numbers of the crowd swelled. Aimlessly following the lights, the crowd bumped into a "fire inspection" of the Haven . . . The area was filled with pretty people with too much time and too much money . . . Kids being raped by lethargy. This mixture of militants and the bored was a volatile one. Push once more came to shove as the cops tried to clear the area in front of the Haven. But this time they were not pushing some druggie from Westchester, but a veteran of a long and tiring march. This kid pushed back. Immediately the cops attacked, truncheons swinging, clearing the area. . . . No longer able to proceed, the marchers now regrouped by the Women's House of Detention. Unwittingly, the cops had created allies and forced them to make a stand.

Outside the House of Detention the chanting continued. Again they were joined by the inmates' shouting from the towers, "Freedom. Freedom." Instantly, almost magically, like a giant fiery tear from heaven, a flaming paper bag drifted down from a high, barred window. This was followed by three more, flames burning brightly against the clear summer night. The crowd cheered at the spectacle. Almost unnoticed, more police arrived on the scene.

. . . The police charged, forcing most of the crowd into 8th Street. Arrests were made. . . . Again another police charge. The police racing into 8th Street, bodies wildly in motion. . . .

The battle lines are drawn. Eighth Street has been liberated. An army propelled by a relentless energy . . . About 40 TPF men wait across the Avenue of the Americas. The air is filled with tension; everyone knows that this Maginot Line will also be crossed. A volley of bottles is shelled upon the police. That is their signal. They charge.* One heroic (crazy?) streetfighter rushes out to meet them, picking his man and felling him with a karate kick to the chin. . . .

Blum wrote that by 2:00 a.m. the streets were finally almost empty, but that "From a window near the top of the House of Detention a solitary voice cries, 'Powah. Powah.'"

Some homosexuals may have known that the after-hours Psychedelic Shack, a gay club, was raided at that same hour, the club left unlocked and later vandalized after suffering $1,000 in damages by police. The following Friday morning police gave the Haven its coup de grace, smashing bars, discotheque machines, railings, speakers, refrigerators, and toilets and searching eighty people. Of the ten arrested, charges of loitering to secure narcotics were dismissed by the court.[11] The *New York Post* quoted the Haven owner's assessment of damages as $75,000. "What does this

* *The Advocate* told that "A black man in a white jump suit, who was standing watching the melee, was ordered by a policeman to move. Confused, he turned the wrong way. He was beaten to the pavement. Another young man got a nightstick across his nose." (September 30–October 13, 1970.)

have to do with a search for narcotics? This is wanton destruction," he said.[12] Don Schanche's observation in *The Panther Paradox: A Liberal's Dilemma* (New York, 1970) is not unsimilar. He states, "there seems little doubt to me that there is an unuttered police conspiracy acting against the Black Panther Party. It doesn't take much imagination to see that kind of lawless police hostility expanding to include the repression of other 'power groups' in our society, such as their own civilian political leadership, the press, disagreeable political parties and any other group that threatens police freedom of action. Such a prospect is far more terrifying than the cries of enraged black children to 'off the pigs.' "[13]

As with the Stonewall riots, there was a Sunday revival attempt. A "Flaming Faggot"* reported, in RAT, that

It was GLF who chose to continue the struggle . . . with the knowledge that a Village Sunday afforded less protection (in the form of tourist bystanders) than a Village Saturday night. Some understandably did not choose to go and maybe as few as fifty of us set out down the dark streets, our chants ringing out on the night air. But approaching the Village, we found that the street people, almost (amazingly) in the same numbers as before, were there, already angry, already thinking of moving out. We were faced with a higher level of anger than some of us had bargained for. And there were clubbings and six more arrested.**

"Only afterwards," said the writer, "did people begin to realize how different it was from the Stonewall riot of a year ago, the one that had begun it all to our complete amazement and joy then that we, too, could move toward revolutionary struggle. Different: because we now accepted struggle as a fact of our lives . . ."[14]

Gay Flames praised GLF members who, over the next forty-eight hours,

were present in Court for each arraignment, and to date, GLF has posted $1500 bail *** and provided lawyers (with sincere thanks to The Lawyer's Commune and The National Lawyer's Guild) and aid to each and every person arrested, without question. Incidental expenses taking people to and from hospitals, money for car-fare and food for those without funds, etc., have amounted to another $100-odd. None of this money has gone to GLF members: only four of the people arrested belonged to GLF and none of those required bail or financial assistance.[15]

In a *Come Out!* report, Martha Shelley regretted damages done to stores and automobiles, and pointed out that "Several of the people on the march are of the opinion that agents provocateurs were among us—throw-

* Of a GLF men's consciousness-raising group which used that name.
** Monday's New York *Daily News* cited eighteen arrests from the Saturday-night riot and told that "seven cops were hurt, including one knifed . . ."
*** A women's lib group contributed $250.

ing bottles from the rear while the people up front got clubbed, encouraging acts of violence and vandalism for which others got blamed." [16]

The New York Times, which took little notice of the protest and riot, reported instead a Sunday news conference held at the Church of the Holy Apostles, where a group of eleven GLFers and Radicalesbians detailed reasons for the protest march by homosexuals.[17] In the meantime, Gay Activists Alliance (which did not participate, as an organization, in the riot: at 18th Street, president Jim Owles had the GAA banner folded and told Activists they were on their own if they continued) sought a new meeting with police officials. Owles spoke to GAY: "The anger and frustration of the gay community is more understandable when you take into account that despite promises of coordination and support, solutions were not forthcoming from the establishment. The police again picked prime hours on a weekend night, the very night of our protest demonstration . . . There should be some sort of cease fire, with both sides realizing the things we want cannot be attained by matching violence with violence." [18] The men of *Gay Flames* could not foresee any post-election/after-summer ceasefire: "The real reason for the stepped-up police activity is that the pigs are up-tight at the new sense of pride and militancy emerging from the gay community. Have you watched your brothers and sisters on the streets recently? Being gay, talking gay, walking gay, wearing buttons, holding hands, kissing hello or good-bye. Coming out of the closets and out of the shadows." [19]

■

At a Gay Activists Alliance meeting on August 6, Arthur Evans rose to speak for the Political Action Committee. He was angry. GAA had held a dance in the spacious subcellar of New York University's Weinstein Hall, a freshman dormitory, in early summer but was denied rental permission for a second dance when officials discovered the group was a gay one. He thundered what he felt: "We have a right to use their space! If they deny this right to us, we will attack them: that means we will have a demonstration *or* a sit-in *or* a disruption (however the membership here decides). . . . We were denied the hall because we were a homosexual group—groups use it, homosexual groups thus far have not. They never ask anybody whether they are a heterosexual group. The very fact that that question has been asked us is a form of oppression; there's no reason why *anybody* should ask us, as a group, whether we are homosexual or heterosexual.

"Secondly," he went on, "that university is a part of the community of Greenwich Village, and has, in the opinion of the Political Action Committee, a responsibility to that community. A large proportion of that community is gay; the university has consistently done absolutely nothing for the gay community. We are in desperate need of space—for dances, for business meetings . . . They have denied us that space because we are gay. In the opinion of the committee that is a form of oppression, it must be challenged. If they resist, they must be confronted and disrupted!"

Jim Owles strode to the front of the room and added: "NYU, besides that, also receives an indirect subsidy from every gay person in New York because it enjoys a tax-exempt status. And if they can discriminate, then in my opinion they can't expect me indirectly to subsidize them. Furthermore, they have used their right—as a university, and with the powerful public they have—to expand whenever they want to, simply to take a huge chunk of our community (of the straights' community, too) and build it into a gigantic parking lot or new library or new lounge . . . In other words, they've been taking and taking and taking. It's about time they started giving a little bit."

Randy Wicker differed with the two speakers: "If you go down to NYU and start getting aggressive, I'm reminded of the old civil-rights dictum 'Bricks through windows don't open doors.' We get a lot of adverse publicity; NYU is disrupted; homosexuals sit in the lobby of Weinstein Hall; *'there was a small ruckus when YAK supporters jumped on the GAA people and a window was broken . . .'*; everyone in the Village immediately says, 'GAA spells trouble! And as a property owner, even if I might consider renting to them, I'd better not because we know that violence and disruptions occur where they are.' " *

GAA was able to find a church hall for its next dance, and, busy "politically," did not press NYU further. The Christopher Street Liberation Day Committee did, however. An all-organization gay group that coordinated the June 28 celebrations of the Stonewall riots, its members had not disbanded until they might commence plans for 1971 but hoped, as an ongoing club, to initiate legal, medical, and housing services for the gay community. Dances would provide needed funds. In negotiations with the Student Governing Association of Weinstein Hall, CSLDC scheduled a series of Friday-night "Dance-a-Fairs" in the subcellar, August 7 to September 4. NYU officials, who learned that the dances were for homosexuals, overruled the student commission following the third dance;

* Wicker's fears of Villagers' distrust of gay militancy were to be proven correct. Following the raids on gay after-hours clubs and the late-August riots, straight *and* homosexual residents and owners of licensed, legal gay bars complained to the chairman of the Greenwich Village Urban Action Task Force about "homosexual ruffians" and noise and obscenities shouted in the streets. One lesbian, a Village resident, said, "The Village is a powder keg which might explode at any minute. If the backlash succeeds here, the whole town is going to close up tighter than it did in 1960." (GAY, October 26, 1970.)

In summer 1970, Los Angeles GLF distributed to fellow-gays a mini-flyer: *"Residents have the Right to Sleep and You have the Right to Cruise! Cruise Early or on Business Streets:* The local residents have complained to the police department that and people talking late at night on the side streets. They are not complaining about you are disturbing them at night with cars speeding up and down residential streets what you are doing and do not want the *Vice* to come down on you. We are here to protect you and to show the police department that we do not need the "vice squad" to solve our community relations."

203

the university insisted that students had no right to deal with non-university organizations.* GAY detailed how,[20] "through the offices of Mrs. Bella Abzug, the Committee retained the services of an NYCLU lawyer. Discussions between the Christopher Street Liberation Day Committee and the NYU administration saved dancing space for August 21st and negotiations were to be held regarding any further dances at the Weinstein facility."

The Mattachine Society had earlier been rebuffed, similarly, by NYU in an attempt to rent Town Hall, a subsidiary unit of the university, "for an evening of special entertainment for its members and the homosexual community in general." MSNY reported that the Chancellor of the university feared "bad publicity and bad press." The society sought aid from Mrs. Abzug, Representative Edward Koch, and the New York Civil Liberties Union.[21]

GAY continued, that "Because of the many legal technicalities and restrictions imposed by the NYU administration with regard to these negotiations, Gay Student Liberation–NYU, the on-campus gay group, decided to hold the dance scheduled for August 28th." Earlier that week, CSLDC had asked GSL if they, as an NYU organization, would sponsor the dance. *Gay Flames* records that "GSL agreed and went to the administration. For any other chartered student group, it would have been automatic, but these people were *homosexuals* and for the Deans that was a horse of a different sex." [22] The GSLers "were informed that now it had been decided to close all NYU facilities to all gay social functions until it (the administration) had decided whether or not *homosexuality is morally acceptable!* The basis given for this decision was said to be NYU's responsibility to impressionable freshmen who, the Vice-Chancellor in charge of student affairs was willing to acknowledge, *could* swing both ways!" [23]

At 8:30 p.m., Friday, August 28, twenty-four hours before their Times Square protest march, gay liberationists circled, furious, in front of Weinstein Hall. Shouting "NYU is really through!" and "Free Bobby!" and "Gimme a G . . ." they swung hastily lettered signs: NYU IS A SEXIST PLOT!—TO LOVE, GAYS MUST FIGHT!—WE WILL FIGHT FOR A PLACE TO EXIST! A composite of GLFers, Committee members, Gay Activists, Radicalesbians, and the university's own GSL paced together, ogled by a growing crowd of spectators. *Gay Flames* recorded what happened:

About 9:30 the City Pigs arrived. There wasn't too much they could do except block off University Place. In fact, they played it pretty cool. (Must

*Had CSLDC been a student group it might have fared no better. *Mattachine Times* has reported that "GLF at the University of Michigan was refused use of the Student Union for meetings after the director objected to a 'guerrilla theatre' performance" in which it participated. "The issue is sticky, as the director may not have authority to deny use of the building to a group recognized by the Student Government Council, as GLF is." (August 1970.)

have thought we were all students—not "just" people off the streets.) The Kampus Kops were pretty up-tight and they called around until they got Mr. Hogg. Supposedly, he was the highest NYU man in town. The Kops told him that the weather was threatening and so he trotted out of his closet to see if he could avert the thunderstorm.

About 20 of us went on over to Dean Whiteman's office. Hogg asked who represented us and we told him it was all or none. We went on in to the plushly carpeted office. Hogg tried to "reason" with us, like the sweet liberal he was. But 6,000 years of persecution has turned gay people off to reason and this movement is not "reasonable" any more.

We told him it was Weinstein Hall or stormy weather. He looked at us and he knew we meant it. We weren't hiding in our closets and we had a foot wedged in his. So, after a little while, he gave in and said we'd have it. We ran back over and told the people who were still marching the news. Another win for GAY POWER. We have met the enemy and the hall is ours!

We had to wait a while until the Kops found the key, but we got in. Then a brother went off to get a stereo. And other sisters and brothers went for ice and beer. We danced even without the music. And we rapped with each other. Everyone was just about as stoned as we'd been on June 28.[24] *

But the NYU capitulation was merely a tactical retreat, and its decision to allow neither non-university homosexuals nor its own Gay Student Liberation to hold dances in Weinstein stood pat. On Sunday evening, September 20, at about 10:00, members of GSL entered the general meeting of Gay Liberation Front to recruit volunteers for an immediate sit-in in the Weinstein subcellar. A contingent of seventy strong, including members of CSLDC, Radicalesbians, Gay Activists,** Gay Youth,*** and others, was ensconced within an hour in the dormitory's deserted depths. The occupation was to last five days. RAT observed that "Fairly soon, the press showed up, but GSL policy was to hand out a press release and not to give interviews to the sexist press. . . . Soon, everyone was settled in. One lesbian drank coffee and read The Bust Book, in obvious anticipation. A groupuscule of gays formed a flying squad to produce and distribute leaflets along the Drag Strip, that is, Greenwich Avenue and Christopher Street, and soon the entire gay community was represented. During the next five days, gays from all over the city came to sit a while in Weinstein Hall." [25] RAT told how

The freshman class were somewhat disconcerted, but not nearly as much as the House Commission [a group of graduate students]. The students voted overwhelmingly to support the gay occupation, and to treat the gays as their guests in the dormitory. Some sent down blankets, for the Administration had turned up the air conditioning in an effort to freeze people out. . . .

* Gay Scene noted that it "was not a total victory for the Committee since the air-conditioning mysteriously went off and no one could be found to repair it"! (No. 4.)
** GAA as an organization did not support the sit-in.
*** GY was an under-21 group of gay liberationists; see pages 214–16.

Every once in a while, some straight student would come down to the laundry room to peek at the freaks, and sometimes he or she would stop to chat the next time. Many of us spent time explaining our life styles, scrounging for doughnuts, and passing out whatever information we had about things on the outside . . .

Arthur Bell of GAA, who passed many hours at the sit-in, wrote [26] that on Tuesday at Weinstein, "a floor by floor vote was taken and the two-to-one decision among the students was to support the sit-in, to allow Weinstein to open its facilities to Gay Student Liberation; a unanimous decision was reached about not calling the cops." On Wednesday night, sit-ins met with a newly formed New York University Liberation Front and sent out a call for more "squatters" from the gay community.

Gay Flames called the occupation "long and grueling"—although many sit-ins went home to sleep, returned when they could spare a few hours, others curled up on tables and doubled chairs as best they could.

But more than anything it was gay; it was different from other sit-ins. Long lines of gay people bunny-hopping to "Power to the people!", chanting, dancing, stomping, high on the people . . . " 'cause there ain't enough pigs/in the whole wide world/to stop gay liberation/from serving the people/POWER!" We played charades. We played spin-the-bottle—all kinds of us together— transvestites, middle-class people, students. A lot of barriers and fears were broken down. We were coming together. In love—together. Strong and proud together.[27]

Thursday evening, Bell recorded, "An important meeting was held at Weinstein with the squatters and the student body. The students drew up a contract supporting the sit-in and honoring a dance that we would schedule for the following night. After the dance, we were to negotiate again for further action." But on Friday, after five days of hesitation, the "Administration fucked up both the students and the gays—and in the long run, themselves. They called the cops and busted 29 people who were in Weinstein that early afternoon." RAT sympathized that students had been led by the administration to believe that they could run the dorm as they chose, then officials "chained up the subcellar, and informed people that it was to be closed until Monday noon, and that the contract between the students and the Gay Student Liberation was voided. So much for student autonomy." That afternoon, a leaflet nevertheless announced "GAY PROTEST RALLY–DANCE, 8:00 p.m., Weinstein Hall"; ran through the week's sit-in story; and revealed that the "administration gave us only 10 seconds to leave, then the TPF Pigs [*Gay Flames* recounted how, "Hitting their clubs against their hands, they started counting"] 'escorted' us out"—"We left peacefully but we will be back."

The Saturday *New York Post* attested [28] that "Some 400 Gay Liberation supporters showed up outside the dorm last night, determined to have their dance. School guards refused to admit them to the building, so they took to the street outside and challenged TPF police to move them. Instead the cops shut the street to traffic and waited out the crowd . . ." It marched and chanted and sang. *Gay Flames* recalled that "At one point, plainclothes pigs followed some straight pot-smokers into the crowd and dragged them out. Quickly the gays surrounded them to try to help. But the pigs pulled out their pieces, hitting one sister with a gun butt [or brass knuckles; accounts differ] and threatening to shoot if the gays did not move back. One brother, trying to get the names of those arrested, was himself arrested for 'assault.' " Though some street transvestites wanted to remain on the Weinstein steps, the crowd of gays dwindled away in early-morning hours. Saturday night saw only some leafleting and anti-climactic pacing.

The NYU student daily, *Washington Square Journal,* took favorable note of the gay sit-in. On Tuesday, September 29, it presented [29] the "other side" in an explanation by Dr. Allan Cartter, Chancellor of the university, who wrote that "the situation had passed beyond the bounds of an internal matter of students' rights and responsibilities." He affirmed that "The residence halls have never had the authority to rent out facilities to outside groups," though the "University had stated that it had no objection to the use of the sub-cellar by recognized student groups primarily for NYU students." He observed that Gay Student Liberation, "reported to have only half a dozen members, was acting—as events later indicated—as a front for the outside agencies."

In Wednesday's *Journal,* Colleen Sullivan reported [30] "a quiet press conference" on the steps of Vanderbilt Hall by some twenty representatives of gay organizations. They had arrived at the law school to present their demands to President James Hester, who was not in his offices. Some of the women and men marched in a circle, chanting "Diamond Jim Hester, Diamond Jim Hester, Where are you, where are you? Hiding in the closet, hiding in the closet, We see you, we see you, at NYU." Sullivan quoted a gay spokesman, Jim Clifford, who was also an NYU employee: "The Village is the largest gay ghetto in the world, and the University, as a guest in this community, should take its responsibility to the community seriously. That's why our demands are focused on community needs."

Leafleted, the "GAY DEMANDS" were:

```
WHEREAS NYU IS LOCATED IN THE LARGEST GAY GHETTO IN THE
WORLD, POSSESSES LAND, BUILDINGS AND MONEY, AND USES POLICE
AND OTHER LIBERAL INSTITUTIONS TO MAINTAIN ITS POSITION OF
EXPLOITING AND HOLDING POWER OVER THE GAY COMMUNITY AND
EVERY SURROUNDING COMMUNITY,

WE DEMAND:   1)   Space for a 24-hour gay community center, to
                  be controlled by the gay community
             2)   Any community center space demanded of NYU
                  by other communities
```

3) Open enrollment and free tuition for gay people and all people from the communities NYU oppresses

4) Open employment for gay people and all people NYU oppresses, with adequate pay as determined by employees

5) Facilities and funds for 24-hour child care centers controlled by the communities.

WHEREAS NYU CONTROLS BELLEVUE BUTCHER SHOP,* WHICH EXPLOITS GAY PEOPLE AND OTHER OPPRESSED PEOPLE IN THE NYU GHETTO,

WE DEMAND: 1) An end to the oppression of homosexuals and all people in Bellevue Psychiatric Prison -- the end of shock treatment, drugs, imprisonment and mental poisoning

2) Free medical care, dental care and preventive medicine under community control, including free abortion controlled by community women, with no forced abortion and no forced sterilization, without regard to age or obtaining permission from anybody

3) Open employment for homosexuals and all people in the communities NYU oppresses, with adequate pay as determined by employees, including 24-hour child care for employees' and patients' children, controlled by the communities.

WHEREAS NYU ALLEGES TO BE AN EDUCATIONAL INSTITUTION,

WE DEMAND: 1) NYU stop teaching lies and myths about homosexuals

2) Homosexual history and culture and the truth of gay oppression be taught in every area of study

3) Students in medicine, nursing, education, law, social work, etc., be taught how those professions oppress gays and be educated to work against the mechanisms of oppression

4) All NYU students, employees and faculty have the right to be openly gay, without fear of retaliation by NYU.

Gays' biggest pitch was yet to come. On Monday, October 5, they let NYU have it, in three separate demonstrations from noon to mid-evening. From the West Coast, *The Advocate* told: [31] "At noon, 25 demonstrators picketed Loeb [Student Center] carrying signs reading, NYU MUST SERVE THE COMMUNITY, COME OUT OF YOUR IVORY TOWERS AND INTO THE STREETS, GO GAY—BEAT NYU, and AN ARMY OF LOVERS CANNOT LOSE. The demonstrators chanted 'Gay Power' and '2–4–6–8, NYU teaches

* Issue No. 7 of *Gay Flames* presents an interview by Arthur Bell and Sylvia (Rey) Rivera (of STAR; see page 209) with a black male transvestite, GAY PRISONER IN BELLEVUE. See also Don Jackson's DACHAU IN AMERICA, in *Gay Sunshine*, November 1970; and KONCENTRATION KAMPS FOR GAYS, *Gay Flames*, No. 8.

hate.' " In mid-afternoon, a silent vigil of about thirty gays watched outside the 30th Street psychiatric division of Bellevue Hospital. At 8:00 p.m., an assemblage of sixty persons heard gays speak, outside Loeb Student Center, condemning the NYU decision to ban gay dances on the grounds that homosexuality was not moral or a valid life-style.

The October 5 gay protests, as well as the Weinstein Hall sit-in, lacked the full support of the homosexual community and its organizations and may have had little immediate effect on NYU and Establishment American thinking. It was a beginning. Interestingly, it realized Angelo d'Arcangelo's expostulation [32] in *The Homosexual Handbook* two years previous:

. . . as homosexuals we must avoid and discourage any organization that discriminates against homosexualism in any way, because as citizens we are guaranteed "life, liberty and the pursuit of happiness." Therefore, any organization, federally funded—or to be more explicit, for which we pay through taxes—that attempts to chastise or discriminate against the free citizenry because of sexual habits or preferences or even inclinations, is unfair, illegal, and un-American. . . . The wonderful equality we enjoy as Americans is the equality of oppression.

■

RAT remarked that during the Weinstein Hall sit-in, "Some homeless transvestites ate a square meal for the first time all summer in the student cafeteria." [33]

Street transvestites sparkled at the subcellar protest. It was they who, in Queens director Lee Brewster's assertion about the Stonewall riots, "stood up and yelled first and the loudest" [34]; their support of gay protests increased in proportion as homosexual organizations chucked off anti-"femme" prejudices. Out of the "Weinstein Affair" came an organization, Street Transvestites for Gay Power, later renamed STAR, for Street Transvestite Action Revolutionaries. STAR leafleted, "You people run if you want to, but we're tired of running. We intend to fight for our rights until we get them."

In October 1969, the first of the new organizations for transvestites and/or transsexuals was founded by Lee Brewster in New York. To GAY, Brewster gave his reasons: "Not one of [the gay organizations] is working for the drag queen, with the exception of the Erickson Foundation, which concentrates on transsexuals, not drags. It is now time for the 'drag' to place a little of 'her' energy and talent to support an organization that has 'her' as the CENTRAL figure . . ." [35] In a prospectus for Queens, Brewster cited two problems:

1) RIGHT TO CONGREGATE: The license for a drag ball or Masquerade/Costume ball clearly states that no men dressed in the female attire will be admitted as guests, under penalty of law.

a. We will attack the law shortly on the grounds it shows discrimination as it doesn't mention women in men's clothes.

b. That it is not enforced and everyone is under the opinion that it is legal, or that the police are collecting graft, to keep them from raiding the places.

2) RIGHT TO DRESS AS WE SEE FIT: We feel that the wearing of a particular article of clothing does not make one a criminal.

a. We hope to get a ruling adopting the law at present used in the state of Hawaii. This states that one may wear the clothes of the opposite sex as long as he does not deceive others. The wearing of a button stating that one is a male takes away all criminal aspects of wearing drag in the streets.

But Queens members, and other transvestites, had more in mind than costume balls and cross-dressing. In the first issue of Queens' magazine, DRAG, appeared: *"A Patriot for Me,* a play by John Osborne, opened October 1, 1969 to most unusual opening night activities. For the first time in Broadway's history a play was picketed by female impersonators! Several courageous impersonators donned their gowns, carried their signs, and marched up and down in front of the Broadway Theatre. Comments were extremely favorable about the female mimics, who stated their cause to interested passers-by and patrons." [36] The British play, pointedly anti-homosexual, featured a fin-de-siècle drag ball.

Angela Douglas (Key), a founder of Transvestite-transsexual Action Organization relates why she opted out of GLF: [37]

A number of transvestites and transsexuals participated in gay power demonstrations held by the Gay Liberation Front and other organizations in the Los Angeles area during 1969–70; over a period of time, these persons discovered that the members of GLF and other groups, as a whole, were not interested in preserving transvestism; indeed, many of the male homosexuals were extremely antitransvestic and wished for transvestites to participate in GLF actions solely for the shock value afforded by their presence.

Several transsexuals attended GLF meetings and demanded that the GLF take some action to have a transsexual clinic formed in the Los Angeles area similar to the one in San Francisco, and were ignored.

Neither was action taken by the GLF to end the discrimination against transvestites in many of the gay bars and clubs.

When a young male tv was brutally beaten by the LAPD and imprisoned for three months, the GLF totally ignored it, although it was brought to their attention several times. The tv had participated in three GLF demonstrations.

Douglas, a transvestite-becoming-transsexual, had worked in Los Angeles GLF in late 1969. Seeing a need for a separate organization for transvestites and transsexuals, she made announcements in February 1970 that such a group, called TAO, would organize. By late spring its several members participated in Gay Power demos as a group. Weekly meetings were rap sessions about their common problems. Douglas recalls that " 'Coming out parties' were held, where transvestites could meet and many of them wear the clothing they desired for the first time in their lives in the presence of other persons. . . . Individual transvestites, who had never gone out in public, were literally taken by the hand by more experienced tvs until they were able to adjust." No fees or dues were required. Douglas tells that

Businesses which accepted transvestic customers were listed and made available to members, welfare officials were contacted and several pre-operative transsexuals were able to obtain badly needed financial and medical assistance, and members instructed each other in the art of makeup, carriage . . . Feminine clothing was exchanged between members.

The GLF was contacted by several women's liberationists over the problem of transvestites and transsexuals who were participating in feminist groups. GLF contacted TAO, and several meetings were held and the problem discussed.

TAO's recommendations to women's lib were printed in *Come Out!*'s TRANSVESTITE & TRANSSEXUAL LIBERATION:

Transvestites: Male transvestites should not participate in Women's Liberation unless they publicly proclaim themselves as male transvestites and agree to any special limitations or conditions which may be imposed upon them by the particular feminist group.
Transsexuals: Partial and complete male to female transsexuals should be allowed to participate in Women's Liberation without any discrimination.[38]

But, Douglas added, "The overall consensus of the group seemed to be that transvestites and transsexuals should organize among themselves."

In June, TAO members attempted "to raise support for a massive demonstration against the film *Myra Breckinridge,* but this failed, and on June 28, shortly before the Christopher Street West parade in Hollywood, several TAO members picketed the theater showing the film and distributed leaflets demanding that the producers of the film donate a percentage of the profits to transsexual research." TAO's objections to the film were: "using a non-transsexual to portray a transsexual character, while hundreds of transsexuals were available; misinforming the general public about transsexualism; and simple exploitation of transsexualism." Douglas notes that "There has been no response from the film's producers."

Douglas was on hand when, following the June 28 parade, the Los Angeles homosexual minister Troy Perry (see Chapter 13) was arrested for "blocking the sidewalk." At his arraignment the next morning, she

observed a male to female pre-operative transsexual being arraigned with other *male* prisoners. The preop had been brutally beaten during the night by heterosexual male prisoners and this had been observed by Perry. Perry had

211

arranged for the transsexual's release. A few days later, during Perry's week-long hunger fast, Douglas met with a California state representative and demanded that action be taken to end the mixing of male to female transsexuals with heterosexual male prisoners in California. The representative was shocked and promised to take immediate action.

A third group, which placed emphasis on transsexuals, had its first meeting September 1, 1970, in New York City: T.A.T., for Transsexuals and Transvestites. It was a "non-profit organization designed to help transsexuals with sex-reassignment, and together with transvestites to bring about a better understanding of what the two groupings are and what characterizes each." Judy Bowen, a male-to-female pre-operative, was a founder of the group.

Gay militant organizations have eradicated much of the sexism that offended their more "masculine" sisters and more "feminine" brothers. A Philadelphia GLF newsletter protested, in August 1970, *"WHO LIKES DRAGS?* Gay Liberation Front welcomes any gay person, regardless of their sex, race, age, or social behavior. Though some other gay organizations may be embarrassed by drags or transvestites, GLF believes that we should accept all of our brothers and sisters unconditionally. Who are we to put up the butch ideal for society when some of our brothers are not, nor do they intend to butch it up for society." [39] A member of the New York GLF 17th Street commune told, in *Gay Flames*'s "Gay Liberation Packet." * how many male New Homosexuals have renounced the "butch" ideal:

Many of us in GLF *are* traitors to our sex, and to this sexist society. We reject "manhood," "masculinity," and all that. Rather than run from the "feminine" qualities we discover within us (and within all men), we are beginning to embrace them, and search for new ways to express our "masculine" and "feminine" natures without getting into role playing. Some of us wear makeup, dress in drag, or get our sex changed—the ultimate surrender of male privilege! Our means differ, but together we are shedding the levis and leather jackets that secured us in our closets, and with them, our fear of being recognized as "faggots." [40]

As, out of Angela Douglas's GLF experiences, TAO had begun, so did the Gay Liberation Front spawn Third World Gay Revolution, for non-white homosexuals, female and male. By the end of summer, TWGR, only a few weeks old, had two consciousness-raising groups—and a leaflet statement (in English and Spanish), "The Oppressed Shall Not Become the Oppressors," which affirmed that, struggling to become "men," "Third World men have always tried to reach this precarious position by climbing on the backs of women and homosexuals," and described the new group's

* Pamphlet No. 11, "An Introduction to Gay Liberation," by Guy Nassberg. The article is a revision of one originally published in New Haven's underground paper *View From The Bottom.*

212

threefold oppression: "1) We are oppressed as people because our humanity is routinely devoured by the carnivorous system of Capitalism. 2) We are oppressed as Third World people by the economically inherent racism of white Amerikan society. 3) We are oppressed by the sexism of the white society and the verbal and physical abuse of masculinity-deprived Third World males."

Advocating that "the system must be changed," that "Socialism is the answer," TWGR published its goals and beliefs in *Gay Flames*.[41] They were, in brief:

1) We want the right of self-determination for all third world and gay people, as well as control of the destinies of our communities. . . .
2) We want the right of self-determination over the use of our bodies; the right to be gay, anytime, anyplace. The right to free physiological change and modification of sex on demand. The right of free dress and adornment. . . .
3) We want full protection of the law and social sanction for all modes of human sexual self-expression.* . . .
4) We want liberation for women. We want free and safe birth control in-formation and devices on demand. We want free 24-hour child care centers controlled by those who use them. We want access for women to fill all edu-cational opportunities. We want truthful teaching of women's history. We want an end to preferential hiring against women and oppressed national minor-ities. . . .
5) We want the abolition of the bourgeois nuclear family.

We believe that it perpetuates the false categories of homosexuality and heterosexuality by creating sex roles and sex definitions. The nuclear family propagates capitalism. The woman is an instrument of production. . . .
6) We want a free educational system that teaches us our true identity and history, and presents the entire range of human sexuality without advocating any one form or style; that sex roles and sex-determined skills not be fostered by the schools; that language be modified so that no gender takes priority. . . .
7) We want full employment for third world and gay people. . . .
8) We want decent housing, fit for the shelter of human beings. . . .
9) We want all third world and gay people, when brought to trial, to be tried by a people's court with a jury of their peers from their community. A peer is a person from similar social, economic, geographical, racial, historical, environmental and sexual background. We have been and are being tried by all-white sexist juries that have no understanding of the average third world gay woman or man. . . .
10) We want an immediate end to police brutality and murder of third world and gay people. . . .
11) We want all third world and gay men to be exempt from military service. We also want an immediate end to military oppression both at home and abroad.

* In *Come Out!*, December 1970–January 1971, the statement was altered to "for all human sexual self-expression and pleasure between consenting persons, including youth."

We believe that third world and gay people should not be forced to fight in the military service to defend a racist and sexist government that does not represent us. . . .

12) We want an end to all organized religions because they aid in the genocide of third world and gay people by teaching hatred and superstition.

We believe that organized religions are an instrument of capitalism, and therefore an enemy of the people. . . .

13) We want a new society—a socialist society. We want liberation, food, shelter, clothing, transportation, health care, employment, and utilities for all. We want a society where the needs of our people come first. . . .

As GLF had given birth to organizations for transvestites and transsexuals and for Third World people, so did it sire Gay Youth—for those under-21's who decided it would be easier to relate to less-than-adults; non-student adolescent gays who found GLF largely unappealing had available no place to relate to their homosexuality. Student Homophile Leaguer Bob Martin had affirmed, in *Gay Power,* that "Most of the city's homophile groups won't touch young kids for fear of being labeled 'dirty old men/women.' As far as I know only the college groups and GLF are willing to help these kids out." [42] Ian Edelstein told *Come Out!* that members of Gay Youth "felt distinct differences between their attitudes and those of old Homosexuals on various sexual, social and political issues"; they intended, also, to avoid "rhetoric" and "political ideologies." [43]

Gay Youth's goals were, as a flyer detailed, "both political and social (with an accent on social). We wish to bring together young gay people who have so far been out of touch with the gay community and gay life in general, as well as all young gays." A consciousness-raising session was to be part of GY general meetings. On "Homosexual News,"* over New York radio station WBAI, Mark Segal, a nineteen-year-old leader of the organization, has attested to the difficulty of gay consciousness for the gay under-21: "At first I was having sex with somebody but I didn't realize that I was gay. It was just something I was doing. Then I realized I was gay, and thought, 'My God, I can't tell my parents!' . . . This sort of hits you. I don't think most people know they're gay when they're first having sex with another man or woman." [44] "Most important of all," stated GY's leaflet-introduction, "our group gives a chance for young gay people to make gay friends their own age, and to meet people in similar situations." The group planned to recruit members from high

* In late summer 1968, WBAI announcer Charles Pitts went on the air after midnight using his real name and speaking as a homosexual. A month after, the station started a once-a-week half-hour series, "The New Symposium," which was devoted to interviewing homosexuals; sometimes its producer-moderator and his assistant (Baird Searles and Pitts) merely discussed news of homosexual interest. A year later, Pitts and Pete Wilson were co-producers. In spring 1970, the show's name was changed to "Homosexual News," but its time span was reduced to fifteen minutes.

schools, by means of the press, within the gay community, and "wherever young people congregate." In late 1970, Gay Youth was organizing in Philadelphia,* San Francisco, Chicago, Tampa, Detroit, and Ann Arbor.

New York GY has considered "age chauvinism." Segal argues that "A lot of groups are asking for the sodomy law to be retracted—it's all right for two consenting adults, twenty-one years or older, to do it as long as they are not hurting each other. . . . What about younger people?"

The first issue of New York GY's *Gay Journal,* in November 1970, showed its consciousness of the gay liberation movement. It listed "Gay Movement News," including:

- Louisville, Kentucky—The University of Kentucky has a class in gay liberation with the consent of the administration.
- Seattle, Washington—Seattle GLF has launched an educational program in the streets.**
- Boston, Massachusetts—Boston GLF has been leafleting all the major shopping centers and subways concerning gay liberation.
- Hartford, Connecticut—Kalos [Society] held a confrontation picnic demonstrating the right of gays to assemble freely in the City of Hartford.
- Tallahassee, Florida—The GLF group at [Florida State University] has not received recognition by the administration to organize and hold meetings on campus. They need support. Right on, brothers and sisters!
- Denver, Colorado—Denver GLF has organized guerrilla theater activity for educating college students on campus.
- Sydney, Australia—A Sydney GLF *** is being formed and members are being recruited.
- Chicago, Illinois—There has been a split in Chicago GLF over policy. A new group was formed: The Chicago Gay Alliance. The new group believes in working within the American system and GLF does not believe this will work. . . .

* Philadelphia GLF leafleted that "GY will serve in the following capacities. 1) To act as a basic introduction to GLF; 2) Trying to relate to ourselves as fellow oppressed human beings and not just as sexual objects; 3) 'Coming Together' in the sense of getting our heads together, determining where we are in the gay world, and finding alternatives to the depressing scene at Rittenhouse Square and all that it connotes."

** Seattle GLF was quoted in *Gay Sunshine* (August–September 1970) describing how it "leafleted the Unitarian Church when they held their recent convention in Seattle and voted favorably on a proposal to legalize homosexual-bisexual behavior."

*** GY was inaccurate. *The* [Sydney] *Old Mole* printed CAMP (Campaign Against Moral Persecution) Inc.'s announcement on October 26. Admitting that they felt like saying "2—4—6—8, Gay is just as good as Straight!", co-founders Christabel Poll and John Ware insisted that "we would get nowhere at present if we got out in the streets and shouted it. . . . We concluded that, at this stage, as far as the wider society is concerned, we should concentrate on providing information, removing prejudice, ignorance and fear, stressing the ordinariness of homosexuality and generally reassuring and disarming those with hostile attitudes. Concerning homosexuals, we think a policy of development of confidence and lessening of feelings of isolation and guilt, where they exist, is vital."

In *Come Out!,* Martha Shelley, who spoke at an April rally in Grant Park at the invitation of University of Chicago Gay Liberation, noticed the lack of a strong Left in that city. Illustrating further Chicago gay liberation's lack of unanimity, she pointed out that "Chicago is a city of neighborhoods, with no central area like the Village, so there is a North Side GLF and a Hyde Park GLF, and GLFs on every campus in northern Illinois." [45]

Gay liberation got started in Chicago after a UC student put an advertisement in the student newspaper asking, "Tired of prejudice? Do something about it! Gay Liberation now!! Call . . ." Henry Wiemhoff, who placed the ad, has outlined Chicago gay lib's 1969–70 history: [46]

Beginning in December 1969 as a group of ten, male and female, University of Chicago Gay Liberation developed an ideology and program of social and personal liberation, and adopted as its slogan, "Out of the closets, into the streets." In a series of actions, we danced as Gay people at University straight dances, picketed a notorious Chicago policeman as he spoke to the Women's Bar Association in the Loop, and held the city's first public Gay dances, first on campus and then at the Coliseum, attracting up to 2,000 at a time. Together with the ACLU, we successfully challenged the Vice Squad's policy of defining Gay dancing as public indecency and therefore subject to arrest. We found ourselves repeatedly on radio and TV talk shows and were invited to speak to high school sociology classes.

Having established a precedent for Gay dancing, we then demanded that the bars allow dancing, and when they refused, called a boycott and began a picket of the Normandy, the largest. After several negotiating sessions, they acceded to the demands, which also called for no discrimination against women, no hustling of drinks, and the freedom to express physical affection. When, on the day the agreement was to go into effect, the owners announced there would be no *slow* dancing, plans were made to invade the bar *en masse* and dance slow anyway. Word got back to the owners, and they capitulated.

UC Gay Lib participated in the Mobe anti-war demonstrations in April, supplying a large contingent and several speakers at the rally. During the Student Strike in May, UC Gay Lib, as part of the "close it down and open it up" demand, held a Gay Guerrilla Dance on campus (in spite of the explicit denial of permission by the University), which was open to *all* members of the community (not just students) and which was dedicated to victims of oppression everywhere. Concurrently, *Boys in the Band* was leafleted nightly, we put out a special Gay Lib supplement in Chicago's underground paper, the *Seed,* and we began coffee-hour discussions in the dorms on campus. We also developed a Study Group which began an in-depth analysis of oppression, making use of a critique we made of [Carl] Wittman's *Manifesto,* and of works of Marcuse, Engels, etc. . . .

Gay liberation not only spanned the country—as GY's *Journal* certified—but was producing palpitations in America's conservative heartland.

GLF New York, in the wake of its Weinstein Hall–NYU troubles, got a Midwestern invitation—in Minneapolis, FREE: Gay Liberation of Minnesota was holding a first "Regional Gay Convention," October 9–11. Planned, at the start, to embrace homophile/gay lib organizations in a ten-state area, FREE had invited all the nation's homosexual groups after a request by members of the gay men's caucus at the Panther-sponsored Revolutionary People's Constitutional Convention in Philadelphia a month before.

FREE had spent four months planning workshops on a variety of topics: how to establish campus gay groups; police–gay relations; "Gay Lib and Other Homophile Groups: Can They Work Together?"; establishing courses on homosexuality in colleges and high schools; etc. FREE had, moreover, invited speakers such as Conrad Balfour, Minnesota Commissioner of Human Rights, who "has publicly championed gay rights and will seek extension of job and housing discrimination laws to cover Gays next year." [17]

Primarily at the urging of gay lib representatives from New York, San Francisco, and Chicago, the convention junked the workshops *and* the speakers: "We didn't come here to listen to a bunch of straights," said a New Yorker. "This is the time for us to get our own heads together." Among the speakers passed over, correspondent Lars Bjornson informed *The Advocate,* "was Paul Goldman, the Chicago lawyer who guided the successful Illinois effort to repeal sodomy laws for consenting adults. . . . Other 'non-speakers' included the Rev. James Siefkus, director of congregational social concerns for the American Lutheran Church, who is working for healthier attitudes toward gay people in his church, such as the statement adopted July 2 by the Lutheran Church in America*; Prof. William Howell, president of the Speech-Communication Association of America, who hoped to discuss Gay Lib's rhetoric; Jerrold Winters, counselor at a mental health center in St. Paul, on Gays' personal problems; and Sandra Purnell of Minneapolis Women's Lib"!

The sixty men and twenty women who attended** spent the entire convention—except for a Saturday-night dance—hearing reports about

---

* At its Fifth Biennial Convention in Minneapolis, the church voted approval of the following statement: "Scientific research has not been able to provide conclusive evidence regarding the causes of homosexuality. Nevertheless, homosexuality is viewed biblically as a departure from the heterosexual structure of God's creation. Persons who engage in homosexual behavior are sinners only as are all other persons—alienated from God and neighbor. However, they are often the special and undeserving victims of prejudice and discrimination in law, law enforcement, cultural mores and congregational life. In relation to this area of concern, the sexual behavior of freely consenting adults in private is not an appropriate subject for legislation or police action. It is essential to see such persons as entitled to justice and understanding in church and community."

** From Madison, Milwaukee, Mankato (Minn.), St. Louis, DeKalb (Ill.), Iowa City, Ann Arbor (Mich.), Lawrence (Kan.), New York, Chicago, Minneapolis, St. Paul, San Francisco, Philadelphia, and Washington, D.C.

what each gay lib organization was doing and rapping on racism and sexism. Plans were also gone over for the Panthers' Revolutionary People's Constitutional Convention in Washington, D.C., November 27–9.

GAY reported that the women,

who met separately all during the convention at a private home 15 blocks away, sent a delegation to the men to demand that the men deal with their sexism by giving priority, in their plans for the Panthers' convention, to "the problems of Lesbians and of the Third World . . ." and by choosing two women and two Third Worlders as delegates for every white male delegate.

Those demands prompted one male, who had earlier complained that "women have entirely too much importance in this conference," to stalk angrily from the room. He returned 15 minutes later to renew his complaint.

Later, the convention acknowledged the validity of the women's demands but, after a rap session with five of the women on Sunday, chose no delegates and urged everyone who could to go to Washington for the Panthers' sessions.[48]

Despite the scrapping of his workshops and the turning away of his speakers, James Chesebro, FREE's convention coordinator, was not disappointed: "I think it's great that we could have people come halfway across the country to discuss, seriously, honestly, and in detail, the issues of racism and sexism." But, he hinted, "I think the reports we heard show that New York, Chicago and San Francisco standards apply to those cities. I mean, there are some things that are just not appropriate to do in Lawrence, Kansas . . ."[49] The men of *Gay Flames* disagreed:[50] "Gay people are getting it together and we'll soon be holding hands walking down Main Street U.S.A., if the folks in Iowa City and Lawrence win the battles they've already initiated."

Gay people got it together again at the Revolutionary People's Constitutional Convention in Washington, D.C., on Thanksgiving weekend when carloads from New York, Boston, Chicago, Milwaukee, Ann Arbor, Tallahassee, Los Angeles, Berkeley, Yellow Springs (Ohio), and Philadelphia used the chapel of American University as gay headquarters. The Panther-sponsored convention, which had contracted to hold its meetings on the campus of Howard University, had "dissolved into chaos when the university banned it at the last minute, saying the convention organizers had not lived up to their contract. Government pressure was widely suspected as the real reason," contended *The Advocate*.[51] *The Black Panther* reported that $10,824.06 had been demanded by university officials for rental of three campus buldings over the three-day weekend but that only a portion of the fee had to be pre-paid. Three days later, the university officials asked that the entire amount be rendered in advance.[52]

A majority of the gay women met with some seven hundred women in a sort of rump session at Trinity Church during the scattered convention—most of the Panthers were at St. Stephen's—but some stayed with the gay men. *Gay Flames*[53] told that "long meetings dedicated to the adoption of a gay platform for the constitution were interrupted for vital discussions of racism and sexism." Finally, the (revised) Third World Gay Revolution platform "was adopted by the group as the basis of a national gay liberation program. . . . Gay people formed a 15-member delegation under the leadership of Third World people and women, which attempted to make contact with the Panther leadership at St. Stephen's church on Saturday night, and to present the 16-point program to the Panthers. This delegation gave gay people the experience of women and men, Blacks, Latins and Asians and Whites, working collectively in a practical revolutionary context, though the chaos and crowd kept the delegation from completing its task." *

During the convention weekend, "The gay struggle was more than organizational," *Gay Flames* recalled. Four gay men—one black, one white, two Puerto Rican—went to Washington's Zephyr bar-restaurant. One wore a bit of makeup. Without explanation, the management refused them service. They left, returned later with thirty or more gay males to mix with the thirty straight patrons. "When the manager recognized the people he had refused service," *The Advocate* noted, "he again ordered them to leave. Gays and others began filtering toward the door, but a fight erupted when management, security guards, and several patrons attacked one Puerto Rican and two black Gays. Glasses were thrown, windows broken and other damage done in the free-for-all which developed. Two Zephyr employees were reportedly seriously hurt. None of the Gays sustained more than minor injuries. Police arrived and arrested four persons, released them, and began to beat two black Gays. The Blacks were rescued by the others, and eventually all the Gays left without being arrested. However, a Volkswagen bus with 12 of the Gay men in it was stopped by police leaving the area of the bar, and all 12 were arrested on charges of assault, illegal entry, and destruction of property. . . . The 12 were released Saturday on their own recognizance." A trial was scheduled for December 23.

A few weeks before the convention, three New York GLFers and a member of Chicago Gay Liberation disembarked from a Cuban freighter at St. John, New Brunswick. With four hundred other young Americans, half Third-World and half white, they boarded waiting buses to return to the United States—following six weeks' training, as one wary Miami radio station had it, in guerrilla warfare.[54] They had, instead, as members of the third contingent of the Venceremos Brigade, worked for four weeks on Cuba's Isle of Youth harvesting, planting, and fertilizing citrus fruit trees and made a fourteen-day tour, all food, lodging, and transportation provided, of the Cuban mainland.

* Not all GLFers at the convention fully supported the Black Panthers. Tracy Knight resigned the chair at one point announcing that "Louisville GLF was dissociating itself from the Panthers. She said her group would also split with the national Gay Liberation Movement if it supported a Panther-written constitution." (*The Advocate*, December 23–January 5, 1971.)

"Why go to Cuba?" Laurie Zoloth, a member of the first contingent (winter 1969–70), asked in the *Plain Dealer* on June 4.[55]

First off, because it's so important to find out, first hand, just how the first communist experiment in the hemisphere is going, to talk to the people there— to PARTICIPATE in the revolution. . . .

. . . If we want to talk about the revolution in this country, we have to be aware of both the exciting successes of Cuba, and some of the human problems they are working to overcome. When they say Venceremos! (We shall win!) it is with a clearheaded appraisal of the difficulty of that effort. It's important for us to share in that experience, that dedication, to understand that the Cuban Revolution and ours are vitally linked. It's important to touch, see, hear, feel, WORK, in the elusive vision of the Revolution we carry around in our heads.

Venceremos Three left St. John for Cuba on a chicken boat in late August 1970. On the week-long voyage to the Caribbean, the GLFers were open about their homosexuality, wore the Front buttons. To hide their sexual orientation was not only undesirable, but impossible: the four were known to Movement members from New York and Chicago. Earl Galvin, one of the New York GLFers, told *Come Out!*, "There are also a few straight men who are wearing GLF buttons and we generally have strong support from almost all of the women and a great number of men." [56] The GLFers gave copies of *Come Out!* and Carl Wittman's Manifesto to straights who wanted them.

On the ship's arrival in Havana, Galvin related,[57] "the docks were crowded with people dancing and singing. All of us on the boat were doing the same. We took buses across Havana Province to board another boat to take us to the Isle of Pines. In all the little towns along the way were signs saying WELCOME VENCEREMOS BRIGADE. People in the streets everywhere to greet us." Renamed the Isle of Youth and spoken of as "the first Communist region in Cuba," [58] * the island to which the Brigade came was the site of a notorious prison that held Castro and other revolutionaries in 1953. Southwest of the Cuban mainland, it had been nearly devastated by a hurricane eight years before; today, repopulated and converted by volunteer youth groups into a great citrus garden, it has windbreaks to protect the crop, valuable for fruit and sugar.[59] At 2:00 a.m., the boat from Havana Province docked on the island. Trucks with their headlights on flashed a welcome; a couple of thousand people, estimates Galvin, sang as the Americans joined them, loaded the visitors with flowers. On the way to their camp, the Brigade passed other camps where trucks were out, headlights on, to give greeting.

The Brigade's camp, inland among the island's endless orange groves, was being developed as a new school for farm machinery operators. Four

---

* Galvin explains that in mainland Cuba about 30 per cent of the land is still small, privately owned farms. In the largely unpopulated Isle of Youth this is not the case.

dormitories housed the four hundred visitors; other facilities were a huge dining room, a laundry, a recreation room, a library, a basketball court, an outdoor stage, and an open-air movie. A dam-made lake with a small beach was available for swimming. Doctors and dentists were provided. The Americans' day began at 5:00 a.m., when they rose. Following breakfast, by 7:00 they were on trucks setting off for nearby groves. Work stopped at 11:00, and siesta included lunch and relaxation until 3:00. From 3:00 to 7:00, when midday heat was over, work resumed. After supper there were movies and dancing. During the Brigade's second week on the island, about sixty Vietnamese and Laotians, many of them students, worked in groups with the Americans.

The gay liberationists experienced no problems with their Cuban hosts, who knew of course that GLF was one of the Movement groups with the Brigade. In *"¡Soy maricón, y me gusta!"* ("I'm a fag, and I dig it!"), *Gay Flames* reported [60] how, in fact, a Cuban delegate to the Youth Assembly at the United Nations had encouraged gay people to join Venceremos Three. But "we cross our fingers when we think of our beautiful [commune] brother, openly gay, surrounded by straights, working for the common good on an island that has no gay bar nor proud gay community where he can seek shelter." The gays' problems, confirming *Gay Flames,* arose within the Brigade itself—which was by no means of one mind. Galvin marveled, in *Come Out!,* that "it looked for a bit as though we were on the verge of a 6-way war. Blacks vs. Puerto Ricans, Chicanos vs. Whites, men vs. women [and because] we have the support of almost all of the white people (weak though it may be for many), GLF became a sort of 'white' issue. There are 3rd world gay people on the Brigade, but they are mostly very closety and tend to be the most vocal in opposition to the 'bullshit movements'—i.e. Women's Lib and Gay Lib."

After his return from Cuba, Galvin explained: [61] "There just were some people who couldn't deal with that whole thing, there were some people who just couldn't believe that there were gay people there. . . . The main problems were with some of the super-butch revolutionaries, those who portray this whole revolutionary image of the strong, heavy Movement type." Of these, Third World men were more outspoken than whites, said Galvin. "And," he believed, "the most vocally anti-gay people were gay people who weren't accepting their own selves yet, who were still being forced into that whole thing." Galvin related in addition how, during his first week in the island dormitory, the man in the bed across from his yelled, teasingly, each night, "There's a faggot in my bed." One night, when Galvin walked into the dorm, the man was telling another he needed some "homosexual repellent"—"We've got mosquito repellent, we need homosexual repellent!" Galvin stepped over and said, "You don't need it. You've got it in your blood—you repulse us just as you are!" A few days later, the man came over and asked to shake Galvin's hand, telling the GLFer that he was "starting to think about the whole thing."

The gay liberationists' work on the Isle of Youth was twofold: to

221

participate in the Brigade's functions and to convince the Brigade that homosexuals were capable human beings and valuable fellow-revolutionaries. Even their idle time was filled with explanations, arguments; and they contributed their thoughts at meetings, told the history of gay liberation at "presentations." Galvin elucidated some of the results of the gays' efforts: "At the [Revolutionary People's Constitutional] convention in Washington, we met so many people from the Brigade who have 'come out' since—even people from the previous Brigades. That's the most important thing, *I* think. But besides that, there's the whole thing that all of those people who were with the third contingent, their heads can never be the same. Regardless of what they think. I don't know whether their thinking has been improved, or their attitudes have changed for the better or the worse. But at least they've recognized some force to deal with, they can't ignore the whole gay thing anymore. And neither can the Cubans!"

■

In the earliest issue of *Come Out!*, New York GLFer Lois Hart had pled: "We need a place, my friends and I, we who call ourselves GLF. We need space to be together—to meet, to rap, to eat, to dance, to dig each other and plan our work. It would be a place for our paper, communal dinners, meetings and dances—space where we can begin to break down our fragmentation—to create a communal environment closer to our needs and purposes." [62] Exactly a year later, the center was found: a 4,500-foot loft on West 3rd Street. It held open house on December 4, 5, and 6 for the New York gay community.

The Gay Community Center was not a GLF undertaking, but a GLF-affiliated project by a collective of two women and twelve men representing the Front and STAR who saw the center as, more than a Front project, "a place for Gay people to come together to love and learn and create a feeling of community." They specified, in an introductory leaflet,[63] that "The collective will take responsibility for coordinating the functioning of the center; intermediate groups will work with the collective to concentrate on specific services, such as classes, dances, lighting, food, day care, cleaning, etc.; the Community will be the Center—the Center exists for the Community. There will be weekly Community meetings where the Community will define what the Center is to become . . ."

New York gay liberationists had a home.

11

. . . the conspiracy of private industry
and government against homosexuals in the
area of employment is at the heart of the
problem we face today.
—Jim Owles, in "Employment Discrimination Against Homosexuals,"
July 14, 1970

For the sciences of chemistry and physics, the *lambda* symbolizes a complete exchange of energy—that moment or span of time witness to absolute activity.

An ancient symbol brought to application centuries from its origin, lambda is the eleventh lower-case letter of the Hellenic alphabet. The Lacedaemonians, or Spartans, bore it on their shields, a people's will aimed at common oppressors.

Likewise, members of Gay Activists Alliance uphold it as their symbols before the nation. It signifies a commitment among men and women to achieve and defend their human rights as homosexual citizens. Activism is the operative term. Political involvement that is both assertive and effective is GAA's prime thrust. In the struggle against oppression a cultural bond develops, suffused with human energies. The lambda now affirms the liberation of all gay people.*

A leaflet which—together with a copy of the constitution and the explanatory "What Is GAA?"—the visitor could pick up at a table by the door when he paid his $.50 donation. Also near the door, by summer 1970 he could buy a lambda T-shirt (sweatshirt in winter) or button. Tacked to the wall, above the chairman's table, the visitor saw the 4 x 7, royal-blue banner with a yellow lambda and the letters GAY ACTIVISTS ALLIANCE.

He might become a member tonight, if this was his third meeting "within a period of six consecutive meetings"—provided he had gone to at least one committee meeting and to an orientation session held by the Orientation Committee. GAA was proud of itself and of its accomplish-

---

* The symbol has not been adopted by Gay Liberation Front, which has no standard emblem. GLF buttons—and there have been several—generally feature a raised fist.

ments, wanted prospective members to learn that pride. How often at general meetings a newcomer would rise after an hour or so and—as if primed by the Activist leaders—would interrupt, to overflow, "I've been gay for some time, but really until tonight I can say that I never felt proud of myself, never felt proud of being gay, and I just want to tell you . . ." A thrill through the crowd, a pause, the verge of common tears, and the members would applaud—him, themselves . . .

By December 1970, there were two hundred "active" Gay Activists, male and female. And a constant stream of visitors—men and women who couldn't quite yet make militant motions but who wanted to know what was going on. GAA loved visitors, invited them to serve on committees and join actions. They were merely reminded that "Only members may vote on the following motion . . ."

The visitor might have been surprised that GAA's president did not chair, but sat with other members while his appointed parliamentarian presided, the club secretary at the parliamentarian's left hand. Called at the start of meetings to make his President's Report, he returned to the audience and might not speak unless recognized by the chair. GAA had dethroned its president in constitutional amendments of July 30, 1970: the organization needed a dynamo to speak for it to the straight community, it did not need such a man to chair its meetings. As parliamentarian Marc Rubin tactfully suggested, "He's the spokesman of the organization, and the chair inhibits that role."

The visitor might have been equally curious that an entire meeting could be devoted to committee reports, as GAA's was. But committees were the working heart of Gay Activists Alliance, and their week's work, brought to the floor of the general meeting each Thursday, was GAA's "old" *and* "new" business. It was debated, accepted, or thrown out. Committee business was the business of GAA.

The visitor would be asked to join a committee; a sign-up list would be circulated. Males or females loosed hands to sign. In late summer 1970, the "GAA Committee List" (available at the door) outlined the purposes of each:

1) POLITICAL PROJECTS: To recommend to GAA the setting up of new political committees which will be assigned specific political projects, and to recommend to GAA needed changes in the mandates of political committees already established.

2) POLICE POWER: To recommend tactics to GAA to resist systematic police oppression of homosexuals.

3) AD HOC 1970 ELECTIONS: To recommend to GAA the strategy for demonstrations & lobbying directed toward candidates in the municipal, state & federal elections of 1970. Also to oversee the carrying out of such approved strategy. The mandate of the committee will expire on Election Day, 1970.

4) MUNICIPAL FAIR EMPLOYMENT LAW: To recommend strategy to

GAA for demonstrations & lobbying in order to effect passage in the City Council of a bill outlawing public & private job discrimination against homosexuals—and to oversee the carrying out of such approved strategy.

5) FAIR TAX: To recommend strategy to GAA for challenging those elements of the tax structure which oppress homosexuals, and to oversee the carrying out of such approved strategy.

6) LEGAL COMMITTEE: To recommend legal strategy to GAA & to oversee the carrying out of such approved strategy.

7) NEWS: To provide the mass media with information about GAA & its committees.

8) LEAFLET & GRAPHICS: To edit and *distribute* all street leaflets for GAA & all of its committees. To hold and operate the mimeograph machine. To design & distribute posters and other artifacts relevant to GAA policies.

9) FUND-RAISING: To recommend strategy to GAA for a systematic fund-raising drive through mass mailings & other devices. To oversee the carrying out of such approved strategy, except through means of social events.

10) SOCIAL AFFAIRS: To recommend dances and other social events to GAA in order to raise the political consciousness of the homosexual community. To promote the unity & morale of GAA members & to oversee the carrying out of such approved events. All profits from such events belong to GAA.

11) ORIENTATION: To run orientation sessions, to act as hosts at all GAA functions & to make recommendations to the executive committee as to how members should be recruited.

12) AD HOC HARPER'S MAGAZINE ACTION: To recommend strategy to GAA for carrying out the approved action against *Harper's Magazine* regarding a response to the publication of Joseph Epstein's "The Struggle for Sexual Identity."

The visitor might also pick up a list of "GAA Committee Meetings This Week."

Dick Michaels, editor of *The Advocate* and guest at an October meeting, returned to Los Angeles to comment:[1]* "We were impressed by the orderly structure of the GAA, by the rules observed by the various members at the meeting, by the large number of worthwhile projects going on—maybe a few too many for them to handle well. We were impressed by the good humored and calm way they conducted themselves, even when they disagreed wtih each other. . . . They conducted the business at hand efficiently and with dispatch. It was refreshing . . ." Michaels added that he was "impressed also by the great political awareness of Gays in New

* Visitors have come not only to observe, but to preserve the essence of GAA meetings on film. One of the earliest was Guidance Associates, a visual affiliate of Harcourt Brace Jovanovich, which planned spring 1971 filmstrips on "The Second Largest Minority." On September 3, the American Program Bureau videotaped (for CBS-EVR cassettes) a part of its pilot program "Repression in America" at a GAA meeting. University of California students filmed the club meeting of August 20.

York—by how well informed they were. Perhaps New Yorkers," he said, "are simply more 'political animals' than the West Coast variety. If so, we could do with a few imports."

■

A reader of GAY, in midsummer 1970, might have noticed the advertisement

GAYS STEP FORWARD
GAY ACTIVISTS ALLIANCE

wants to hear from gays

whose rights have been violated

in any way because of their

homosexuality. Let's take it

to court.

Legal Action Committee . . .

Gay Activists Alliance had never devoted its entire efforts to in-the-streets confrontations with police and politicos. The work of the Legal Action Committee is a case in point, though its behind-the-scenes actions have followed up raids, riots, and arrests. Chairman Ken Burdick, taking a dual view of his committee's functions, has attempted not only to give legal defense to members and friends who might be arrested during approved GAA actions or while acting as GAA agents on approved organizational assignments, but has planned legal offense to create cases (e.g., a sodomy test case *) whereby homosexuals may achieve full civil rights.

* At the prompting and with the cooperation of the Mattachine Society of Washington, the ACLU of the National Capital Area was, in early 1971, in final stages of preparation for a test case against the sodomy laws of the District of Columbia. On or about February 1, a civil suit was to be brought before a three-judge Federal district court by four volunteer plaintiffs—two male couples (a female couple originally included had dropped out). The plaintiffs planned to attest, through affidavits, to their commission or intended commission of acts of private, consensual, adult sodomy in violation of the DC sodomy statute. MSW president Franklin Kameny has told that "Previous correspondence with the Chief of the Morals Division of the Metropolitan Police Department has elicited the statement from him that he cannot guarantee immunity from arrest for commission of these acts. The plaintiffs will allege fear of arrest and request that the court issue an injunction against enforcement of the sodomy law on grounds of its unconstitutionality, based, probably, upon the First, Fourth, Fifth and Ninth Amendments, and other Constitutional provisions."
Kameny stated that "This case will avoid the weaknesses of other such test cases

226

The committee quickly established good working relationships with the American Civil Liberties Union, the New York Civil Liberties Union, the Association of the Bar, and the Council of New York Law Associates and has had as many as eight attorneys furnishing GAA with legal assistance and advice.

One of the Legal Action Committee's most challenging projects was the defense of nine men who decided to sue the City following their false arrests on the morning of the Snake Pit raid. Burdick reported [2] that "the arrested persons were charged with disorderly conduct, and, though all charges against them were dropped at their arraignments, a suit was legally possible because the City had neglected to get signed waivers from the individuals releasing it from responsibility in the illegal arrest." After several postponements, new hearings were set up for January 21, 1971.

A made-to-order committee project was the incorporation of GAA under New York State law. Burdick stated that the "application has been rejected by the office of the Secretary of State and the matter will have to be taken to court in an attempt to get a reversal of that decision. The GAA attorney plans to file the suit in mid-January 1971." GAA's needs for corporation status were, according to the committee chairman: "1) to protect the organization's officers from lawsuits made against them as individuals and arising out of public dealings of the organization; 2) to ensure that procedures followed within the organization are in keeping with accepted business practices; and 3) to confront the straight community as a legitimate and openly pro-homosexual political pressure group."

An early case for the committee was that involving Gay Activist Rey (Sylvia) Rivera. Rivera was holding a GAA petition up to be signed, on 42nd Street, when a policeman told him to move on. Rivera refused, in order to have the signature completed, and was arrested, charged with disorderly conduct. After several hearings, his case was finally thrown out of court in September 1970 because the arresting officer failed, three times, to appear.

When chairman Burdick rose, at Gay Activists meetings, to make his committee report muffled whistles and light applause from GAA men usually greeted their slender, mustachioed idol. Once, as he leaned back,

---

which have involved arrests and/or which have included a married heterosexual couple among the litigants. Arrests create a prejudicial aura," he believed ."The very real possibility exists that, if given the opportunity, the courts will merely carve out an enclave of special rights for heterosexual couples, leaving homosexuals completely out in the cold."

The DC case would take any of three possible courses. It could be won at the district court level and not appealed, in which case the DC sodomy law would be struck down. It could be won at the district court level and appealed, "in which case an effort will be made to persuade the Supreme Court to strike down all such laws," Kameny has determined. Or it could be lost at the district court level, in which case it *would* be appealed to the Supreme Court on the broader basis. (Letter to the author, January 1971.)

bare-legged in denim shorts, against the parliamentarian's table, even vice-president Barbara Glover gave her sapphic approval: "You look just as good from the back side, honey!" On August 6, Burdick's Legal Action Committee report stirred up antagonism as well as approval. Club president Jim Owles and Political Projects Committee chairman Marty Robinson crossed swords unexpectedly. Burdick wanted to tackle "expungement." *

"By expungement," he explained, "I mean that we have organized a suit that will attempt to remove the arrest records of four individuals who have agreed to join the suit. They were arrested in the Snake Pit raid, but the charges against them were dropped; they are suing the City. However, in the State of New York there are no procedures for removing your record of arrest, even if the charges against you are dropped or if the case ultimately goes to court and you are found innocent. Even though in the eyes of the law you have been found innocent, your name is still on record as having been arrested.

"In twelve states in the Union, as of now, expungement procedures are already in effect. These have been established by statute; in other words, they have been passed by the various state legislatures or have been established by precedent through a court decision. We would like to bring New York into this group of twelve states where expungement procedures are available . . ."

Recognized by the chair, Robinson rose briskly: "One of the GAA Five Demands is that bonding companies no longer have the right to deny you a bond, which you need in order to work in jobs like those on Wall Street. The way they get at you is that they look up your arrest record—you see, they fingerprint you now on Wall Street. So if you've been busted or arrested—much less convicted—that is open information. Therefore, once the bonding company sees that, then you are automatically denied your bond and your right to work. So that Ken's suggestion is important in relation to the Wall Street problem. Also in relation to the fact that investigatory agencies find out if people are homosexuals and pass it on quietly to the employer **—which is something we have to cut

* *The New York Times* tackled it, too, on Sunday, December 6, 1970, in an article by Fred Graham, F.B.I.: WHEN SHOULD ITS ARREST RECORDS BE EXPUNGED?
** A story carried in GAY (July 27, 1970) and *Gay Scene* (No. 2) told how Jim Owles had released the contents of his sharply worded letter to Vincent Gillen, president of Fidelifacts of Greater New York, on June 19:

The letter states: "We have been made aware . . . of your investigations into the sex lives of thousands of human beings." Owles attacked the practice of selling this "information" (regarding homosexuality, extramarital relationships, etc.) to personnel departments of clients of Fidelifacts and other pre-employment investigatory agencies. "Since certain companies bar homosexuals from employment (thusly *creating* a situation in which those involved with those companies could become possible targets of blackmail), do you feel that your services contribute to the worsening of this injustice? Would your agency favor a governmental ban on employment discrimination against homosexuals thereby freeing them from any threat of 'blackmail.' (I would think that a position on this issue is incumbent upon you since your agency has capitalized on the use of this type of information) . . ."

off. . . . This sort of arrest, where you have a criminal record for merely being arrested—not convicted . . . if we can expunge such matter from the records, it would be greatly to our benefit in a number of fields that are already well within our club interests, and therefore I feel that the case is practicable. I definitely feel that we should get into it."

A visitor to the meeting added, "I think that this is an action which is basic to the problems not only of gay people but to anybody who poses a threat to the status quo and therefore invites police harassment!"

Recognized, the club president rose to advise that he was "against projects of this nature, projects for which we will have very little *active* participation. In other words, almost all the work will be done by lawyers. It sets a dangerous precedent, I think, for the organization in that it will make us more and more an organization that appropriates money or provides a study group . . . an organization of people who *listen* and who vote on paper resolutions. It's not something that calls for activism, we won't have a chance to get out and fight for it."

Another GAA member rose "to answer Jim's objections on two fronts. First, it seems to me that he says we shouldn't be 'messing' with this because we're a *political* organization. And yet, if one thing seems clear"— and he referred to the trial of the Chicago 7—"it is that the judicial process and the political process in this country are pretty much the same. The laws in this country are what the politicians want, and if we're going to attack politicians we might just as well attack the laws, because the politicians make the laws. The second point is about the matter of 'participation'—he feels we'll only be benchwarmers. It seems to me that there are plenty of other things we can do as well. There is *no reason why we should,* if we have a good case and a lawyer who is willing to do it for us free, plus a Legal Committee that is enthusiastic about it, and if we believe that the goals are to the benefit of all of us (and anyone who has been busted will understand this, believe me!)"—at this point, loud applause—"and have the resources at our command and the people willing to do it, *refuse to take this on.* There is no need to limit ourselves. This is still a fundamentally political, homosexual-oriented action!" The members applauded as he finished.

Arthur Evans stood: "I believe that it is bad, for several reasons, for this group to undertake it. First is the relationship between political power and legal protection. In our society, you can have all the legal protection you want: you can have the courts abide by all legal precedent, you can have the judges recognize your rights, *and that can mean NOTHING! Everyone who has been involved in the movement knows that these things can mean NOTHING!* If you are not organized into a powerful political constituency that will deliver fear into the hearts of the politicians—who realize that you will disrupt them if you don't get your way—all your legal rights are shit!"

Then, speaking of the State of Illinois, where sex between consenting adults is no longer proscribed, Evans went on: "Everyone knows, who has been in Chicago, that the situation is nevertheless worse there than it is here. There is a simple reason: homosexuals in Chicago do not have political power. Where homosexuals are feared as having the possibility of political power they have their rights. . . . We should not undertake a lawsuit unless it has immediate *political* advantages for homosexuals in New York. This has none. Perhaps in the long run. Now, no."

■

In an editorial, QQ magazine complained, "We homosexuals have been denied basic rights since the Year One. . . . We are treated worse than second-class citizens—but must pay straight taxes and fight straight wars." [3] In *The Advocate,* Tom Biggs protested, "Income taxes support the very government by which we are ostracized." [4]

GAY reported that, in Detroit,

A woman publicly attacked the Gay Liberation Front and the administration of the University of Michigan . . . for a GLF dance held recently using university facilities.

In a letter to the editor of the Detroit News, Mary G. Watts said the dance marked "a new low in the misuse of university facilities."

She said the university's president, Robben W. Fleming, should have prevented the use of the university for the dance. "Taxpayers built the university's facilities at an average cost of $2,000 per student per year. Taxpayers also pay for destruction perpetrated by students," she said in her letter.

The letter continued: "We have watched the school's administration buy peace at any price from militant groups. Apparently the Gay Liberation Front got the same treatment."

"How long will taxpayers put up with this sort of thing? This is the most disgraceful situation yet!" concluded the letter.[5]

GAY felt that no comment was necessary . . .

GAA president Jim Owles told a *New York Times* interviewer on June 27, 1970: "Then there is the question of various churches in gay communities, which do not open up their doors to meetings of homosexuals * (or to other minority groups, for that matter) . . . churches that sit empty six days out of the week. Some of us go to these churches, others pay taxes and subsidize these churches—which are tax-exempt. Yet they aren't of use to us at all."

Gay Activists Alliance saw an opening for a new and important attack on straight society. In midsummer the Fair Tax Committee began work under the chairmanship of Eric Thorndale.

On October 15, the committee recommended to the GAA general meeting "that the following goals be included among the stated goals . . .

* Though some have, most notably the Church of the Holy Apostles, which has hosted, concurrently, GLF, the West Side Discussion Group, and GAA.

230

and that whenever GAA publishes or issues any list of its basic goals, either in a leaflet or in statements to politicians or to the media," they be included:

1) An end to the discriminatory policy of taxing the incomes of single persons at higher rates than the incomes of married persons.* In short—an end to income tax discrimination against single persons.

    Comment: This income tax discrimination rewards those who conform to a particular sexual life-style—specifically, the life-style of the heterosexually married. It penalizes those who do not conform. *It penalizes practically all homosexuals.* This discrimination cannot be justified on any grounds. Many living-expenses (rent, electricity, gas, telephone, kitchen utensils, furniture, household maintenance, etc.) are less per person for a man and wife than for a single person living alone. It is the husband-and-wife combination that can better afford a higher rate of tax, especially when both husband and wife are earning income and filing a joint return. Yet it is the single individual—and for our purposes the homosexual individual—who is taxed at the higher rate. The result of this discrimination is to penalize sexual nonconformists and in effect compel them to subsidize heterosexual marriage.

2) Recognizing that antihomosexual propaganda is always political in its consequences, we demand strict enforcement of the Internal Revenue Service code as it applies to the revocation of the tax-exempt status of those tax-exempt institutions that engage in political propaganda against the rights of homosexuals. In shortened form—revocation of the tax-exempt status of institutions that engage in antihomosexual propaganda.

    Comment: This goal is sometimes labeled antireligious. It is not. Many of the major church groups do not engage in antihomosexual propaganda. However, those institutions, religious or psychiatric, that do engage in this kind of business—those that find this business lucrative—should not be exempt from the law. It is also argued that this goal would deny to antihomosexual institutions their First Amendment rights. Our answer is that it would not. We must distinguish between First Amendment rights and the privilege of exemption from tax. We would not infringe upon anyone's right to fulminate against us. But we must recognize that an exemption from tax is in effect a subsidy, and we have every right to demand that our money not be used against us. This past September the municipalities of Orange and East Orange, N.J., revoked the tax exemption of the Elks because of discrimination against citizens who are black. "The tax-exempt status of the Elks places an added burden on the taxpayer," said the Mayor of Orange, "and I strongly object to it because it forces the citizens who are being discrimi-

---

* GAY noted, on August 10: "The Mattachine Society of New York reports that at least five gay couples in metropolitan New York have filed joint tax returns. Two of the couples received refunds promptly. Computers failed to notice that the partners were of the same sex. One couple, in nearby New Jersey, was investigated by the IRS. The others heard nothing. New York Mattachine referred the New Jersey couple to a skilled New Jersey tax lawyer. IRS officials informed them that they must be married to qualify for a joint return. The couple replied that they had been living openly as a couple for years, long enough to qualify as common-law marrieds . . . [and] a date has been set for them to appear with their lawyer for further confrontations."

nated against to share the burden." GAA should follow the same reasoning in regard to institutions that are antihomosexual. Finally, it is sometimes argued that this goal is not sufficiently relevant to homosexual liberation. Actually nothing is more relevant. The essence of political power is the power to tax and to exempt from tax. We must aim for our share in the control over that power. The tax committee is recommending that GAA serve notice to politicians and to the media that institutions that engage in lobbying or propaganda against homosexual rights must forfeit their tax-exempt status. It is not good politics to place one's persecutors' interests ahead of one's own.

The resolutions were overwhelmingly adopted.

■

"Presented by the *Gay Activists Alliance* to the *New York City Commission on Human Rights*" and dated July 14, 1970, the pamphlet was introduced by GAA president Jim Owles, was sixteen pages long and annotated, contained two appendixes, had been researched by Richy Aunateau's Fair Employment Committee. It was entitled "Employment Discrimination Against Homosexuals," and commenced,

Most companies, as well as most governmental agencies, will not hire or will fire individuals who are found to be homosexual, or who possess "homosexual tendencies." This injustice, in the past, has been perpetrated on those homosexuals who were considered "obvious types." However, in the past several years, the problem has become drastically more acute and is headed in a direction aiming at not only a complete stripping of the gay community of its right to individual privacy and the right to work, but also aims at a situation where heterosexuals also will be (and in cases already reported, are) subject to dismissal on unfounded grounds of alleged homosexuality—clearly then, this is a universal, hazardous, and unjust situation.

The source of this growing problem: the ever increasing use of investigatory techniques and of investigatory agencies by personnel departments of most large companies. As John Cye Cheasty (a former Secret Service, Internal Revenue, and Navy Intelligence man—now an investigator for Fidelifacts of Greater New York) points out, ". . . more and more companies are making 'extensive pre-employment checkups' before hiring such people (applying for managerial positions) . . . 'I think that industrial intelligence is one of the fastest growing businesses in the United States today. . . .'" [6] Jerry M. Rosenberg [7] reports that Retail Credit Company alone, with files on more than 45 million people in the United States, sends out 35 million reports each year to "users"—personal information, in many cases, reports of homosexuality.

How is this information obtained? Vincent Gillen, founder of Fidelifacts of Greater New York (a former FBI agent), [to] executives of the Association of Stock Exchange Brokers two years ago: " 'Establishing that someone is a homosexual is often difficult,' he noted, but 'I like to go on the rule of thumb that if one looks like a duck, walks like a duck, associates only with ducks and quacks like a duck, he is probably a duck.' " [8]

The pamphlet itemized other methods of intruding into individuals' private lives (which companies like Fidelifacts might sometimes use, too): direct questioning methods, checks into draft records, lie detector tests, checks into police records for arrests.

Under "CHECKS INTO DRAFT RECORDS," the pamphlet stated that

It is the practice of many corporations to require a job applicant to sign a "waiver" (for release of information of applicant's selective service records) on the applicant's *application* for employment, refusing even to consider the application unless the waiver is signed. If hired, the applicant is employed on a "provisional" basis pending results of investigations—including the selective service records check. Should the investigation reveal that the applicant indicated "homosexual tendencies" on his selective service medical report, the provisional employee would often be fired on the basis of this information alone. (It should be noted that if a [homosexual] does not indicate "homosexual tendencies" on this medical report and does enter military service, he is eligible for dishonorable discharge as well as faces purgery complications.)

From Vance Packard's *The Naked Society,* the pamphlet excerpted a description of the lie detector test for homosexuality:

. . While the machine is on they ask one or more of these questions:
"Have you had any past or present physical ailments we should know about?"
"Are you holding back something important that was not covered in the examination?"
"Are you holding back information, any incident or condition, which might open you up to blackmail?"
One of the men added, laughing, "If you really throw the homo question to them directly while the machine is on the needles really jump." [9]

The pamphlet illustrated how "HOMOPHILE ACTIVITY" was a possible danger to employment: "There have been a number of cases of individuals fired as a result of their activity in the homophile movement—activity intended to help win freedom and equality for homosexuals, used as an excuse to deny freedom and equality for those persons involved in this political cause. (Note should also be made here of the fact that one is not necessarily homosexual if he is a homophile.)" A news item, HOMO BROADCASTER WANTS HIS JOB BACK, was cited from *Gay Scene:* [10]

Thom Higgins, a 19-year-old announcer for the Radio Talking Book Network, operated by State Services for the Blind, claims that he was fired from his job because he's homosexual. He has appealed to the Minnesota Commissioner of Human Rights and the state chapter of the American Civil Liberties Union to act in his behalf in getting his job back.

Mr. Higgins has been serving as publicity director of Fight Repression of Erotic Expression (FREE), a University of Minnesota organization of homosexuals. He contends that he was fired by Stanley Potter, director of State Services for the Blind, when he notified him that he would be taking part in a FREE press conference. Mr. Higgins asserts he was told "his sexual preference would be acceptable for a staff member were it not to become public knowledge" and that "the blind in Minnesota could not as a minority group stand to be associated with an overt homosexual."

"NOBODY is immune to the threat of antihomosexual practices as long as they are legal," the pamphlet stressed, "—these practices may be used against any person regardless of his sexual orientation, at any time and in some cases without his knowledge." It observed that GAA had considered furnishing complimentary subscriptions to GAY and *The Advocate* to members of the New York City Commission on Human Rights so that they might keep abreast of developments in the gay community. But after further consideration, the organization "decided not to follow through on this gesture on the grounds that it would subject members of the Commission to possible loss of their insurance and possible inclusion of this 'derogatory' information in their checkup reports—which they are not permitted to review or see." The pamphlet declared, for example, that "Allstate Insurance Company* which bases much of its information on this kind of circumstantial evidence, 'not only deny or cancel the insurance (if they turn up any "evidence" of homosexuality) but file a copy of the report with the police, the credit bureau, *the employer* and the insurance bureau' "! [11]

The committee's pamphlet concluded,

Discrimination in the area of employment is only one of many injustices perpetrated against homosexuals. However, the Gay Activists Alliance feels that any meaningful movement for equality is contingent upon the achievement of economic security for homosexuals. For how many people would be willing to say aloud, "I'm free" if it would result in being fired with little chance of decent employment in the future? How many employees now leading double lives in all occupations can assert their dignity as human beings by lifting the cloud of secrecy around their lives, knowing that such an assertion would result in a cutoff of income and financial ruination? **

* In the *New York Post,* November 5, 1970, a feature-interview with Jim Owles noted his assertion that ". . . companies—Owles specifically cited Consolidated Edison and the New York Telephone Co.—'ask you to sign a waiver releasing your draft records to find out if you're gay.' "

** One member of GAA's Political Action Committee felt strong enough, at a meeting of the committee after the Rockefeller Five rally, August 5: "What it boils down to is this: What's more important—your self-respect, your dignity, your liberation? Or your job? It's not an easy thing to do, [but] I've gotten to the point where my job is secondary to GAA."

As "RECOMMENDATIONS FOR ACTION," the committee asked the New York City Commission on Human Rights:

1) to pass a strong resolution supporting the right of equality for homosexuals in employment
2) pending legislative action by the City Council and state legislature, to broaden the definition of "sex" in the City Human Rights law to include "sexual orientation" and this, therefore, to be declared illegal grounds for discrimination
3) to pass a strong resolution urging the City Council and the state legislature to add "sexual orientation" to the list of illegal grounds for discrimination in both the City and State Human Rights laws
4) to urge legislation by both the City Council and the state legislature barring dissemination of information, by both city and state governmental agencies and by private investigatory agencies, relating to sexual orientation or private sexual activities of persons with the intent of influencing a decision by any prospective employer to employ or not to employ said persons in the city and state of New York, or with the intent of influencing a decision by any employer to discharge said persons in the city or state of New York
5) to urge the state legislature to revoke archaic sodomy statutes thereby removing justification of employers to discriminate against the hiring of homosexuals or the firing of homosexuals on the basis of criminality
6) to urge the City Council and the state legislature to pass legislation requiring that any waiver for release of selective service records of an employee or prospective employee include a stipulation that medical records included in these records are not to be released to any employer or private investigatory agency or any insurance agency operating in the city and state of New York
7) to urge the City Council and state legislature to pass legislation making it unlawful for any employer in New York City and New York State to request or receive information regarding sexual orientation or private sexual activities of any employee or prospective employee from any agency either private or governmental, and to require that no such information may be elicited from the employee or prospective employee directly or by lie detector tests, psychological tests, or any such test designed to elicit such information by any employer or prospective employer in the city and state of New York.

After release of the pamphlet to the New York City Commission on Human Rights on July 14, members of the GAA Fair Employment Committee met frequently with the Commission's chairman, Eleanor Holmes Norton. Committee chairman Richy Aunateau detailed [12] that Mrs. Norton had, recently,

released a statement that she was in favor of measures which would bring employment discrimination against homosexuals to an end in New York City. But, under existing law, the Comission could not effectively deal with cases of discrimination on the basis of sexual orientation—legislation by the City Council would be necessary.

The problem now was, basically, how to get the City Council to deal in earnest with the issue. We decided that GAA must attempt to move the Commission into open and public hearings on the matter, there to confront offending employers and "pre-employment" investigatory agencies in order to focus public attention on discrimination against gays. Such public attention could prompt the Council to action—with the inside help of councilmen favorable to it.

Councilman Eldon Clingan, minority leader of the Liberal Party and an at-large delegate from Manhattan, and Carter Burden, an up-and-coming Democratic Party star representing the 4th District in Manhattan, were the initial insiders on whom the Fair Employment Committee largely depended. A draft bill was drawn up by Councilman Clingan's office which in effect was an amendment to the Administrative Code of the city. If passed, the new law would give the Human Rights Commission the power it needed to act in cases of discrimination against gays in both private and civil service employment. The law would also restrict discrimination in labor unions and by employment agents, and could conceivably restrict investigatory agencies in their "selling" of information about sexual orientation to employers.

"In the meantime," wrote Aunateau, "the GAA committee worked closely with Gay Activists Alliance of Long Island, the Alliance's first off-shoot organization, in their uncovering of overt discrimination by the Suffolk and Nassau counties' Civil Service Commissions." Aunateau described how

The Suffolk County medical report (given to all prospective county employees) was an exact duplicate of the Federal Government's Standard Form 89, that infamous "check list" which includes the "homosexual tendencies" question so familiar to those who apply for IV-F draft classification. Jim Owles and Doe Hansen, president of Long Island GAA, released a joint statement to the press through the Fair Employment Committee. It read, in part:

> Should one tell a fib and check "no" on "homosexual tendencies" all is not yet settled. The application asks whether or not a person has ever been denied life insurance ("if so, give details"). Many life insurance companies will openly admit that they will refuse insurance to persons should they uncover "evidence" of homosexuality. Further, the application inquires into draft status and military record—a "waiver" clause for release of draft and military medical records is included on the application, and *must* be signed before the application is processed.
>
> The G.A.A. is in the process of determining strategy to oppose this extraordinary intrusion into the privacy of employees and prospective employees of county government . . .

The press release was widely reported by newspapers and radio on Long Island and put the Suffolk County Civil Service Commission in the position of having to answer the club (they would not, prior to the release, have any dis-

236

cussion with GAA). On September 10, A. John Willis, Executive Director of the Commission, told the *Long Island Press:* "Only in certain jobs in very sensitive areas would the medical examiner want to know the answer to that question." [13] According to Willis, a "sensitive area" was, for example, the county children's shelter. But even in such cases, Willis asserted, only the doctor examining the applicant would be concerned about the area's "sensitivity," not he as Commissioner.

In response to the flurry of publicity, Gay Activists Alliance of Long Island was pledged political support in fighting this offensive hiring discrimination by members of the New Democratic Coalition and by some members of the Long Island Moratorium Committee, as well as by a number of politicians running for office in November 1970.

The Long Island action brought to light an interesting discrepancy. The director of the Nassau County Civil Service Commission informed the GAA committee, "We are unaware of any stated policy regarding the hiring of persons found to be homosexual. Except where the law permits and requires persons of a specific sex because of the duties involved in the performance of the position, the matter of sex is not a consideration of employment." [14] When interviewed by the *Long Island Press,* however, the Commission's answer was qualified: [15]

> The homosexuality question "is unproductive," noted Adele Leonard [executive secretary to the Commission] . . . "It's like years ago when they asked if you planned to overthrow the government. If you were planning to do something like that, you weren't going to say so." Similarly, she said, "I don't think a homosexual who wants a job caring for little boys would level with you." Mrs. Leonard noted that an application for a lifeguard job had been turned down by her department recently because of a history of homosexuality.

Aunateau's Fair Employment Committee meanwhile collected six signed statements from homosexuals recently fired by the New York City Board of Education. The Board, nevertheless, refused to communicate with the committee either in person or by correspondence. Nor would private employers whom the committee had discovered were guilty of discharging gays do so. The committee decided to address a memo-letter to Councilmen Eldon Clingan and Carter Burden, as well as to Eleanor Norton. Its subject: "justification for the use of the subpoena powers of a City Council committee or a Human Rights Commission investigation into employment discrimination against homosexuals." Aunateau related:

Mrs. Norton had already indicated to the committee her unwillingness to use her subpoena powers. But the committee was determined to have subpoena powers invoked by one city agency or another. Should the City Council fail to use these powers, the GAA committee was prepared to demand that the Mayor order the City Investigations Department to check into the matter thoroughly. The issue has not been settled, but the question of making such inquiries of the Board of Education, etc., is a hot one in light of recent investigations by the Manhattan District Attorney into the illegal "sale" of confidential police records to investigatory agencies (who in turn re-sell this information to employers). . . . In the opinion of the Fair Employment Committee, a full-scale investigation into all aspects of discrimination against gays in employment would uncover an enormous amount of such scandalous practices.

"There is a misconception on the part of the New York homosexual community as a whole," Aunateau insisted: "Mayor John Lindsay has *never* issued any executive order barring discrimination on the basis of sexual orientation in New York City employment. Instead, the city's civil service department issued a policy decision in 1967 to that effect which covered only certain city jobs. 'Sensitive' jobs were excluded from the policy decision—which seems to be very much like the official policies of most civil service departments throughout the state (and is very similar to the policy followed by Nassau County when it disqualified its lifeguard). In other words, the much-hailed policy decision—which is reversible, at any rate, should there be a change of city administration—merely brought civil service practices up to date with the rest of the state on the matter." But, the committee chairman declared, "Mayor Lindsay could at any time issue an *executive order* which would cover all jobs in the city as well as jobs in those companies doing business with the city. Such an order would cover teaching positions in public schools . . ." Aunateau revealed that

According to a representative of the United Federation of Teachers who has given the Fair Employment Committee a great deal of advice and helpful hints, there has *never* been a case of a homosexual teacher molesting a student in the city of New York. There have been, however, cases of heterosexual teachers who have molested students. Why, then, are gays excluded from this "sensitive" job? Neither the Board of Education nor the Board of Examiners, the latter having jurisdiction over unlicensed and untenured teachers, can seem to justify its objections on any grounds.

Many of the instructors who have been dismissed from the public school system (usually because a check into their draft records indicated "homosexual tendencies") and who submitted personal testimonies to the committee are now working successfully as private or parochial school teachers. One such, whose name and circumstances must be kept confidential until a fair employment law is passed to protect him, has written us:

. . . there is no doubt that I would have been far better paid in the public school system. Today, I earn perhaps one-third of the money I would be earning under the Board of Education, Emotionally, the strains I have suffered have been more painful than the loss of material benefits. In the Board of Education's manner of furtively excluding me from employment, they have acted with indiscretion and a lack of integrity. I suspect very few victims of discrimination (such as homosexuals) are willing to wait a year before they find that they are "unacceptable" for a position. . . .

By December 1970, the Fair Employment Committee had concluded that Gay Activists Alliance must commence zaps against offending employers and investigatory agencies. Aunateau believed that "Public actions against these offenders is the best way to gain publicity and create an awareness of the problem of discrimination against homosexuals." The committee began, in addition, to bring the fair employment issue to the primarily "straight" New York City areas outside Manhattan: Queens, the Bronx, Richmond, and Brooklyn. A first team went to Alexander's shopping center in Rego Park, Queens, on December 21, to meet Christmas shoppers. It carried petitions: ". . . to the President of the New York City Council, WE, THE UNDERSIGNED, SUPPORT EFFORTS IN THE NEW YORK CITY COUNCIL TO PASS LEGISLATION BARRING DISCRIMINATION ON THE BASIS OF SEXUAL ORIENTATION, IN PUBLIC AND PRIVATE EMPLOYMENT, IN THE CITY OF NEW YORK . . ." and two flyers. One flyer asked "Write to your councilman urging him to help in the passage of such legislation . . . Contact the FAIR EMPLOYMENT COMMITTEE of the GAY ACTIVISTS ALLIANCE if you have any information regarding employment discrimination and offenders, or if you are in a position to help present personal testimony before the CITY COMMISSION ON HUMAN RIGHTS. . . ." A second flyer—for "PERSONAL TESTIMONIES"—requested a statement including information about "1) position held; 2) reason for dismissal (actual and official); 3) how information regarding sexuality found by employer; 4) job performance and promotions before information found; 5) effects of dismissal on future employment prospects; and 6) all other relevant information."

Aunateau enunciated, at year's end: "The battle for the fair employment bill will be the first legislative battle fought by the gay liberation movement in New York City. Prospects for its passage seem hopeful."

■

Points 3 and 4 of GAA's Five Demands (page 150) related to fair employment, when Jim Owles, Arthur Evans, Phil Raia, and sweethearts Marty Robinson and Tom Doerr—hoping to present them—sat-in at headquarters of the New York Republican State Committee on June 24. The trial of the five men—become, to gays, the "Rockefeller Five"—was scheduled for August 5, the New York Criminal Court building at 100 Centre Street in downtown Manhattan.

GAA members distributed an estimated 35,000 leaflets * that broadcast the day of the trial and a gay protest rally for the Five Demands. To equal if not greater effect than the leaflets was the club's pre-rally, Saturday, August 1, in Sheridan Square. For more than an hour, Gay Activists stood on a straight chair borrowed from Bella Abzug's campaign headquarters and aimed a bullhorn at passing Villagers. Evans intoned: "Very often, concerns will not employ people who are homosexuals or who, in their opinion, appear to be homosexuals. We want a law on the books of

* Jim Owles opposed the creation of a GAA newsletter, or newspaper such as *Come Out!*, not only because of the pressures of the club's almost-constant political activity but "because it would make it convenient for people to know what is going on at GAA from the safety of their closets!"

the State of New York making this a crime, punishable by imprisonment and fine. . . . We want an investigation of the New York State Liquor Authority. The Authority is controlled, run for, and paid for by members of syndicates who want the State Liquor Authority to continue the economic exploitation of homosexuals. . . . The answer we got from the Republican Party of the State of New York and the Governor of New York was *the police*—the only answer that the Governor of this state has when a minority which is long oppressed stands up and demands its rights." Morty Manford: "The politicians in this state must, and *shall,* realize that continued neglect and disregard for their homosexual constituents will result in their failure to be re-elected . . ." Robinson: "For too long have homosexuals been excluded from the political process. . . . The time has come now for you to show your mind, to show it on the streets so that the Governor can see, can see that the times have changed and homosexuals have changed . . ." Manford: "We ask you to support the Rockefeller Five in their demands. Come down to 100 Centre Street . . ."

At 9:00 a.m., four days later, "the New York homophile community went with them to the courthouse door," reported the New York Daughters of Bilitis *Newsletter.* "The turnout was good, considering that most of us have to work on Wednesdays—about fifty men and women walking in a big scraggly ellipse, chanting, carrying signs like ROCKY HAS A HAPPY—WHY CAN'T WE? . . ." [16] Others, held aloft, spoke: ROCKY'S SIN IS SILENCE; ABOLISH SODOMY AND SOLICITATION LAWS; END ENTICEMENT AND ENTRAPMENT; BONDS FOR GAYS, NOT BONDAGE; JOBS SHOULDN'T ASK BEDROOM QUESTIONS; GAY CRIMES AREN'T . . . The five men passed under an inscription on the Criminal Court building façade, "EQUAL AND EXACT JUSTICE TO ALL MEN OF WHATEVER STATE OF PERSUASION" . . . and went inside.

"When we were called," recalls Owles, "we went up there holding hands, and the members who were in the court stood up. The judge noticed that we were holding hands, but he said nothing—which was unusual. . . . What he did ask was what the lambda meant (and unfortunately our lawyer didn't know what it meant). One of the members told him what it meant: homosexual liberation."

"After the case was postponed [John Glendinning, treasurer of the Republican State Committee and plaintiff, did not appear *]," Gay Activist Arthur Bell told WBAI "Homosexual News," [17] "about one third of the courtroom walked out. . . . It was quite a mind-blowing sight, I might add. We were covered by CBS cameras!" Jim Jensen, on WCBS-TV's "Six O'Clock Report," [18] spotlighted network reporter Gloria Rojas's interview with a GAA member. The Gay Activist explained, "We're de-

---

* In fact, no representative of the Committee appeared on September 29, date of the retrial, and the case was again postponed—to October 29. When, again, no complainant appeared, the Five were given a D.O.R. (dismissal on recognizance) and charges were dismissed.

manding that Governor Rockefeller make himself sensible to his gay constituents. We're calling for an end to entrapment throughout the state, calling for a fair employment law, calling for an end to raids of bars, calling for the repeal of the sodomy and solicitation laws . . ." Rojas: "Do you feel that the movement is taken as seriously as other minority movements?" The Gay Activist: "Among many quarters I'll have to admit we're not taken seriously yet, but we will be."

Some protesters had picketed while the Five met the judge. Gay Activist Cary Yurman reported to GAY [19] that one passerby, asked by another what was going on, replied, "There are a bunch of people over there. They're demonstrating for love." Picketers saw defeated Democratic gubernatorial candidate Howard Samuels pass by in a limousine and wave his support with a V sign.

The Five exited Criminal Court to a huge welcome, followed by a rally in Foley Square Park and speeches by Gay Activists Morty Manford and Arthur Evans, GLFer Hank Ferrari, Hiram Ruiz of Florida State University GLF (Tallahassee), and Isabel Miller of New York DOB. Some women's liberationists had joined the GAA, GLF, and DOB protesters. Manford acknowledged, "We are proud today to have participation from all areas of the political spectrum. Certain issues transcend political ideologies. We all share our civil oppression. . . ." Evans, of the Five, declared, ". . . today we know that not only is gay good, gay is angry! We are telling all the politicians and elected officials of New York state that they are going to become responsible to the people. We will make them responsible to us, or we will stop the conduct of the business of government." [20]

Some participants in the rally returned to Criminal Court to continue picketing through the lunch hour. Owles maintains, "We freaked out a lot of people down by 100 Centre Street: it was about the last thing they expected* . . . gays marching around with signs and some of the chants we had":

> "Rockefeller, Rockefeller, where are you?
>   where are you?
> When we need the law changed, when we need
>   the law changed,
> Where are you? where are you?"

Bella Abzug, Democratic Congressional candidate for the 19th District, sent a telegram to the rallyers, which was read by Marty Robinson. A day before the rally, Representative Edward I. Koch had posted a letter:

---

* GLFer Gerald Hansen asserts, "One of my dreams is a GLF booth near the statue of Washington in lower Manhattan," and adds that the area is so conservative, "if someone comes along with a new soft drink it almost causes a riot."

Dear Mr. Owles:

I have your letter of July 30 and I did receive a flyer on the subject when walking through Sheridan Square on Saturday. I would like you to know my position with respect to the five items which are the subject of your demonstration.

1) I believe that consenting sexual acts between adults is a private matter and should not be subject to statutory regulation.

2) I believe that police practices which include entrapment of homosexuals are wrong. You may be aware of the fact that I brought this entire matter of entrapment and harassment to the attention of Police Commissioner Leary by letter dated March 18, 1970, a copy of which I enclose. I ultimately received a response from the Police Department which indicated that entrapment and harassment were barred by the Police Commissioner.

3) I believe as you do that the fair employment statutes should prohibit any discrimination based on an individual's private sexual preferences.

4) I believe as you do that bonding companies should not be permitted to discriminate against homosexuals.

5) I believe as you do that state liquor authority policy should be reviewed. With respect to harassment, I refer you again to my letter to Commissioner Leary. . . .

12

Homosexuals, long oppressed because they have been a silent minority, are now, through such militant activist organizations as the Gay Activists Alliance, demanding the civil rights that inherently belong to all citizens of the United States. I wholeheartedly endorse this goal.

—from a statement to GAA by Adam Walinsky, candidate for New York State Attorney General, 1970

The parliamentarian opened the meeting. After the secretary's reading of the minutes. Jim Owles forewent his President's Report, deferring to Police Power Committee chairman Eben Clark. Curious. A hush.

"We've done a study, and we've discovered that in the past five years there have been only four major and violent confrontations with the police, in New York City: one in Harlem, one in Bedford-Stuyvesant, one in Spanish Harlem, and one in Greenwich Village at the end of our protest on 42nd Street. In each of the first three confrontations, Mayor Lindsay made immediate statements on television and then went immediately into the streets to appease the people and to calm the streets. To cool everything. However, after the fourth confrontation—which was the gay confrontation—Mayor Lindsay not only did not come out into the streets to cool things, he didn't even make a public statement or even accept the fact that something had gone on.

"Two weeks ago we voted to zap Mayor Lindsay, since our attempts to have a meeting with him have been denied continuously. We wanted to get from him a public statement on the police harassment of the gay community. On this last Monday we began our zap program on Mayor Lindsay. Thirty of us joined him in attending the opening of the Metropolitan Opera House [September 14]. The confrontation was very fast, but not without effect. *The New York Times, Women's Wear Daily,* and WCBS News gave it coverage.* However, the best news came at a meeting I had with Carter Burden, who is the City Councilman for the Upper

---

* GAY reported: "As the Mayor and his wife entered the lobby at 8:15 p.m., onlookers gave subdued applause. Then, without warning, a GAA member jumped in homosexuals?' The demonstrator was immediately apprehended and pulled away by front of him, shouting, 'What are you going to do about ending police harassment of police. Other demonstrators began to chant, 'End police harassment! End police harass-

East Side. He mentioned that he had heard of the zap not through the papers but through the political grapevine and from one of Lindsay's aides. So obviously the zap was very successful in that area.

"I think Monday was only a warmup. It's proved to us that Mayor Lindsay is vulnerable. So the Police Power Committee would like to propose a second zap action, which would take place tonight.

"Mayor Lindsay is speaking at a peace rally. Since his policy, as of now, seems to be peace for Vietnam but no peace for homosexuals in New York City, I feel that a confrontation would be very good this evening. I would like to take a group over now, from here, to confront him.

"It's been published in the press and invitations have been sent out to individual groups concerned with the peace movement that Lindsay will be speaking, along with Bella Abzug and several other candidates. It's going to be at the Eisner and Lubin Auditorium, which is in the Loeb Student Center by Washington Square Park. If we vote upon taking this action this evening, then I would like everybody who is interested in joining the zap—which should be as many people as possible—to go over there now. We have worked out a zap action. It would involve our waiting until Mayor Lindsay is on the speaker's podium, at which time we would walk in in force, down the aisles, and attempt to seize the microphone. The more people we have, obviously, the much more successful the attempt will be.

"For those of you who don't know what a zap is, it's a confrontation in public with an official—this official being Mayor Lindsay. At the confrontation, this one, we simply ask that he make a public stand on our questions of police harassment. It's a successful thing. GAA has done it in the past and will continue to do it. It's a very good political maneuver. It's a very powerful thing. We are one of the few groups in New York City to seem to take advantage of it. . . . Now I'll turn over the floor to any discussion of this zap action tonight . . ."

A member suggested that when—and if—GAA members captured the microphone the Mayor might give them "one of his political excuses." Then, "do we just remain there on the stage?"

Clark replied, "No. Our intention would be for one person to go to seize the podium. We have several people who have agreed to make the attempt, with prepared statements to be read so that we may gain the confidence of the audience. The statement would say that 'We are sorry to interrupt this meeting. It is not by choice. We are forced into it because we have not been able to meet with Mayor Lindsay and this is the only opportunity which we have to voice our problems.' At which time, if he attempts to leave, he will embarrass himself publicly—it's going to be

---

ment!' The Mayor smiled and moved hurriedly into the theatre. 'GAY POWER!' shouted the demonstrators after him . . . 'All right boys, you made your point,' said an irritated, balding employee of the Met. 'Will you leave now?' Police escorted the demonstrators off the plaza." (October 12, 1970.)

covered by the press, and everybody in the audience will see what's happening immediately, and we will make a statement to the audience, 'You see what our problem is,' and then leave en masse.

"If Mayor Lindsay stays but refuses to answer the question that we ask—which is 'Why do you not control the police force in New York City, and when will you come out with a public statement on police harassment of the gay community?'—then we will go into a chant of 'Answer the question, answer the question!' "

A GAA member was concerned that New York University had a security guard, which might present trouble. Clark: "I can only say from past experiences in zap actions that, of those of you who undertake this action tonight—and I hope you all will—no one will be arrested! What will happen is that, if someone fails to reach the podium, in that event he will be thrown out—possibly by regular police, possibly by college security forces, but he will just be let outside." At the suggestion that the Gay Activists take along a lawyer, Clark reassured, "The only people who are attempting to seize the podium are people who have volunteered their services. Anybody who joins us in this zap action tonight will merely be a participator marching down the aisles. You won't be asked to seize the podium. Nobody who joins the zap action other than those who volunteered their services would be risking possible arrest."

Randy Wicker rose to object that GAA would be "interrupting a peace meeting with several speakers, one of whom is our friend Bella Abzug." Clark answered that the statement that GAA had been forced into the action would prevent misunderstanding, but Wicker countered that the Activists would be confronting the Mayor in an audience of "his supporters."

"We will *not* be confronting Lindsay in front of his supporters— this is not a Lindsay rally, this is a peace rally. There will be a helluva lot of people there who don't give a shit about Mayor Lindsay. They are there because they want peace in Vietnam."

John Rash worried that the gay community's disputes with NYU over dances at Weinstein Hall had not been forgotten: ". . . I think that if this comes off, unless it is made absolutely crystal clear that it's not against the *university* it will damage the relationship—which may be improving." Clark again insisted that the statement from the podium would suffice as an apology for the interruption, that "this is what we as citizens are forced to do . . ."

Leo Martello contributed, "We are not there so much to zap Lindsay as we are to dramatize our plight. This is the only recourse open to us."

The president rose to speak of an encounter just that week with Arthur Goldberg, who would not answer several GAA questions. "Bella said, 'Go ahead, Arthur, answer him!' I'm sure she'll say the same thing tonight." Owles was sure that students in the audience would support the zappers. "*They* won't like his evasive smile. I don't think they'll stand for it like the people at the Metropolitan Opera did."

A duplication, then a multiplication, of quiet voices: "Let's go!" "Let's go!" "Let's go!"

A vote was taken. The motion to attempt the action carried unanimously. To wild applause.

But now, Clark had instructions to give: they would meet at Washington Square Arch, away from Loeb Student Center where their action might be anticipated—"Lindsay might recognize us (he knows several of our faces!), pulling up in his limousine." A truck could take some of the members. Others had cars. Several could share taxis.

Clark detailed: "When we enter Loeb Student Center, no matter how many aisles there are, we want to fill all of them. (I'm under the impression that there are two aisles to go down.) We want to march down toward the stage chanting 'End police harassment!' so that the minute we enter the auditorium people know the number we're doing—we're not going to enter chanting 'Gay Power'! We want our point to be made, that we are there protesting police harassment, from the minute we enter, so that if we're not completely successful in the zap, people at NYU will not simply say, 'Well, those fucking faggots are just doing a heavy Gay Power number.' "

Together-laughter . . .

"Secondly, if we are successful in seizing the podium, then if Lindsay capitulates and says he will meet with us we want to leave immediately en masse. But the signal to leave will be whenever the GAA member who is on the podium leaves the podium. (*Not* if he's thrown off the podium!) We do an immediate about-face and march—not quietly: we chant 'Gay Power!' on the way *out* of the Student Center, we want to make it very clear that when we leave we are very together. We want it to have been very obvious to the people there that we were there for one reason: not to disrupt the meeting, but to get our grievances to Lindsay in the presence of the public.

"If Lindsay refuses to answer any questions that are put to him by the speaker who has gotten to the podium, please immediately go into the chant of 'Answer the question!' and continue this chant until Mayor Lindsay comes over to the podium or splits. If he splits, we have a planned statement to give to the audience, which will let them know that 'Even here, you see what happens—he splits without making a public statement.' That's all."

Exeunt.

The 50-odd Gay Activists stood, later, at a corner near Loeb, unable to join the rally—speeches had begun and the doors were locked. As Lindsay's limousine approached a side entrance to the Loeb stage, an Activist spotted him. A rush, shouts of "End police harassment!" and he scurried inside. Dennis Altman, an Australian gay and visitor to the meeting, reconnoitered to locate a balcony exit, but, inside, was told by a guard that the "balcony is not being used tonight." Around the block containing the student center, the disgruntled Activists picketed, chanting, until the rally should end.

The *New York Post,* GAY, and *Gay Scene* told what happened next. In GAY,[1] Randy Wicker related that Morty Manford managed to gain admittance (Wicker—with his video machine and press card—and writer Leo Skir also entered):

Manford approached the stage as Lindsay spoke, mounted the platform, stood next to the mayor, apologized for interrupting and commenced his statement (amid a chorus of boos from those in the audience) "Mayor Lindsay has failed to restrain his police . . ." At which point a plainclothesman pushed him back off stage. Lindsay interrupted his speech, which was being covered by local and national press and which was essentially a carefully worded statement regarding those domestic needs which are being neglected because of the Vietnam War.

"Anyone who felt he had something to say, please come forward and I will relinquish the microphone," Lindsay interjected.

An organizer of the rally took the platform to decry "the attempted disruption of this meeting which has so long been in planning." He received thunderous applause from those present.

". . . To attack one of the few men in this city who are still willing to listen is also a grievous error. I would now like to ask Mayor Lindsay to continue his remarks." (Thunderous applause once more.)

Lindsay continued a few minutes more but once again, GAA's Morty Manford came down the aisle and mounted the platform.

"You said anyone could speak." Manford commenced looking at Lindsay, who nodded, then stepped back and surrendered the podium to him.

Manford apologized once again for interrupting the meeting only to be greeted by a chorus of boos. "We have tried to meet with the Mayor but have not been successful," he charged, "so we have to confront him publicly in this manner."

Over 400 gays had been arrested in the midtown area, held overnight and then released, he said, and these people were thereby burdened with a police record which can cause trouble in finding employment. He noted he himself had been arrested as "an observer." . . .

"We have 100, 150 people outside who want to come in here and talk with you," he noted, then challenged Lindsay: "What are you going to do, Mayor Lindsay, to control your police, to keep them from harassing homosexuals?"

Lindsay continued to stand to the side conferring with three or four aides. The audience noise was disruptive enough that Manford leaned forward to be better heard through the mike.

"One in ten people participate in homosexual sex. In New York, that number might be more like 20%," he speculated. "We constitute a large voting bloc. If Mayor Lindsay ignores this voting bloc, he has no future as Mayor or as a presidential candidate in 1972." His comments ended, Manford walked offstage to scattered applause.

Lindsay returned to his speech, at first continuing to talk about Bridges for Peace, the sponsoring organization, and only very slowly and indirectly getting around to answering Manford's charges.

"Those who are dissatisfied, who have complaints . . . should see my aide Barry Goetterer as soon as possible," Lindsay replied, then went on to add that sometimes someone who heads a large bureaucracy, as he does, finds it impossible to keep in touch with every group.

Meanwhile, Loeb Student Center guards had allowed the GAA demonstrators to come into the lobby and listen to the proceedings in the hall, over a loudspeaker situated there.

As Lindsay left, several GAA members approached him asking about homosexual civil rights. Lindsay kept smiling, shaking hands, saying "Glad to see you" to one and all as he worked his way through the crowd to his limousine.

Arthur Evans, a GAA activist, stood in front of Lindsay's limousine to block its exit but a security man simply picked him up by the belt and back of his pants and tossed him aside . . .

As the meeting ended and the students filed out, the GAAers stood to one side of the Loeb Student Center steps chanting, "WE NEED YOUR HELP! WE NEED YOUR HELP!" . . .

A little more than a month later, GAY headlines announced LINDSAY AND WIFE ZAPPED BY GAY ACTIVISTS; MRS. LINDSAY OBVIOUSLY SHAKEN.[2] For *The New York Times*[3] Charlotte Curtis pictured the gala event: a first benefit of the New York City Cultural Council. "The gathering, which included a preview performance of 'Two by Two' at the Imperial Theater and supper afterward at the Metropolitan Museum of Art, began—as all such occasions having virtually anything to do with the Metropolitan have lately—with pickets." She meant New York Museum Action, a group hoping to halt the museum's expansion into Central Park, who stood outside the theater. Mrs. Edwin I. Hilson, chairman of the event, was greeting guests inside.

Mr. and Mrs. Lindsay entered the lobby without being noticed by Mrs. Hilson, but she soon saw them and called out. At the point when she joined them, "for the inevitable photography, perhaps a dozen men from Gay Liberation [Gay Activists Alliance] . . . began to shout at them. 'Homosexuals need your help,' they yelled five times in unison, then, 'End police harassment, end police harassment, end police harassment. . . .' The Mayor looked straight ahead. Guests jamming the lobby pushed and shoved each other to get into the theater. The Mayor's bodyguard pushed back. Theater employees rushed to shove the demonstrators outside. Mrs. Hilson was frightened. 'My God, they came right at us,' she said. 'Anything could have happened. . . .' "

On October 12, GAY's editors had pondered,[4]

While we have been quite enthusiastic about the many accomplishments of

248

the New York Gay Activists Alliance, we find ourselves disenchanted by GAA's latest "action": zapping Mayor Lindsay on opening night at the Metropolitan Opera.

Did the demonstrators who stepped in front of the Mayor and his wife expect that he would say to her, "You go inside dear. I'm going to sit by the fountain and chat with the fellows from the Gay Activists Alliance."

We do not doubt but that the Gay Activists Alliance is impatient. We are all impatient. . . . If some activists are so impatient that they are ready to abandon several years of improved relations with the Mayor's office because of recent police harassment, we feel that this is indeed tragic. . . .

Now, reviewing the Imperial Theater confrontation, the editors stated that "zapping is generally unproductive, we feel, in rectifying any grievances which homosexuals may have and could easily turn a friend into an enemy," [5] but editorialized: [6] "There seems to be some question as to whether or not John Lindsay, the Mayor of New York City, is a friend to the homosexual community. . . . Is the Gay Activists Alliance choosing the best method of approach? Hmmmmmm."

He is a short man, unprepossessing and mild-mannered. One might think he is a mousey, hen-pecked milquetoast, a professional failure. The impression remains when he speaks. . . . Then one feels the quiet authority and inviolable dignity, and recognizes a tremendous strength.

Thus Dick Leitsch painted Howard Regis Leary, THE STRONG ARM OF THE LAW, for GAY readers: [7] a New York City police commissioner whom Leitsch first met in 1966 and under whose commissionership, "Any allegation or charge I ever made through Mattachine of police abuse, corruption, or harassment, was always carefully checked out." Four Gay Activists visited Leary on July 27.

With Commissioner Leary were First Deputy Police Commissioner John Walsh and other top police officials. Recounting recent raids on afterhours bars, harassment and verbal abuse of individual homosexual citizens, Jim Owles met them full on: "We're here to ask you what can be done. Your actions make it difficult for a civil rights organization such as ours, that is trying to reform the establishment. When we work against a background of such police tactics, they tend to undermine our efforts and to drive the gay community into the hands of extremists."

Owles agreed with Leary's answer that "If someone is selling liquor without a license, we have to stop them. We have a duty." The GAA president emphasized that GAA's concern was "that homosexual patrons should be left alone when police take action against such establishments."

Marty Robinson complained of syndicate control of gay bars—even of legitimately run gay bars: "Such bars should be tolerated . . . We want to see legitimate bars where there's no guy at the door with a cigar in his face saying to kids, 'Welcome to your life—this is it, your subculture, your subterranean existence.' Commissioner, our desire *now* is that anyone who's honest can get into business and stay in without a shakedown, and can get police protection. But we must have police protection for this to be possible." Deputy Commissioner Walsh promised, "You can get all of the police protection we can give here." Owles added that "GAA is pressing for an investigation of alleged collusion between the State Liquor Authority and organized crime. Meanwhile, whatever struggles there are between the police and the syndicate, we simply ask that homosexual patrons not be used as pawns in between."

Before leaving, the Gay Activists "brought forward a demand for a police directive barring the use of offensive epithets"—they remembered the Snake Pit raid—"by police against gays." Commissioner Leary answered, "With your cooperation, we'll write such an order. We don't want police to harass or intimidate or use objectionable language. If we have constant communication and your cooperation, we can take corrective action in these areas. We appreciate the sensitivity of your position. And while we are duty bound to enforce the law, it needn't be in an offensive manner. If policemen are lacking in basic psychological awareness of your community,* we must apologize for that. Let's arrange to have another meeting at your convenience so that we can continue with constructive communication." [8]

GAA was angry when what seemed a reinvigorated election-year/end-of-summer wave of arrests troubled the New York gay world in July and August. Had the negotiations been merely sweet talk? GAA was shocked when what began as a GLF-GAA combined protest in Times Square turned into New York's second series of gay riots on August 29 and 30. The Activists' meeting, that following Thursday, was a tense one.

Owles: "I think we have to accept more and more of these things when we have a city administration that turns a deaf ear to our demands . . . I can understand the frustration and alienation of many of the people in that demonstration at the end, when they started to fight back. . . . This week we tried to set up a number of meetings, we tried to get a comment from the Mayor's office, but for the most part we were given

---

* In a letter published by ....*another Voice* (Central Ohio Mattachine Society newsletter), a policeman in Orlando, Florida, commented: "Police officers are exasperated at having to engage in vain efforts to enforce laws that aren't justified by present-day conditions. The resolution of society's sex problems has been left to the policeman, who has neither the time nor the training to cope in any scientifically oriented way with the sex offender. . . . Those laws that have been shown by new knowledge to be obsolete should be stricken from the books. Only then will mistreatment of sexual minorities come to an end." (December 1969–January 1970.)

a runaround.* As saddened as he was irked by the Mayor's silence, the new series of zaps would be poor consolation: "I want you to know that we are going to be following the Mayor around. There is not going to be the old game-playing anymore, where a small group of, us grab hold of his arm, saying, 'Hey, look, talk to us.' That's out. We are going to escalate. We are going to bring much more pressure than we ever have."

Robinson: "So we went back to Leary, and again—in violation of his 'Open Door' policy—he gave us no appointment. We called up the Mayor and we spoke to the Mayor's people and we were told, 'No appointment. No comment. Go see Eleanor Holmes Norton of the Human Rights Commission.'"

A few weeks later, Gay Activists Owles, Eben Clark, and Arthur Evans, accompanied by City Councilmen Carter Burden and Eldon Clingan, were guests of Deputy Mayor Richard Aurelio. GAY stated that "The meeting followed two public confrontations by GAA members, of Mayor Lindsay," and published a part of the dialogue: [9]

Aurelio: I am not aware of any harassment prior to the demonstration. Without individual badge numbers, names, squad car numbers and precincts, I can only regard this information as hearsay.
Arthur Evans: While I served as a GAA observer on 42nd Street, I was arrested with three other GAA members. All of us were illegally arrested. We took badge numbers. . . .
Eldon Clingan: There are many other problems facing the homosexual community besides police harassment. I have been working with GAA on a fair employment law to protect homosexuals. It would be beneficial if Mayor Lindsay would speak out in favor of such a bill.
Aurelio: Mayor Lindsay has never been on the wrong side of a civil rights question.
Eben Clark: We're here to discuss the need for a meeting with Mayor Lindsay.
Aurelio: My office can handle any problems which might arise in the community. GAA has established two liaisons with the Mayor's office, which is more than any other group of people in New York has.
Eben Clark: We feel that the Mayor should hear about our problems from the lips of homosexuals! How can you expect us to believe that you can accurately relate our problems to the Mayor when you are so naive about the problems of the community? . . . You have avoided every question put to you, not only by GAA, but by these two City Councilmen as well.
Aurelio: I am sorry to hear that, but I have more to consider than just the homosexual community. . . . Perhaps if you have problems, you may

* On Monday, September 1, in response to a complaint by the Mattachine Society of New York, a police representative had visited MSNY headquarters. Michael Kotis, MSNY president, detailed police harassment of homosexuals on 42nd Street and Third Avenue; a "campaign against after-hours bars"; harassment of meetings of the Daughters of Bilitis; "intimidation of the radical elements of the gay community"; and "violation of an individual's right to have a telephone call made for him when arrested." (GAY, September 21, 1970.)

establish rapport with local police precincts and a great deal might be accomplished in this manner.

Arthur Evans: We have attempted to establish liaisons with police and the gay community, and police promises to GAA have never been fulfilled. It is now the policy of GAA to deal only with elected civilians to whom police are answerable.

Aurelio: I feel that you will find you can work through local precincts. I will issue a press release stating that I have met with GAA representatives, but I doubt that the papers will print it.

GAY did, after calling the Deputy Mayor's offices for a copy of the release: "Deputy Mayor Aurelio and Councilmen Eldon Clingan and Carter Burden met with four members of the Gay Activists Alliance to hear their grievances regarding discrimination, denial of civil liberties and other problems. They were urged to continue their discussions with the City Commission on Human Rights and to provide the City Administration with specific instances of harassment."

■

On August 6, GAA secretary Arnie Kantrowitz read from his minutes: "The president reported that a delegation from GAA visited the Executive Committee of the New Democratic Coalition, which represents 20 per cent of the Democratic Party in New York State. At our request, NDC has set up a special committee on homosexual rights, which will have two GAA representatives. This committee will pressure for acceptance of our demands of New York State; GAA will be allowed to leaflet inside the NDC convention hall."

In an August 13 story for the *Village Voice,* GAA public relations man Arthur Bell argued that GAY IS POLITICAL AND DEMOCRATS AGREE. "That the Democrats, in the shape of the New Democratic Coalition, were responsive," he said, "and the Republicans, in the form of the New York Republican State Committee, were not, may be indicative of where the gay vote goes in November. New militant gay groups such as Gay Activists Alliance are reaching into politics and getting to the homosexual whose concern may not be political, but who knows that Bella Abzug is pro-movement and Leonard Farbstein anti."

Interviewed by WBAI's "Homosexual News" commentator Pete Wilson, Bell told what he discovered at a first NDC convention at Robert Wagner Junior High School a few days after the coalition agreed to form a homosexual rights committee:[10]

"From Arthur Goldberg I got a very evasive answer. When I asked Goldberg if we could set up an appointment, he said—and I quote— 'I'm always available to conduct a decent conversation. That was no way

252

to approach me.' " * About Adam Walinsky: "He said that he would make a statement, work something out, particularly in the area of police harassment, before the campaign is over." Richard Ottinger, United States senatorial candidate, "did say that, if he had a platform, he would include a statement about homosexuals and would answer to some of the demands that we were making of the NDC." Bell asked one of Ottinger's opponents, the incumbent Charles Goodell, "What are you going to do about us? Are you going to acknowledge the fact that we're alive?" Bell handed him the five GAA demands, and he replied, "Thanks very much. I'll look into it."

Activist Bell remarked, of the NDC convention, that "most of the people who talked about freedom of the individual and all of the good things that we're supposed to expect of our good politicians neglected to mention homosexuals. They completely avoided the subject, they were all for rights for the black people and for the Chicanos and for women and for everybody—'We'll do it, we're wonderful people'—but no mention at all about homosexuals."

On September 19, the Activists' Ad Hoc 1970 Elections Committee mailed, primarily to Democratic and Republican candidates for New York State and Federal legislatures as well as elective State executive offices, a letter with enclosure:

Dear Candidate:

In certain areas of New York City close to thirty percent of the electorate is homosexual or bisexual. In most urban and suburban areas throughout the state, the homosexual minority counts for approximately ten percent of the electorate. Although the Gay Activists Alliance does not endorse political candidates, it does inform the homosexual electorate of candidates' positions on homosexual rights.

The enclosed questionnaire gives you the opportunity to express your feelings on these vital subjects. In turn, it provides us with the information we need to enable us to perform our role. These questionnaires have been sent to all but a few of the major party candidates who are running for office within the city and the state. In order to be considered valid, the questionnaire must be signed by the candidate. Please send it back to us in the enclosed envelope within ten days.

Thank you for your cooperation.

Sincerely,
Jim Owles
President, Gay Activists Alliance

The Federal enclosure asked:

* GAA planned to approach the candidate again on October 17 at Broadway and 86th Street, but canceled the confrontation when he issued a supportive statement.

253

1) Would you support an end to discrimination against homosexuals in obtaining federal security clearance?

Yes..................................No..............................

2) Do you support the right of homosexuals to serve in the armed forces?

Yes..................................No..............................

3) Would you work for an end to income tax discrimination against single persons?

Yes .. ..No ....

4) Would you support the revocation of the tax-exempt status of those tax-exempt institutions (religious, psychiatric, and educational) that defame homosexuals and lobby against them?

Yes..................................No..............................

5) Would you work to oppose governmental collection of data on the sexual preference of individuals?

Yes..................................No..............................

6) Would you favor ending the State Department's policy of denying visas to foreign homosexuals?

Yes..................................No..............................

7) Would you favor ending the policy that often denies to foreign-born homosexuals the privilege of obtaining American Citizenship?

Yes..................................No..............................

8) Would you work for a federal fair employment law which prohibits the refusal to hire and the firing of employees solely on the basis of their homosexuality?

Yes..................................No..............................

Remarks:

Signature...

And the State enclosure queried:

1) Do you favor total repeal of the New York State Sodomy and Solicitation laws?

Yes.... ....No..............................

254

2) Will you work for an end to police harassment and entrapment of homosexuals?

Yes................................No................................

3) Will you work for an end to police harassment of bars and other public facilities catering to homosexuals?

Yes................................No................................

4) Would you support an investigation of the State Liquor Authority concerning its harassment of bars and other public facilities catering to homosexuals?

Yes................................No................................

[5), 6), 7), and 8) were near-duplicates of numbers 8), 3), 4), and 5) of the federal questionnaire.]

9) Would you work for an immediate investigation of the insurance and bonding companies which practice discrimination against homosexuals?

Yes................................No................................

Remarks:

Signature..

Invitations to visit its meetings were extended by GAA to many candidates. On October 8, New York City Assistant Commissioner of Commerce and Industry Arthur Kessler represented Charles Goodell, incumbent and candidate, R, for United States Senator. Three candidates for the Manhattan 63rd State Assembly District spoke to the Gay Activists on October 15: Stephen Casko, C; Charles Drew, R; and incumbent William Passannante, D. Two Thursdays later, George Spitz, D, candidate for the Manhattan 26th State Senatorial District, visited the club.

The earliest visit to Gay Activists Alliance was made by deputy campaign manager Ethan Elvin, for Richard Ottinger, candidate, D, for United States Senator, on September 24. Mr. Elvin advised, "I think that the reasons you should be with Dick Ottinger partly have to do with Ottinger, partly have to do with what's going on in this country, partly have to do with the other two candidates running for the same office. Dick Ottinger has been a fighter for civil liberties, rights of people to be left alone, to live their own lives the way they choose, ever since he has been in public life. He's fought on the right side of every civil libertarian issue: he fought against the House Un-American Activities Committee, he's fought for civil rights, he's fought for poor people, for black people, for Chicanos, for Puerto Ricans. . . . And he's fought these battles consistently—he hasn't been an opportunist who one year was on one side of the issue, another year was on the other side of the issue. He didn't play the kinds of games of being for half-way measures and trying to make excuses to both sides in an issue. He's been very much out in front. . . . He's been outspoken consistently against political repression in this country. Especially recently, with the kind of problems we've been experiencing with the Nixon-Agnew-Mitchell regime."

Mr. Elvin assured GAA members, "In terms of what *you're* concerned about, in this organization, I could tell you that Dick Ottinger will support an investigation of the police department, and an investigation of the SLA for the kinds of police riots that we saw at the Haven, the kinds of police riots that we saw at the Stonewall last year. And that he supports a revision of the penal code as it affects any sex practices of anyone."

Backing GAA-type militancy, Ottinger's representative urged, "Like, with any other oppressed group of people, you gotta do what you're doing now: you gotta get together and yell. Nobody yelled much before, so, yeah, you can yell at us—the politicians who didn't do anything—but part of the burden is with you because you didn't do anything before . . ."

Marc Rubin, parliamentarian and chairman of the meeting, made certain the deputy campaign manager knew that "GAA does not endorse political candidates. GAA will never recommend to its constituency that it vote for a particular political candidate. What it *can* do is report on a candidate's stand. And then leave it up to them." Jim Owles rose, to add, "Once we have heard from as many candidates as possible and received their replies to the questionnaire, we are going to put out a leaflet to the community . . ."

Before Mr. Elvin left the meeting, an Activist referred back to the "position papers" the campaign manager had assured them Ottinger would publish: "I want to know if the word *homosexual* will be used and our grievances not just be lumped in with penal reform and some other nebulous term that will cover all of us! If we're going to our constituents and speak of Ottinger we've got to have some definite comments in these position papers and not on the sixty-fourth page of the *Times*!" . . .

As candidates began to mail back the GAA questionnaire—many did so with a letter-comment in addition—GAY headlined VAST OUTPOURING OF POLITICAL SUPPORT,[11] told that "The Gay Activists Alliance of New York City has successfully elicited answers from nearly one-third of New York's candidates . . ." * GAY published a letter from New York State

---

* Marc Rubin, Elections Committee chairman, revealed that the return was nearer 25 per cent. Questioning candidates' views on homosexual civil rights was no new tactic for the homophile world; MSNY and groups in other cities have done so for years. Percentage of response, however, had never been greater than in the New York 1970 elections. By comparison, the Dorian Society of Seattle reported, "Out of 73 questionnaires mailed to both Republican and Democratic candidates competing in the September 15 primary, only five bothered to respond. . . . All five of the responses were from Democrats, and four of the five were positive." (*The Columns Northwest*, September 1970.)

Attorney General Louis Lefkowitz to Jim Owles, sent as a substitute for the questionnaire and non-committal, which said, "I am opposed to illegal harassment of any citizen in any place." Adam Walinsky, Lefkowitz's opponent for the attorney generalship, was more precise:

I endorse the rights of every individual, whatever his political, religious or social affiliation, to live his life free of political, social and economic harassment and oppression. Specifically, I recommend repeal of the Sodomy and Solicitation Laws as they refer to homosexuals. I support extending to homosexuals the existing Fair Employment laws relating to private, public and governmental establishments. I deplore police harassment of homosexuals. I am opposed to the collection of data on the sexual preference of individuals by governmental agencies.

GAY's election issue (as did *The Advocate*'s) listed the candidates who had responded to the Activists' questionnaire and indicated their answers to each item. GAY included several of the candidates' "remarks": [12] Shirley Chisholm (incumbent and candidate, D, for Brooklyn's 12th Congressional Districts)—"Homosexuals are human beings and should enjoy all liberties and opportunities afforded all other citizens." Martin Fine (candidate, R, for State Assembly, Manhattan)—"Most of the questions are too broad and ambiguous to permit a yes or no answer." Charles Drew (candidate, R, for Assemblyman, Manhattan)—"Every man and woman has a right to do his or her 'own thing' with regard for the rights of others!" George Spitz (candidate, D, for State Senate, Manhattan)—"I endorse the Wolfenden Report (Great Britain)." Antonio Olivieri (candidate, D, for State Assembly, Manhattan)—"All of these are perfectly reasonable proposals which I will support." Stephen Solarz (incumbent and candidate, D, for State Assembly, Brooklyn)—"Keep fighting!"

GAY was unable to note gubernatorial candidate, D, Arthur Goldberg's opinions about GAA demands. Following a mid-October meeting with Elections Committee chairman Marc Rubin and Marty Robinson, Goldberg issued a statement for release October 25:

Homosexuality has been treated by our society as a criminal problem, with harsh and discriminatory laws, for too long. I believe that all issues concerning consenting relations between adults in private are mishandled when they are dealt with adversely in the legal area. Questions of fair employment, bonding, police harassment and other, related matters should not be answered negatively for a man or woman just because his or her private life involves homosexuality. Present laws and present attitudes are wrong. The law must change and social attitudes must change. I will work to these ends if I am elected.

In the *Village Voice,*[13] Activist Arthur Bell called it "a major breakthrough in the political-sexual arena that Gay Activists Alliance occupies. It is the first time a gubernatorial candidate has come out openly in favor of homosexual rights." Bell had voiced dismay over WBAI on August 14 [14] that "Rockefeller is completely inaccessible—you cannot get near him, you cannot get his itinerary!" But Marty Robinson, Morty Manford, and several other Gay Activists—including a GAA photographer, Richard Wandel—did on Thursday evening, September 24, as the Governor left the Georgian Room of the Piccadilly Hotel. Wandel told GAY that Rockefeller "said that he has little knowledge of the New York State sodomy laws" and "gave the gay demonstrators his personal assurances that the State Liquor Authority was completely honest and that New York's gay bars were not controlled by mobs or syndicates." An October issue of GAY [15] described how

GAA members, mingling with Rockefeller's audience, shook the hand of the smiling governor and asked for a statement on gay civil rights.* For a moment he furrowed his brow, and put his arms around a homosexual activist, and briefly expressed his concern.

Rockefeller quickly tired of this, however, and breaking away from his questioner, grabbed for another hand to shake. He was surprised to find that it was that of another GAA member with the same question and demands. As the Governor proceeded to move toward the exit, he was repeatedly stopped by GAA members. His look of affable concern turned to one of uneasiness and annoyance.

At about 10:00 that night, the group of Activists burst into their own meeting, removing unfamiliar ties. Robinson exclaimed, Oliver Hazard Perry–like, "Rockefeller's capitulated! The state is ours!"

In another article in its election issue, U.S. SENATE CANDIDATES SUPPORT HOMOSEXUAL STRUGGLE, GAY presented Richard Ottinger's and Charles Goodell's statements. Most Gay Activists favored Ottinger, but the incumbent, Goodell's, views were eagerly awaited. They were: [16]

The Constitution of the United States guarantees every citizen not only the right of free expression but the right of privacy. The sexual conduct of consenting adults should not be the subject of legislative regulation. It also should not—as it so often is today—be grounds for discrimination in employment for an individual who is otherwise fully qualified. Nor should it be grounds for discrimination in housing or in other civil rights. People's private sexual conduct, like their private opinions, should not be the subject of governmental investigation. Information on an individual's private sexual activities should not be a subject on which files are kept or information is stored.

* The Governor's managers had told "the Mattachine Society that Rockefeller would make his views known when the State Legislature presented him with a bill for sodomy-law repeal and for homosexual equality. Mattachine officials noted, however, that this was done several years ago in the passage of New York's new penal code which abolished homosexuality as a crime. *Rockefeller vetoed this part of the new code.*" (GAY, November 23, 1970.)

These Constitutional principles are today clearly being abridged and denied in reference to homosexuals, and I therefore support efforts to secure their basic rights under the Constitution.

Tax laws, welfare laws, and other legislative provisions now contain wholly indefensible discrimination against all single persons. I have fought in the Senate to eliminate that discrimination. I have supported legislation designed to provide single persons with tax and welfare treatment similar to that accorded married individuals. And I have introduced a Single Room Occupancy bill which would provide housing for low income single adults.

The weeks before election day 1970 were hectic for Gay Activists. Secretary Arnie Kantrowitz kept a list of GAA activities, which he believed was incomplete because of "much behind-the-scenes work . . . e.g., the writing and production of leaflets, the writing, production and dissemination of press releases, etc. . . . the work of all the supportive committees like Social Affairs and Fund-Raising":

Oct. 13—Confrontation of candidates at Greenwich House to seek commitments on support for gay civil rights.

Oct. 14—Meeting with Deputy Mayor Richard Aurelio and City Councilmen Carter Burden and Eldon Clingan.

Oct. 16—Demonstration at Gold Rail Bar to protest ejection of a gay for putting arm around a friend. Demo in cooperation with GPC,* GPCCNY,* GLF.

Oct. 17—Private meeting with City Council Minority Leader Eldon Clingan on drafting of fair employment bill.

Oct. 17—Marshal training for marshals at gay demonstrations. Quaker House.

Oct. 23—Demonstration at 100 Centre Street, for trial of Ruth Simpson, president of DOB; demo to protest police harassment of gay organizations; in cooperation with DOB and other gay groups.

Oct. 23—Heavy leafleting campaign to inform gay community of candidates' stands on gay rights, since the press won't publish results.

Oct. 24—Concentrated effort to reach media with news of GAA's role in obtaining candidates' statements.

Oct. 25—Marc Rubin on WBAI-FM *re* election issue of gay rights.

Oct. 25—Visit to *New York Times* to protest their refusal to print the statements of Goldberg, Ottinger, and Goodell.

Oct. 27—Sit-in at *Harper's* magazine to protest publication of J. Epstein's anti-gay "The Struggle for Sexual Identity" and to ask for pro-gay policy, possibly including publication of articles in rebuttal.

Oct. 27—Visit to "Dick Cavett Show" (ABC-TV) to disrupt taping in order to pressure for equal time to respond to the show's many anti-gay

* GPC (Gay People at Columbia) succeeded Student Homophile League there; GPCCNY, modeled informally after GPC, was chartered in autumn 1970 at City College of New York, a unit of CUNY.

comments. Plans discovered, negotiation resulted in scheduled appearance of two GAA representatives on the November 27 show.

Oct. 28—Arthur Bell and Pete Fisher on WNET-TV "Free Time" *re* election issues and gays.

Oct. 28—Press conference to inform media of candidates' stands on gay rights; drew few press representatives, though Bonnie Lubell of the New Democratic Coalition, candidate Antonio Olivieri, and Councilman Eldon Clingan were there. Resulted in a reading of Goldberg's, Ottinger's, and Goodell's statements on ABC radio.

Oct. 28—Confrontation of Mayor Lindsay at Imperial Theater to protest police harassment, etc.

Oct. 29—Second retrial of Rockefeller Five, arrested for sitting-in at Republican State Committee headquarters. Dismissal on Recognizance.

Oct. 31—Meeting with Eleanor Holmes Norton, chairman of the New York City Human Rights Commission, to arrange the format of forthcoming Commission public hearings in support of a homosexual fair employment bill.

Nov. 3—Heavy leafleting outside polls. Special attempt to seat Olivieri in Manhattan 66th State Assembly District.

A GAA press release pamphlet* dated October 24 was circulated to all major news media; it carried copies of major candidates' complete statements in support of gay rights; a list (including Adam Walinsky) of Manhattan, Brooklyn, and Bronx Congressional and State candidates who were "particularly positive in their response"; samples of the Federal and State GAA questionnaires; and a description and history of Gay Activists Alliance and its tactics. Jim Owles's statement informed, "Our efforts have been systematic. We issue no endorsement, and all candidates were given equal opportunity to respond. . . . The quantity and quality of our show of political support is a landmark for our movement, that was born with new vitality and militancy so recently. Therefore, these official political positions are of interest not only to homosexuals but to all citizens . . ." But evidently not of enough interest: only *The New York Times* responded, with a blushing three-paragraph article, 3 CANDIDATES SUPPORT RIGHTS OF HOMOSEXUALS, midway down page 18, on October 27, 1970. HOMOSEXUALS IN REVOLT had made page one on August 24.

GAA leafleted as it never had before, and told GAY that "Voters may secure last-minute information by calling (212) 371- . . ."[17] One of the Activists' earliest leaflets advised, "REGISTER AND VOTE GAY . . . Gay Activists Alliance is canvassing candidates for city, state, and federal office . . . USE YOUR VOTE ON NOVEMBER 3; DON'T THROW IT AWAY! Look for the forthcoming information from GAY ACTIVISTS ALLIANCE . . ." In an attempt to inform frequently unpolitical East Side gays, one early leaflet announced,

* MSNY's Action Corps (see page 272) in *Right On!*, No. 1, concurrently issued excerpts from major candidates' statements in support of gay rights.

CANDIDATES SPEAK OUT ON

HOMOSEXUAL RIGHTS

The GAY ACTIVISTS ALLIANCE - (GAA) - systematically questioned all East Side Democratic and Republican candidates concerning homosexual rights. GAA asked such questions as:

> Would you favor repealing the N.Y. sodomy and solicitation laws?
> Would you favor ending police entrapment of homosexuals?
> Would you favor extending the existing fair employment **laws** to homosexuals?
> Would you favor ending income tax discrimination against single persons?

Here is where the two major parties' candidates from the East Side stand: (Figures indicate percentage of questions answered favorably)

GAA makes no endorsements -- You decide for yourself.

OLIVIERI (D): 100% * 66th A.D.	HANSEN (R): Refused to answer questionnaire or to issue statement. 66th A.D.
BERLE (D): No response to questionnaire. Favorable statement issued. 64th A.D.	FINE (R): 53% 64th A.D.
STEIN (D): 88% 62nd A.D.	LYNCH (R): No response. 62nd A.D.
SPITZ (D): 100% 26th S.S.	GOODMAN (R): Refusal to answer questionnaire or to issue statement. 26th S.S.
KOCH (D): 100% 17th C.D.	SPRAGUE (R): 75% 17th C.D.

Candidates' statements and signed questionnaires are on file at GAA office.

GAY ACTIVISTS ALLIANCE

  * Eben Clark, chairman of GAA's Police Power Committee, was leafleting one day in Olivieri's district when he discovered the candidate speaking to voters at a street corner. Olivieri, who knew Clark, stopped speechmaking, announced GAA's presence, reiterated his support for gay rights, and thanked the Activists for letting

In a second East Side leaflet, on election day GAA again announced the positions of Olivieri, Hansen, Spitz, Goodman, Koch, and Sprague. A comprehensive two-page leaflet excerpting major candidates' statements to GAA was distributed throughout gay areas and gathering places in the Manhattan, Brooklyn, Queens, and Bronx boroughs.* It included, most significantly, a complete list of the candidates who "have responded favorably on the question of homosexual rights. AN ASTERISK [and capital letters] INDICATES PARTICULARLY STRONG SUPPORT." It began: "MANHATTAN . . . Congress—* BELLA ABZUG . . ."

Mrs. Abzug won. From the list of thirty-six, so did the following: (Manhattan) *EDWARD KOCH, Manfred Ohrenstein, Sidney Von Luthor, Andy Stein, William Passannante, Peter Berle, Richard Gottfried, *ANTONIO OLIVIERI, *ALBERT BLUMENTHAL, Franz Leichter, Stephen Gottlieb; (Brooklyn) *SHIRLEY CHISHOLM, Donald Halpern, Brian Scharoff, *STEPHEN SOLARZ, Leonard Simon; (Queens) Jack Bronston, Arthur Cooperman; (Bronx) James Scheuer, Jonathan Bingham, Abraham Bernstein, Seymour Posner, and Oliver Koppell. Statewide candidates for Governor, Arthur Goldberg, for Lieutenant-Governor, Basil Paterson, for Attorney General, Adam Walinsky, and for United States Senator, incumbent Charles Goodell and Richard Ottinger—all supporters of gay rights—were defeated. Gay Activist Marc Rubin alleged that "Their tallies were probably very little affected by their support for gay rights or by our leafleting these. I wonder what would have resulted if Representative Ottinger or Senator Goodell had made their supportive statements an integral part of their campaigns. Statistical analysis of the State Senatorial and State Assembly races produced an interesting fact: Where only one of the two major-party candidates supported us, he usually won his election. Seventy-four per cent of such races were won by candidates who added their support of homosexual rights to their campaign policies. Political support for these rights was not, therefore, the kiss of death that many people thought it would be; it turned out to be an asset. It is quite possible that a more courageous public stand on the part of one of his opponents could have defeated [Conservative] James Buckley.** This would have given homosexuals throughout the state a basis of choice between his two ideologically similar rivals."

Gay Activists Alliance considered its greatest coup the Olivieri victory on Manhattan's East Side. Rubin explained: "Antonio Olivieri, the liberal-Democratic candidate for the 66th State Assembly District, returned to us

---

all Eastsiders know where he stood. "This from a man running against an entrenched incumbent," observed Election Committee chairman Marc Rubin. Following his victory, Olivieri bought a "compliments" ad in the program of "Echoes of the Left Bank," a musical benefit for GAA sponsored by Gay People at Columbia.

* Statewide candidates for Governor, Lieutenant-Governor, Controller, Attorney General, and U.S. Senator were not included on the list.

** Buckley, a third-party candidate running against two liberals, received approximately 39 per cent of the state vote.

one of the most forthright statements of support and provided us with the miracle we had only dreamed would occur. The 66th A.D. has a very large number of homosexual residents. Tony Olivieri was running against an attractive young Republican incumbent, Stephen Hansen, who refused—despite our very strong attempts—to give gays any kind of a statement. On one of my visits to the Hansen headquarters I told his secretary that his refusal to answer us was both arrogant and politically 'stupid.' The results on election day supported my appraisal. Although GAA never endorsed Olivieri, we did let homosexuals in the district know that he had responded and had made his endorsement publicly and frequently, while his opponent had remained silent. Olivieri won by five hundred votes in a district that had not sent a Democrat to the Assembly in fifty-six years. Mr. Hansen became the only defeated Assemblyman incumbent in New York City. He won this signal honor through his refusal to acknowledge that Gay Power could be translated, at the polls, by an aware electorate, into Gay Political Power. . . ." *

■

That GAA had also a social, or "fun," side was obvious to the hundreds of homosexuals who attended its first dance, in the subcellar of NYU's Weinstein Hall on June 26—a highlight of Gay Pride Week. Other summer and autumn dances followed, generally at St. Peter's Church, complete with raffles from which a gay could win a subscription to GAY or QQ, dinner at Fedora's, Braggi kits . . . GLFers were quick critics of what they deemed GAA's "capitalist" orientation. Nor did they like mixing old and new rock music: " 'Old' music has the gloom of faggotdom!" said one GLF commune member. At one dance, "Women were almost totally absent," Jim Clifford noticed—"It was a sexist dance." Nor did he approve the darkened dance floor: "If you want to do what we're doing in the dark, it implies a sense of shame—people are afraid to look other people in the face when they're being sexual!"

Gay Activists did not join a July 4 march by homosexuals in Provincetown, but made the trek there for a "Solidarity March" on Labor Day. Of the earlier march, GAY reported that the Provincetown Selectmen (Town Council) summarily denied the request to parade. In a telephone interview with GAY, Selectmen Chairman Marion Taves cracked, "Are they coming on a ferry boat?" and hinted, "We didn't know what sort of group intended to descend on the town. We were afraid it might be just a bunch of the cheap exhibitionistic types who wanted to horse around." [18] Ignoring the refusal of permit, on Independence Day 150 gays representing Homophile Union of Boston, GLF Boston and GLF

* In late summer 1970, American gays had two state lobbyists for homosexual rights: Robert Vain, of Human Enlightenment (Wilmington), registered with the Delaware legislature; and Jerry Curtis, of Homophile Action League (Philadelphia), with the Pennsylvania legislature.

New York and the Lavender Menace,* MSNY, Boston Student Homophile League, the Boston DOB, and Graduate Student Homophile Association of Harvard University "paraded through this resort town while thousands of enthusiastic tourists roared approval." [19] (Provincetown has long been a summer mecca for Eastern homosexuals.)

Their signs read: STRAIGHT OR GAY—WE'RE ALL JUST PEOPLE; COME OUT—YOU HAVE NOTHING TO LOSE BUT YOUR SHAME; "LOVE AND THEN DO WHAT YOU WILL" . . . ST. AUGUSTINE; COME OUT—MARCH TO YOUR OWN DRUMMER . . . And they carried scores of pastel balloons that bore their message: "GAY IS LOVE." It was Labor Day, and nearly two hundred gay women and men marched in Provincetown "not to protest grievances, but to demonstrate solidarity among gay groups in the Bay State . . ." [20] In the forty-five-minute parade through the heart of the Cape Cod hamlet, groups which had marched two months before were joined by Boston University Homophile Club, Homophile Group at MIT, the Council on Religion and the Homosexual–Boston, and by out-of-town gays from Homophile Action League of Philadelphia, the Mattachine Society of Washington, and Gay Activists Alliance. With the last of the marchers, GAY remarked, "was a sign to remind onlookers that a rainstorm had cleared just before the march was to begin. It read, GOD LOVES US—SEE THE SUN!

As summer ended, films and the media, too, had begun to understand that "Gay Is Love." A photo-advertisement in the *New York Post* on September 18 captioned unabashedly, "Hiram Keller and Martin Potter are lovers in Nero's Rome in 'Fellini Satyricon,' at the Apollo, Art, Midtown, Trans-Lux 85th and other theaters." Harold Fairbanks previewed for *The Advocate,* November 25,[21] a Commonwealth-United remake of *The Picture of Dorian Gray* with homosexual episodes; Hammer Films's *The Vampire Lovers,* with a lesbian bloodsucker ("Imagine the alarm of the townspeople when they discover she has been putting the bite on her victims, not in the usual spot on the neck, but a little to the south of it!"); and *There Was a Crooked Man,* in which "Hume Cronyn and John Randolph were a pair of elderly homosexual prisoners in a territorial prison in the Old West. Playing their roles as a frontier 'Odd Couple,' both actors manage to steal the picture from veterans Kirk Douglas and Henry Fonda." Best news of all was CBS-TV's "Medical Center" on September 23. The story of a "brilliant researcher being smeared by anonymous letters accusing him of homosexuality," Paul Burke as the guest star shocked heterosexuals *and* homosexuals when, "immediately before the first big commercial break, [he] looked straight into the camera and said, 'I am

---

* A Lavender Menace wrote, for *Come Out!* (September–October 1970), that one night "the cast of the Provincetown Playhouse announced between one-act plays that they were going to commemorate the arrival of pilgrims who sought freedom by giving money to oppressed groups. They had decided on HELP and the Panthers, but had discussed Indians, etc., etc. (no mention of homosexuals). We confronted the senior member of the cast at intermission. 'Can't you see all the oppressed homosexuals in this town? the Indians have left.' "

a homosexual.' " *The Advocate's* Carl Driver praised Burke "for avoiding the traps of camping or playing the role super-butch. Unlike so many shows which have dealt with this subject, the protagonist . . . did not become a travesty of a human being." Granting that the "dialogue ran from the trite to the contrived" and that homosexuality was described as a "condition," Driver took into consideration that the show reached millions of homes in prime time and noted, moreover, that *"TV Guide* chose the week it was on to run a major interview with ["Medical Center" star] Chad Everett," drawing more attention to the program.[22]

Bar owners had to be taught that "Gay Is Love." *The Advocate* reported how, on September 26, "the operators of the Farm, a popular Santa Monica Strip bar, yielded to GLF demonstrators* and gave patrons the right to hold hands and put their arms around each other above the waist. Despite continued GLF insistence, however, the Farm declined to condone even a quick, casual kiss. Since the Farm agreement, several other bars along the Santa Monica strip have made essentially the same concessions." A Los Angeles GLF flyer yelled, "Victory! The Farm is liberated! . . . Another groovy freedom brought to you by the GAY LIBERATION FRONT." *The Advocate* hailed a greater breakthrough in the East:

In New York, about 25 male and female homosexuals held what was described as an "affectionate action" [GAY termed it a "kiss-in"] Oct. 16 at the Gold Rail Bar . . . Gay couples entered the tavern and proceeded to kiss and embrace each other as a protest over the ejection of two male homosexuals earlier in the week. The couple had kissed each other while sitting at the bar.

At that time a bartender in the predominately straight establishment informed the Gays that "there is no room for any display of affection here." A heated argument quickly developed between one of the gay patrons and the bartender, who allegedly threw a glass of beer at the homosexuals and ordered them out.

Members of several local groups, including New York GLF, the Gay Activists Alliance, and Gay People at Columbia, participated in the Friday night action. . . . Most of the straights who were in the bar at the time of the demonstration seemed to approve of it.[23] . . .

GAY recorded that "The owners, taking exception to the action of their employee several nights earlier, said hand holding and light kissing would be permissible between homosexuals but that heavy petting and tongue kissing would be forbidden between homosexual patrons as it was between heterosexual patrons." [24]

Meanwhile, gays in Ithaca, New York, "with a little help from a police captain . . . backed down a local bar-owner who didn't care to serve homosexuals." Cornell GLF president Robert Roth and several friends

* Picketers carried signs, "THE FARM" TREATS US LIKE ANIMALS; FOOTBALL PLAYERS GRAB ASS, WHY CAN'T WE?; IN "THE FARM," IT'S TOUCH AND GO . . . (*Gay Sunshine,* October 1970.)

had been told to leave Morrie's Bar by the owner, Morris Angell, who explained that he ordered the group out only because it was closing time.

Roth, however, said Angell had told them he didn't want "their kind" in the bar, and to "get out and not come back." Roth said Angell had allowed several other patrons to stay past the normal 1 A.M. closing time.

The next night, Roth returned to Morrie's with GLF members and a large crowd of supporters. While several hundred waved placards and shouted, "Power to the people!" on the sidewalk outside, 50 crowded into the bar to confront Angell.

Angell ordered them out and the doors locked, shouting, "This bar is closed. Finish your drinks and leave."

Several shoving matches broke out between bar employees and the protesters, and the bar's bouncer brandished a baseball bat at some of the GLF people.

"Leave the bouncer alone," cried one of the group. "All we want to do is talk with Morrie."

Angell waited about 10 minutes and then called the police.

Ithaca Police Capt. Raymond Price, who responded to the call, discussed the situation briefly with Angell and a GLF spokesman, and then told Angell, "You can't insult these people. You can't just refuse to serve them."

"In two years here, we've never caused any trouble at all," Roth said.

"I never said I had any complaints," Angell replied. "I don't say you're welcome, but I'll have to serve you."

"If he refuses to service us, he's going to have to close the bar," said Janis Kelly.[25] . . .

■

September 14, 1970

Dear Mr. Morris:*

We are writing in response to Joseph Epstein's** article, "Homo/Hetero: The Struggle For Sexual Identity," published in the September issue of *Harper's*. The Gay Activists Alliance, finding this article uninformed, biased, and, more important, offensive to our organization and to all homosexuals, feel it is our obligation to insist upon an article of rebuttal in a forthcoming issue of *Harper's Magazine*.

The Gay Activists Alliance is a militant, non-violent political coalition dedicated to securing and protecting homosexual civil rights. Many members of GAA are professional writers and publishers, and with this knowledge we trust that *Harper's* will reasonably consider our demand to be represented in an article to be published in the January 1971 issue. We propose an article of approximately 7,500–10,000 words, consistent with the literary standards of

* Willie Morris, *Harper's* editor-in-chief.
** Epstein has written essays and reviews for *The New Republic, Commentary,* and other magazines.

Harper's and GAA, to be submitted and literarily negotiated to the mutual satisfaction of both parties.

To this purpose, we ask that *Harper's* reply to this letter, no later than September 22, 1970, designating a meeting between a *Harper's* representative and spokesmen of the GAA *Harper's* Action Committee.

We look forward to your prompt reply.

> Sincerely,
> Peter Fisher, Chairman
> *Harper's* Action Committee
> Jim Owles, President
> Gay Activists Alliance

New York homosexuals were almost as angered by the photographs of heavily made-up male mannequins as they were by the inanity of Epstein's attempt to describe something about which he, admittedly, knew next to nothing. "My ignorance makes me frightened," he said. His ignorance made them wrathful.

"I do think homosexuality an anathema, and hence homosexuals cursed . . ." he had written. And, "If I had the power to do so, I would wish homosexuality off the face of this earth." Epstein concluded, "There is much my four sons can do in their lives that might cause me anguish, might outrage me, that might make me ashamed of them and of myself as their father. But nothing they could ever do would make me sadder than if any of them were to become homosexual. For then I should know them condemned to a state of permanent niggerdom among men, their lives, whatever adjustment they might make to their condition, to be lived out as part of the pain of the earth." [26] Homosexuals were in part amused, at his confession of fear. But they were, above all, appalled. No Billy Graham had ever sounded more convincing! *

Harper's replied, at first, that they would consider an article in rebuttal, but the several submitted by Gay Activists failed to please. Nor would they commission a pro-homosexual article by a writer of their choice.[27]

They didn't know GAA was coming. Gay Activist Gale McGovern recalls how, at 9:00 a.m., Tuesday, October 27, "In the reception area one group of us set up a table with coffee and doughnuts, others spread out and leafleted every desk in the company. As people came in to work, we walked up to them, offered a handshake, introduced ourselves, saying,

---

* Activist Eric Thorndale has suggested that the "chronic affliction of *Harper's* is cultural lag." In a *Harper's* of August *1*870 (Vol. 41, No. 243) Thorndale discovered an eight-page unsigned diatribe against female suffrage. "The natural position of woman is clearly . . . a subservient one," the magazine stated. If women were given the right to vote: "They will sell their vote any day for a yard of ribbon or a tinsel brooch." (Pp. 438, 445.) "If this kind of cultural lag is not willfully vicious," Thorndale insists, "it is at least—like the Epstein article of a century later—cheap, canting, pretentious, and wrong."

'Good morning, I'm a homosexual.* We're here to protest the Epstein article. Would you like some coffee?' " Startled, the incoming employees accepted a cup and a doughnut. Maybe a leaflet, such as the two-page collection of derogatory quotes from Epstein's article which ended: "DO YOU BELIEVE THE THINGS MR. EPSTEIN SAYS ABOUT HOMOSEXUALS ARE TRUE? DO YOU BELIEVE THAT HARPER'S SHOWS JOURNALISTIC RESPONSIBILITY IN PUBLISHING SUCH MATERIAL?"

In a second leaflet, "GAY ACTIVISTS ALLIANCE STATEMENT ON HARPER'S MAGAZINE," the magazine was accused of

```
--IRRESPONSIBLE PUBLISHING. Harper's chooses an article on
the basis of its content and intent as well as its literary
merit. To select an article which is blatantly discrimina-
tory toward homosexuals is for Harper's to clearly associate
itself with this type of opinion.

--INCOMPETENT EDITORIAL JUDGMENT AND GUIDANCE. Pointing out
faulty logic and poor scholarship is one of the major tasks
of the competent editor. Obviously this was not done in the
case of the Epstein article.

--TASTELESS EXPLOITATION. Feeding the fears of the unin-
formed with half truths, resorting to innuendo, and presenting
slander in the form of pseudo-scholarship are the worst forms
of yellow journalism. The photographs used on the cover and
within the magazine reinforce the content of the article and
are demeaning to homosexuals. The use of such photos is a
type of sales exploitation completely inconsistent with
responsible journalism.

--MANIPULATIVE PSEUDO-LIBERALISM. Harper's has chosen to lend
its reputation and prestige as a magazine espousing liberal
causes to Epstein's fear-mongering attack on homosexuals and
has presented such overt prejudice as acceptable and enlight-
ened. This can only be viewed as an attempt to increase
public hostility toward homosexuals and to make it even more
difficult for them to secure and protect their political
rights.

--CHEAP AND UNACCEPTABLE TOKENISM. In response to a flood of
outraged letters from its readers, Harper's has thought to
bypass its responsibilities by printing several of these
letters in its November issue. A series of letters is a
wholly inadequate way of redressing the imbalances of a preju-
dicial feature story, offensively illustrated on the cover of
the magazine. This is tokenism of the most obvious and
insulting type
```

Outside, passersby and incoming employees were given an invitational or preparatory flyer, "WHAT ARE HOMOSEXUALS LIKE?" It told that, "As

* In autumn 1970, the Homophile Action League of Philadelphia began a campaign to let the straight world know homosexuals were around: in subways, on signboards, auto bumpers, etc., they pasted stickers and hung posters announcing THE PERSON STANDING NEXT TO YOU MAY BE A HOMOSEXUAL. WHY ISN'T HE FREE? (*Gay Scene,* No. 4.)

a service to the people of New York and the readers of *Harper's* Magazine, GAY ACTIVISTS ALLIANCE has arranged to make a group of homosexuals available to meet with the public, to meet with those who would like to test the truth of the remarks which appeared in *Harper's*. All those who are interested in rapping with us are encouraged to drop in and join us in our Surprise Visit to *Harper's* offices on the 18th floor of the Park Avenue Building, 2 Park Ave., any time today. Coffee will be served; stop by on your coffee break. Bring a sandwich on your lunch hour—have lunch with a homosexual at *Harper's*. . . ."

McGovern tells how Pete Fisher, chairman of the Ad Hoc *Harper's* Magazine Action Committee, "had carefully planned and explained the tone he wanted the day's action to strike: civilized, intelligent, educational, consciousness-raising, hospitable—no demands, no threats, no damage to offices or files."

The tiny reception room was soon invaded by television cameras,* as the Activists, accompanied on guitars by Tom Doerr and Pete Fisher, sang the chairman's gay-meant compositions: "Be Yourself," "Stand With Me," and "The Time Is Now." Through the day, the Activist hosts and *Harper's* editors rapped. *Harper's* thought that Epstein's "piece was not anti-homosexual, that it was 'literary' and not 'political' and therefore could not have 'political' effect, so why why why (dear G–d!) did political us bother them?" wrote Leo Skir for GAY.[28] McGovern amplifies, "They kept coming back to their view that the article was a literary work devoid of political content; we insisted that it was a political work devoid of literary merit."

McGovern remembers the pleasantness of the confrontation, and the "sense of brotherhood among all homosexuals who stayed and who visited." She even noted "a feeling of tentative communication between the gays and the straight office workers from other companies in the building—many of them were talking to a homosexual for the first time and were fascinated by our spirit of freedom: they could ask anything they had ever wondered about and here were live homosexuals who weren't embarrassed to answer . . . We punctured a lot of myths."

The women and men in lambda T-shirts and sweatshirts left the magazine offices in late afternoon, assured that *Harper's* would "actively consider finding" an article favorable to homosexuals. Strange. It didn't matter so much now.

GAA began to Meet the People more and more frequently as 1970 ended. Especially on television. Activists' unofficial PR man Arthur Bell relates that [29]

About the third week of October I received a call from the producer of a new news telecast show to run Mondays through Fridays, 7:30 to 8:00 p.m.

* WOR-TV followed the Gay Activists in and filmed for about an hour. Mid-morning, a camera crew from WABC-TV arrived, and mid-afternoon WNEW-TV. Two GAA members taped the whole day's activities.

on WOR. Mel Shastock, the producer, got sicced on to me by the *Voice*. The station wanted to do an in-depth study of gay liberation as one of their first special-coverage spots—could he and his camera crew come over in an hour.

It was all very casual. I sat on the living-room couch and Bill Ryan, the WOR anchorman, asked several questions. They taped for about an hour.

The following day they phoned and said the film came out beautifully—now could they come to one of our meetings. They also asked if they could follow me to work with their cameras: a sort of day in the life of a living, breathing homosexual. They claimed that the coverage they had was, by its own accord, taking a direction: the human aspect of the homosexual (as opposed to political, angry, etc.). They would stretch it out to a three-part series.

The program was aired on November 17, 18, and 19; each segment ran about five minutes. In the first segment Bill Ryan interviewed Bell.

His opening spiel ran, "Sometimes, when the weather is nice, Mr. Bell walks to work. There is nothing to distinguish him from other New Yorkers except that he is an admitted homosexual." He asked me what the liberation movement was after. My answer was: giving homosexuals a feeling of identity—that for the homosexual to mold himself into a place in heterosexual society is an antiquated idea, it's not bad to be gay, gay is good.

Ryan then said that the word *gay* turns straight people off. I asked him if it turned him off. He said yes. I asked him to question himself as to why it did, and apologized because I was interviewing him. . . . He asked me what the social problems of being a homosexual are. I said, I'm sorry, I didn't think the problems were with being gay but often came from a world that thought anything alien to its own way of life was out of kilter. Problems are an individual thing. He asked about the lack of fulfillment of not having children. I answered that one by telling him I was perfectly fulfilled without having kids; in fact, I rather dislike children.

Ryan asked Bell about job discrimination, then finally informed listeners that "Arthur Bell is quick to point out that he is not a spokesman for all homosexuals, but that there is an organization that is speaking for many—the Gay Activists Alliance. . . ."

On Wednesday's, second segment Bell's voice told about the spectrum of homosexual activists while the camera examined a variety of faces at the Gay Activists meeting. As Bell described the *Harper's* sit-in, the cameramen followed the protesters into the building, down the hallways, talking to executive editor Midge Decter; then Ryan outlined GAA's complaints about the Epstein story.

The third installment focused on Barbara Gittings, homophile activist and member of GAA. She spoke about her homophile activities and of the problems peculiar to the lesbian, to whom both women's and gay lib called. Closing the final segment, Ryan asked Bell "the ridiculous question 'Will you ever be completely happy?' My response, if I remember correctly,"

Bell maintains, "was 'I'm happy when my work is going good, when my lovelife is going good, when I'm attuned to the world. With me, being attuned is never constant; therefore I can never be completely happy. Can you?' . . . The following Monday, Lem Tucker, head of WOR news, called to say that their program went up five points with this show. Hooray for Gay—we're box office!"

The Gay Activists' ultimate coup was an appearance on the "Dick Cavett Show," ABC-TV, November 27, with Phyllis Diller, James Earl Jones, and Nora Ephron. "We welcome, please, Marty Robinson and Arthur Evans* from the *Gay Activists Alliance*," Cavett intoned with musical come-on, joked uncomfortably to put his visitors at ease—the star wasn't—and asked "What are you really after?" For the next forty minutes Cavett and TV America heard Evans and Robinson—and Dick Leitsch of Mattachine, introduced later—pose the problems of the nation's once-"invisible" minority—its most deprived. Robinson answered, "Heterosexuals live in this society without any scorn—they live openly, their affection is idolized in movies, theater. Homosexuals want the same thing: to be open in this society, to live a life without fear of reprisal from anybody for being homosexual—to live a life of respect." At one point Evans explained that "We're faced with a kind of cruel alternative: if we deny our emotions, don't show them in public, and appear to be straight, then we can have a career; but if we're open, and show our affections the way heterosexuals do, and lead an open sexual life, then our careers are ended. We feel that it is repressive and unjust that we have to face that alternative. There is no reason why we can't be full people, both economically and in terms of our feelings! . . . This is a matter of political rights, our Constitutional rights, which we have under the Declaration of Independence: 'Life, liberty, and the pursuit of happiness.' We should have that, too, don't you think?" he asked Cavett.

Evans detailed how homosexuals must work to gain those rights: "We've a phrase called 'coming out'—gay people, when they first realize that they're gay, have a process of 'coming out,' that is, coming out sexually. We've extended that to the political field. We feel that we *have* to come out politically, as a community which is aware that it is oppressed and which is a political power bloc feared by the government. Until the government is afraid of us—afraid of our power—we will never have our rights. The Federal Government is based on a power structure: it doesn't matter what the laws say. The Constitution gives us our rights already. If that were enough, we'd be free people today. Until we have power, we'll never be free."

The guests spoke of the 1970 elections, of Mayor John Lindsay, and of the Epstein article in the September *Harper's*. Evans fumed, about the last, "A point that was really offensive, to my mind, was the statement by Joseph Epstein that homosexuality is a curse, which should be wiped

* Robinson and Evans were chosen by the Cavett Show staff from a group of volunteers selected by an ad hoc GAA committee.

271

off the face of the earth. . . . If someone had said that about the Jews or the blacks, *Harper's* magazine would have been burned to the ground. The fact that they said it about homosexuals was left unnoticed by the press, or by any politician or spokesman for society. . . . People sit back and say, 'Oh, how 'bout that.' " Robinson: "I can say, to Mr. Epstein, that my own personal experience as a homosexual is that of a happy human being. My homosexuality is one of the assets of my life: I *like* my life-style, I love my lover, I'm happy being what I am . . ." Leitsch: "It's a hideously pitiful article . . . I felt sorry for him more than I did angry at him."

A comment of Cavett's, to audience and guests alike: "I don't know what we can learn from this, exactly . . ." [30] But that he did and his audience did, Gay Activists Alliance was confident.

■

The first full year of gay militancy was closing.

Mattachine, in response to it, had established an Action Corps. GAY took note, on September 7: [31]

The Action Corps will be responsible for MSNY's participation on picket lines and in demonstrations; staffing literature tables; distributing flyers and pamphlets; manning the office staff; and suggesting actions and organizational policies.

Michael Kotis, President of MSNY, described the new development as follows: "Mattachine has always tried to be a full service organization for the homosexual community, and activism is a part of that service. . . . This is an attempt to keep Mattachine relevant . . . and also to make us more effective in dealing with society's prejudice and oppression on an individual basis and in conjunction with other gay organizations in the New York Homosexual Community Council."

The need for an NYHCC had been suggested by Kotis at an April 30 meeting of the Daughters of Bilitis to which delegates of GLF, GAA, SHL (Columbia University; now Gay People at Columbia), and West Side Discussion Group had gone to describe their organizations. Shortly after, NYHCC began to meet. In *Come Out!*,[32] Bernard Lewis and Martha Shelley stressed how it

sprang up out of a need which it felt was not being met: a need for organizations to resolve misunderstandings among themselves, as reflected in the reluctance of a number of organizations to relate to the June 28th March out of what proved to be an unfounded fear that some organizations were planning violence. The Council is concerned not with individuals, but with organizations; organizations all having the same goal, the liberation of women and men homosexuals, but sometimes differing in methods of action. Thus, when a misunderstanding arises, communication will be possible through meetings of the Council, which can be called by any one of the participating organizations at any time. . . . There are to be no officers, no treasury. . . . The Council sees itself as a center through which new ideas can be channeled to and from organizations and from one organization to others.

An "informal confederation of New York City's homosexual civil rights, membership organizations," it would "meet at regular intervals and/or at the request of any member organization . . ."

Though by unofficial estimate, Gay Liberation Front had more than a hundred organizations scattered throughout the nation—some of them less radical, more system-oriented, than the Fronts in New York, San Francisco, Los Angeles, Chicago, and Philadelphia—as the year ended a "conservative," GAA-type homosexual activism was catching on. GAA of New York had a chapter of about fifty members at Hempstead, Long Island, and had extensive contact with gay liberationists in upstate New York. The *Mattachine Midwest Newsletter* [33] remarked in October that

Perhaps the most significant development on the local scene during the last month is the division which has occurred in the local Gay Liberation movement. . . . On Sunday, September 27, a group calling itself the Chicago Gay Alliance read a statement explaining its position in leaving Chicago Gay Liberation. CGA had originally considered becoming a caucus of Gay Liberation, but the Alliance finally decided that two independent groups could probably function more effectively than one group with a somewhat disabling conflict of philosophy.

Both groups feel that they are primarily concerned with gay problems, but they differ in their interpretations of how the concerns of the gay community can best be served. CGA felt that Gay Liberation had become too involved in Movement politics, both locally and nationally, to the extent that its political activity was turning off most gay people and preventing effective work within the larger gay community. . . .

Those remaining with Chicago Gay Liberation tend to view the oppression of gays as including a large political component. They feel that such oppression is inseparably tied to the oppression of other minorities and that discrimination and oppressive institutions must be fought on a broad front including both personal and political components. . . .

Wasn't it inevitable?

Dennis Altman, Australian teacher and several months' visitor to the gay militant scene—East and West Coasts alike—told *Come Out!:* [34]

I regret the lack of contact that seems to exist between GAA and GLF. . . . To me the two are complementary, not rivals. (Although I am conscious that it is far easier to write this for a man than a woman; it is impossible to ignore the extent to which GAA is male-dominated . . .) Each fulfills different functions; it would I think be silly to deny that GAA has a certain political efficacy, just as I would hope they can recognize the extent to which GLF and the various groups it has spawned . . . has provided a means whereby gay people can redefine themselves and come to terms with the extent to which we have internalized the shit straight society has thrown at us. I value the sensibility that GLF has taught me toward racism, sexism, etc., but I would wish we could combine this with some of the sense of political efficacy of GAA. . . .

As a middle-aged visitor to a Gay Activists meeting once said, "I go to both GLF and GAA. I think both have a value."

13

And Jonathan made David swear again
by his love for him; for he loved him as
he loved his own soul.
—I Samuel 20:17

The sign said, FAGOTS—STAY OUT. Old-timers remember it had hung
there for more than thirty years, over the bar at Barney's Beanery, a
"sleazy but fashionable" little rambling bar-resturant in West Hollywood.
To remove that sign would be Los Angeles GLF's first major action.

On the night of February 7, 1970, a crowd of over one hundred
gays—from GLF, the Committee for Homosexual Law Reform,* CHF,
the Homosexual Information Center, and Social Workers for Peace
—descended on the offending tavern. Management had refused GLF's
request to remove the sign, had even post six additional signs within
the restaurant in weeks preceding. That night, the gay contingent leafleted and picketed. "Heckling was minimal," Douglas Key told the *Los
Angeles Free Press*.[1] "A drunken customer fell out of the cafe and ranted
for a few minutes, then joined the picket line, singing a ribald English army
song with homosexual connotations. A man shouted repeatedly, 'I like
girls, not boys,' and was answered by a lesbian GLF monitor. 'So do I,
mister.'" Key noted that hundreds watched the three-hour demonstration
and that drivers of passing cars shouted "Gay Power!" and flashed V signs.
Chants of "Barney's dead—take down the sign!" and "Barney's beans are
death on queens!" "The demonstration was bathed in a sans souci aura
with laughter and joking coming from the pickets. Men kissed, embraced
and walked hand in hand. . . . Music blared from a number of transistor
radios, and some pickets danced as they picketed." There were no problems
from police. Key wrote that, "Members of the Hollywood Sheriff's department spoke with GLF officials prior to the demonstration and offered
their services in a protective capacity." At about 10:00 p.m., picketing

* CHLR, successor to the Committee for Homosexual Freedom in Los Angeles,
started in late 1969 as an ad hoc committee directed by Troy Perry. It has demonstrated frequently for an end to California laws restricting the private sexual behavior of consenting adults. (Jim Kepner, in a memo to the author, December 19,
1970.)

275

halted, and the gay group adjourned to a nearby parking lot to rap. Six of them, led by Rev. Troy Perry of CHLR and Morris Kight of GLF, entered Barney's, announced their sexuality, and requested service. They were served immediately, then dialogued with the bartender and the new owner about the moral validity of the sign. When they had finished their drinks, the gays left. The sign still hung.

The Advocate [2] told that

When the first demonstration started, the Beanery was in the process of being purchased by Irving Held, a large, genial, nervous man, with a mercurial temper. He didn't seem to mind the picket lines—he promised free beer to any of the pickets who cared to come inside—and there was little evidence that the several dozen marchers seriously hurt his business. . . .

. . . Held played the host well. But after the third demonstration, about 30 or more demonstrators left just a token group of pickets on the narrow sidewalk out front, while most entered the bar and occupied most of the seats. Held began to appear very nervous. . . .

The demonstrators were scrupulous about being quiet, orderly and non-hostile (several were ardently explaining their case to other customers), but they were *not* drinking very fast . . .

So Held put hand-lettered signs on some tables announcing a price increase. And several persons complained that when they handed over a dollar bill, they were not given change. . . . Held seized glasses that were more than half-filled from some and told them to reorder or leave. Then he refused to serve those who did reorder. . . .

Held attempted to eject one young man who was at that moment alone at a table. The young man refused to leave and was then rejoined by companions. Half-empty beer mugs had been cleaned off the table, and Held ordered them to buy another round or leave. He refused to serve them at the table, and when Cliff Lettieri, chairman of HELP [Homophile Effort for Legal Protection*], got up to go to the counter for refills, Held again said they would have to leave because all four seats at the table weren't filled.

Cliff returned with the beers, and Held knocked one from his hand. This dampened the hand-lettered sign Held had placed on the table announcing the new price. He demanded $5 payment for the sign. Then he called the Sheriff's deputies.

Lettieri handed someone a brochure describing HELP's legal service. The owner snatched it from his hand. . . . The owner snatched Lettieri up from the table and began to swing.

The Sheriff's deputies arrived at that moment and pulled Held off, telling him to cool down. He demanded that they arrest various demonstrators, while several of these were demanding that Held be arrested for assault and for various license infringements.

At the officers' suggestion, the demonstrators went back outside and joined the pickets for another hour, vowing to return the following week.

* Founded, L.A., 1968, as a result of a raid on a Wilmington gay bar, HELP guaranteed legal aid to members, especially when they were victims of police raids.

But they felt optimistic. And they returned the following Friday, a large group, early in the evening. Most of them went inside for "a few very slow beers."

"Meanwhile," noted *The Advocate,* "the Rev. Troy Perry and two others had, separately, entered protests against a granting, by the State Alcoholic Beverage Committee, of a liquor license to the new owner." Perry had written:

. . . I am filing this complaint because of a very offensive sign that is displayed in the place of business that reads "FAGOTS STAY OUT." This sign is evidently directed at members of the homophile community . . . and it rates, in my opinion, with the same type of signs displayed some twenty-five years ago, in other establishments of Los Angeles, that made reference to the race, color and creed of individuals, such as: WHITE ONLY, NIGGERS STAY OUT and NO MEXICANS OR DOGS ALLOWED IN THE BUILDING.

This sign is a direct violation of some of our civil rights laws, enacted in the State of California and also the Federal Laws. And, as a citizen of the State of California, residing in Los Angeles, I herein petition for a hearing in this matter.[3] . . .

The ABC had by now written Held that there would be a hearing on the granting of his license. Further, consulting attorneys, Cliff Lettieri, and others were requesting that the Sheriff's officers arrest Held on charges of assault. That night,

The group spread out through the bar and restaurant. Held kept his temper this time but called the Sheriff's officers repeatedly, asking them to arrest this one or that one. The regular customers began more and more to side with the demonstrators. [Held] tried to have Perry arrested because the minister refused to pay $2 for a cup of coffee.

. . . The dozen Sheriff's deputies were getting tired of the whole affair. It obviously was an explosive situation which could lead to real trouble. And it didn't seem worth it!

Then it was all over. The deputies went back into the kitchen with Held— for a long time. They first had asked spokesmen for the demonstrators just what they would accept.

Kight, Perry, Lettieri, and others said we had no desire to turn the Beanery into a gay establishment, that they would leave peacefully if the signs came down, and that charges against Held would be dropped. They also said they would like to have the signs.

After about an hour of conferring, an employee came out and took down the original sign over the bar, but left it face out on the back bar. There were cheers, and a few grumbles from diehard regulars, and some doubt that the sign was down to stay.

A few minutes later, the new signs, all on cardboard, came down, and these were handed to the demonstrators. The old wood sign was taken out of sight.

The group had a last rousing cheer out front, then disbanded.[4]

■

"Can a man who gets down on his knees to suck cock also kneel to worship his god without feeling hypocritical or schizophrenic? Should one devoted to the former forget the latter, considering himself an abomination in the sight of the Lord?" asked John Francis Hunter in GAY.[5] The Rev. Troy Perry, gay founder and pastor of Los Angeles's Metropolitan Community Church answers "Yes!" to the first, "No!" to the latter.

Perry—who had picketed Barney's, led about two hundred Angeleno gays through the city's Civic Center on November 16 to protest California's sodomy laws, and on a rainy January 11 marched at the head of nearly three hundred homosexuals in a candlelight procession along Hollywood streets—was a militant well known to gays when Hunter interviewed him in GAY's March 29, 1970, issue. Three and a half months later TIME devoted a column and a half to the handsome thirty-year-old preacher; *Newsweek* featured him October 12. TIME told how the father of two sons and minister had separated from his wife *and* the church when he found he could not conquer his homosexual desires. One night in 1968 Perry bailed a fellow-homosexual out of jail, tried to comfort him. "It's no use," the youth wept. "No one cares for us homosexuals." "God cares," replied Perry. But the young man persisted, "No, not even God cares." Perry had found—refound—his calling.[6]

Perry, whose pulpit style, in Hunter's words, "is that of a fire-eating Fundamentalist hooked on Hubert Humphrey happiness pills," met with his first gay congregation—twelve people—on October 6, 1968.* Not quite two years later he had helped establish his fourth Metropolitan Community Church: besides the mother church in Los Angeles, there were MCCs in San Francisco, San Diego, and Chicago. He had helped set up an MCC mission in Phoenix, and was hoping to establish missions in Tucson, El Paso, and Dallas. In late 1970, the L.A. church had nearly five hundred members and over one hundred associate members, or "friends." A first general conference of the new domination was called in September.[7]

The doctrine of Metropolitan Community Churches—Perry was raised a Pentecostal in rural Florida—is a general Protestant one. The church embraces the sacraments of "baptism by the water and the holy spirit" and "holy communion or the Mass, which is the partaking of bread and wine . . ."[8] On his visit to Perry in Los Angeles, Hunter recorded that MCC's

* MCC of Los Angeles held services in a movie theater for nearly two years; on October 13, 1970, it purchased its own building, a church with a 600-person capacity near the University of Southern California campus.

278

activities and services besides Sunday morning worship include prayer meetings and Bible classes; an "Alcoholics Together" group; a class for the deaf; marriage ceremonies (performed for couples who have been together for at least six months); a ladies' auxiliary designed partly to counsel wives, mothers or sisters of homosexuals; and a Rescue Squad which responds to telephone hot-line pleas from homosexuals in immediate trouble—whether it be with the law or themselves when a love affair has ended and rejection has become overwhelming . . .

But Perry "exhorts his followers like a hip Billy Graham to hold their heads up, face up to what they are and what they can do to build a better life, and cry 'Amen!' to positive living." [9]

The MCC founder is frequently a guest speaker or interviewee to gay and straight groups across the nation. On the "Virginia Graham Show," summer 1970, Perry asserted that "the purpose of his church was not to convert people to homosexuality, but to provide a place where homosexuals could pray. 'Forsake not the assembling of yourselves together,'" he quoted from the New Testament when Miss Graham queried why gays needed a church of their own, and explained how unwelcome the open/covert homosexual was/felt in the church.[10] But, Perry has stated, "Many times in the Press, we are referred to as a Church for Homosexuals as though we believe in the doctrine of separation. We do not! . . . We are not the 'Gay Church,' we are the 'Church of the Living God'"[11] The MCC monthly magazine bears the name *In Unity*.

In April 1969, Perry with eight of his congregation joined a sympathy demonstration for San Francisco's Committee for Homosexual Freedom at the Los Angeles division of States Steamship Lines. In a November 1970 New York appearance, sponsored by MSNY, in the Summit Hotel "The Rev." illustrated how his peculiar blend of old-time religion and gay militancy quelled a lady detractor at the steamship demonstration. He related: "I had on my collar. And a little lady came over and I said, 'Here, madam, would you like one of our leaflets?' And she hit me with her purse! And like a fool, instead of stopping, I said, 'Madam, are you *sure* you don't want one?' And she hit me again! She said, 'If I had my way all of you perverted individuals would be locked up, in jail, and the key thrown away!' I said, 'Madam, that's a wonderful Christian attitude you have.' She looked at me and she said, 'Do you know what the book of Leviticus says?' I said, 'I sure do! It says that it's a sin for a woman to wear a red dress, a man to wear a cotton shirt and woolen pants, for you to eat shrimp, oysters, or lobster—or your steak too rare.' She said, 'That's not what I mean!' I said, 'I know that's not what you mean, honey, but you forgot all of these other sins, too, that's in the same book of the Bible.' She said, 'Do you know what St. Paul said?' I said, 'I sure do. He said for women to be silent, not to speak.' She said, 'That's not what I mean either.' I said, 'I know it's not, honey, but Paul hated women: he said that women were not to teach, preach, they were not to serve *any*

279

sort of authority over a man.' I said, 'Where would our women's liberation groups be, if we listened to the Apostle Paul?' She said, 'Well, that's not what I mean still.' I said, 'I know it's not, honey.' I said, 'Not only that, but Paul was a great fella. He met a slave one time, and the word of God says that he converted this slave, made him a happy *Christian* slave— he didn't try to get him into Canada by the Underground Railroad, he sent him back to his master *still a slave!* Paul wasn't against slavery.' And I said, 'Not only that, he said if a man hath long hair, it's a shame unto him. Now, if we're going to close the doors of the church to the hippies just because they have long hair'—I said—'I can't believe that.'

"She said, 'All right, smarty. What did *Jesus* think?' I said, 'Now there's a weirdy for you. Now if he had lived in this day and age, the way you people label individuals, you would have labeled *him* a homosexual right off the bat!' I said, 'I don't believe Jesus was a homosexual. But I know you people. Here was a guy that was raised by a mother with no father— typical homosexual syndrome—never married, and ran around with twelve guys all the time. Not only that, he wasn't above having bodily contact with another man: John the Beloved lay on the breast of Jesus at the Last Supper. Not only that, but a *guy* betrayed him with a kiss!! Doesn't that make you want to puke?' Well, of course she was just white as a sheet by then. I said, 'Madam, not once did Jesus say, "Come unto me, all ye heterosexuals—who have sex in the missionary position with a member of the *opposite* sex—and you can become our true followers." Jesus said, "Come unto me *all* that labor and are heavy laden and I will give you rest." ' And I said, 'Once he was asked, "What is the great commandment!" And he said, "The great commandment is this: you're to love the Lord thy God with all of your heart, your mind, and your strength. And your neighbor as yourself, which is the second part of the commandment." ' "I said, *'That's* what Jesus says . . .' "

Perry's churches for homosexuals (heterosexuals are not excluded) have been criticized for their encouragement of separatism, also because they do not *fight* the doctrinal discrimination against gays in other churches —instead, gather unto themselves all gays who feel oppressed in the "straight" church. Said SIR's Tom Maurer on a May 1970 visit to FREE in Minneapolis: "I know entire churches that are homosexual—they're terrible. If one goes to a straight church and is accepted, that's something, but if one goes to an entirely homosexual church and is accepted, that's nothing. I don't like to see gay ghettoes." [12] Meanwhile, Father Robert Clement established the gay American Church, based on the restored Gallican rite of A.D. 576, in New York later that summer; the Homophile Social League of Washington, D.C., sponsored an all-homosexual service at All Souls Unitarian Church there on September 27 [13]; and Rabbi Herbert Katz conducted an opening service on November 6 for New York's new gay House of David and Jonathan. "Homosexual Citizen" columnists Lige Clarke and Jack Nichols, citing Perry's slogan, "The Lord is my shepherd and He knows I'm gay," suggested: [14] "The prime enemy of the homosexual has always been the Church. We hoped at one time that gays would learn to abandon absurd vestiges of superstition and dogma. Troy Perry, the good gay reverend, has proved our hopes in vain. Jesus lives in a homosexual church! People need him. Christians burned us at the stake in the name of God. But man, it seems, is the eternal masochist. Bow down before *power,* real or imagined. Queer, isn't it?"

Clarke's and Nichols's fears of a mass migration of American homosexuals to the new gay churches were fanciful—despite leaflets such as MCC San Francisco's, urging, "TAKE A TRICK TO CHURCH TOMORROW!!! . . . a relationship with another person can be motivated by more than sex . . . it can be motivated by love!" Many gays, like GLFer Jim Clifford, have felt ashamed even meeting in church facilities as the New York Front did *: "It's a closet kind of thing." (Yet it is interesting that Daughters of Bilitis, one of the few non-student gay groups in Manhattan that met *outside* church property, has been harassed repeatedly by New York City police.) Other gays are less restrained than Clifford. Picketing St. Patrick's Cathedral on November 20, members of GLF and STAR carrying posters that read GOD IS GAY and THE CHURCH IS THE REAL PERVERSION remembered that the church had given up its matches, ropes, and nails and become the homosexual's friend only shortly before psychiatrists assumed his chastisement. *Gay Power* [15] had recorded how in Hollywood on March 8,

Hate exploded at Blessed Sacrament Church on Sunset Blvd. Catholics emerging from communion spat on Gay Liberation Front members who were peacefully picketing the church. Virulent hatred was unmistakeably evident on many Catholic faces—"You ought to be lined up against a wall and killed with a machine gun," said a woman with two small children. "For 2¢ I'd like to kill them all," said a father. . . .

With such strong hate vibes, GLFers marched the picketline in silent dignity, turning the other cheek to the threats of murder, insults and spit falling on them. . . . "We are not afraid," answered one Gay, "after what you have done to us, we have nothing to fear." . . .

One homosexual carried a sign BEFORE CHURCHIANITY GAYS WERE FREE; another, THIS USED TO BE OUR FATHER'S HOUSE . . .

In issue nine the *San Francisco Free Press* [16] reported a semiludicrous but deeply symbolic costumed action by writer Don Jackson and Morris Kight, a founder of GLF Los Angeles.

L.A., Feb. 23. His Holiness Pope Morris I went to the First Congregational Church in Los Angeles to tack a bill for 90 billion dollars on the door. The amount represents $10,000 for each of the 9 million homosexuals which his-

* Probably the greatest number of American homophile/homosexual organizations meet and have social affairs in church facilities. Even during the first Revolutionary People's Constitutional Convention, New York GLFers were housed in Germantown Presbyterian Church in Philadelphia.

torical records indicate were executed at the instigation of the clergy. The Gay Pope said, "The Congregational or Puritan Church is particularly guilty; they murdered thousands of people for sodomy in New England during the 17th and 18th centuries."

As he left the church, The Pope remarked, "I hope the straight Christians will pay their just bill and then learn a little bit about love—doing it in the missionary position all the time is a sin and an awful bore." . . .

A few days later, on March 1, "Pope Morris" led picketers at three Los Angeles churches. The gays told churchgoers as they left services, "Christ never condemned us," "Love thy neighbor," "The church is guilty of genocide." GAY reported that "Members of Christ Unity were warm and receptive. 'Wonderful!' one churchgoer said. Another said, 'Christ is with you,' and another, 'Thank you!' " [17]

In the *Berkeley Barb,* October 9–15, Leo Laurence reported [18] how gay activist Rev. Jim Rankin said, "Get beyond tokenism" to the First Unitarian Church in San Francisco, that GLF "is not asking to be 'accepted,' we want you to embrace what we are doing."

Unitarians tell us: "You're a nice person . . . but shut up about it!" Rev. Rankin is talking about the usual liberal bullshit that's been coming down at local "movement" churches; i.e., First Unitarian and Glide Methodist.

"Back it up!" Rankin says to the followers of Thomas Starr King, who have nice rhetoric, but do damn little to show their willingness to ". . . bring an end to all discrimination against homosexuals . . . bisexuals," as ordered by the 1970 General Assembly of the Unitarian Universalist Association.

Signs were posted last Sunday inside the church: "FAGGOTS 'NOT WEL-COME.' "

That's where it's really at, contrary to the public statements published by Herb Caen in the KKKronicle. . . .

■

In Los Angeles on June 12, 1970, what *The Advocate* [19] termed "the first marriage in the nation designed to legally bind two persons of the same sex" was performed by the Rev. Troy Perry.* Joined in a simple double-ring ceremony were two young women, Neva Joy Heckman and Judith Ann Belew. A legal test of the marriage was expected.

The rites were conducted under a provision of California law that allows a common-law marriage to be formalized by a church ceremony and issuance of a church certificate when the couple have been together two years or more. Neva and Judith had been together just over two years.

* *The Advocate* (July 8–20) noted that "Rev. Perry said he had no immediate candidates for a second wedding, but his lover, Steve Jordan, caught the bride's bouquet."

Issuance of the certificate by MCC completed the law's requirements.

No marriage license is required under this provision, bypassing Los Angeles County Clerk William G. Sharp, who said . . . that he would not issue such a license to persons of the same sex "under any circumstances."

California law, like that of many states, does not specify that marriage partners be of the same sex. It does require, however,

that the couple be asked if they accept each other as husband and wife.

Rev. Perry, therefore, had Neva make this altered version of the vow:

"I, Neva, take thee, Judith, to be my wedded *spouse,* to have and to hold from this day forward, for better and for worse, for richer and for poorer, in sickness and in health, to love and to cherish, according to God's holy ordinance, *to serve in the office of husband* until death do us part, and thereunto I give thee my troth."

Judith made the same vow except to say "wife" instead of "husband."

Instead of declaring them husband and wife, Rev. Perry pronounced "our sisters, Neva and Judith," to be "living in the offices of husband and wife."

County Clerk Sharp, who planned to ask the California legislature to alter the marriage statutes to specify that partners be of the opposite sex, had had a great increase in inquiries from homosexuals since two men in Minnesota applied for a license on May 18.[20]

Mike McConnell and Jack Baker made national headlines, as did Kentuckians Tracy Knight and Marjorie Ruth Jones, in coming months. Both men were twenty-eight, McConnell a Ph.D. in Library Science and Baker a B.S. in Chemical Engineering with an M.A. in Business Administration. Baker was just completing a degree in law. The two had met in graduate school at the University of Oklahoma, had been lovers three years before applying for their marriage license. Baker stated in Minneapolis's *Pro/Con,* January 1971: "Ever since my lover and I applied for a marriage license . . . we have been asked a thousand times: 'Why don't you just live together and not make such a show of the whole thing?' There are several reasons why we are testing the marriage laws and why living together 'in sin' is not a satisfactory arrangement." [21] The reasons all had to do, Baker has contended, with the fact that the legal system in this country uses the institution of marriage as a distribution mechanism for certain rights and privileges that can be had solely by entering into a contract of marriage.

He has justified his and McConnell's right to be wed on five grounds: [22]

First, procreation cannot be the only standard used to legally recognize a significant love relationship. The first book of the Bible, the Book of Genesis, speaks of marriage at three different passages. Only once (Gen 1:28) does it mention procreation in conjunction with marriage. At two of the three passages (Gen 2:18 and 2:24), the Bible speaks of marriage in terms of a

283

love bond or a love union between two people. That's how we look at marriage. We feel it's the relationship, i.e., love and concern that is important—not procreation. We look at marriage as a commandment of God to love one's companion. In our view, sex is a natural extension of love and a child is the biological result of sex between a man and a woman. But a child is by no means necessary to create a valid marriage. It is more important that people learn to share their lives with someone who will help them grow and mature, someone who will share their happiness and their troubles. We feel the state is out of line with both the Constitution and the Bible to insist that there must be children involved or contemplated in a relationship before it will recognize a marriage. Such an insistence is hypocritical because most states allow marriages between senile couples, imbeciles and sterile people. We believe love knows no gender.

Second, any relationship that promotes honesty, self-respect, mutual growth and understanding for two people and which harms no other person should be accepted by the law. Relationships which foster harmony among the participants remove disharmony from the community. And conversely, relationships that foster disharmony among the participants increase the disharmony in society. Since society has an interest in maintaining order, it is to society's benefit to recognize and encourage harmonious relationships. There is no biological reason why the participants in a harmonious relationship have to be of the opposite sex. Therefore, we believe the state is unwise to set up artificial criteria when there is no compelling reason to do so.

Third, sexual preference is not a reason to deny a couple inheritance rights, property privileges or tax benefits. The institution of marriage has been used by the legal system as a distribution mechanism for many rights and privileges. These rights and privileges can be obained only thru a legal marriage . . . we believe that it is a violation of the spirit and mandate of the Constitution to use sex preference as a basis to deny one couple certain rights that are granted to another couple.

Fourth, homosexuals are entitled to the same rights enjoyed by heterosexuals. We demand the same rights as a matter of principle. We insist that Gay people be given *ALL* rights granted to heterosexuals, no more but no less. This includes, but is not limited to, the right to hold the hand of, dance with and kiss the object of one's affection in public. We think that when any minority allows itself to be denied a right that is given to others, it is allowing itself to be relegated to a second-rate position. We don't advocate that all Gay people exercise all rights, e.g., legal marriage, but we think as a matter of principle, all Gay people should have the option to exercise their rights if they so choose.

Fifth, the desire of two human beings to be joined in a permanent love relationship ought to be recognized with full legal dignity. We consider it a slur for the law to say that our relationship is not to be recognized because there are no children involved or contemplated. Such insults should not be tolerated. We feel we have a constitutional and a God-given right to love the person of our choice. That is a right that is above the law. Therefore, it is not the place of the law to say that some choices are better than others.

For *Pro/Con* readers, Baker emphasized his third rationale, expanded it in five ways:

The surviving spouse of a heterosexual couple can inherit the other's property automatically as a matter of right (assume here for simplicity there are no children). There is no hassle; the law directs what to do with the property of deceased persons where there is no will. For a Gay couple, however, there is no such right. When one party dies, the other's property goes to the desceased's family. This arrangement has been known to cause bitter lawsuits especially when the Gay couple made joint payments on, say, a car or a house but title remained in the name of one person only.

A heterosexual spouse can inherit through his or her deceased partner. For example, if grandmother Tillie dies leaving a large estate that the deceased party would have taken if alive, then his family would inherit just the same. Not so with a Gay couple. A Gay person cannot inherit his deceased lover's grandmother's estate under any circumstances.

Wills are not all that beneficial. If a Gay person leaves all his property to his lover, his family may contest the will on the grounds of undue influence and succeed in breaking it. This is especially true if there is much money involved.

In some states (not Minnesota) there is a form of ownership of property that is reserved solely to married couples. It's called "Tenancy by the Entirety." It guarantees that the property will go to the surviving spouse despite claims of creditors. Gay people can hold property in "Joint Tenancy," i.e., co-owners, but creditors can get to the property and thus there is no guarantee the surviving "spouse" will end up with it.

The surviving spouse of a heterosexual couple can sue a third person who wrongfully killed the partner. The ability to do this comes from the "wrongful death statute" and is available only to legally married couples. But Gay couples have no such right. For example, if a third person wrongfully kills my lover, I am without his companionship and without any legal remedy to redress the wrong. A good friend of mine had this happen to him. A doctor killed his lover through negligence and he could prove it. But he couldn't sue the doctor because they weren't "married." His lover's parents were old and didn't want to go through the ordeal of a lawsuit. He was without his lover and without any way of redressing the wrongful death.*

McConnell's and Baker's marriage bid was to initiate Minnesota's first important case of job discrimination against a homosexual. In a flyer explaining its SAVE MCCONNELL Campaign, FREE—of which both men were members—described how:

---

* Baker does not specify lower insurance rates or the joint tax advantages of being legally married. In GAY (December 15, 1969), Randy Wicker complained, ". . . my lover and I paid $2000 more in income taxes last year because we had to file separate returns as single males. If we could have filed jointly, our tax load would have been reduced by nearly one-third."

In February, Jim * McConnell applied for a library position in the University of Minnesota Library system. In April, McConnell interviewed with Dr. Hopp, Associate Director of the O. Meredith Wilson Library. On April 27, Dr. Hopp officially offered McConnell the position of Head of Cataloging Division of the St. Paul Campus Library. In no way did the letter indicate that the appointment was conditional upon the approval of any University committee or the Board of Regents. Dr. Hopp has not been able to fill the position for over one year and McConnell was led to believe that he was one of the first candidates who did possess the qualifications for the position.

On May 18,** McConnell and Baker walked into the Hennepin County Court House in Minneapolis to apply for a license to marry. GAY told how they "were sworn to an oath that they were fully aware they sought a union between two males—far different terms from the usual oath." [23] The clerk, however, withheld granting the license until he could confer with County Attorney George Scott. On Scott's advice, the license was denied on May 22. "Citing a 1949 State Supreme Court ruling declaring the state to be a third party to marriage contracts," GAY observed, "Scott, who is a candidate for the Democratic-Farmer-Labor Party endorsement for governor, said: 'It is the duty of the state, in the conservation of public morals, to guard the marriage relation. To permit two males to marry,' he said, 'would result in an undermining and destruction of the entire legal concept of our family structure in all areas of law.'"
FREE continued:

On June 24, six days before McConnell was to begin his active work in the library, Mr. R. Joel Tierney, University Attorney, informed McConnell that the Faculty, Staff, and Student Affairs Committee of the Board of Regents had voted not to recommend his appointment and that McConnell should not report for employment on July 1. McConnell had already turned down another employment offer, resigned from his present position, allowed his apartment lease to expire, severed financial ties, and made provisions for a permanent relocation from Kansas City to Minneapolis. The letter from the University Attorney provided no reason for failing to approve the appointment yet the Attorney says that McConnell can request an appeal hearing on July 9. Without knowing why the appointment was not approved, preparation for the hearing becomes extremely difficult. . . .

They were to learn why soon—if they'd ever wondered. The Board of Regents issued a statement finding McConnell's "personal conduct, as represented in the public and university news media . . . not consistent with the best interests of the university." [24]

* McConnell was called by his middle name, Mike, but the two men used "Jim" in all publicity about the license application in hopes that the university would not make the connection.
** In a letter to the author, October 21, 1970, Baker told that the marriage application was his birthday present to McConnell; "it was timed so the pictures would appear in the local papers on his birthday—May 19."

On September 20, *The New York Times* announced, HOMOSEXUAL WINS SUIT OVER HIRING: "Declaring that 'a homosexual is a human being,' a Federal judge has ruled that the University of Minnesota may not refuse to hire a person merely because he is an avowed homosexual." Backed by a local chapter of the American Civil Liberties Union, McConnell had gone to court in late August. Federal District Judge Philip Neville had taken the matter under advisement. On September 19, Neville ruled, saying: [25]

An homosexual is after all a human being, and a citizen of the United States, despite the fact that he finds his sex gratification in what most consider to be an unconventional manner.

He is as much entitled to the protection and benefits of the laws and due process fair treatment as are others—at least as to public employment in the absence of proof and not mere surmise that he has committed or will commit criminal acts or that his employment efficiency is impaired by his homosexuality. . . .

The courts have abandoned the concept that public employment and the opportunity therefore is merely privilege and not a constitutionally protected right. . . .

To justify dismissal from public employment, or . . . to reject an applicant for public employment, it must be shown that there is an observable and reasonable relationship between efficiency on the job and homosexuality * . . .

McConnell did not begin work, however. By a vote of the Board of Regents, the University of Minnesota appealed to the United States Court of Appeals for the Eighth Circuit. His job was kept open until the court might decide. GAY remarked: "At his own press conference Baker—McConnell's lover—estimated that the original suit and appeal are costing the university about $6,000. He asked 'whether or not it is a wise use of public funds to spend thousands of dollars in an effort to deny human rights instead of defending civil rights.' In any event, McConnell's side will be argued free of charge by volunteer lawyers for the ACLU . . ." The Minnesota Library Association meanwhile asked the American Library Association "to look into the James M. McConnell case and to censure the University of Minnesota board of regents if it finds the regents discriminated against McConnell just because he's gay." [26]

On October 22, Baker and McConnell were plaintiffs in another case. Their lawyer, Michael Wetherbee's, brief began: "This memorandum is in support of the motion for the issuance of a writ of mandamus to require Gerald R. Nelson as Clerk of District Court of Hennepin County, to issue a marriage license to plaintiffs. . . ."

* "Judge Neville cited the 1965 and 1968 Scott decisions regarding federal employment in which, in his words, 'an admission that one is a homosexual, standing alone and without evidence of any practice thereof, will not justify the Civil Service Commission in refusing to certify him as eligible for employment based on a determination of "immoral conduct."'" (GAY, October 12, 1970.)

Selecting portions of the Minnesota Statutes, Chapter 517, he italicized to prove his points. From the M.S.A., section 517.02, he noted:

"Every male person who had attained the full age of 21 years, [note the comma] * and every female person who has attained the full age of 18 years, is capable in law of contracting marriage, if otherwise competent. . . ."

Wetherbee remarked, "For present purposes, then, section 517.02 can be read as follows: Every male person who had attained the full age of 21 years is capable in law of contracting marriage, if otherwise competent. . . ."

A lengthy M.S.A. section, 517.03, told what marriages were prohibited:

"No marriage shall be contracted while either of the parties has a husband or wife living; . . . ; *nor between persons one of whom is a male person under 18 years of age or one of whom is a female person under the age of 16 years*; . . ."

Wetherbee observed that "section 517.03, despite its lengthy detail in prohibiting certain marriages, does not prohibit marriages between two persons of the same sex, though a clause to that effect could easily have been inserted. It is to be concluded, then, that had the legislature desired to prohibit marriages between persons of the same sex, it would have inserted that prohibition in section 517.02."

Citing subdivisions 1 and 3 of M.S.A., section 517.08, which contained information to be asked of license applicants by the county clerk, Wetherbee showed that *"There is no requirement that applicants for a marriage license state of which sex they are on the application form. Thus, there is no legal way in which the county clerk can become cognizant of the sex of the applicant."*

Wetherbee's brief argued through eighteen pages. At a hearing on November 9, the plaintiffs appeared before District Judge Stanley Kane with witnesses-in-their-behalf Minnesota Human Rights Commissioner Conrad Balfour; Rev. Tom Maurer of San Francisco, former coordinator of the Kinsey Institute Research Project on Homosexuality; Jerrold Winters, a St. Paul social worker who has counseled both gay and straight lovers; and Mrs. Barbara Knudson, sociologist at the University of Minnesota. Their comments, dismissed as irrelevant, were cut off and the license denied in a ruling on November 18.

One part of the Minnesota marriage statutes, M.S.A. section 517.07, read:

"Before any persons shall be joined in marriage, a license shall be obtained from the clerk of the district court of the county in which the woman resides, or, if not a resident of this state, then from the clerk of the district court of

* The brackets and bracketed materials are Wetherbee's.

any county and the marriage need not take place in the county where the license is obtained."

Furthermore, said Judge Kane, "this law [that of marriage] is not to be read in isolation from the other laws governing the marriage relationship in the areas of divorce and annulment, probate and property law, inheritance and tax laws and regulations, and notably the law governing the rights and privileges of married women. In this overall view, it must be concluded that the legislature did not intend to authorize or permit such marriages." [27]

The Advocate [28] stated that McConnell, Baker, and Wetherbee

had attempted to raise a federal constitutional issue in the case, but the court ruled that they had failed to comply with a Minnesota rule of civil procedure requiring proper notice to be given to the state attorney general when a constitutional question is raised, and therefore the decision was strictly on state law.

However, Wetherbee said after the Nov. 9 hearing that "the court never reached the question of constitutionality" because Judge Kane cut off testimony of several experts for the plaintiffs into gay life-styles, emotional matters, and discrimination as "immaterial and irrelevant."

Baker, himself a law student at the University of Minnesota, had said the next step in the event of an adverse ruling from Judge Kane would probably be an appeal to the state Supreme Court.

Because District Court left the constitutional issue open, however, he said after the Nov. 18 ruling that he and McConnell may go directly to U.S. District Court. In any case, he said, there is no question that they will appeal.*

Gay Scene reported,[29] autumn 1970, that

British law is being tested by Carole Mary Lord, 23, and Terry Floyd, 24, who were married in a civil ceremony at the Southbend England Registrar's office recently. James Cotier, who married them, said: "This is a bona fide wedding until it can be proven otherwise." Both the bride, who wore white, and the groom, who wore a suit, are female. A wedding certificate showed that Terry is a "bachelor." . . .

The police have not questioned them, and thus no charges have been made. . . . RIGHT ON, YOU TWO!

It wasn't so easy for Tracy Knight, twenty-five, or (Mrs.) Marjorie Ruth Jones, thirty-nine, who applied to Jefferson County Clerk James Hallahan in Louisville, Kentucky, on July 7. Eric Pianin of the *Louisville Times* related how Hallahan, who conceded that state law did not specify the sex of marriage partners, refused to issue the license because their marriage would "lead to a breakdown in the sanctity of government,"

* Don Rundquist, a friend of the plaintiffs, states that "they have already received the assurance of nine priests [Baker is a Catholic] in the Minneapolis area that they would marry the couple when they receive the license . . ."

would jeopardize society's moral fiber, and, warned the clerk, "It could spread all over the world"![30] On November 12, 1970, Stan MacDonald of the *Courier-Journal* affirmed that "One of the most unusual trials in Kentucky history began in Louisville yesterday: an attempt to determine whether the Jefferson County clerk can legally refuse to issue a marriage license to two women who want to marry each other." He noted that "The women . . . gave the court several reasons for wanting to marry, including love, legality and financial security."

According to MacDonald,

Bruce Miller, the Jefferson County Attorney, became confused during his questioning about which of the two was to be the "wife" and who was the "husband." . . .

Before the testimony and questioning began, Jefferson Circuit Judge Lyndon R. Schmid objected to the attire worn by Miss Tracy Knight . . . Schmid found her beige pantsuit "offensive to the court" and said she must change her clothes if she wanted \to attend the trial. "She is a woman and she will dress as a woman in this court," Schmid said.

Miss Knight left the courtroom and returned wearing a green dress. . . .

In his initial statement, Stuart Lyon, an attorney for the two women, argued that Hallahan has no authority under state law to deny a marriage license because of sex.

Lyon also contended that Hallahan's action violated individual rights under the First Amendment of the Constitution, which protects freedom of expression and association.

Miller, representing Hallahan in the case, indicated after the two-hour session that he will argue that state laws never intended that marriage licenses be granted to persons of the same sex, even though this is not specifically spelled out.

The small courtroom was filled with about 25 onlookers who chuckled occasionally and were once sternly reprimanded for doing so by Judge Schmid. Many were college-age and members of the Gay Liberation Front.

Edwin S. Segal, the anthropology professor, was the first to take the stand. He told the court that some women in other cultures marry each other. As examples he named the "Nupe, Ibo and Nuer" peoples of Africa. They married, he said, largely for "inheritance."

"I can see no disruption to what we now consider normal marital relations . . . by allowing marriage between two persons of the same sex," he said.

Schmid declared that the court was only concerned about "this culture," not African cultures.

Dr. Sandor Klein, a Louisville clinical psychologist, testified that he recently examined the two women and had concluded that "neither at this point would be able to have a normal heterosexual relationship." . . .

In her testimony, Miss Knight agreed with Klein's findings. She said she could have a "social" relationship with men but not a "physical" one.

She said marriage to Mrs. Jones would provide "security and companionship." She said it was cheaper for two persons to live together, and added, "I can save on taxes and insurance." [31] . . .

The *Louisville Times* observed that Mrs. Jones told the court, "I'm a Lesbian and I'm very much in love with Tracy."

Miller proposed that the marriage would harm the well-being of Mrs. Jones's three children, two of them grown and the youngest, fifteen, who lived with his mother. Mrs. Jones agreed that publicity from the trial might hurt them. The women were nevertheless determined to appeal higher if their case were lost.

Gays by and large sent "Right on!" 's to Heckman, Belew, McConnell, Baker, Knight, and Jones, but were divided in their opinion on the advisability of legalized homosexual marriage. Ralph Hall exclaimed, in *Gay Power*: [32] "Homosexual marriages submitting to the guidelines of so-called conventional rites must be classed as reactionary. The gay lib movement does not need these kinds of tactics. We're involved in rational warfare, not irrational. Now, don't you agree it isn't relevant to gay liberation when we start imitating meaningless, bad habits of our oppressors and begin instituting them? That *isn't* the freedom we want. That isn't *our* liberation. That *isn't* the equality we want. And that *ain't* revolutionary. . . ." Martin Dennison III told GP readers: [33]

Another Cause-with-a-capital-C that keeps coming up every so often is the Right of Homosexuals to Marry—to Marry each other, that is. For some reason, lesbians seem to be more prone to this one than the gay boys; but they aren't immune, by any means. They loudly demand, in violent manifestos in all colors of typewriter ribbon, the right to have a religious ceremony solemnizing their union, to adopt children, own property in common, etc., etc., etc. (None of them has ever gone so far as to include the right to prosecute one's erring partner for adultery, but I'm expecting to see that one included any day now.)

Leaving aside all considerations such as how suitably a child could be reared in a homosexual home, or the fact that most modern women are trying to *escape* the legal and other restrictions of marriage, so that it's funny to see these "enlightened" lesbians trying to get *into* them . . .

Concern,[34] speaking for the Southern California Council on Religion and the Homophile in June 1969, felt that "Such union could help conscientious homosexuals to have the sex life they require without the promiscuity heretofore too characteristic of their kind." The magazine granted that "homosexuals are in more of a dead-end situation than are heterosexuals. So long as there is no institution of responsible, monogamous union available, the homosexual's situation encourages him to multiply sexual attachments and to promiscuity." Franklin Kameny averred, in *The Same Sex: An Appraisal of Homosexuality* (Philadelphia, 1969), that "homosexuality is far more a matter of love and affection than it is commonly considered to be; and heterosexuality is far more a matter of physical lust than our culture, with its over-romanticized approach, admits it to be. Actually, homosexuality and heterosexuality differ but little, if at all, in this respect." [35]

Straights had mixed opinions. Queried "Is marriage between men all right?" in the street by the *San Francisco Chronicle*'s Novella O'Hara,[36] Marie Hagopian's answer was typical: "Isn't that kind of a weird idea? I guess maybe it isn't. Actually, if people are in love, well, then they should be allowed to marry. Whatever makes them happy. I don't think you can make rules about people's emotions. About who they can or cannot love. So maybe it's a good idea. Yes, I'm for it." GAY revealed how the Rev. Morris Russell, vicar of St. Matthew's in Auckland, New Zealand, believed the Christian church should find a way to bless the relationship of two homosexuals who want to be wed.[37] *The New York Times* reported on August 10 that Mrs. Rita Hauser, United States representative to the United Nations Human Rights Commission believed laws banning marriage between two persons of the same sex were unconstitutional. The *Times* stated that, "Speaking on 'Women's Liberation and the Constitution' at a section meeting of the American Bar Association, Mrs. Hauser said that such laws were based on what she called an outdated notion that reproduction is the purpose of marriage. She argued that overpopulation had made this rationale outmoded." [38] The *Times* had reported,[39] however, that on July 25 the Rev. Gino Concetti warned, in the Vatican, that gay marriages "are simply moral aberrations that cannot be approved by human conscience much less Christian conscience." Gays wondered how he knew. Moreover, reported Nancy Tucker,[40] Washington correspondent exclusive to *The Advocate,* "President Nixon 'doesn't think that people of the same sex should marry,' the White House told the ADVOCATE Aug. 12. Presidential Press Secretary Ronald L. Ziegler said the President 'hasn't been for it, he's not for it, and he won't be for it.' "

Notwithstanding, the Family Guidance Center of the Metropolitan Hospital, New York, expanded its marriage counseling service to include gay "marrieds." [41] And Father Robert Clement of the New York American Church began religious services for gays who wished to exchange vows. From the foreword of his "Service of Holy Union": [42]

The soul of Jonathan was knit with the soul of David, and Jonathan loved him as his own soul. And Jonathan stripped himself of the robe that was upon him and gave it to David. Then Jonathan and David made a covenant, because he loved him as he loved his own soul.

From *The Vows:*

I, (John), take thee, (James), to be my beloved, to have and to hold from this day forward, for better for worse, for richer for poorer, in sickness and in

292

health; to love and to cherish in the sight of God: and thereto I pledge thee my word. . . .

■

René Guyon: "The trouble to which the psychiatrists have gone to explain . . . nature in terms of convention, health in terms of mental disease, is scarcely to be believed. . . . The distinctive method of its system is that every time it comes across a natural act that is contrary to the prevailing conventions, it brands this act as a symptom of mental derangement or abnormality." [43]

Thomas Szasz: "In stubbornly insisting that the homosexual is sick, the psychiatrist is merely pleading to be accepted as a physician. . . . [W]e may safely conclude that psychiatric opinion about homosexuals is not a scientific proposition but a medical prejudice. . . . It is clear that psychiatrists have a vested interest in diagnosing as mentally ill as many people as possible, just as inquisitors had in branding them as heretics. The "conscientious" psychiatrist authenticates himself as a competent medical man by holding that sexual deviants (and all kinds of other people, perhaps all of mankind, as Karl Menninger would have it) are mentally ill, just as the "conscientious" inquisitor authenticated himself as a faithful Christian by holding that homosexuals (and all kinds of other people) were heretics. We must realize that in situations of this kind we are confronted, not with scientific problems to be solved, but with social roles to be confirmed. Inquisitor and witch, psychiatrist and mental patient, create each other and authenticate each other's roles. For an inquisitor to have maintained that witches were not heretics and that their souls required no special effort at salvation would have amounted to asserting that there was no need for witchhunters.[44] . . .

On May 14, 1970, psychiatrists became the hunted. An invasion by a coalition of gay and women's liberationists interrupted the national convention of the American Psychiatric Association in San Francisco "to protest the reading of a paper by an Australian psychiatrist on the subject of 'aversion therapy,' a system of treatment which attempts to change gay orientation by keying unpleasant sensations (such as electric shocks) to homosexual stimuli.* By the time the meeting was over, the feminists and their gay cohorts were in charge . . . and the doctors were heckling from the audience." [45]

GAY called it A MUCH NEEDED ZAP, and editorialized: "Homosexually

* Don Jackson reported in *Gay Power* (No. 19) that the treatment consists ["According to Dr. Kay Thomas"] of showing the patient nude, provocative photographs of handsome men. An electric shock is administered with each photo. In the nauseous drug therapy, the patient is sexually aroused by a man, and then forced to take a nauseous drug. 'It is nothing new,' said Dr. Thomas. 'It is just Pavlovian conditioning—you might call it brain washing. It does work in many cases, but it would be equally effective if it were used to cure heterosexuality.'"

inclined people have much to fear from the entrenched dogma of today's psychiatric establishment. We cannot stand idly by while so-called 'scientists' prepare the groundwork for electric shock treatments. To do so would be to masochistically assist evil headhunting shrinks to bring *Brave New World* closer than ever." [46]

Californian Gary Alinder told *Come Out!*: [47] "Walking into the enemy's inner sanctum is an enlightening experience. . . . We found out how tuned out the shrinks are." He described the main convention meeting as "a refugee camp for Nixon's silent majority. It was 99 and 44/100 per cent white, straight, male middle-aged, upper middle class. . . . They have no qualms about male chauvinism, they've never even thought about it." Alinder noted that their agenda was to feature ". . . a panel about American Indians which concentrates on suicide by them rather than genocide by us . . . learning about aversion treatment for homosexuals—but not considering whether homosexuality is really a psychiatric 'disease' . . . hearing about drugs, new drugs and old drugs—but not the way drugs are used to tranquilize people who are legitimately upset . . . hearing about psychiatry and law enforcement but not about how our society uses police to oppress people and prevent change . . . discussing sexuality and abortion—but not the way sex roles are used to oppress women."

GAY detailed the gays' takeover: [48]

Dr. Nathaniel McConaghy of the University of New South Wales had come all the way from Australia to deliver his paper, and when the protesters started booing, he pleaded with them for a hearing.

Ironically, McConaghy is of the school which does not regard homosexuality as a mental aberration, and he told the demonstrators so. "This paper is the result of six years' work," he said. "Let me have my half-hour to report on it."

One woman leaped to the stage and demanded to use the microphone. Without identifying herself, she lashed out against McConaghy's paper.

"There is an alternative to this horrible, barbaric, disgusting, sadistic technique," she said. "That is, that people who are upset about something get together and talk about their problems among themselves."

[Alinder] . . . "I want to know what room the women can have to meet together in, and I want to know now." The chairman went on to the next speaker. Another woman got on the microphone: "I don't believe you heard, we want to know what room we can have and we want to know now."

[GAY] . . . Shouts and boos . . . from the front rows, which the demonstrators had largely taken over, and from further back came shouts of counterprotest.

"Shut up," cried a psychiatrist near the front of the hall, and others joined in with ill-concealed hostility: "Get out," "Be quiet," "We don't want to hear you."

One man dressed as a priest [the Rt. Rev. Michael Itkin] . . . protested against "oppression," which, he said, "has been going on for five fucking thousand years."

Konstantin Berlandt, of Berkeley GLF, paraded through the hall in a bright red dress. Paper airplanes sailed down from the balcony. With two papers still unread, the chairman announced adjournment.

GAY told, "A slim young man in tight white jeans with shirt open to the navel leaped to the podium and shouted, 'The liberated meeting of the American Psychiatric Association is now in session.' This time it was the doctors who were the hecklers, several of whom engaged in a furious shouting contest with a Women's Lib member trying to get the floor. 'Don't shake your fucking finger at me,' the woman shrieked. 'I'll shake whatever I please,' retorted one doctor, his face livid."

[Alinder] . . . We are in a room of enraged psychiatrists. "They should be killed," shouts one. "Give back our air fare," shouts another.

Maria DeSantos reads from a Women's Liberation statement: "Women come to you suffering from depression. Women ought to feel depressed with the roles society puts on them. . . . Those roles aren't biological, those roles are learned. . . . It started when my mother threw me a doll and my brother a ball. . . ."

Michael Itkin reads the Gay Liberation demands.* . . . Knots of people talking loudly all over the room. Shrinks coming up asking us what we want. . . .

[GAY] . . . One girl spoke to her part of the floor about the passes made at her under the guise of psychiatric examination. Another accused Dr. Leo Alexander of Boston, one of the most eminent psychiatrists today, of assaulting her, and he stormed the stage to protest the injustice of her charge . . .

Alinder wrote that he found Dr. Irving Bieber, Professor of Psychiatry at New York Medical College, in a later convention panel entitled "Transsexualism v. Homosexuality: Distinct Entities?" and blasted the New Yorker:

"You are the pigs who make it possible for the cops to beat homosexuals: they call us queer; you—so politely—call us sick. But it's the same thing. You make possible the beatings and rapes in prisons,** you are implicated in the torturous cures perpetrated on desperate homosexuals. I've read your book,***

* Alinder reported that "One of Gay Liberation's demands to the convention was the abolition of psychiatry as an oppressive tool."
** Randy Wicker noted, in GAY (December 4, 1970), how "Five prisoners at the Queens House of Detention have been indicted on charges of first degree sodomy for forcing homosexual inmates into sexual acts during the takeover of the jail during early October. . . . Four homosexual prisoners were forced to engage in sexual acts with one another while the inmates looked on, and then were attacked by the five and sexually abused."
*** Irving Bieber et al.: Homosexuality (New York, 1962).

Dr. Bieber, and if that book talked about Black people the way it talks about homosexuals, you'd be drawn and quartered and you'd deserve it."

Bieber answers: "I never said homosexuals were sick, what I said was that they have displaced sexual adjustment." Much laughter from us: "That's the same thing, motherfucker." He tries again, "I don't want to oppress homosexuals; I want to liberate them, to liberate them from that which is paining them—their homosexuality." That used to be called genocide. . . .

On June 23, eighteen women and men of Chicago Gay Liberation nonplused a workshop on "Family Medicine" at the national convention of the American Medical Association in the Midwestern capital. Dr. Charles Socarides, New York psychiatrist and Arch-Enemy Number Two of the American homosexual, was their prime target. Scattering themselves throughout the meeting hall, the gays waited until Socarides began to speak. "As soon as he said the word 'homosexual,'" wrote Step May of CGL, "one invader shouted 'homosexuals are beautiful' and ten others jumped up to distribute the prepared leaflet. We then settled back with our arms around each other to hear all about ourselves."

Time and again during his address, the gays challenged, "That's a moral judgment!" or "You're making things up!" or "Do you cure your straight patients of heterosexuality?" Socarides emphasized how physiologically adapted the male and female of the human species were to each other. A gay yelled, "A woman's breasts don't fit into a man's chest!" May told how,

After Socarides finished, one furious doctor demanded to know by what authority we were attending the session. Another doctor suggested that the issue that the Gay Liberation people were raising should be given legitimacy, and that one homosexual should join Socarides and the other authorities on the panel. A gay guerrilla raised the objection that there were women homosexuals and men homosexuals and that both groups would have to be represented. A gay woman and a gay man then took their places on the panel [49] . . .

New York Mattachine vice-president Bob Milne took his place, later that summer, on a panel discussion treating homosexuality, theology, and psychiatry at the State University of New York College of Nursing (Downstate Medical Center) in Brooklyn. Before an audience of nurses Milne and Father William Frederickson, a Catholic priest, crossed swords.

Father Frederickson spoke of two parishioners who were "sad men" and "laden with guilt." This was all Milne needed. "In the ensuing dialogue, [he] made clear that the parishioners in question did not suffer 'guilt' because of their homosexuality, but because they'd been *made* to feel guilty by 'The Vacuous Vatican, the Forever Fallible Fathers (vs. Galileo, Darwin, Freud, etc.), No-Fun Fundamentalists, Billy Bible-Bigot Grahams, and Rabid Rabbis.'" [50]

The *Mattachine Times* [51] affirmed how MSNY's

man marshalled and machine-gunned his facts: pointed out the popes who were practicing homosexuals; reviewed the history of homosexual prohibitions from Sodom in the Genesis myth (wherein the Jews promoted the practical purpose of procreating their persecuted and decimated race) to Henry VIII's incorporation into common law of ecclesiastical "sin"; revealed the fact that Jesus never once in line, chapter or verse condemned homosexuality; quoted Kinsey's statistics that proved clergymen have the highest homosexual percentage of any of the professions . . .

GAY detailed [52] how the gay spokesman

then launched into the lexicon of psychology to illuminate the etiology of homosexuality, the genes, hormones, the ontogenetic and phylogenetic evolutionary evidence, the geographical, historical, the cross-cultural, cross-species proof of the basic bisexual nature of man. He concluded with a caustic technical critique of quack psychiatrists.

The Catholic priest clasped his hands prayerfully, but getting no reply turned to an instructress for a more pragmatic assist. "I'd hoped the (mission) psychiatrist would be here to help me out" . . .

Gay liberation had not finished with the psychiatrists. A few months later GAY revealed: LOS ANGELES GAYS INVADE PSYCHOLOGISTS CONFERENCE: "GUINEA PIGS" RISE UP IN PROTEST—an on-the spot report by Tony DeRosa of L.A. GLF. *The Advocate* proclaimed, PSYCHOLOGISTS GET GAY LIB "THERAPY." [53] To a lecture on aversion therapy at the 2nd Annual Behavioral Modification Conference, on October 17, went GLFers and other gays who had arranged with Dr. Albert Marston of the University of Southern California (one of the sponsors) Psychology Department "for anyone willing to identify himself as a homosexual or member of GLF to be admitted to the session without paying a $10 fee." *The Advocate* related:

Some 140 persons were watching a film being shown by British psychologist Dr. M. Phillip Feldman of the University of Birmingham when GLF activists in the audience raised shouts of "Barbarism!" "Medieval torture!" and "This is disgusting!"

Lights were turned up and nearly a third of the audience, led by October GLF chairman Tony DeRosa, Don Kilhefner, Morris Kight, and Steve Beckwith, marched to the stage in the Music Room of the Biltmore Hotel. . . .

"I had hoped we could get through with Dr. Feldman's film and presentation and open some dialogue and discussion," Dr. Marston told the audience and the demonstrators.

"How can you have dialogue when you've got us up here as a show?" Beckwith objected.

Up to this point, there had been little reaction from the rest of the audience—many, but not all of them, practicing psychologists.

There was a brief exchange between Kight and Dr. Feldman, with Kight describing the aversion techniques worked out by Dr. Feldman in research with homosexual males between 1962 and 1966 as "primitive medieval torture."

In the first part of his lecture, before the film, Dr. Feldman had stressed the ethical responsibility involved in using such techniques and had said that they were used only on homosexuals who had sought help and whom the researchers had been convinced genuinely wanted to change.

"I do not serve as the agent of society. I'm not here, either in America or in England, to do society's bidding. I'm here to help people who ask for this.

"This means we didn't keep in treatment any patients who were referred by the law or by the courts. I thought this was totally wrong. If it became clear early in treatment that they didn't want to change, we let them out through the back door. I can say this here, I couldn't say it in England."

Kight, however, took the tack that the very existence of such techniques was a threat.

"Gentlemen, and ladies, you are a party to this. You must be responsible . . . With this kind of treatment, you could make a Tory, you could also make a Nazi, you could also make any number of things."

Dr. Feldman protested that in the interrupted film, "I make just this point."

"Then, sir, Dr. Feldman, you should not have allowed this. You should have said to homosexuals, 'So what?' "

Kilhefner took over the microphone and said, "I'm a firm believer in free speech. But what you people out there call free speech, in fact has been a monologue for over a half century. And we would like to start a dialogue."

He said the GLF would print Dr. Feldman's speech at its own expense for those who wanted to read it later, "but right now the GLF is suggesting . . . that this session this morning be reconstituted. That if a dialogue is to begin, let it begin now. You have been our oppressor for too long, and we will take this no longer.

"We are going to reconstitute this session into small groups," he said, "with equal numbers of GLF members and members of your profession, and we are going to talk this morning—talk as you have probably never talked with homosexuals before, as equals. We're going to talk about such things as homosexuality as an alternative life style."

Kilhefner was interrupted by protests from the audience and the session rapidly turned into a shouting match. Kilhefner had the advantage of the microphone and continued to make himself heard above the uproar.

"We paid money to come here and listen to Dr. Feldman," one man shouted.

"If you believe in free speech, why don't you practice it?" a woman psychologist challenged the demonstrators.

Kilhefner plowed on, ignoring the protests.

"We're going to be talking about what you as psychologists are going to do to clear up your own fucked minds."

"I'm not a psychologist," a young Black in the audience yelled.

"This is what we're going to be doing, baby," Kilhefner kept on. Anybody who "can't dig it, we ask you to leave," he said. "Is this straight?"

"We ask you to leave," a man said loudly. "Yeah," a woman shouted, triggering applause.

298

"Sorry, buddy . . ." Kilhefner began. He was almost drowned out in a rising storm of boos, protests, and handclapping. Through it he kept shouting, "No more, baby, no more, baby!"

Some members of the audience got up and left. Others drifted in from the corridors to see what was going on. Kilhefner eventually gave up the microphone and several other GLF members attempted to speak.

Finally, Kight came forward and attempted to chide the audience for reacting angrily to the invasion. "Is this any tribute to your professionalism . . . You have a rare opportunity to talk to homosexuals who are terribly proud of it."

Dr. Marston spoke up at this point to say, "I think most of the people attending the regular conference agreed with me that we would, in fact, like to talk to members of the GLF. Our position is, that in order for the points to be made by the GLF, particularly for a lot of the audience who knew little about homosexuals, little about this treatment that you feel is so terrible, and do not know the isues, that it would be very valuable for them to see the rest of the film and hear what Dr, Feldman has to say."

This set off shouts of protest by the Gay Libers.

"We are here fighting for our lives," said Lee Heflin, pushing in to take the microphone. "This is the same situation that happened in Nazi Germany. You wonder why we are here with hostility. You are wanting to burn our brains out because you don't like the way we live."

After several minutes, Dr. Marston managed to get the microphone back.

"The professionals in the room are, for the most part, very sympathetic towards the GLF, and are mainly concerned with tactics. I don't want to close the ears of the people in this room who can be helpful, who can go out in the general public and be of great service to the GLF. And this is the only reason that I ask that you agree to their conditions for this dialogue and simply wait probably no more than a half hour or 45 minutes to hear the end of Dr. Feldman's film."

The argument went back and forth for several minutes more. GLFer Ralph Shafer said, "Ever since I was five years old, I've been reading books about homosexuality written by psychologists and psychiatrists, and I've been seeing films . . . and we're sick and tired of it . . . Now we want to be treated like human beings."

This got applause from the demonstrators and from many in the audience. But the audience as a whole was not won over and the uproar went on.

Kight took the mike to say he understood the police had been called, and asked in wondering tones, "You're proud of the fact that you have called police on people who want to talk? You believe in that? All of you who approve of the police being here, applaud."

A wave of applause came from the audience.

"You're nothing but a living martyr," yelled a young woman who later identified herself as Cheryl A. Bartlett, a therapist at Fairview State Hospital in Costa Mesa. Kight protested, but she kept on.

"You are a living martyr to what you think is right . . . Listen, buddy, when Dr. Feldman came in here, he said we're going to be dealing with a situation on a voluntary basis. We want to deal with people who come to us and say, 'I feel anxiety, I feel hostility, I feel tensions, because I am what I am, and I want to change.'

"You people are happy, go your way, God be with you."

Miss Bartlett's comments set off the loudest uproar of the session. Beckwith objected that if there were any homosexuals who felt anxiety, it was because of what society had done to them.

Dr. Feldman had left the hall hurriedly. DeRosa told GAY readers what followed: [54]

Dr. Marston: "There will be no arrests, there will be no arrests. We have reached a compromise. It is now 10 o'clock. Let us spend the next hour in small groups discussing this thing. At 11 o'clock we'll hear the rest of Dr. Feldman's presentation."

Applause. The audience reluctantly and nervously moves the neatly rowed chairs into loose circles.

"Can we still see the movie at 11?"

"Yeah, baby, yeah, baby."

The rap sessions go well. The behaviorists prove to be intelligent people and now seem truly interested in rapping with us. I wander from group to group and everyone seems deeply engaged in conversation. Some of the questions evoke automatic responses ("But you can't have *children,* and we can." "We don't *have* to have children, *you* will have our children for us. We're not a different species, we're all human beings. Creating children is part of your lifestyle, it is not part of ours. You will have gay children and you will have straight children, etc. etc. etc.") but most of the talk proves meaningful and constructive.

11 o'clock.

Morris Kight: "Ladies and gentlemen, thank you. That wasn't so bad, was it?" (Applause) "Now, 25,000 large meetings such as the one you have had here today happen in Los Angeles each year. Most of them come and go, and nobody but the families of those involved know that they came to Los Angeles. Now, you can't say that you came to Los Angeles and it wasn't noticed, because *we* noticed you—and the Associated Press and United Press noticed you, and this little episode that we had with you this morning is going out on the wires right now, and everybody in the country is being told that psychologists and homosexuals were *talking* together and we think that's news. I would like to thank, in the name of Gay Liberation Front, the kind people who had the good sense to send the police away. It would have been exceedingly inconvenient for us to have been in jail this weekend, but we were prepared to do so and had set up procedures to handle it should we have been arrested. We would, in turn, have charged you with disturbing our peace, as you have disturbed our peace lo these many years. Because we cannot and will not allow it to be disturbed anymore. This is the unique thing that the Gay Liberation Front does. We no longer apologize because we have nothing to apologize for. When we say 'We're Gay and We're Proud,' we *mean* it. We *are* proud! Now, we do not say that heterosexuality

300

is wrong or evil. If you think that it is, get Dr. Feldman to cure you! Thank you, thank you again for coming to our consciousness raising sessions today!"

Don Kilhefner: "I don't think anybody need be deluded that now we'll just go away, that we've had our fun for the morning, because it isn't that type of revolution that we're engaged in right now. This is just the beginning and we'd like to make you aware of the fact that anytime any conference is being held where our lives and our people are being discussed, we are going to be there. Now, I encourage you, if you are involved in planning these future discussions, that you make an attempt to invite us. I guarantee that if you don't make an attempt to invite us, we will invite ourselves. This is just the beginning. You are going to see a lot more of us; you are going to hear a lot more of us. *My* only concern this morning is that you're all back in your nice little rows passively listening to somebody when you were actually talking and actively learning a short while ago."

Dr. Feldman returns. The overthrow of the session that morning has obviously shaken him. Militant homosexuals are not something he had bargained for. He decides to forego showing the rest of the film and settles instead for a series of mundane slides, filled with statistics and diagrams. Words like "improved" and "not completed" indicate clearly that his treatment is not a success. Dr. Feldman stumbles over words, stares at the slides for minutes without speaking and often seems unable to continue.

During the question and answer period which follows, Gay Liberation Front proves so strong that Dr. Feldman is soon reduced to mumbling "I don't know, I don't know."

In a speech to the assembly shortly after it reconvened, moderator Dr. Albert Marston said: "We have a responsibility for education. If, in fact, we are aware, sensitive professionals who know that homosexuality is not a sickness, who know that the homosexual life style is a legitimate alternate lifestyle, we have a responsibility not simply to know it and sit with our hands crossed, but to educate our fellow professionals and to educate the general public. We have to begin looking carefully at how we allocate our priorities and we have to consider whether we can do greater social good doing research on some aspects of homosexuality which we can learn from the Gay Liberation Front."

RIGHT ON!

14

I have a recurring daydream. I imagine
a place where gay people can be free. A
place where there is no job discrimination,
police harassment or prejudice. A place
where love rules instead of hate. A beautiful
valley in the mountains . . . A place where
a gay government can build the base for a
flourishing gay counter-culture and city.
—Don Jackson, in "Brother Don
Has a Dream"

The *San Francisco Chronicle* noticed that he coined a phrase, "Blatant
is beautiful." [1] *The Advocate* worried that he felt, "As violence shall
oppress us, so shall it liberate us." [2] Charles Thorp, twenty years old, "an
attractive-ugly boy with long black hair and the build of a lithe hustler"
(as Dennis Altman has described him for SIR's *Vector* magazine [3]),
English major at San Francisco State College, active in the formation of
the Committee for Homosexual Freedom a year and a half before, chairman
of the San Francisco State Gay Liberation Front, keynoter and organizer
of the National Student Gay Liberation Conference held at SIR Center
August 21, 22, and 23, 1970. The *Chronicle* headlined, HOMOSEXUAL
CALL FOR MILITANCY; *The Advocate* insisted, NO SUPPORT FOR THORP
"VIOLENCE" SPEECH, KIGHT SAYS. His address—verbally—sounded an
alarm, an alarm that Thorp had perhaps not intended; Thorp had, said
Altman, who visited the conference, "an enormously verbal inarticulate-
ness. One of the seniors of SIR claimed he is 'mad' but he was, I think,
totally wrong. Charles is perfectly sane in the context of the new counter-
culture." Morris Kight heard in Thorp's speech "not so much calling for
violence as predicting its inevitability if 'oppression' of Gays does not end
in the near future."

Thorp's keynote speech was a masterpiece of inspiration/annotation
(he cited Sartre, Frantz Fanon, Bob Dylan, Mao Tse-tung). Throughout
he opposed *Homosexuality* to *Gay:* the former a lifeless sexual identity
given by an antipathetical straight society, the latter the self-designation for

a "Whole-entity" (Thorp) and life-style. Thorp saw the gay life-style as essentially demonstrative: "We are all Blatant, unless we're ashamed of being Gay . . ." He elaborated, that

The straight establishment has taken any notion of identity from us by trick-ortreating us into believing that we are a sexual entity, therefore, we'll suck cock and be quiet (you will see it is hard to speak with a cock in the mouth). Also, this helps in their minds to put them in the right no matter how they treat us. For in our Judeo-Christian Society the only way one may kill and treat his neighbor like dirt is to reduce his official standing to less-than-human or to that of animal. If the "other society" can believe that we are a sexual entity . . . then they may think of us as animals and treat us as they wish. I'm sure you've heard that phrase time and again: "you're just animals all you think about is sex." It is important to notice how many people think of us as "its." This is their way of linking us to the animal world for an animal can be eaten in a civilized world not humans. So our people are killed and their bodies and souls eaten till there is no existence for us. . . . One of the most effective tactics that straights use on us is our own belief that we are sexual entities; that way we can be easily kept in "our place." Our place being the three Big B's the Bars, the Beaches and the Baths. These are to keep us happy, controlled and patrolled. Also the straights perform their "pervert hunts" (equal to Salem easily) shame us and kill a few to keep the "flock" down. Then back at the homestead the "men" pump the women full of little perverts to be thrashed for another generation: except that this is where it all ends!

THIS PUNISHING OF OUR PEOPLE EITHER *ENDS* OR (AS IT WAS IN NEW YORK * AND SO IT SHALL BE . . .) *THE FIRE NEXT TIME!!* . . . . . to quote James Baldwin.[4]

The three-day conference that followed drew delegates not only from California campuses but from as far away as Texas, New York, Oregon, Virginia, and Nebraska. Altman told *Vector* that the discussions and workshops stirred little dissension: ". . . there was a strong tendency to affirm everybody's thing, a willingness to suspend criticism in a search for unity. The exception came when the delegates from San Diego talked of abolishing laws relating to *adult* sexual behavior which produced heartfelt cries from non-adults to fuck whom they please."[5]

■

Jonathan Black was not thinking of Thorp-type physical challenges to American straight society when, in his reportage of Christopher Street Liberation Day for the *Village Voice*,[6] he analyzed:

* The complete speech was printed in the *San Francisco Gay Free Press* (successor to *San Francisco Free Press*), Vol. 2, No. 11, as I.D., LEADERSHIP AND VIOLENCE.

The black experience is safely compartmentalized; we're not about to change color or culture. But there is nothing stopping the heterosexual going gay. Who *is* a latent homosexual? That is the threat posed by gay liberation. It is a challenge to all our macho chauvinism, a challenge to shed our protective skin and open up all the insides. The implications of gay liberation are not that everyone is gay, or that everyone should be gay ("you can't *knit* a homosexual," said one GLFer), or even that everyone must have a gay experience. The implications are that we must begin to cope with our own non-sexist loves and affections, and not let our sexual preferences distort and color our entire emotional life. To that extent, gay liberation is not a problem, but perhaps the most profoundly revolutionary movement that we are in touch with.

Homosexuals have always felt, deep in their hearts, that they were ahead of straight society in sexual thinking—if only because they might have tried to conform but didn't. "We stand outside of society," Larry Powell told *Concern* in February 1967, ". . . but it appears that we are not in back or to one side, but in front. The rest are moving toward us and can learn a great deal from us about what to expect." [7] Equipped with this extra-societal sexual knowledge, many homosexuals have, luckily, been thinkers. New York writer-editor Edmund White has decided: [8]

All homosexuals are philosophers. Which is a fact I've sometimes discovered to my dismay when I've dragged home An Innocent Farm Boy or A Menacing Motorcyclist and prepared myself to dive into a fantasy. Hopefully, the fantasy may last through the sex, but afterwards I invariably detect beneath the innocence or the menace a detached, analytic, self-conscious turn of mind. I had expected to participate, for one spectacular moment, in pure, unreflecting action. I thought I was getting James Dean or Marlon Brando, but ended up in the cold embrace of Bishop Berkeley or Immanuel Kant; for every homosexual, whether he be a truck-driver or a defense attorney, has at least one big theory, one theory he's forever building, modulating, extending, scrapping or revising: Why am I gay?

Gay liberationists like Charles Thorp may have stopped asking why, but, philosophers, they have gone on "extending," "modulating" . . . generally about sex and/or love. Gays have been forced to promiscuity, and in psychological defense some have aped the faithfulness syndrome of straight married life so fixedly that, one mild transgression by lover, and—, *pow!*—they're back on the promiscuity trail once again. A vicious circle? Perhaps. But Thorp rationalized it—and suggested a future-shocking lifestyle?—in "To My Community, Lovers," signed as customarily "charles p. thorp (bold soul sister)":

```
My lover, Brian, asked me the cum-y question, "How do you measure
    love ?"The answer to which i'm recording because it is community
    i am talking about- community dig.

Brian: "How do you measure love?"
Charles: "o, by... by time. Right, there are three dimensions by which
```

```
             i can measure nails,boards and houses, but how am i to
             measure home. i guess in a different dimension. The fourth
             dimension is time and it never occurred to me, but i measure
             my love by time. What i mean is i call my lovers; forever
             lovers, transient lovers, and lovers of the moment.All those
             terms are measurements in a sense , measurements in time.
             My love is the fourth dimension of Man/boy."
Brian:    "Explain the terms."
Charles:"Well a forever lover is what my first lover, Keith, and i are
             and something you are become...ing..."
Brian:    "But Keith and you were together only 2 years."
Charles:"right. together is 3 dimensions, 2years is a decadent fourth
             dimension. We were together(lxwxh) for 2years, but it is
             forever because we loved forever (measure of our love) when
             we were together. In other words forever is how deep the love
             is when in deed you were together. So when i vowed i'd love
             Keith forever i fullfiled it by loving him that deep. We broke
             apart for growth and it changed nothing essential.
             As for transient lovers they were lovers that lasted a few
             weeks, a few months and the love was determined greatly on
             that time basis. We shared and loved for awhile and passed
             on our ways like residents of the tenderloin . We were tender
             we  were animal we were             tenderlove
             together we were gone. We were the space between forever. Since
             there was no space there we loved in a zoneless way that gave
             us a parking ticket and it is in that contradiction that we
             we arrived and departed, the lovers, the transient, the lover.
             As for lovers of the moment,, , there are those and at that
             many that call them tricks. But that is not Gay that is their
             unhappiness showing through their kool-ade stand. Tricks
             sounds too much like Drags' Christmas (Hall0(ctober)ween(31).
             They are during those shared fondling moments my lovers...
             very definitely my lovers. i treated them with as much love
             and depth as i would my forever lovers, on their first night.
             i gave them all the love i could and we who traveled lonely
             concrete or lonely alcohol-caves separate are together -
             communion - love. Communi(cation)ty is what we are. We are
             all our people possible lovers so we are a community of lovers.
             Because in those moments i spend breathing Hard and biting
             flesh with these lovers i realize and over       that we
                                                     over and
             are community, we are lovers. So when i have said in the past
             we are an army of lovers, it is a time element too. It is from
             oppression and hate of my love(r)s that we are an army. And
             in time we will win and in time the battles will all be
             fought and won...time will have taken its toll on these lovers
and          we will no longer be an army of lovers just a community of
-            lovers.But now we must be an army to defend what we love.
¹ⱼ           Do not let them harm your lovers. Anyone in our community
'ⱼ           who is attacked(murdered) by the pigs must be defended(revenged)
-            as a dead lover. Weep revenge fight as if you lost forever.
be           cause you have. i love you time immeasurable. i love, i love
"            through you...as a child passes through forever'. My reaching
             is unending to my needs, to my love, to my community."
Brian:    "smiled" that he knows i know
```


In the October *Gay Sunshine*,[9] Nick Benton apotheosized homosexual
soixante-neuf but his implications were that the non-sexist/non-oppressive
position would equally benefit heterosexual partners:

. . Sex between persons of the same sex is the cultural antithesis to the most
fundamental presupposition of the whole Western capitalistic mentality, which
is derived from one fundamental act—"missionary position" (male atop female)
sexual intercourse.

The "missionary position," penis in vagina for the explicit purpose of the creation of offspring, is the first presupposition of everything Western culture represents. From it are derived the concepts of purposeful existence, patriarchy, capitalism, nationalism, imperialism, fascism. From it come the thought patterns of active/passive, dominant/submissive, I/you, we/they, top/bottom, greater/lesser, win/lose and on and on and on . . .

An absolute antithesis of this presupposition is an orgasmic sexual act between persons of the same sex. And on that level, a most perfect antithesis, it seems to me, is the act of 69-ing involving two persons of the same sex.

As a presupposition for social existence, this act is absolutely mutual, and absolutely pleasure, rather than purpose, oriented. It is an absolute act of mutuality and pleasure, then . . . or of mutual affection apart from any purposeful motive above and beyond the mutuality shared by the two partners.

Any orgasmic sexual act between partners of the same sex can be an expression of this mutuality, but the act of 69-ing seems the most symbolically perfect.

Evidence of its perfection is that the totality of its mutuality creates the condition for the expansion of the act to include more than two persons without subtracting from anyone's degree of complete involvement: expansion into a community of persons sharing in the same orgasmic act of mutual affection. It is at the point of such an expansion that barriers of age, physical appeal, and ultimately even gender, can be overcome for the participants, and the possibility of a total community of all persons of the human race participating in total mutual affection can be actually experienced.

As such this symbolic model may be the most revolutionary act in which a human being in Western culture can engage.

It is an extension of the equally revolutionary Jesus-concept of "love your enemy" to cover the physical-sexual-orgasmic totality of man. *"The enemy" in Western culture is, ultimately, every other person of the same sex that one could not use in copulation for the purpose of creating offspring to strengthen one's own position in the world.* [Italics mine.]

The homosexual revolution is the Jesus revolution, and it is total. . . .

In SOME THOUGHT AFTER A GAY WOMAN'S LIB MEETING for *Come Out!*,[10] Sue Katz, like Benton, saw the "missionary position" as "an institution. In an oppressive society like Amerika, it reflects the same ideology as other major institutions. It is goal-orientated, profit- & productivity-orientated. It is a prescribed system, with a series of correct & building activities aimed toward the production of a single goal: climax. It's also a drag. . . ." Her substitution for it, equally revolutionary, was SENSUALITY:

. . . Physical contact and feelings have taken a new liberatory form. And we call that SENSUALITY. The women's movement in general, especially at the beginning, and gay feminism now is a fantastically sensual experience for me. I love my body and the bodies of my sisters. Physicality is now a creative non-institutionalized experience. It is touching and rubbing and cuddling and fondness. It is holding and rocking and kissing and licking. Its only goal is closeness and pleasure. It does not exist for the Big Orgasm. It exists for feeling nice. Our sensuality may or may not include climax. If it does include genital experience, that may or may not be the beginning or the ending of the experience. It may be anywhere or nowhere. To make good love with women, I don't want to have to "produce" anything. Except pleasure. . . . The sensuality I feel has transformed my politics, has solved the contradiction between my mind and my body because the energies for our feminist revolution are the same as the energies of our love for women. When we feel good about someone we may sleep together. . . . If we feel good in a group we may have a pajama party, which would be called an "orgy" inside the institution of adult sex. . . .

Sensuality is something that can be very collective. Sex is private and tense. Sensuality is something you want your best friends to feel and act on with your other best friends. Sex is something you want power and territorial rights over. Sex is localized in the pants and limited by that. Sensuality is all over and grows always. Sex is pinpointed in the pants because the penis is there and the penis is, if not the material source, the material basis for power in Amerika. If you don't have capital you get fucked over by those who do. Unless you attach yourself to someone who has it so that you can serve them in exchange for protection (known as marriage). Sperm is coin. And that whole system of exchange necessarily excludes us as lesbians. . . .

More than suggesting for homosexuals and/or heterosexuals new forms of sex/sensuality, Craig Schoonmaker of *Homosexuals Intransigent!* has predicted a Homosexual Era (the solution to overpopulation problems?) in a reconstruction of Genesis: [11]

IN THE BEGINNING THERE WAS ONE, AND THE ONE WAS GOD: God was One and the One was the Universe. God was alone, and grew lonely. So He parted the Universe from Himself, and there were Two.

God delighted in the Universe, for it was He, yet it was not He. God gave substance and detail to the Universe, setting forth all that was in Him. And as God created, He created in twos: earth and heavens, night and day, good and evil, life and death, the living and the nonliving, beast and Man, Man and Woman. And all life he commanded to arise from One. The humblest He decreed will remain One thru their time, ending their solitary existence to repeat the miracle of One parting self from self to become Two. But each of these Two, innocent of God's plan, wanders from the other, and each is alone. But to ever more exalted creatures God gave ever more awareness of His plan.

Man, God's favored child, He made a microcosm of Himself, imparting to Man multifarious splendor, and rendering him able to sense God's plan. God created a creator, gave him dominion over the earth, and Intelligence that he might rule wisely.

In Man flowed on the pattern of Two: two eyes, two ears, two nostrils; two arms and hands, two legs and feet; two lips, two breasts, two buttocks, two testes—each of the pair like unto the other. But God gave Man one head, one mouth, one penis, one anus. And Man was incomplete as one, as was God's plan. For God intended that Man should not live alone but should seek out another.

And God divided the history of the world into two parts, the heterosexual and the homosexual, and He numbered their days.

He commanded the heterosexuals to go forth across the earth to establish Man's dominion over the world and build his numbers that he might thereafter create a Civilization worthy of that dominion God willed. Thru all this time of spreading and multiplying, the Heterosexual Era, God willed that homosexuals should dwell in the background, guardians of a future as yet unsensed; puzzle to the contemplative whom God was preparing for the New Era.

When Man achieves dominion over the earth, then shall God's will emerge and the puzzle be made clear.

For God commanded the homosexuals to halt the increase in Man's numbers; to restore Man to balance with all God's other creatures and with himself; to prevent Man from becoming a mortal plague upon the world; and to build from a hardwon culture, a Civilization reflecting God's wisdom and His will.

Man Multifarious shall merge into Man Multifarious, as each seeks out another like unto himself. And instead of numbers, Unity and Peace shall spread across the earth. Thus shall Man emulate God the Universe. Thus shall Man glorify the miracle and mystery of Two sprung from One, of Two being One yet One being no longer alone.

The Homosexual Era will arrive when Man is about to destroy himself and the world God gave him mandate over, and will pass only as the world passes.

In the end, God will gather all His creatures to Himself, and He and the Universe will again merge, one into the other. All that is, will be One: The One will be God. God will be the Universe. And the Universe will be Peace.

In GAY's SETTING STYLES FOR STRAIGHTS, June 1, 1970, Dick Leitsch posited that

The ones who make the laws, who keep up the efforts to stamp out homosexuality, are those with obvious homosexual problems (and some with other sexual hangups, such as impotence, sado-masochistic tendencies and frigidity). They hate the thought that somewhere, somehow, somebody might be enjoying sex.

A common cry of the homosexual oppressor is "If we accept homosexuality as a viable alternative, everyone will become a homosexual!" This translates like this: "If you take away the laws and social sanctions against homosexuality, my defenses against my homosexuality will no longer be valid."

If one has them. In which case, homosexuals see no reason why one should not cast them aside and live gay—or "bi." Though few homosexuals can honestly conceive of a Homosexual Era—albeit its inauguration could not frighten *them*—many gays and straights forecast bisexuality: "Exclusive homosexuality," wrote Black for the *Voice*, "after all, is just as repressive and dehumanizing as exclusive heterosexuality."

Suzannah Lessard, in her *Washington Monthly* December essay, "Gay Is Good for Us All," [12] viewed the sexual utopias that women's lib and gay lib—and even other movements—anticipate when "the king" is no longer restricted by his "king-male role":

The vision of these sexual freedoms is not a very full one, a kind of comprehensive liberation in which all oppressed groups unbind each other for a hazy new purpose. Reasonable as the idea is, it seems to exist in a thin, improbable future.

It also seems to include the seeds of disasters, such as large numbers of people, having no role assigned to them, going out of their minds for lack of identity—like a lot of bureaucrats without their bureaucracy. But as things change, the vision firms up and even becomes a little part of reality—like the Panthers' trying to accept the Gay Liberation people. A large part of it all lies in just getting used to separate ideas, such as that homosexuals are just as good as heterosexuals. . . .

■

It took two successive issues of *The Advocate*, September 30 and October 14, to do justice to Rob Cole's exemplary coverage of COLLISION IN SAN FRANCISCO: the story of NACHO's "liberation," August 26-8, 1970. Columnist Jim Kepner editorialized further in NACHO IN FUTURE-SHOCK.[13] MSNY delegate Dick Leitsch, who wrote the convention summary for *Mattachine Times*, could not understand why the convention's organizers had not anticipated the invasion by gay liberationists—"similar troubles have plagued nearly every convention and conference in the last year." [14] What was more, Charles Thorp's National Student Gay Liberation Conference had ended, in the same SIR Center that was to house NACHO, just three days before.

To explain, in part, the gay radicals' determination to change NACHO, Leitsch posited that

Over the intervening years, NACHO had become a bureaucracy, and was on its way to becoming a super-organization. A Credentials system had grown up within NACHO, which had the power to decide who was eligible to attend Conference meetings and who was not. Many organizations objected to NACHO setting itself up as a judge of orthodoxy in the movement, and more disliked NACHO's growing tendency to speak for the movement and, in effect, commit member organizations to policies or actions which would possibly be disapproved by the membership or Boards of the member organizations. . . .

Gay liberationists were adamant that NACHO allow free entry to any interested homosexual and institute one-man (woman)/one-vote procedures rather than maintain voting by organizational delegates.

Kepner told how the conference-that-was-not-a-conference began/didn't begin: "The chairman stalled on convening the meeting to give the insurgents their say. The first day being also Women's Strike Day . . . seven angry homosexual women . . . came in demanding that our male-dominated movement pay more attention to women's unique problems. The assembled group voted heavily to back Women's Lib. But this was nearly scuttled by the appending of a demand that we also support the Black Panthers and 'the revolution,' which the assembly had not had a chance to discuss. . . ." Rev. Jim Rankin, in Berkeley's *Gay Sunshine*,[15] described the non-convention as "three terrible, joyous days of open, honest battle." The women's liberationists, he underscored, "broke the underlying battle into the open. The radical-conservative conflict became bitter indeed, and when the meeting formally convened and refused entry to the radicals, they just moved in and took over." Kepner detailed how it happened:

Friday morning, most GLFers slept late. The conservatives . . . hastily chose a new nine-man committee to run NACHO until the 1971 Conference in NYC. . . . The insurgents didn't hear of the committee's existence until next day.

When the GLF arrived in force, the meeting was discussing this writer's motion to open conference membership to all interested parties. An ironic ultra-left/ultra-right coalition wanting to exclude all heterosexuals from the conference was defeated. After endless amendments and substitutions, open membership, for next year, was approved, and a new vote was started to do it now.

Then, under black and red flags, the GLF marched in shouting, and drove out most delegates [there had been a report that one radical had brandished a gun]. They then discussed reconstituting the Conference. (During all this one Gay Lib woman was running around town trying to round up Panthers, newsmen, Gays, or women to bust down the doors which were already open.) Some delegates threatened to call the police—the unpardonable sin! SIR spokesmen insisted that the hall was rented to NACHO only and that non-delegates must behave or leave—but were welcome to meet in another room.

After one screaming hour, the insurgents withdrew, and the few remaining credentialed delegates reconvened. The chairman tried to adjourn until next year, but the delegates instead voted to open the conference on a one-person, one-vote basis—an action which ought to have come much sooner.

Some delegates then left. They'd paid heavily in fees and travel expenses to come to NACHO, and objected to sharing with freeloaders. Then, one quarter of the original delegates and several insurgents quickly shouted through several wordy partisan resolutions, supporting the Panthers, demanding an investigation of homosexuals killed at Dachau, and so forth . . .

NACHO seemed dead. At least, reported Leitsch, "It was agreed that the NACHO structure and all of the bureaucracy had to go. Everyone agreed that the Conferences had to be returned to their original state, and that the only organization NACHO should have would be a committee to plan the next year's meeting and make the necessary arrangements. The Credentials Committee had to be abolished, and the Conference opened to anyone who wanted to attend. The Planning Committee would consist of nine people, preferably three from each of the 'regions' of the country, and a Business Manager." Leitsch hoped that as a part of the 1971 conference ample time would be set aside for gay and women's lib seminars and workshops to give everyone a chance to "do his thing."

Rankin pronounced, perhaps precipitately, of the 1970 NACHO conclave:

This was the battle that ended the homophile movement. It began twenty or more years ago, it produced men and women of great stature, it had its martyrs, it made possible to a large degree everything that a new movement is going to do. It was a noble thing. We respect it. We love those who were a part of it. They were brave and strong when it was difficult. We fear having to match their stature in our own situations. But it is now time to move on, and the ground rules and basic assumptions of that movement are no longer acceptable or effective.

The central conflict was on how to deal with reality. Or perhaps there was some question as to what was reality. The struggle was not over strategy or a question of there being many roads to the truth. It was that there was a deep division as to what the goals ought to be. At every major point of the conflict it could be clearly seen that the two broad groups differed on the most basic level, and tactics had nothing to do with it. Indeed, it was often possible to have both groups espouse the same tactics from their own perspectives.

The older group felt it had to justify itself to the world, become part of it, let straights into leadership roles, keep the movement a "one-issue" trip, be wary of dealing with youth, and in general, conform to the reality the heterosexual oppressor imposed. The others replied that the whole thing must be turned upside down, for the values had been inverted: "Don't adjust your mind: reality has a flaw in it." Right on!

As if to justify the radicals' "victory," on Friday night as the conference concluded, State Assemblyman Willie Brown (D, San Francisco) told 450 conventioneers assembled for dinner at California Hall that the gay community "must begin to identify with all of the minority groups existing in this society, must begin to understand that we have a common enemy." *The Advocate* [16] related how,

In a heavily applauded speech, he also said that both Gays and Blacks "must learn to do our bickering inside our own house, must resolve our disagreements behind our own doors. It is wholesome for us to debate the issues, to argue about the measures that we must take to try to save this society. . . .

311

Those arguments should not at any time give comfort to those persons who are our enemies. . . ."

Brown, author of California Assembly Bill 701, which would abolish penalties for homosexual acts performed in private by consenting adults, conceded that many in the gay community consider it an "Uncle Tom" bill.

"That bill will not become an *un*-Tom bill, as a matter of fact that bill will not be enacted, until somehow, every single, solitary community in the state of California becomes as organized from the gay standpoint as is San Francisco.

"Let me assure you, when the passage of that bill occurs will be the time when I will probably move on to the next step, which will be the removal of all laws that attempt to legislate morality."

(Brown's bill had been bottled up in committee during the last legislative session, died automatically at the legislature's adjournment. He had promised to reintroduce it in the next session.)

Brown did not call for violent revolution. He believed, however, that the only way for minorities to achieve their goals was by getting together. Suzannah Lessard later reiterated this faith, to *Washington Monthly* readers,[17] adding that "When people realize they're all up Queer Street together, the bonds of kinship can grow denser and stronger than any of the divisive factors of class, or caste, or suit, or kind." Brown warned: "If the Panthers, if the Women's Liberation, the Gay Liberation, the NAACP, the Jewish community, the church community, the un-church community, the old, the student dissenters . . . if they can't come together in the same room to plan, and be tolerant of each other in their common quest to change the minds of people in the society, there will not be a society."

■

It was bound to come. Gay separatism and/or nationalism was/were quite logically byproduct(s) of the more limited derring-do of gay liberation.

In an essay, "I AM HOMOSEXUAL," * Craig Schoonmaker of *HI!* voiced the complaint of the gay separatist/nationalist:

But there has seemed no alternative to accepting our second-class status. We are just a minority—an amorphous, unconsolidated minority at that, hiding from itself as much as from the intolerant majority. And in our society, it's not good enough to be a minority, because the majority rules.

Well, there *is* an alternative: we must become the majority. I don't mean that we should wage an aggressive campaign to convert people to homosexuality . . . but rather, that we should designate certain geographical areas for demographic takeover by homosexuals. We should leave the farms and

* Written at the request of Dr. Ian Maw, assistant professor at Rutgers University, to be part of a guidance counselor's handbook.

villages, the small towns and small cities, and come to specific neighborhoods of specific big cities. We should take over entire election districts and cities, and vote our people in to speak militantly for our rights. The blacks have done it. Puerto Ricans, Italians, Irish, and others too. It works.

According to Alfred Kinsey's studies, one of every six men and one of every eight women in the U.S. is predominantly or exclusively homosexual. The U.S. having a population of some 210 million, that means that some 30 million citizens are predominantly or exclusively homosexual. For those 30 million gay citizens, there are zero Congressmen, zero Senators, zero state legislators, and zero local government officials to speak out regularly for their interests. Odd, don't you think? Oh, there are homosexuals in government, but they don't dare acknowledge it and agitate for homosexual rights. One can almost—almost—excuse them: according to a Harris poll, 63 percent of the people of the U.S. regard homosexuals as "harmful to American life." You can see how tenuous the position is of any gay politician whose constituency is predominantly heterosexual. So we must have gay constituencies. And we must create model neighborhoods, a model society, to show heterosexuals how fine and decent homosexuality can be.

We should create men's neighborhoods and women's neighborhoods, despite the outcry that to do so is perverse. Of course it's perverse to heterosexuals, because heterosexuality requires ready access to the opposite sex. But the opposite sex is at best irrelevant and at worst a grievous annoyance to homosexuals. In a homosexual world, there is absolutely no reason why women *have* to be part of a man's life. One need *not* have friends of the opposite sex or of the opposite sexual orientation to be a healthy, valuable person. One does *not* have to go to bed with a woman to be a man. Exclusive homosexuality is *not* sick. Nor is it sick to want to live in a gay neighborhood, work with gay people, socialize with gay people—even with gay people of the same sex. Heterosexuals do not think it a sickness to live, work, and socialize with only (presumed) heterosexuals—they think the whole world IS heterosexual, and they're very happy that's the case. So homosexuals have no reason to doubt their sanity just because they may think it would be perfectly lovely to live in a world without straights or women. (Women, please make adjustments to your own terms throughout.)

It is absurd to argue that a world without women would be an intolerable bore. *Not* all men are alike. The world would *not* be somber and dull without "a woman's touch." The brilliance of art created by men is bright enough to light up an all-male subworld. The sparkle of bright men's fashions and crackling conversations is fully up to the alternative posed in a mixed world. Men have no reason to be ashamed of themselves, to feel inadequate without women.

Is this not the real argument behind the anti-separatist diatribe?: Man is inadequate, man without woman is less than man; man was made for woman and woman for man. Who says so? Heterosexuals, that's who. Why should we believe it? Because we are told to. By whom? By heterosexuals, of course.

How deep-seated heterosexual conditioning is! We can never escape it unless we remove ourselves from it. . . .

For New York City, Schoonmaker's plan was to "Create a homosexual majority in Manhattan's 19th and 20th Congressional Districts—which we have designated the 'First Gay-Power District.' This area will be organized homosexually, men creating an all-male environment on the West Side between 60th and 96th Streets, the 'First Homosexual Men's Neighborhood'; women creating a women's neighborhood (to be set later). The remainder of the District may be divided into other men's and women's neighborhoods later, or perhaps be sexually mixed. A homosexual majority will enable us to elect outspoken representatives to public offices at all levels of government, and to create social institutions valid for homosexuals." [18] Schoonmaker's homosexual-separatist goals were not purely political: "The point of establishing a homosexual majority is to make possible not merely defense of gay people's rights but also the repair of minds damaged by heterosexuals' pressures, and the creation of a new, healthy, *homosexual* mentality." [19]

A broader, non-city dream of gay takeover to establish a gay counter-culture, a refuge for persecuted homosexuals, and a gay tourist mecca was Don Jackson's. Presented first at the Berkeley gay lib conference, December 28, 1969, later printed as BROTHER DON HAS A DREAM by a number of underground newspapers,* Jackson's plan confessed:

I have a recurring daydream. I imagine a place where gay people can be free. A place where there is no job discrimination, police harassment or prejudice. A place where love rules instead of hate. A beautiful valley in the mountains, remote enough from cities so we will not be hassled, yet close enough so transportation is rapid. A place where a gay government can build the base for a flourishing gay counter-culture and city.

If only two hundred pioneering gays can be found, my dream can come true.

The Constitution of the State of California sets up 58 counties. Vast powers are granted the county governments by the constitution.

There is a county in California where 200 gays would constitute a majority of registered voters. If they were to register to vote 90 days before the election, a great prize would be theirs; the primary powers of government, two hundred millions per annum in tax revenues, freedom at last.

It would mean gay territory. It would mean a gay government, a gay civil service, a county welfare department which made public assistance payments to the refugees from persecution and prejudice. It could mean the establishment of the world's first gay university, partially paid for by the state, under the California Community College Act. It could mean the establishment of the world's first museum of gay arts, sciences and history, paid for with public funds. Housing could be erected under public housing laws with funds furnished mostly by the state and federal governments. A free county health service and hospital could provide for our sick.

* The perhaps most recent printing was by the *Los Angeles Free Press*, in its gay lib supplement, August 14, 1970.

Under California law, the County Sheriff is responsible for enforcing the laws passed by the Supervisors, and, in effect, such of the state laws as he chooses to enforce. A Gay Superior Court Judge would have great discretionary powers. A Gay District Attorney could choose which laws and which criminals he wishes to prosecute.

A gay publication, expressing gay opinion and community news, could be published and distributed nationally at public expense, under the power granted the Supervisors by the constitution to "publish and distribute publications to advertise the resources of the county, to attract residents, tourists or industry."

This county has revenues of hundreds of millions of dollars. Most of these funds come from state and federal subventions. Not even Congress has the power to cut these off, unless they cut off subventions to every other county in the nation. The amounts the county receives could be greatly increased by taking advantage of the cost sharing programs of the federal and state governments. An influx of poor students enrolling at the gay university or a large number of welfare cases would enable the county to be classified as an impoverished county under federal regulations, thus making millions of dollars in additional federal and state funds available.

The county Board of Supervisors has unlimited powers of taxation. It can levy a property tax in any amount it wishes. Almost all land in this county consists of large land holdings of wealthy absentee owners, except for the third of the county which lies within a national park. Theoretically, the federal government is exempt from the property tax. In practice, it pays taxes like everyone else, calling the tax payment "Subvention in lieu of property taxes." Since the tax rate in this county is one of the lowest in the nation, it is expected that it could be tripled or more without any protest from Washington.

For certain projects, the county can borrow on the credit of the state, and could levy many new types of taxes aimed at nonresidents for increased revenues.

The current population of the county is mostly elderly people who are employed by the county, since county government is the only industry. Most of them would probably move away when the new gay administration took over.

There are four farms in the county. These farmers have been able to appropriate millions of dollars for projects such as building paved roads leading 50 miles to a single farm. After all, the subventions amount to around a million dollars per person per year. A gay government could certainly find more useful ways to spend the bankroll.

The gay colony would have to have certain professional people because of a stipulation saying so in the state constitution—two attorneys to serve as District Attorney and Superior Court Judge, a registered civil engineer to serve as Road Commissioner, four credentialed teachers to serve as the school board, and a doctor to serve as health officer.

The new gay city could bring a large income from the tourist trade. It could become a mecca for gay tourists from around the world, not to mention the straight curiosity seekers who would be interested in visiting such a unique community. Communications media could be relied upon to give the gay colony world wide publicity on account of its uniqueness and the controversy it is sure to cause.

The colony could become the gay symbol of liberty, a world center for the gay counter-culture, and a shining symbol of hope to all gay people in the world. . . .

Alpine County and its capital, Markleeville, a two-store village (population 165), were Jackson's Promised Land. The 723-square-mile east-central California county, ten miles south of Lake Tahoe and whose snows average 453.6 inches per year, lies along the Nevada border, split north-south by the High Sierras. The *Wall Street Journal,* which, along with TIME Magazine, the *San Francisco Examiner,* the *Los Angeles Times,* and other worried media, reported the project's progress in October, told that "Whatever the outcome, people here admit that even the talk of the invasion is the biggest news to hit here since word came in 1863 that Markleeville was in California, not Nevada. Until a state survey was made in that year, the residents had thought they were in Nevada." The *Journal* noted also that "Those bygone days were the golden days for Alpine County. An 1867 business directory listed seven attorneys, two doctors and two blacksmiths in Markleeville alone. Now the county not only has no lawyer or doctor but also lacks a barber and a high school." [20]

Jackson's gay nationalist dream, which came to be called "Stonewall Nation," was slow to catch on, especially in the Bay Area, where he introduced it. Its greatest support was to come from Southern Californians —as was main support for the continuing gay lib movement in California throughout 1970. (Jim Kepner writes that "San Francisco was too comfortable for all but street-gays to sustain a militant program." [21]) In early autumn, a member of the Los Angeles Metropolitan Community Church who had just bought a five-acre lot and cabin in Alpine, distributed an "Alpine Report" he had carefully made. It described the county's topography, roads, and economy for prospective gay migrants, detailed that the county was conservative, with an average citizen's age of forty-three. "There are 49 county employees, 23 state employees, and the rest of the population save perhaps two dozen who run stores or gas stations make their living from motels and related tourist activities, which hit their peak mainly in the hunting and fishing, but for Bear Valley [a resort area forty miles west of Markleeville, population 150] in skiing and summer, season." The Report provided information on Climate, Services, Land for Sale, even Indians: "Many are apathetic and could care less whether gays come or go. Some say they don't favor it, but most said they feel they have been raked over by the present Co. Govt. and welcome any change gay or straight."

"Alpine Report" quoted from interviews with Sheriff Stuart Merrill "who said he would do his duty and protect our lives and property to the same extent he would that of co. residents when we came, but that he wouldn't like doing it"—and other county officials and residents. The

Report warned that "We will be issued building permits but our buildings will be constantly checked to make sure they adhere to the Code. Also we can expect Health Dept. harassment after we move in to see that we stay within that code." Friends and Open Enemies were listed, as well as Possible Weapons That Could Be Used Against Us. One resident said, "Well, you know, my boys are pretty good with their deer rifles." Another, "I hope they come. Hell, 500 more people up here and my business would triple. Of course, I would sell to them. I'm open to the public, aren't I?"

Los Angeles Gay Liberation Front, which had assumed primary responsibility for Stonewall Nation, advised *The Advocate* in November that it had nearly five hundred gays signed up to go. Don Kilhefner, L.A. organizer for the project, specified, "We project the first group of 250 to 300 people going up to Alpine County as of Jan. 1, 1971, to establish residency.* By mid-April, we should be able to initiate the recall procedure, where we will recall all the elected officials in Alpine County, and immediately have a new election in which homosexuals will be elected to all the elective offices in the county." [22] Out of an approximate county population of 450, Alpine had 367 voters.[23]

The Advocate explained that

. . . the requirements for a recall election are complex, but generally a petition signed by a total number of eligible voters equal to at least 20 percent of the entire vote cast at the last preceding election for all candidates for a given office would be sufficient. For some local offices, only 12 percent would be necessary.

Herbert Bruns, a rancher who is chairman of the Alpine County Board of Supervisors, is not laughing about the proposed gay takeover.

"We are all very concerned," he said Oct. 18 in Markleeville . . . "Naturally, we'll do everything we can to prevent anyone taking over our county. The trouble is, with that new State Supreme Court decision and the new election laws, it makes it easier for people to register." . . .

Bruns, three other supervisors, and Dist. Atty. Hillary Cook met [in Sacramento] with Richard Turner, assistant legal affairs secretary to Gov. Ronald Reagan, on Oct. 21.

Turner said there probably was nothing the state could do to keep the Gays out.

"They will receive a hostile reception when they come," said Bruns. "Apples and peaches don't grow very well" in Alpine's cold climate, he said. "No fruit is very welcome up in our particular county."

A newcomer to Markleeville pinpointed the real threat that residents felt: "Most of the folks here work for the county or are on welfare. If the county government is taken over, they're out of jobs." [24] Don Collins

---

* Jim Kepner writes, however, that "the January 1 deadline for moving in was a date pulled out of the hat. We will encourage people to arrive in late spring. No one should arrive in January unless prepared for *severe* climate and probably no accommodations." (Memo to the author, November 24, 1970.)

reported to GAY that the bar of the Alpine Hotel sported a hand-lettered sign, HOMO HUNTING LICENSES SOLD HERE [25]; TIME related how a highway marker read WATCH FOR DEER—HIT A QUEER, that the main street of Markleeville was marked GAY WAY and the tavern called "Fairyland Bar." [26] A sign at the county line was soon to read: QUEER COUNTY. The *San Francisco Chronicle* announced October 27 [27] that the Rev. Carl McIntire, a right-wing fundamentalist, planned to flood Alpine with "missionaries." "Homosexuality must be met head on by the Gospel," said McIntire in his Collingswood, New Jersey, headquarters. *The Advocate* quoted the Collingswood release adding that the preacher felt "the attempt to dignify and legalize [homosexuality] will further corrupt society. A new order, established after they have repudiated our system of morality, could very well become the first U.S. atheist and Communist county"! [28] Collins noted, in *The Advocate,* that "The *Los Angeles Times* recently ran a cartoon implying that Gays moving in would make the county unfit as a place to raise children. The cartoon drew an angry protest from Rev. Troy Perry . . ." [29]

The gay writer-compiler of "Alpine Report" sensed Alpine residents' fears of a "forced rapid takeover military-style," "mass rape of their young," a "large influx of hippie-type degenerates who would sponge off the Co. Welfare and do nothing for the Co.," "drugs and crime in their Co." . . . He suggested that GLF should "Send some articulate straight-looking people (as they are over paranoid about long hairs and hippies and fems) to talk to the people face to face and assure them that we don't want to harm them or their children . . ." GLFer Don Kilhefner's three-point program to counter resistance would take the Report's advice. His plan, reported in full in Markleeville's *Alpine Beacon,*[30] set forth:

"The first thing will be just discussion, dialogue. Simply getting homosexual people to sit down with some of the residents up there and explain what we're doing, why we're there, who we are, and explain to them that we are no threat to them.

"If this doesn't work, the next action will be using all the legal alternatives we have, exhausting all the legal avenues, taking it to court if any roadblocks are put in our way. We already have lawyers looking into this.

"Beyond this, if there is any other harassment of us—by vigilante groups, say, or whatever—we intend to use self-defense. If necessary, we will defend ourselves."

Alpiners, too, drew up plans. On November 12, a day-long hearing in the Alpine County Courthouse established three committees. A first committee would prepare emergency legislation to "kill" the county, merge it with El Dorado County to the north—"Alperado" County? suggested the *San Francisco Examiner* [31]—to produce a population of about 42,000. Sheriff Stuart Merrill headed a second committee to maintain "law and order." A third committee would see to the gays' welfare—if they came.

Dr. Ruth Jolly, U.S. Public Health Service representative and county health officer, would head it. But, *The Advocate* reminded, "Dr. Jolly took a dim view of her prospective 'customers.' "

Alpiners still counted heavily on weather to deter the gay *Putsch;* temperatures in mid-winter Alpine often reach twenty degrees below zero. Property big enough to hold a group of five hundred would be, furthermore, next to impossible to find, with the possible exception, noted Supervisor Bruns, of a tract "over on the East Carson River. If they got in there and we had a good storm, they would never get out." [32] Alpiners spoke of one additional hope: the resort village of Bear Valley and its absentee owners. The lodge and cottage owners were familiar with homosexuals in San Francisco, Los Angeles, and other cities, but nevertheless dreaded a gay takeover. Wallace Jackson, president of the Bear Valley Residents Association, commented *The Advocate,* was sure "his group could muster hundreds of votes by registering people who maintain second homes in the area." "We're watching and waiting, and if necessary, we could register in Alpine . . ." GLFer Morris Kight remarked, out of Los Angeles, that Bear Valley property owners seemed to contemplate "being registered in two places at once. That's not quite cricket." The state registrar's office agreed.[33]

Gay support for the Alpine project was far from unanimous, even west of the Rockies, and in the East the gay nationalists' plan was largely pooh-poohed. Old-line homophile groups and gay militant leftists concurred—for different reasons. Antony Grey had encapsulated old-timers' goals in L.A.'s *Concern,* two years before: "We must neither sct ourselves apart in, nor relegate others to, a sexual ghetto. For it is only by ultimate integration, and not by sexual apartheid, that we shall all of us realize our humanity to the full. Integration, after all, is the goal of the anti-racist believer in equal Civil Rights, and it should be the goal of the sensible sexual reformers also." [34] The Red Butterfly cell of New York GLF arranged a forum, "Which Way to Freedom? Gay Liberation or Gay Nationalism," then revealed its views in a flyer for the Weinstein Affair: "Gay nationalism will not be the answer to the ending of oppression of gay people. It only satisfies the part of our oppression that deals with working in the present system. Gay nationalism's goals are to be oppressed like every other minority in Amerikkka today. We must see our fight in relationship with the fight of other people waging a battle against the common enemy." *Gay Flames* [35] seconded The Red Butterfly, but more gently: "We cannot be free in one county alone. We must be free anytime, anyplace. We must be free as children, as teenagers, as adults, as old people. I'll go to Alpine County to see the vision and live the fantasy. Perhaps, I'll see and touch you there. And maybe we'll return together to the Fathercountry, Straightamerika. To make it over in the image of freedom for all the people. To make it free for us."

Berkeley Gay Liberation Front criticized the project, and withdrew from it, by a two-thirds vote of the membership attending a November

2 meeting. Objections to the Alpine takeover were that it was "sexist" (though L.A. GLFer Don Kilhefner had insisted, "It will not be a strictly male society. Many of our sisters will join us" [36]) and "counter-revolutionary"—that is, a separatist copout. Berkeley's fellow-organization, San Francisco GLF, reaffirmed its support for the project at a November 8 meeting. San Francisco State [College] GLF leader Charles Thorp, who voted for the project,* explained the Berkeley radicals' objections: "Morris Kight, who is an older generation person, came in and said that it was going to be actually working within the system and using the system. And a lot of people think that's counter-revolutionary and is undermining the Gay Liberation movement. I personally think that was a copout, and it's too bad, treating Alpine as a reform. It's not really a reform, it's a major step toward psychic preservation." [37]

Jim Kepner opined, in Los Angeles, "Enthusiasm here may play out. But I frankly expect the settlement to work. The take-over may be something else, but will at least get more publicity than anything Gays have done before. . . ." [38] *Advocate* editor Dick Michaels agreed: "The whole fantastic idea is a marvelous vehicle for publicity, which is perhaps all it's meant to be." He believed, however, that "If we were thinking of doing such a thing, we should prefer to carry it out over a period of years, with Gays moving in a few at a time, setting up businesses and ranches, building homes, and so on—in other words, building an economic base to insure the survival of the 'colonists' among hostile natives." [39]

The remote and underpopulated "pristine wonderland of majestic peaks, verdant pine forests, and crystalline lakes nestled high in the rugged Sierra Nevada" [40] awaited . . .

---

* To aid the Alpine project, Thorp helped organize BAG/FUN (Bay Area Gays for Unification and Nationalism) in September 1970; a sister-organization, the Gay Nationalist Society, was founded in Los Angeles. (*Berkeley Tribe,* October 16–23, 1970.)

15

Where do you send the congratulatory telegram, the Happy Birthday greeting in commemoration of a year of astounding and unprecedented progress toward equality under the law and universal dignity for homosexuals in America?

—John Francis Hunter, in GAY, June 29, 1970

A woman from the Quaker Project on Community Conflict is speaking to an anxious-happy assembly at Alternate U.: New York GLFers, Gay Activists, Philadelphia GLFers and HAL members, DOB women, some under-21's of GY, and others. The hundred-odd sit on untrustworthy folding-chairs, dilapidated sofas, or squat in an irregular circle on the floor. Some are too tense to sit for long, and maneuver a bit like caged lions. A few unfamiliars to AU are more out of than in the group. A *New York Times* editor I am hosting stands with me, listening and writing, by the south wall.

It is a gathering for hasty training of marshals for the Christopher Street Liberation Day parade, June 28, 1970. It is nearly 11:00 a.m. The parade begins at 2:00 . . .

"We must forget our differences. This is no time for politics. We are all here on one central issue. We are having this wonderful thing, this coming out. That's what we're together on. . . .

"Now, there are a few situations which can come up, and we are to be prepared for them, or try to be prepared. Now remember, you're one of the people, the moment you forget that, lose that identity, you've lost everything. When you've got that, you're in. You rap with the kids around you. You let them know where your head's at. Remember, that marshal's band is something you have to live down. The moment you become something you're a bit of a pig to them. . . . Think of yourself as one of the marchers, which you are, and think of all your fellow marchers as potential marshals. Assimilate the two: OK?" [1]

Abruptly a fight breaks out. Two men are shouting at one another. "Cocksucker!" They back away, size one another up. The larger of the two lunges, falls on the other gay.

Instructions have been to "surround," "smother," and several women and men move in. The two combatants rise, smiling—we have witnessed a test.

Later, marshals' instructions complete, most trainees in the room pin on an orange armband initialed CSLD. Some are still studying a Civil Liberties Defense March Pamphlet. All marshals have been equipped with emergency information for the marchers they will attend.

"You're one of the brothers. Remember that. Don't go on a police trip," repeats Barbara, one of the instructors.[2]

The marshals begin to split for lunch. I leave for coffee with my guest.

■

Gay Pride Week, and June 28's Christopher Street Liberation Day festivities in particular, had been planned ostensibly to commemorate the rioting at the Stonewall Inn one year before. More importantly, they were to commemorate the rift in the homosexual community that promoted the riots and that produced clashes a week later between old-line homophile leaders like Franklin Kameny and new militant-minded, hand-holding New York gays who had bussed to Philadelphia for the Annual Reminder, a peaceful picketing, then several seasons old, in front of Independence Hall on July 4. Who was being "reminded," the young gays had thought, the American Congress and people or the weary homosexuals who circled for two hours in a hot sun? It was the last such gay picketing at the national shrine.

Craig Rodwell, of Homophile Youth Movement, and Ellen Broidy, of NYU Student Homophile League, brought an idea to the ERCHO meeting in Philadelphia on November 1 and 2, 1969. The (first) resolution they introduced at the conference, and which passed, read:

RESOLVED: That the Annual Reminder, in order to be more relevant, reach a greater number of people and encompass the ideas and ideals of the larger struggle in which we are engaged—that of our fundamental human rights—be moved both in time and location. We propose that a demonstration be held annually on the last Saturday in June in New York City to commemorate the 1969 spontaneous demonstrations on Christopher Street and that this demonstration be called CHRISTOPHER STREET LIBERATION DAY.[3] . . .

The resolution also proposed that homophile organizations across the nation be urged to hold parallel demonstrations on the same day.

A second resolution established an umbrella committee to plan the demonstration. Each homophile/homosexual group in the East might send a delegate to the committee. Eventually to be called the Christopher Street Liberation Day Committee, it met once in January, finally every night as the week—how the Saturday demo had expanded!—approached. Rodwell and Michael Brown, a GLF founder, spoke convincingly with New York City police to obtain a permit for the march, as well as one for a gay-in in Central Park.*

For weeks, homosexuals were reminded of the big week and great day. GLF's *Come Out!* intoned that "These days mean something special for every lesbian and homosexual. They mark the first time that gays took to the streets angry, proud, joyous—tearing down the prisons in which this sexist society has chained us. They are days to march, to chant, to dance, to love, to rap, to study—with brothers and sisters coming together to openly affirm the beauty of our lives and throw wide open the closet doors which will no longer be nailed shut. . . ."

The Committee announcement, with its flags of female/female and male/male sex symbols intertwined, was stuffed into all comers' hands at Christopher Street and Greenwich Avenue. Gay Activists Alliance leafleted the Village—some members ventured uptown to stash them on YMCA "information tables" and at hospitable bars—with what were to be its "GAY PRIDE WEEK HAPPENINGS":

EROTIC Art Show at the Thompson Gallery at 20 Cornelia Street. From Mon. the 21st thru Sat. the 27th. 6 to 11 P.M.**

RIOT provided by Laurel and Hardy in "Twice Two" and Busby Berkeley's "Gold Diggers of 1933." . . .

GOVERNOR GOES DOWN when G.A.A. members sit-in at Republican State Headquarters. . .

GET A FEEL of G.A.A. and its politics. . . Political Workshop and dancing after our general meeting. . .

DANCE at 5 University Place on Friday the 26th. . . . Refreshments. Donation.

GAY-IN The most beautiful day in history. . . .

---

* At a meeting in September 1970, the Committee initiated plans for the 1971 celebration, anticipating 25,000 gays. The Committee had its Western counterpart in Los Angeles' Christopher Street West, which was encouraging twenty-five similar marches rather than a single, centralized one in L.A.
** With live male sculpture.

The week began with a poorly attended Laurel and Hardy, picked up speed with the GAA sit-in on Wednesday, then met with a minor setback on Thursday night. As Jonathan Black reported for the *Village Voice,* "not all oppression is at the hands of the Silent Majority. Friends in the radical movement itself have sometimes turned up less than friendly." [4] A midnight benefit had been scheduled at the Elgin Cinema in support of the CSLD Committee. In error, the Elgin booked another group for the same night: the Venceremos Brigade. According to Black, the Brigade knew the Committee had prior booking but arrived first. GLF members "showed up at the Elgin, switched off the projector, turned on the lights, and demanded that the Brigade hold its benefit some other night. The Brigade suggested the gays choose some other night, then suggested splitting receipts, both of which GLF rejected. After all, it was Gay Pride Week, not just any Thursday. And as things got tense, reports GLF, the Brigade called the gays faggots and threatened to rape them." [5]

Nearly a thousand homosexuals danced with GAA to open the weekend Friday night till wee hours Saturday in the subcellar at Weinstein Hall, 5 University Place. Meanwhile, at Washington Square Methodist Church nearby, GLF members provided free food, general information, first aid, and workshops on liberation topics to needy and interested gays. Pads for the weekend were made available to out-of-towners low on cash. A bright placard welcomed and dared: GAY LIBERATION FRONT. COME IN AND COME OUT.

At about 1:00 a.m. that night, five young gays suffered more than blows to their Gay Pride when they were assaulted at 14th Street and University Place. Several straights, lurking in a parked car, saw the homosexuals holding hands and called out, "Faggots! Commies! Hippie perverts!" then surrounded them, kicking and beating them to the ground. Bystanders hailed a cruising police car, but at the station house the gays were urged to drop the matter; should they press charges, they "were advised that in all probability the attackers would make a counter-claim against them. Several times the protesting five were advised to avoid trouble and to walk away: the hint was that they themselves might be punished"! [6]

GLF persisted in hospitality and in workshops and rap sessions the following day and after the Sunday Gay-In. At one point Saturday afternoon, a group of Tennessee high schoolers wandered downstairs from a church program to hear Bob Kohler on gay liberation. They "looked at the man from GLF, and somehow he didn't *look* queer. And they looked around, and there were all these men who really didn't seem to have *anything* in common, except they *must* be queer or else why would they be there? . . . so many different *kinds* of queers, even some older men in business suits . . . what did he say? . . . the *gay* people. They'd have to think about that." [7] Two Young Lords visited the church "to check it out," because (according to Kohler) "Man, you people are really gettin' it together!" [8]

324

Around Village lanes that afternoon marched members of the GLF Gay Guerrilla Theatre, sporting huge boards that asserted, I AM A HOMO-SEXUAL. Black, in the *Voice*, described a playlet action they staged here and there and which featured "a drag queen in front of a gay bar. The queen gave a $5 bill to the bar owner who gave it to the State Liquor Authority who gave it to the Mafia who gave it to a policeman who clobbered the queen with his nightstick."

The "GLF News" leaflet directed homosexual women to a Lesbian Center at the Church of the Holy Apostles, which promised "discussions, workshops, music all day: bring food and drink to share." Friday evening saw a workshop on "Women's Liberation, Sexism, and Lesbianism." The next evening brought a communal supper, afterward a dance. GLFers were a comradely bunch, but the Center's activities were "RESTRICTED TO WOMEN."

Sunday.

The sun a blowtorch in a sky bluer than any New York had boasted since the horseless carriage—no gay would remain in the shadows that day—Sheridan Square was gay-militant at 12:30. Placards to be hoisted or worn declared: GAY PRIDE—LESBIANS UNITE!—FEMME and BUTCH—HI, MOM!—HOMOSEXUAL IS NOT A FOUR-LETTER WORD—ME TOO (on a dachshund)—WE ARE THE DYKES YOUR MOTHER WARNED YOU ABOUT—EVERYTHING YOU THINK WE ARE, WE ARE!—SMASH SEXISM—SAPPHO WAS A RIGHT-ON WOMAN—FREE OSCAR WILDE—GAY POWER—I AM A LESBIAN AND I AM BEAUTIFUL . . . Bob Kohler, Tom Doerr, Jim Owles, Becky Irons, Michael Kotis—joyful-serious—were retailing the parade's significance to media men of radio and TV. Michael Brown's pronouncement highlighted front-page *New York Times* coverage of the event and was the *Times*'s Quotation of the Day, Monday, June 29: "We're probably the most harassed, persecuted minority group in history, but we'll never have the freedom and civil rights we deserve as human beings unless we stop hiding in closets and in the shelter of anonymity."

Police barricades to keep gay paraders in the street during preliminaries lined both sides of Washington Place west of Sixth Avenue. CSLD marshals, stationed there and on Waverly Place should the crowd overflow, began to corral city gay powerites and hundreds of others from Washington, D.C., Boston, Cleveland, New Haven, Philadelphia, New Brunswick, Baltimore, and other Eastern cities. The young and not-so-young of old-line organizations such as Daughters of Bilitis, Mattachine societies, and the Institute of Social Ethics (Hartford) would stride with "infant" gay militant clubs whose first birthday hadn't been celebrated. But it was every homosexual's birthday: how many hundreds of non-organization gays, women and men who might someday join, might never join, might even return to their closets at that day's end, now stood proud *or* trembling, *but stood,* under the slim Day-Glo rectangles of MSNY, among the blue T-shirted, gold lambda'ed Gay Activists and mauve T-shirted (shades of the) Lavender Menace, and between the ten- to fifteen-foot banners—unfurled and

uplifted in strong reds and blues and yellows and greens—of GAY LIBERA-
TION FRONT, GAY ACTIVISTS ALLIANCE, PHILADELPHIA [GLF] . . . and, at
parade head, CHRISTOPHER STREET GAY LIBERATION DAY 1970
beside an American flag.

"Gimme a G!"
"G!"
"Gimme an A!"
"A!"
"Gimme a Y!"
"Y!"
"Gimme a P!"
"P!"
"Gimme an O!"
"O!"
"Gimme a W!"
"W!"
"Gimme an E!"
"E!"
"Gimme an R!"
"R!"
"Whatawe want?"
"GAY POWER!"
"Whendawe want it?"
"NOW!"

Rey (Sylvia) Rivera's voice was imperious, his expression selfless, then
and as he cheer-led hoarsely along the sixty-block hike that was to end
over an hour later. It was 2:10. The parade had begun. New giant steps
to follow those giant steps of just a year before.

The Village sidewalks are jammed. I watch the beaming faces of the hip
people, the unbelieving looks of out-of-towners on a Sunday excursion.
Some of us raise the clenched fist of Gay Power, but fingers more frequently spread to a V sign, which is returned. *Mattachine Times* is to
report later [9] that a gay woman "saw a straight couple from her building.
He had a sign saying HAPPINESS TO HOMOSEXUALS and she had one reading LOVE TO LESBIANS. 'What are you doing here?' Alice asked. 'You're
straight.' 'We love a parade,' the wife said." Reports will also have it
that a boy yelled from the pavement, "There's my *mother! Marching!*" [10]
We occupy the far left-hand lane of Sixth Avenue's several. Twenty or
more gays, on the sidewalk, accompany us handing out a welcome note
prepared by the Christopher Street Liberation Day Committee:

Welcome to the first anniversary celebration of the Gay
Liberation movement. We are united today to affirm our
pride, our life-style and our commitment to each other.
Despite political and social differences we may have, we
are united on this common ground: For the first time in
history we are together as The Homosexual Community.
This is the commitment that draws us together; let us
not forget it throughout this, our day.

Placing this commitment above all else, let nothing stand in
our way. We are Gay and proud. No one can convince us
otherwise. Degrading remarks by hecklers or observers are
not important enough to interfere with our goal and don't
deserve a reaction.

The Christopher Street Liberation Day Committee has worked
closely with the New York City Police Dept. and we have
received their full cooperation to insure an orderly and
successful march. Trained marshals are marked with orange
CSLD armbands; they are members of the Gay Community and
are here to serve the people by providing important information such as medical and legal aid, parade routes, and the
location of rest areas. Feel free to ask them any and all
questions; they are here to help you in every way possible.

Every one of us is important. We are showing our strength
and love for each other by coming here today. We are all
participants in the most important Gay event in history.

I have taken a thick handful of the WELCOMEs, but with my right
hand in friend Arthur Evans's I decide to distribute them only after we
reach Sheep Meadow, which is still fifty-odd blocks away.

Only a few spirits are dampened—and only temporarily, thanks to GLFers' radical wisdom—in what Jonathan Black of the *Voice* will term "a mini-confrontation when an 8th Street Black Panther paper-hawker called out 'Get the Panther paper and stop all this foolishness.' Several gays pounced out of the line of march with angry cries of 'listen, brother, cut that shit out!' It all ended peaceably with some tense shouts of 'Right on!' and 'Power to the People!' " [11] Then, just as GLFers pass the Women's House of Detention:

"Free our sisters! Free ourselves!"

South of 14th Street, a man is waving a sign:

SODOM

+

GOMORRAH.

We shriek at him. Today, we've not much tolerance for the intolerant. Besides, at the corner, second and third floors, friendly faces and V signs greet us with cheers from the open windows of Alternate U. We return:

"Say it loud: Gay is proud!"

Non-marching gays are challenged by those of us en route: "Come on out or I'll point you out!" "Join us!" "Come on in, the water's fine!" Approaching 22nd, we see a woman lean out of an office window to throw streamers of film in honor of the marchers. We cheer her.[12] Now crowds of spectators grow thin, and will remain so until we near 42nd Street; I wonder if the now-few, habitual parade watchers we see knew what they were in for when they heeded the invitation of lamppost handbills: NO PARKING SUNDAY. PARADE. —POLICE DEPARTMENT.

By this time many gay men march shirtless in the warm mid-afternoon glow. We are, I am told, fifteen blocks long.

"Two, four, six, eight,
Gay is just [and soon, *"twice"*] as good as straight!"

and

"Hey, hey, whadaya say?
Try it once the other way!"

Spectators blanch, then usually grin. But if they sometimes don't grin, they don't frown either. And they read the WELCOMEs, surprised to receive them. No antagonisms. Has New York ever had such an unhassled protest march? But then, has New York ever had such an ecstatic protest march?

Approaching the crowds of suburbanites lined up at Radio City Music Hall, some of the powerites do a few kicks in Rockettes style,[13] but our

328

mood is anything but effeminate. It is a rocket of do-or-die determination lifted by a joy that none can contain. The do-gooders who perch on an auto top at 57th Street with signs that Jesus can still save us cringe as we pass by laughing but with fire in our eyes—we, perhaps even despite our intended "waywardness," harbingers of a new moral tone, a morality of full sexual pleasure and sensuality that curiously prevents many gay militants from soliciting sex with straights because we refuse to be considered solely as sex objects and that may have prompted GLF's rebukes to gay newspapers which print exploitative photographs of nude homosexual men and women [14] . . .

"Together, together, together, together . . . !"

We have reached the park! Central Park! As we enter, a mustachioed gay yells to a cop who also sports one, "It isn't so bad, is it?" "No!" the cop returns.[15]

"Out of the closets and into the streets!"

now becomes

"Out of the bushes and into the streets!"

and finally, with humor that homosexuals best (?) appreciate, quietly and with some snickering:

"Out of the streets and into the bushes!"

It has been a long walk. And, no apology intended, we are the New Homosexual, we are very very human . . .

Those first homosexual men and women who entered Sheep Meadow and marched to the grassy-rocky rise at its western end turned to view the oncoming parade and were stunned at their achievement: Where had they all come from? There couldn't have been so many gays when the march left the Village! Yet now

Wave on wave of gay brothers and sisters, multi-bannered, of all sizes and descriptions were advancing into the meadow, and a spontaneous applause seized the early marchers . . . For all of us who have been slowly climbing for years toward our freedom, this one last hill which let us look across our dear brothers and sisters was a cup running over. . . . It was as if . . . now at last we had come to the clearing, on the way to the top of the mountain . . . and tho' we knew we still had far to go, we were moving, and knew it.[16]

Lige Clarke and Jack Nichols have expressed similar feelings: [17] "Our eyes filled to the brim with tears as we stood together in Central Park's

Sheep Meadow, hugging each other, cheering wildly, applauding . . . awe-struck by the vast throngs of confident humanity wending their way into a promised land of freedom-to-be."

The New Yorker reported that, to get a clearer view, "One boy climbed on another's shoulders. A third boy looked on approvingly and said, 'You've got the grooviest sign in the whole parade.' " [18] From Jason Gould, in GAY: "We were on top of the world. It was pure exultation. . . . We got to the rock and threw our arms around our friends and kissed. We were gay and out in the open in Central Park, and, by God, we were proud!" [19]

Gays on the march swarmed in—over and around New Yorkers, hip and square, who had chosen the meadow for lunch—till Homosexuality spread across that wide green plain. Gould records that "A chant went up: 'Anyone who's standing is straight!' 5,000 gay guys and girls sat down. Couples wandered around together, arms around each other. Lovers kissed. Heads lit up. The sweet smell of grass was everywhere." Two lesbians, waxing poetic,[20] have remembered that

> *In the Sheep Meadow with kite-streamers overhead the smiles*
> *of the people were important, the smiles of those*
> *unafraid of each other. . . .*

Perry Brass guessed, in *Come Out!,* that it was "possibly the first time love had reappeared in the park on such a large scale since the first Easter Be-In three years ago . . ." [21]

But homosexuals, in their Gay-In bliss, had not forgotten what a long way they'd come—and still intended to go. A WNEW commentator opened an on-the-spot newscast with "Ladies and gentlemen, here we are with the boys and the girls in the band"—to be struck by a chorus of "Fuck you!" 's [22]

An intimate mountain of GAA men professed to be playing sensitivity games. A young queen treated the crowd to a semi-striptease. Under trees near a picket fence at the edge of the meadow four men lying on blankets were kissing—were to kiss for some nine hours—in what was a successful attempt at breaking the heterosexual world kissing record (set most recently by a straight couple in South Africa). Cary Yurman, writing for GAY, later reminisced that "The Rules of the contest prohibited touching except at the lips, and the kiss could not be broken. Tava [Von Will] was fun to kiss, but the first hour was the slowest one. It just seemed to drag on and on." At 4:45, "I attack Tava. We can touch, we can touch. Now how do we get rid of all these people?" [23] The marathon, spon-sored by GAA, featured another pair, Phil Raia and (Garland) Judy Bowen. Contented parkgoers, straight and gay, quietly watched the two male couples.

Kissing and making out, or simply relaxing, lesbians and gay males occupied, *staked out* Central Park that afternoon. GAY's co-editors have recalled that "around us couples cuddled, smiling secure, proud . . . we saw incredulity on the faces of bystanders. For the first time in their lives they were face to face with an overpowering reality: homosexuals can be beautiful sensual beings. . . . Muscular male bodies, stripped naked to the waist, wrestled playfully in the shade. Striking women, beautiful without makeup, kissed in the sunlight." [24] John LeRoy wrote that

It was the grandest demonstration in this part of the country of the homosexual's sense of self-affirmation I have ever seen, and, in a larger sense, it was a celebration of life itself. In no other gathering had I ever witnessed such a radiant glow of genuine freedom, yet without license, disorder, or harassment. . . .

. . . the gay community that had appeared on that Sunday afternoon demonstrated some of the finest qualities of all humanity: they showed that man can be erotically free, but socially responsible; that people can be themselves without any risk of social or political collapse; that man's inalienable right to love his fellow man need never be suppressed.[25]

In *Gay Scene*,[26] Robert Liechti was to capture homosexuals' twilight sentiments on June 28, 1970:

. . . it was all a bit like the time when Martin Luther King surveyed that vast flock of blacks in Washington. We, too, had been to the mountain top and we are not turning back; we had tasted the sweet morsel of glory and it was good . . . to sit in the shade with one's friends after it was all over in the evening's glow; it was glory, indeed. And man, it was beautiful!

The media did not ignore homosexuals this time. Monday's *New York Times* produced an excellent shot of the parade's beginning, announced that THOUSANDS OF HOMOSEXUALS HOLD A PROTEST RALLY IN CENTRAL PARK, Lacey Fosburgh's reportage citing attendance figures from "over a thousand" to 20,000 and quoting three gay leaders. Among them was GAA's Marty Robinson, who declared that the parade "serves notice on every politician in the state and nation that homosexuals are not going to hide any more . . . won't be harassed and degraded any more." The *Daily News* treated the marchers to a full paragraph, estimating 10,000 and naming them—surprisingly—GAY, but adding FOLK for respectability.

In the *Times*'s July 5 Sunday recap, "News of the Week in Review," Fosburgh enriched her expanded article—now headed THE "GAY" PEOPLE DEMAND THEIR RIGHTS and with a photo of the GAY PRIDE poster—to include statements from Becky Irons, a past president of Daughters of Bilitis, as well as Bob Kohler of GLF, who elucidated the new militancy: "This generation of homosexuals knows that the only way to loosen up society and eliminate the fear and disgust we arouse in people is through open confrontation. We're going to get loud and angry and then more loud and angry until we get our rights." The *Times* article boldly enunciated that "The focus of the protest, which brought together almost two dozen divergent groups, was both the laws which make homosexual acts between consenting adults illegal and the social conditions which make it difficult for homosexuals to behave romantically in public, get jobs in government, corporations, banks, airlines, schools or utility companies, or even in some cases rent apartments together."

Not only did major-city media such as the Philadelphia *News* detail the "series of celebrations designed to publicize the new militant fervor among homosexual organizations" (June 29), but an Associated Press release was carried by towns all across America. Readers of the Monday *Youngstown* [Ohio] *Vindicator* were to learn about the march by "3,000" and the "gay-in" in Central Park as well as about the West Coast parade sponsored by Christopher Street West which enlisted "400" gays and their floats. Among magazines, *The New Yorker* described the parade frankly and un-snidely. Nora Sayre, in London's *New Statesman,* not only itemized CSLDay but commented on GLF men's determination to eradicate their male chauvinism and noted that "some of the US Left is beginning to remark that gay liberation is one of the most radical goals of all, since it shakes up such profound questions of equality, rights, and prejudice, and also defies the consumer-trained family unit which perpetuates capitalism." [27] TIME Magazine, blasted however weakly by RASCO the preceding November, confessed: "Homosexuals, as Gore Vidal has noted, are one of the last minorities in the nation about whom it is still safe to make public jokes. That may not last much longer." [28] In the same issue, "The Weekly Newsmagazine" offered homosexuals a column and a half about Los Angeles's Troy Perry and his Metropolitan Community Churches for gays. *Evergreen* and *Mademoiselle* were to run GAA member Leo Skir's fine stories of the celebration in their September issues.

The gay press had a field day. Newsletters of a hundred homophile/homosexual clubs blossomed with new life during the next months. GAY, in succeeding weeks, presented CSLDay news by Jason Gould and by reporter–Gay Activist Kay Tobin, plus CSLDay features by John Francis Hunter, John LeRoy, Stefen Verk, and Angelo d'Arcangelo—each well illustrated. A GAY roving reporter, Charles Costa, discovered that "Gay Pride Week and the U.S. celebration of the Stonewall uprising have created new enthusiasm in gay communities throughout Latin America." Gay bars in Buenos Aires gave free brunches and dances, and posted signs of LIBERACIÓN. Gays in Rio de Janeiro, under a dictatorship that recently derided Michelangelo's statue of David, had little fun, but bars in Lima and Managua did a land-office business. Gays in Panama and Costa Rica planned activities for 1971.[29] (Many European newspapers noticed the event. A director of the International Homosexual World Organization in

Denmark helped arrange a "militant" day in Hamburg; discussions were held in the street and a public debate that evening was televised.[30])

Gay Power outdid its best, topping the treat with GLFer and camera-woman Diana Davies's polished shots. *Gay Scene,* by Robert Liechti's reminiscences, captured homosexuals' deep sense of satisfaction. *The Advocate,* fairest and most news-generous, displayed on its July 22–August 4 front page co-photos of New York and Los Angeles parade beginnings, with more candid shots inside. It also covered, via David Stienecker, the rally of some two hundred Chicago gays at Bug House Square—"a symbol of repression for Chicago's gays"—followed by a march to the Civic Center. Cast members of the Chicago *Hair* helped "Let the Sunshine In." Chief of *The Advocate* Dick Michaels editorialized that, "considering the degree of oppression in that midwestern bulwark of conservatism, that march required even more courage than in liberal Hollywood." Chicago gay liberationists had started the week with a boat cruise on Lake Michigan; Chicago Gay Liberation hosted a conference, with workshops, for Midwestern gay lib clubs and other interested groups Monday, June 22, through Thursday, June 25. Another *Advocate* reporter depicted the San Francisco event in which "Twenty to 30 persons marched up Polk Street from Aquatic Park to the Civic Center the night of June 27"; a gay-in the next day boasted some two hundred homosexuals in Golden Gate Park, however. But "heavy policing blighted the occasion."

Granting that New York City had the . . . LARGEST TURNOUT, LONGEST GAY MARCH, *The Advocate* burst with pride nevertheless about Christopher Street West: "The gay community of Los Angeles made its contribution to Americana on June 28. Over 1,000 homosexuals and their friends staged, not just a protest march, but a full-blown parade down world-famous Hollywood Boulevard." It hadn't been easy. Rev. Troy Perry told New Yorkers in November how the Los Angeles Police Department said gays would have to "put up a bond of one million dollars, another one of a half-million dollars, [and] cash of fifteen hundred dollars to pay the policemen for the day, to protect you people"—the overtime it would cost. "And you're going to have to have at least three thousand marching in the parade." As the gays withdrew, one policeman asked: "Are you going to have a queen in the parade?" Perry replied, "Oh, we're going to have several!" With an ACLU attorney, the gays returned. After an hour and a half, the LAPD came down to $1,500. " 'You've got to put it up—to pay for the policemen who are going to have to work overtime to protect you.' Well," said Perry, "that was Friday afternoon and Monday morning we went to court. We asked the judge to sign a writ of mandate to enjoin the police department to give us our parade permit. We were going to have a parade. Friday, the city had to show cause, to show up in court. They couldn't show cause. And we had our parade!"

Flags and banners floated in the chill sunlight of late afternoon; a bright red sound truck blared martial music; drummers strutted; a horse pranced; clowns cavorted; "vice cops" chased screaming "fairies" with paper wings [a GLF Guerrilla Theatre entry]; the Metropolitan Community Church choir sang "Onward Christian Soldiers"; a bronzed and muscular male model flaunted a 7½-foot live python.

On and on it went, interspersed with over 30 open cars carrying ADVO-CATE Groovy Guy contestants, the Grand Duchess of San Francisco, homo-phile leaders, and anyone else who wanted to be seen, and five floats, one of which depicted a huge jar of Vaseline, another a homosexual "nailed" to a cross. . . . [Lee Heflin, a leader, with Tony DeRosa, of L.A. GLF's caucus Militant Gay Movement, wrote in the gay lib supplement of the *Los Angeles Free Press* [31] that "the float which really struck to the heart of the matter (was) the huge jar of Vaseline. This was the one statement which openly spoke of what homosexuality is all about . . . that men can and do find Supreme Ecstasy by enveloping and being enveloped in each other's bodies."] . . .

Sensation-sated Hollywood had never seen anything like it.* . . .

Crowds lined both sides of the boulevard up to 10 deep along the half-mile-plus parade route . . . realistic estimates put the number of spectators at 15,000 to 20,000. . . .

The spectators appeared for the most part to be either friendly or neutral. There was a light scattering of boos, catcalls, and derisive shouts along the parade route, but applause and cheers followed the convertible in which Rev. Perry ** and his lover, Steve Jordan, were riding, the ADVOCATE staff car, and a number of other parade units. . . .

[One supremely sour note during the L.A. march: Tom Eckler, on his way Sunday to the Metropolitan Community Church, was accosted by two policemen who noticed his button, "GAY POWER/Christopher Street West/ '70." Insisting to them that he was *not* a "queer," but a homosexual, he was frisked, handcuffed, and received a ticket for "lewd conduct with a police officer." [32]] . . .

The GLF float carrying a homosexual on a cross and a large black-and-

---

* Hollywood may be even more impressed in June 1971. Float designs were suggested, autumn 1970, one of which "turns out to be fifteen feet wide, twenty-five feet long, and electrified in the works," said Morris Kight in the gay lib supplement of the *Los Angeles Free Press,* August 14. He also told how "Hotels are calling to offer a package deal of travel, in-town bus, room, and after-the-show champagne dinner. Gay bars are already planning brunch-bus-buffet packages."

** Immediately after the parade, Perry, with Carole Shepherd, president of L.A. DOB, and Kelly Weiser of HELP, began a fast at the corner of Hollywood Boulevard and Las Palmas (scene of frequent police harassment of homosexuals). A week earlier, Perry had told his MCC congregation that he would commence an indefinite fast on the steps of the L.A. Federal Building and would continue fasting until state officials began measures to guarantee sexual freedom for consenting adults. Police arrested Perry, Shepherd, and Weiser for "incitement to riot," a charge later changed to "obstructing sidewalk traffic." (GAY, July 27, 1970.) Perry spent the night in jail without food, left the next day on his own recognizance to fast—and sleep—for the next ten days on the Federal Building steps. He was joined by several parishioners and friends. At 8:00 p.m., July 7, he broke his fast by a symbolic break-ing of bread at the corner of Hollywood and Las Palmas.

white sign, IN MEMORY OF THOSE KILLED BY THE PIGS, spread silence like a pall . . .

Signs carried by the marchers bore such slogans as HOMOSEXUALITY IS NATURAL BIRTH CONTROL; MORE DEVIATION, LESS POPULATION; STOP ENTRAPMENT; AMERICA: IN GOD WE TRUST . . . LOVE IT BUT CHANGE IT; 20% OF YOU ARE US; HICKORY, DICKORY, DOCK, THEY'LL PICK OUR BEDROOM LOCK, THEY'LL HAUL US IN AND CALL IT A SIN, UNLESS WE STOP THEIR CLOCK; THE NAZIS BURNED JEWS, THE CHURCH BURNED HOMOSEXUALS. . . . [TIME called attention to a T-shirted gay who walked a white husky bearing the sign NOT ALL OF US WALK POODLES.[33]] . . .

There was also this . . . clean-cut, college-type boy and a long-haired blond girl who occasionally nuzzled his neck:

He: "I think it's great. There's got to be more love in the world."

She: "I'm all for them. I think everybody ought to be free." . . .

So does every gay militant, GLFer and Gay Activist alike, despite their multi-differences, their alignment vs. non-alignment politics. And they won't wait for evolution.

In the *Philadelphia Free Press* of July 27, 1970, Steve Kuromiya, who celebrated Christopher Street Liberation Day in New York City, tells why:

We came battle-scarred and angry to topple your sexist, racist, hateful society. We came to challenge the incredible hypocrisy of your serial monogamy, your oppressive sexual role-playing, your nuclear family, your Protestant ethic, apple pie and Mother. We came to New York holding hands and kissing openly and proudly, waving 15-foot banners and chanting "HO-HO-HOMOSEXUAL!" In one fell swoop, we came to destroy by our mere presence your labels and stereotypes with which you've oppressed us for centuries.

And we came with love and open hearts to challenge your hate and secrecy. . . .

NOTES

CHAPTER 1

1. "Give Me Liberty or . . ." *Homophile Action League Newsletter* (Philadelphia), August–September 1969.
2. Hans Knight: " 'Other Society' Moves into the Open," Philadelphia *Sunday Bulletin,* July 19, 1970.
3. Tom Burke: "The New Homosexuality," *Esquire,* December 1969, p. 316.
4. Lee Brewster, in a release from Queens, August 1970.
5. George White: "Confessions of the Heterosexuals," *San Francisco Free Press,* November 1–14, 1969; Gary Alinder: "Alternative Culture," *San Francisco Free Press,* November 15–30, 1969.
6. Craig Rodwell, in Breck Ardery's LP recording *June 28: Gay and Proud.*
7. John Francis Hunter: "The Rise of the New Conscience: Gay Pride on Parade," GAY, June 29, 1970.
8. Lige Clarke and Jack Nichols, in their "Homosexual Citizen" column, *Screw,* July 25, 1969.

CHAPTER 2

1. Lige Clarke and Jack Nichols, in their "Homosexual Citizen" column, *Screw,* July 4, 1969.
2. David Bird: "Trees in a Queens Park Cut Down as Vigilantes Harass Homosexuals," *The New York Times,* July 1, 1969.
3. David Bird: "Queens Resident Says the Police Stood By as Park Trees Were Cut," *The New York Times,* July 2, 1969.
4. "Gay Riots in the Village," *New York Mattachine Newsletter,* August 1969.
5. John Francis Hunter: "The Rise of the New Conscience: Gay Pride on Parade," GAY, June 29, 1970.
6. "Gay Riots in the Village."
7. "The Stonewall Riots: The Gay View," *New York Mattachine Newsletter,* August 1969.
8. Ibid.
9. Dick Leitsch: "The Snake Pit Raid: Some Afterthoughts," GAY, April 13, 1970.

10. Lige Clarke and Jack Nichols, in their "Homosexual Citizen" column, *Screw*, July 25, 1969.

11. Ibid.

12. Leo Martello: "A Positive Image for the Homosexual," *Come Out!*, November 14, 1969.

13. Tom Burke: "The New Homosexuality," *Esquire*, December 1969, pp. 316–18.

CHAPTER 3

1. Edward Sagarin: "Behind the Gay Liberation Front," *The Realist*, May–June 1970, p. 17.

2. Foster Gunnison, Jr.: "The Homophile Movement in America," in *The Same Sex: An Appraisal of Homosexuality* (Philadelphia, 1969), pp. 123–4.

3. George Mendenhall, in a letter to the author, September 1, 1970.

4. Charles Alverson: "A Minority's Plea: U.S. Homosexuals Gain in Trying to Persuade Society to Accept Them," *Wall Street Journal*, July 17, 1968.

5. "Cross-currents," *The Ladder: A Lesbian Review*, May 1965, p. 22.

6. "Picketing: The Impact and the Issues," *The Ladder: A Lesbian Review*, September 1965, p. 5.

7. Jim Kepner, in a letter to the author, October 2, 1970.

8. "Raid," *Concern* (published by PURSUIT for the Southern California Council on Religion and the Homophile, L.A.), January 1967.

9. Jim Kepner, in a letter to the author, October 2, 1970.

10. Sagarin: "Behind the Gay Liberation Front," p. 17.

11. Madolin Cervantes: "Is Militancy the Answer?", *Gay Power*, No. 14.

12. Jim Kepner, in a memo to the author, November 23, 1970.

13. FREE Newsletter #2, August 24, 1970.

14. "Why *'Homosexuals Intransigent!'*?", *Homosexual Renaissance* (newsletter of *HI!*, The City College/CUNY), November 12, 1969.

15. Jim Kepner, in a memo to the author, November 23, 1970.

16. Jim Kepner, in a memo to the author, November 13, 1970.

17. Don Jackson: "Homosexual Gov't Planned," *Los Angeles Free Press*, January 9–15, 1970.

18. Marcus Overseth: "Inside Look at Where We Stand," *San Francisco Free Press*, Vol. 1, No. 9.

19. Sagarin: "Behind the Gay Liberation Front," p. 18.

20. Overseth: "Inside Look at Where We Stand."

21. "Kew Gardens Rally," *New York Mattachine Newsletter*, September 1969.

22. Steve Dansky: "Hey Man," *Come Out!*, June–July 1970.

23. Stephen Donaldson (pseud. of Bob Martin): "Student Homophile League News," *Gay Power*, No. 2.

24. Ibid.

25. Marcus Overseth: "Grows Rapidly; What Kind of People?", *San Francisco Free Press*, December 7–21, 1969.

26. Dansky: "Hey Man."

27. Gary Alinder: "Alternative Culture," *San Francisco Free Press*, November 15–30, 1969.

28. Ralph Hall: "Gay Liberation Front," *Gay Power*, No. 5.

29. Jonathan Black: "The Boys in the Snake Pit: Games 'Straights' Play," *Village Voice*, March 19, 1970.

30. Ellen Bedoz: "Afraid of What?", *Come Out!*, September–October 1970.
31. Dansky: "Hey Man."
32. Kathy Wakeham: "Lesbian Oppression," *Come Out!*, June–July 1970.
33. Don Jackson: "Rafferty and Dudley Swim in Cesspool," *Gay Power*, No. 8.
34. Basil O'Brien: "Ga Soirée," *Plain Dealer* (Philadelphia, September 3, 1970.
35. "Minnesota: FREE for All," *San Francisco Free Press*, December 7–21, 1969.
36. "The People's Dance," *Gay Students' Union* (UC; 721 40th Street, Oakland, Cal.), May 25, 1970.

CHAPTER 4

1. "Sociologists Vote on Homosexual Rights," ....*another Voice* (newsletter of the Central Ohio Mattachine Society, now SIR of Ohio, Inc.), December 1969–January 1970.
2. Thomas Szasz: *The Manufacture of Madness* (New York, 1970), p. 176.
3. "An Offensive Voice," *Homophile Action League Newsletter* (Philadelphia), October 1969.
4. Michael Brown, Michael Tallman, and Leo Martello: "The Summer of Gay Power, and the *Village Voice* Exposed!", *Come Out!*, November 14, 1969.
5. Ibid.
6. "Marchi or Procaccino: Jail or Asylum," *Come Out!*, November 14, 1969.
7. Ibid.
8. Ibid.
9. The Gay Commandoes: "The October Rebellion," *Come Out!*, November 14, 1969.
10. "GLF News," *Gay Power*, No. 4.
11. Ibid.
12. Dick Leitsch: "The Gay Vote," GAY, December 15, 1969.
13. Craig Schoonmaker: *"Homosexuals Intransigent!"*, *Gay Power*, No. 9.
14. Ralph Hall: "Gay Liberation Front," *Gay Power*, No. 5.
15. Ibid.
16. Jim Kepner, in a memo to the author, November 13, 1970.
17. Reese Erlich: "Berkeley's Berlandt, Gay Liberation for Gay Dignity," *Los Angeles Free Press*, December 5–11, 1969.
18. Stevens McClave: "Manifesto for Gay Liberation Theatre," *San Francisco Free Press*, October 16–31, 1969.
19. Don Jackson: "Gay Liberation Movement," *Berkeley Barb*, October 10–16, 1969.
20. "Gay Liberation Theatre," *San Francisco Free Press*, November 1–14, 1969.
21. Stevens: "Sir?", *San Francisco Free Press*, November 1–14, 1969.
22. Marcus Overseth: "24 Hours: From Bust to Bail," *San Francisco Free Press*, November 15–30, 1969.
23. Larry Clarkson: "A Fairy Tale," *San Francisco Free Press*, November 15–30, 1969.
24. Don Jackson: "First Bloodshed in Gay Freedom Struggle," *Gay Power*, No. 7.
25. Overseth: "24 Hours: From Bust to Bail."
26. Jackson: "First Bloodshed in Gay Freedom Struggle."

27. "S.F. Cops Arrest 12 Pickets After Melee at Examiner," *The Advocate,* January 1970.

28. Jackson: "First Bloodshed in Gay Freedom Struggle."

29. Overseth: "24 Hours: From Bust to Bail."

30. Jackson: "First Bloodshed in Gay Freedom Struggle."

31. Ralph Hall: "Gay Liberation Front," *Gay Power,* No. 8.

32. Sam Jones: "Gays Picket LA Times," *Los Angeles Free Press,* November 14, 1969.

33. "Los Angeles Times Under Attack," GAY, December 1, 1969.

34. "Gays Picket L.A. Times over Paper's Ad Policy," *The Advocate,* January 1970.

35. Jones: "Gays Picket LA Times."

36. Nancy Ross: "Homosexual Revolution," *Washington Post,* October 25, 1969.

37. Bronick: "In the Streets for the Revolution," *San Francisco Free Press,* November 1–14, 1969.

38. "Gay Liberation Theatre."

39. Dick Leitsch: "Homosexuals Don't Really Exist!", GAY, April 27, 1970.

40. David McReynolds: "Notes for a More Coherent Article," WIN, November 15, 1969, p. 14.

41. Paul Goodman: "Memoirs of an Ancient Activist," WIN, November 15, 1969, p. 7.

42. Marty Stephan: "Deliver Us from Our Friends—Please O Lord," *Gay Power,* No. 8.

43. The Tangents Group, in the gay lib supplement of the *Los Angeles Free Press,* August 14, 1970.

44. Bob Martin: "The New Homosexual and His Movement," WIN, November 15, 1969, pp. 15–16.

45. Randolfe Wicker: "A Businessman Sounds Off!", GAY, December 15, 1969.

46. Leitsch: "Homosexuals Don't Really Exist!"

47. Thane Hampten: "Misplaced in Middle America: A Return to the Heartland," GAY, September 28, 1970.

48. "Don't Pigeonhole Gays, Goldstein Tells NSLU," ....*another Voice,* Vol. 1, No. 2.

49. Jim Fouratt: "Word Thoughts," *Come Out!,* January 10, 1970.

50. Bob Martin: "Student Homophile News," *Gay Power,* No. 2.

51. Franklin Kameny: "Gay Is Good," in *The Same Sex: An Appraisal of Homosexuality* (Philadelphia, 1969), p. 145.

52. John LeRoy: "The Anti-Homosexual in America: Donald Webster Cory," GAY, April 20, 1970.

53. "A Thousand Times, No!", *Gay Flames,* No. 2.

54. Craig Schoonmaker, in a letter to the author, August 17, 1970.

55. Bob Amsel: "Closets Are for Clothes Only!", GAY, December 31, 1969.

56. Nick Benton: "Who Needs It?", *Gay Sunshine,* August–September 1970.

57. Haskel Frankel: "On the Fringe," *Saturday Review,* June 14, 1969.

58. "'Homosexual Handbook' Names Dozens of Living Showbizites as Such," *Variety,* March 5, 1969.

59. Jim Kepner: "The World of Pat Rocco," GAY, June 1, 1970.

60. As reprinted in "Lesbians as Bogeywomen," *Come Out!,* June–July 1970.

61. Donn Teal: "Does America Have Stage Fright?", GAY, February 2, 1970.

62. Ibid.

63. Bob Martin: "A Gay Musical Romp with Hang-Ups," *Gay Power*, No. 14.

64. Teal: "Does America Have Stage Fright?"

65. Douglas Dean: " 'Puppy Dog' Tale Identifies with Gays But Lacks Dramatic Conflict, Growth," *The Advocate*, July 8–21, 1970.

66. Clive Barnes: "Theater: 'And Puppy Dog Tails' Opens," *The New York Times*, October 20, 1969.

CHAPTER 5

1. Bob Martin: "ERCHO Meeting Adopts Radical Manifesto," *The Advocate*, January 1970.

2. Foster Gunnison, in a letter to *Playboy*, printed August 1970, p. 46.

3. "ERCHO Spring Conference," *Gay Power*, No. 7.

4. Martin: "ERCHO Meeting Adopts Radical Manifesto."

5. Foster Gunnison, in a letter to Bob Kohler, December 21, 1969.

6. "Whither the Movement?", *Homophile Action League Newsletter* (Philadelphia), November–December 1969.

7. Foster Gunnison, in a letter to Bob Kohler, December 21, 1969.

8. Foster Gunnison, in a letter to the author, August 1970.

9. Jim Kepner: "Angles on the News: Reform and Revolution," *The Advocate*, June 24–July 7, 1970.

10. Madolin Cervantes: "Is Militancy the Answer?", *Gay Power*, No. 14.

11. Kepner: "Angles on the News: Reform and Revolution."

12. K. R. Newell, in a letter to *Vector* (SIR, San Francisco), printed July 1970.

13. Michael Itkin: "Homosexual Liberation and Nonviolent Revolution," *Gay Power*, No. 7.

14. Charles Alverson: "A Minority's Plea: U.S. Homosexuals Gain in Trying to Persuade Society to Accept Them," *Wall Street Journal*, July 17, 1968.

15. Charles McCabe: "The Fearless Spectator: Gay Is Good?", *San Francisco Chronicle*, October 1, 1970.

16. Steven Roberts: "Homosexuals in Revolt," *The New York Times*, August 24, 1970.

17. Don Neal: "President's Message," "Anewsbits" (newsletter of the Society of Anubis, Azusa, Cal.), August 1970.

18. Ed Jackson: " 'New Left' Not for Gays, Darden Says," *The Advocate*, May 1969.

19. Rob Cole: "Radicals' Dilemma: The Leftists They Woo Call Them 'Faggots,' " *The Advocate*, September 16–29, 1970.

20. Douglas Key: "Gay Lib Front Meets; Plans to Picket Barney's Beanery," *Los Angeles Free Press*, February 6, 1970.

21. "Leroi Jones Calls Gays 'Fake,' " GAY, December 15, 1969.

22. LeRoi Jones: "To Survive 'The Reign of the Beasts,' " *The New York Times* (Arts and Leisure), November 16, 1969.

23. "Leroi Jones" (editorial), GAY, December 15, 1969.

24. The Red Butterfly: "Gay Liberation" (GLF; New York, 1970).

25. Jim Fouratt: "Word Thoughts," *Come Out!*, January 10, 1970.

26. Foster Gunnison, in a letter to *Playboy*, printed August 1970, p. 46.

27. Foster Gunnison, in a letter to William Wynne, July 25, 1970.

28. Martha Shelley: "More Radical Than Thou," *Come Out!*, January 10, 1970.

29. "Looking Ahead," *Homophile Action League Newsletter* (Philadelphia), January–February 1970.

30. "Whither the Movement?"

31. "The Homosexual: Newly Visible, Newly Understood," TIME, October 31, 1969, p. 62.

32. Stevens: "November 15," *San Francisco Free Press*, November 15–30, 1969.

33. Don Jackson: "Gay Liberation Peace March," *Gay Power*, No. 7.

34. Michael Itkin: "The Homosexual Liberation Movement," *San Francisco Free Press*, December 7–21, 1969.

35. Ralph Hall: "Gay Liberation Front," *Gay Power*, No. 7.

36. "GLF News," *Gay Power*, No. 4.

37. Ralph Hall: "Gay Liberation Front News," *Gay Power*, No. 3.

38. The Red Butterfly: "Gay Liberation" (GLF; New York, 1970).

39. Lois Hart: "GLF News," *Come Out!*, January 10, 1970.

40. Marcus Overseth: "Inside Look at Where We Stand," *San Francisco Free Press*, Vol. 1, No. 9.

41. Ralph Hall: "Gay Liberation News," *Gay Power*, No. 9.

42. Hart: "GLF News."

43. Overseth: "Inside Look at Where We Stand."

44. Fouratt: "Word Thoughts."

45. "Anti-Thanksgiving March Stuns Exploiters, Ends in Good Vibes at SIR," *San Francisco Free Press*, December 7–21, 1969.

46. "An Interview with New York City Liberationists," *San Francisco Free Press*, December 7–21, 1969; also, RAT, August 12–26, 1969.

47. Douglas Key: "Gay Power Groups Pull It Together," *Los Angeles Free Press*, December 19, 1969.

48. Overseth: "Inside Look at Where We Stand."

49. Jim Kepner: "Gay Lib Conference Attracts Hundreds," *The Advocate*, March 1970.

50. "California Teachers Union Adopts Homosexual Resolution," *Homophile Action League Newsletter* (Philadelphia), March–April 1970.

51. Carl Wittman: "Refugees from Amerika: A Gay Manifesto," *San Francisco Free Press*, December 22–January 7, 1970.

CHAPTER 6

1. Jonathan Black: "The Boys in the Snake Pit: Games 'Straights' Play," *Village Voice*, March 19, 1970.

2. Dick Leitsch: "The Snake Pit Raid; Some Afterthoughts," GAY, April 13, 1970.

3. "Patrons Tell of Raid from Inside," GAY, April 13, 1970.

4. "Responsible Cop Cops Out," GAY, April 13, 1970.

5. "Patrons Tell of Raid from Inside."

6. "The Morning of the Snake Pit: An Interview by Arthur Irving" (pseud. of Arthur Bell), *Gay Power*, No. 13.

7. "Patrons Tell of Raid from Inside."

8. "The Morning of the Snake Pit: An Interview by Arthur Irving."

9. Black: "The Boys in the Snake Pit: Games 'Straights' Play."

10. Arthur Irving (pseud. of Arthur Bell): "Gay Activists Alliance News and Other Events," *Gay Power*, No. 13.

11. Leo Martello: "Raid Victim Impaled on Fence," *The Advocate,* April 29–May 12, 1970.

12. Allen Warshawsky: "Take Good Care of My Brother," *Come Out!,* April–May 1970.

13. "500 Angry Homosexuals Protest Raid," GAY, April 13, 1970.

14. "Responsible Cop Cops Out."

15. "Snake Pit Raid" (editorial), *Gay Power,* No. 13.

16. "Who's Guilty?" (editorial), *Screw,* March 22, 1970.

17. Nat Hentoff: "Reader's Comment," *Village Voice,* March 19, 1970.

18. "Political Club Acts to Halt Raids," GAY, April 13, 1970.

19. "Congressman Koch Questions Police Bar Raids," GAY, April 20, 1970.

20. "Congressman Koch Is Cool!" (editorial), GAY, April 20, 1970.

CHAPTER 7

1. Franklin Kameny: "Gay Is Good," in *The Same Sex: An Appraisal of Homosexuality* (Philadelphia, 1969), p. 144.

2. "Gays in Louisville Choosing Sides over Liberation Group," *The Advocate,* October 14–27, 1970.

3. Foster Gunnison, in a letter to William Wynne, July 25, 1970.

4. "Homophiles Need Support" (editorial), GAY, April 13, 1970.

5. Leo Skir: "We're Freakin' On In!", *Mademoiselle,* September 1970, p. 195.

6. Dick Leitsch: "Politicians Make Strange Bedfellows!", GAY, May 25, 1970.

7. "Councilman Greitzer Yields to Gay Activists," GAY, June 1, 1970.

8. Kay Tobin: "Gay Activists Confront Politicos," GAY, March 15, 1970.

9. Arthur Irving (pseud. of Arthur Bell): "Gay Activists Alliance News and Other Events," *Gay Power,* No. 11.

10. Ron Hollander: "Gays Picket City Hall," *New York Post,* March 5, 1970.

11. "Onward to City Hall," *Gay Power,* No. 12.

12. "Gay Activists Confront City Hall," GAY, March 29, 1970.

13. "Will Mayor Lindsay Listen?" (editorial), GAY, March 29, 1970.

14. "Is ABC-TV Against Us?" (editorial), GAY, March 29, 1970.

15. Nancy Ross: "Homosexual Revolution," *Washington Post,* October 25, 1969.

16. Frank Keating: "Pleasure Palace," QQ, Winter (1969–1970), p. 9.

17. Lige Clarke and Jack Nichols, in their "Homosexual Citizen" column, *Screw,* January 19, 1970.

18. "Police Continue Entrapment at Continental Baths," GAY, February 16, 1970.

19. Lige Clarke and Jack Nichols, in their "Homosexual Citizen" column, *Screw,* January 19, 1970.

20. Lige Clarke and Jack Nichols, in their "Homosexual Citizen" column, *Screw,* January 26, 1970.

21. "Boston Gays Present Demands," GAY, April 20, 1970.

22. "Gays Voted Role in Rights Parley," GAY, May 11, 1970.

23. "Gays Toss Out NBC-TV," GAY, April 27, 1970.

24. Arthur Irving (pseud. of Arthur Bell): "Gay Activists Alliance News," *Gay Power,* No. 15.

25. Grace Glueck: "For Museum Birthday, Good Cheer and Cake," *The New York Times,* April 14, 1970.

26. Arthur Irving (pseud. of Arthur Bell): "Gay Activists Alliance News," *Gay Power,* No. 16.

27. "GAA Confronts Lindsay at Channel 5," GAY, May 11, 1970.

28. Sandra Vaughn: "Lindsay & Homosexuals: An Edited Encounter," *Village Voice,* April 23, 1970.

29. "GAA Confronts Lindsay at Channel 5."

30. "N.Y. Rights Commissioner Backs Employment Demands," GAY, May 18, 1970.

31. Ibid.

32. "GAA Meets with City Brass," GAY, May 25, 1970.

33. "Telephone Company Discrimination Charged," GAY, December 15, 1969.

34. "Pan American's Perversions" (editorial), GAY, August 3, 1970.

35. "Honeywell, Inc. Admits Job Bias; Betty Crocker Says Gays Welcome," GAY, August 31, 1970.

36. "Three Big Companies Say They Hire Gays," *The Advocate,* September 30–October 13, 1970.

37. "Mickey Spillane Fears 'Fags' Takeover," GAY, May 25, 1970.

38. "Dear Abby Says 'Gays Not Sick!' ", GAY, July 13, 1970.

39. Hans Knight: " 'Other Society' Moves into the Open," Philadelphia *Sunday Bulletin,* July 19, 1970.

40. "Bella Abzug Assists Harassed Youths," GAY, June 8, 1970.

41. Arthur Irving (pseud. of Arthur Bell): "Zapping with Carol; Hello Bella," *Gay Power,* No. 18.

42. "Bella Abzug, Congressional Hopeful, Bids for Gay Vote," GAY, June 15, 1970.

43. Arthur Irving (pseud. of Arthur Bell): "On a Clear Day You Can See Bella Abzug," *Gay Power,* No. 19.

44. Eric Thorndale: "Fugitives from the Syllogism," *Gay Power,* No. 19.

45. Kay Tobin: "GAA Confronts Goldberg, Blumenthal," GAY, June 29, 1970.

46. Kay Tobin: "GAA Tackles Five More Candidates," GAY, July 6, 1970.

47. "Bella Abzug, Gay Rights Candidate, Wins Primary," GAY, July 13, 1970.

48. "Bella Abzug's Victory" (editorial), GAY, July 13, 1970.

49. "Rao Blasts Koch on Police Issue," GAY, April 27, 1970.

50. "Bella Abzug, Gay Rights Candidate, Wins Primary."

51. "Samuels on Law Reform," *Mattachine Times,* July 1970.

52. "Is There Hope for the Governor?" (editorial), GAY, July 13, 1970.

53. John LeRoy: "Blossoms on the Boob Tube," GAY, July 20, 1970.

54. Ibid.

55. "5 Gay Activists Arrested in Sit-In," GAY, July 13, 1970.

56. "Wall Street Purge Causes Job Losses," GAY, March 15, 1970.

57. "5 Gay Activists Arrested in Sit-In."

58. Timothy Ferris: "A 'Gay' Sit-In at GOP HQ," *New York Post,* June 25, 1970.

CHAPTER 8

1. Robin de Luis: "The Sunday Night Meeting," *Come Out!*, September–October 1970.
2. Ellen Bedoz: "Afraid of What?", *Come Out!*, September–October 1970.
3. "What's Going On Here?", *Gay Flames*, No. 3.
4. "To Serve the Community," *Gay Flames*, No. 1.
5. Gary Alinder: "My Gay Soul," *Gay Sunshine*, September 1970.
6. "Why Gay Lib on April 15th?", HUB (newsletter of Homophile Union of Boston), May 1970.
7. "A 35-Year-Old Guru Ministers to Hippies of Northern California," *The New York Times*, September 21, 1970.
8. "The Liberators" (editorial), QQ, Summer 1970.
9. "News," *Come Out!*, June–July 1970.
10. Step May: "What's Wrong with Sucking?", in *Gay Flames*'s "Gay Liberation Packet," November 1970.
11. Tony Diaman: "GLF Walkout," *Come Out!*, September–October 1970.
12. Randolfe Wicker: "The Wicker Basket," GAY, August 24, 1970.
13. Bob Kohler: "Gay Liberation Front–New York," *Gay Power*, No. 15.
14. "News."
15. Kohler: "Gay Liberation Front–New York."
16. "News."
17. Ibid.
18. "Gay Liberation," *Plain Dealer* (Philadelphia), July 30, 1970.
19. Kate Millett: *Sexual Politics* (New York, 1970), p. 30.
20. Lois Hart: "Black Panthers Call a Revolutionary People's Constitutional Convention: A White Lesbian Responds," *Come Out!*, September–October 1970.
21. "Gay People Help Plan New World," *Gay Flames*, No. 2.
22. "No Revolution Without Us," *Come Out!*, September–October 1970.
23. "Lesbian Demands, Panther Constitutional Convention, Sept. 5, 1970," *Come Out!*, September–October 1970.
24. "No Revolution Without Us."
25. "Philly Convention," RAT, September 11–25, 1970.
26. Joseph Modzelewski: "Police Keep Their Distance as Panthers Meet," New York *Sunday News*, September 6, 1970.
27. "No Revolution Without Us."
28. Ibid.
29. "Black Militants Oust S.F. Gay Lib," *The Advocate*, October 28–November 10, 1970.
30. "Gays Attacked in Philly," *Gay Scene*, No. 4.
31. "Gay Brothers Attacked in Philly," *Plain Dealer* (Philadelphia), September 3, 1970.
32. "Panthers Get FREE Nod," *The Advocate*, November 25–December 8, 1970.
33. Angela Douglas: "Panthers Still Biased Against Gays, Women," *The Advocate*, November 11–24, 1970.

CHAPTER 9

1. Pat Maxwell: "Lavender Menaces Confront The Congress to Unite Women," *Gay Power*, No. 17.
2. "Lavender Menace Does It: Two Views," *Come Out!*, June–July 1970.

3. Sidney Abbott, in an interview, December 2, 1970.

4. Maxwell: "Lavender Menaces Confront The Congress to Unite Women."

5. Rita Laporte, in a letter to *Newsweek*, printed April 6, 1970, p. 4. She is Director of Promotion, *The Ladder*, Box 5025, Reno, Nevada 89503.

6. Kay Tobin: "Daughters of Bilitis Confronts Feminist Issues," GAY, August 3, 1970.

7. "A Redstockings sister": "I Am 23, A Mother, and A Lesbian," RAT, August 9, 1970.

8. As reprinted in "Lesbians as Bogeywomen," *Come Out!*, June–July 1970.

9. Elsa Gidlow: "Sisters Take a Stand," *Women: A Journal of Liberation*, (Baltimore), summer 1970.

10. As reprinted in *Gay Sunshine*, October 1970.

11. Reprinted as "A Letter from Mary," in *Gay Flames*'s "Gay Liberation Packet," November 1970.

12. Martha Shelley: "Stepin Fetchit Woman," *Come Out!*, November 14, 1969.

13. "Women's Liberation," RAT, April 17, 1970.

14. Shelley: "Stepin Fetchit Woman."

15. As noted in "Is Harriet Van Horny?" (editorial), GAY, May 4, 1970.

16. Suzannah Lessard: "Gay Is Good for Us All," *The Washington Monthly*, December 1970, p. 42.

17. "Radicalesbians," *Come Out!*, December 1970–January 1971.

18. "The Woman-Identified Woman," *Come Out!*, June–July 1970.

19. "Radicalesbians."

20. Ibid.

21. Ibid.

22. "GLF Women," *Come Out!*, December 1970–January 1971.

23. Ibid.

24. Tobin: "Daughters of Bilitis Confronts Feminist Issues."

25. Martha Shelley: "Confessions of a Pseudo-Male Chauvinist," *The Ladder: A Lesbian Review*, June–July, 1970, pp. 18–19.

26. "Pasha": "Women Together," *Gay Sunshine*, October 1970.

27. Del Martin: " 'If That's All There Is . . .': Female Gay Blasts Men, Leaves Movement," *The Advocate*, October 28–November 10, 1970.

28. Judy Grahn: "Lesbians as Women," *San Francisco Free Press*, December 22, 1969–January 7, 1970.

29. "Sappho Was a Right On Woman," *Ain't I A Woman?*, October 30, 1970.

30. From page 14 of *Ain't I A Woman?*, October 30, 1970.

31. Tobin: "Daughters of Bilitis Confronts Feminist Issues."

32. Contained in *Sisters* (DOB, San Francisco), December 1970.

33. Rita Laporte: "The Undefeatable Force," *The Ladder: A Lesbian Review*, August–September 1970, p. 5.

34. Ti-Grace Atkinson, in an "Article Prepared for the New York Times Op-Ed Page, Lesbianism and Feminism: Justice for Women as 'Unnatural,' " December 21, 1970. Publication rights belong to New York DOB.

35. "Policemen at DOB," *Newsletter* of Daughters of Bilitis/New York, November 1970.

36. "Back to the Closet?" (editorial), *Newsletter* of Daughters of Bilitis/New York, November 1970.

37. "Women's Lib: A Second Look," TIME, December 14, 1970, p. 50.

38. From a Women's Strike Coalition NEWS FLASH leaflet, "Action in Support of Kate Millett."

39. Judy Klemesrud: "The Lesbian Issue and Women's Lib," *The New York Times*, December 18, 1970.

CHAPTER 10

1. "From Limp Wrist to Clenched Fist," *Plain Dealer* (Philadelphia), June 4, 1970.

2. "Village Unisex Club Suffers Harassment," GAY, September 21, 1970.

3. Randolfe Wicker: "The Wicker Basket," GAY, September 21, 1970.

4. "Village Unisex Club Suffers Harassment."

5. "East Side Harassment," *Mattachine Times* (New York), August 1970.

6. Randolfe Wicker: "The Wicker Basket," GAY, August 17, 1970.

7. "East Side Harassment."

8. "Arrests Continue Upward Spiral," GAY, September 14, 1970.

9. "Scenes," *Village Voice*, August 26, 1970.

10. Howard Blum: "Gays Take On the Cops: From Rage to Madness," *Village Voice*, September 3, 1970.

11. "Police Damage Totals $1,000 in Bar Raid," GAY, September 21, 1970; "Police Destroy $20,000 in Private Property: Wield Crowbars in Raid on the Haven," GAY, September 28, 1970.

12. Cy Egan: "Village's 'Haven' Raided," *New York Post*, September 4, 1970.

13. Don Schanche: *The Panther Paradox: A Liberal's Dilemma* (New York, 1970), pp. 224–5.

14. A "Flaming Faggot": "We're Not Gay, We're Angry," RAT, September 11–25, 1970.

15. "Money Needed for Bail," *Gay Flames*, No. 4.

16. Martha Shelley: "Gays Riot Again: Remember the Stonewall!", *Come Out!*, September–October 1970.

17. C. Gerald Fraser: " 'Gay Ghettos' Seen as Police Targets," *The New York Times*, August 31, 1970.

18. "New Gay Riots Erupt in Greenwich Village: Demonstration Ends in Violent Melee," GAY, September 21, 1970.

19. "Pigs Play It One Way," *Gay Flames*, No. 3.

20. "NYU Breaks Gay Dance Contract," GAY, September 21, 1970.

21. "MSNY/NYU," *Mattachine Times* (New York), September 1970.

22. "NYU Bows to Gay Rage," *Gay Flames*, No. 1.

23. "NYU Breaks Gay Dance Contract."

24. "NYU Bows to Gay Rage."

25. "Out of the Closets and into the Subcellar," RAT, October 6–27, 1970.

26. In a mimeographed leaflet which Arthur Bell distributed at a Gay Activists Alliance meeting on October 1.

27. "Gays Siege NYU; Demonstrate! Monday, Oct. 5," *Gay Flames*, No. 5.

28. Jay Levin: "Sad End for Dorm Gay Gala," *New York Post*, September 26, 1970.

29. Allan Cartter: "The Weinstein Affair," *Washington Square Journal* (NYU), September 29, 1970.

30. Colleen Sullivan: "Diamond Jim Hester, Where Are You?", *Washington Square Journal* (NYU), September 30, 1970.

31. "Demonstrators Challenge New York University Policies," *The Advocate*, October 28–November 10, 1970.

32. Angelo d'Arcangelo: *The Homosexual Handbook* (New York, 1969), p. 193.

33. "Out of the Closets and into the Subcellar."

34. Lee Brewster, in a release from Queens, August 1970.

35. "Drag Queens to Form Their Own Organization," GAY, December 1, 1969.

36. "Drag Queens Picket Broadway," DRAG, No. 1, p. 13.

37. Angela Douglas (Key), in a letter to the author, autumn 1970.

38. Angela Douglas (Key): "Transvestite & Transsexual Liberation," *Come Out!*, September–October 1970.

39. "Who Likes Drags?", *Philadelphia Gay Liberation Front–Newsletter*, August 9, 1970.

40. Guy Nassberg: "An Introduction to Gay Liberation," in *Gay Flames*'s "Gay Liberation Packet," November 1970.

41. "3rd World Gay Revolution Platform," *Gay Flames*, No. 7.

42. Bob Martin: "Under the Groves," *Gay Power*, No. 8.

43. Ian Edelstein: "Gay Youth Liberation," *Come Out!*, June–July 1970.

44. Mark Segal, on "Homosexual News," WBAI (New York), October 13, 1970.

45. Martha Shelley: "Report: Chicago Gay Lib," *Come Out!*, June–July 1970.

46. Henry Wiemhoff, in a questionnaire returned to the author, September 1970.

47. Lars Bjornson: "Experts Frozen Out at FREE Convention," *The Advocate*, November 11–24, 1970.

48. Erik Larsson: "Radicals Split Directions of Mid-Western Conference," GAY, November 23, 1970.

49. Ibid.

50. "Around the Nation," *Gay Flames*, No. 6.

51. "Chaos Marks Panther Meet," *The Advocate*, December 23–January 5, 1971.

52. "Statement by the Black Panther Party on the Feeble Attempt of the Pigs of the Power Structure to Crush the Revolutionary People's Constitutional Convention," *The Black Panther*, December 5, 1970.

53. Ron V., Giles K., and Allen Y.: "Gay Tribes Come Together in the Nation's Capital," *Gay Flames*, No. 8.

54. As told to the author by Earl Galvin, taped January 3, 1971.

55. Laurie Zoloth: "Come to Cuba," *Plain Dealer* (Philadelphia), June 4, 1970.

56. Earl Galvin: "Letter from Cuba," *Come Out!*, December 1970–January 1971.

57. Ibid.

58. Zoloth: "Come to Cuba."

59. Ibid.

60. "¡Soy maricón, y me gusta!", *Gay Flames*, No. 3.

61. As told to the author by Earl Galvin, taped January 3, 1971.

62. Lois Hart: "Community Center," *Come Out!*, November 14, 1969.

63. "Gay Community Center," mimeographed by the collective, late 1970

CHAPTER 11

1. "Refreshing Visit" (editorial), *The Advocate*, October 28–November 10, 1970.

2. Ken Burdick, in a report to the author, December 1970.

3. "The Liberators" (editorial), QQ, Summer 1970, p. 5.

4. Tom Briggs: "What Price Gay Freedom?", *The Advocate,* August 19–September 1, 1970.

5. "GLF Spurs U. of Mich. Controversy," GAY, July 13, 1970.

6. Vance Packard: *The Naked Society* (New York, 1965), p. 42. (Pamphlet footnote 3.)

7. Jerry Rosenberg: *The Death of Privacy* (New York, 1969), p. 44. (Pamphlet footnote 4.)

8. Alan Westin: "The Career Killers," *Playboy,* June 1970, p. 233. (Pamphlet footnote 5.)

9. Packard: *The Naked Society,* pp. 53–6. (Pamplet footnote 8.)

10. "Homo Broadcaster Wants His Job Back," *Gay Scene,* No. 1. (Pamphlet footnote 10.)

11. *Gay Power,* No. 8. (Pamphlet footnote 15.)

12. Richy Aunateau, in a report to the author, December 1970.

13. Marsha Kranes: "The Gay People Have a Gripe: Fight Homosexual Question in Suffolk Job Blank," *Long Island Press* (Jamaica), September 10, 1970.

14. Adele Leonard, in a letter to Jim Owles, July 9, 1970.

15. Kranes: "The Gay People Have a Gripe: Fight Homosexual Question in Suffolk Job Blank."

16. "The Rockefeller Five and Gay Protest," *Newsletter* of Daughters of Bilitis/New York, September 1970.

17. Arthur Bell, on "Homosexual News," WBAI (New York), August 14, 1970.

18. As reported by WCBS-TV News, 6:00 p.m., August 5, 1970.

19. Cary Yurman: "GAA Protests Rocky's Silence," GAY, August 24, 1970.

20. Ibid.

CHAPTER 12

1. Randy Wicker: "The Wicker Basket," GAY, October 26, 1970.

2. "Lindsay and Wife Zapped by Gay Activists," GAY, November 23, 1970.

3. Charlotte Curtis: "Cultural Gala: Diamonds and Pickets," *The New York Times,* October 30, 1970.

4. "Mayor Lindsay at the Opera" (editorial), GAY, October 12, 1970.

5. "Lindsay and Wife Zapped by Gay Activists."

6. "John Lindsay: Our Friend?" (editorial), GAY, November 23, 1970.

7. Dick Leitsch: "The Strong Arm of the Law," GAY, October 12, 1970.

8. Kay Tobin: "Police Commissioner Howard Leary Meets with GAA," GAY, August 17, 1970.

9. "NYC Deputy Mayor Meets Gay Spokesmen," GAY, November 9, 1970.

10. Arthur Bell, on "Homosexual News," WBAI (New York), August 14, 1970.

11. "Vast Outpouring of Political Support," GAY, November 9, 1970.

12. Ibid.

13. Arthur Bell: "Candidates Uphold Gay Rights," *Village Voice,* October 29, 1970.

14. Arthur Bell, on "Homosexual News."

15. Richard Wandel: "Rockefeller Ignorant of Sodomy," GAY, October 26, 1970.

16. "U.S. Senate Candidates Support Homosexual: Ottinger & Goodell Make Statements," GAY, November 9, 1970.

17. "Vast Outpouring of Political Support."

18. "Provincetown Council Denies Permit," GAY, July 13, 1970.

19. "Gay Groups March on Provincetown," GAY, July 27, 1970.

20. " 'Gay Is Love' in Provincetown Parade," GAY, October 12, 1970.

21. Harold Fairbanks: "Many New Movies a Little Gay, Like 'Dorian Gray,' " *The Advocate*, November 25–December 8, 1970.

22. Carl Driver: " 'Medical Center' Treats Gay in Sensible, Mature Manner," *The Advocate*, October 28–November 10, 1970.

23. "Bar in N.Y. 'Liberated' by Gay Kiss-in," *The Advocate*, November 11–24, 1970.

24. Randolfe Wicker: "The Wicker Basket," GAY, November 23, 1970.

25. "Cornell GLF Forces Ithaca Bar to Serve Gays," *The Advocate*, November 25–December 8, 1970.

26. Joseph Epstein: "Homo/Hetero: The Struggle for Sexual Identity," *Harper's*, September 1970, pp. 42, 43, 51.

27. Randolfe Wicker: "The Wicker Basket," GAY, November 9, 1970.

28. Leo Skir: "Breakfast at Harper's: An Inside View of a Sit-In," GAY, November 23, 1970.

29. Arthur Bell, in a letter to the author, December 4, 1970.

30. From the "Dick Cavett Show," ABC-TV, November 27, 1970.

31. "Mattachine Forms Action Corps," GAY, September 7, 1970.

32. Bernard Lewis and Martha Shelley: "Let a Hundred Flowers Bloom," *Come Out!*, September–October 1970.

33. Bob Stanl: "Homophile Homefront," *Mattachine Midwest Newsletter* (Chicago), October 1970.

34. Dennis Altman: "One Man's Gay Liberation," *Come Out!*, December 1970–January 1971.

CHAPTER 13

1. Douglas Key: "Gay Liberation News Roundup," *Los Angeles Free Press*, February 13, 1970.

2. "Gay Groups Win: Signs Come Down at Barney's Beanery," *The Advocate*, April 29–May 12, 1970.

3. Troy Perry, in a letter reprinted in *In Unity* (magazine of the Metropolitan Community Church, L.A.), April 1970.

4. "Gay Groups Win. Signs Come Down at Barney's Beanery."

5. John Francis Hunter: "The Lord Is My Shepherd and He Knows I'm Gay!", GAY, March 29, 1970.

6. "Hope for the Homosexual," TIME, July 13, 1970.

7. Rob Cole: "Just Call It Metropolitan Community Church U.S.A.," *The Advocate*, March 29, 1970.

8. Ibid.

9. Hunter: "The Lord Is My Shepherd and He Knows I'm Gay!"

10. "Troy Perry on Virginia Graham Show," GAY, September 28, 1970.

11. Troy Perry: "The Pastor Speaks: Dr. King and the Homosexual Community," *In Unity*, May 1970.

12. "Maurer on Sexuality," *mpls free* (from FREE), May 12, 1970.

13. "First D.C. Gay Church Service Held," *The Advocate*, October 28–November 10, 1970.

14. Lige Clarke and Jack Nichols, in their "Homosexual Citizen" column, *Screw*, October 26, 1970.

15. "Catholic Hate Trip," *Gay Power*, No. 13.
16. Don Jackson: "$90,000,000,000 Demand," *San Francisco Free Press*, Vol. 1, No. 9.
17. "Gay 'Pope' Steps Up Campaign," GAY, April 20, 1970.
18. Leo Laurence: " 'Embrace Us!' Gay Lib Tells Unitokeners," *Berkeley Barb*, October 9–15, 1970.
19. "Two L.A. Girls Attempt First Legal Gay Marriage," *The Advocate*, July 8–21, 1970.
20. "Clerk Wants Tighter Law Against Gay Marriages," *The Advocate*, June 24–July 7, 1970.
21. Jack Baker: "Everything You Wanted to Know About FREE (But Were Afraid to Ask)," *Pro/Con* (Minneapolis), January 1971.
22. Jack Baker, in a letter to the author, October 21, 1970.
23. "Two Men Apply for Marriage License," GAY, June 15, 1970.
24. "Gay Librarian Wins Court Case," GAY, October 12, 1970.
25. Ibid.
26. "Librarians Ask McConnell Case Probe," *The Advocate*, November 11–24, 1970.
27. Lars Bjornson: "Judge Nixes Marriage Bid," *The Advocate*, December 9–22, 1970.
28. Ibid.
29. "British Females Marry," *Gay Scene*, No. 4.
30. Eric Pianin: "Hearing Held on Women's Bid to Wed," *Louisville Times*, November 12, 1970.
31. Stan MacDonald: "Two Women Tell Court Why They Would Marry," Louisville *Courier-Journal*, November 12, 1970.
32. Ralph Hall: "The Church, State & Homosexuality: A Radical Analysis," *Gay Power*, No. 14.
33. Martin Dennison III: "All That's Gay Does Not Glitter or We Have a Lunatic Fringe, Too," *Gay Power*, No. 4.
34. John Jones: "A Homosexual Christian Faces His Problem," *Concern* (published by PURSUIT for the Southern California Council on Religion and the Homophile, L.A.), June 1969.
35. Franklin Kameny: "Gay Is Good," in *The Same Sex: An Appraisal of Homosexuality* (Philadelphia, 1969), pp. 131–2.
36. "Question Man: Is Marriage Between Men All Right? By O'Hara," reprinted by permission of the San Francisco Chronicle and Chronicle Syndicate in *The Advocate*, August 5–18, 1970.
37. "Anglican Minister Backs Gay Weddings," GAY, June 8, 1970.
38. "Homosexual Marriages Defended by U.N. Aide," *The New York Times*, August 11, 1970.
39. "Vatican Aide Condemns Homosexual Marriages," *The New York Times*, July 26, 1970.
40. Nancy Tucker: "Nixon Nixes Same-Sex Marriages," *The Advocate*, September 2–15, 1970.
41. "Gay Marriage Counseling," *The WSDG Newsletter* (West Side Discussion Group, New York), November 1970.
42. Randolfe Wicker: "The Wicker Basket," GAY, August 31, 1970.
43. René Guyon: *The Ethics of Sexual Acts* (New York, 1948), pp. 270–1.
44. Thomas Szasz: *The Manufacture of Madness* (New York, 1970), pp. 173, 174, 175–6.
45. "GLF and Women's Lib Zap Shrinks," GAY, June 8, 1970.
46. "A Much Needed Zap" (editorial), GAY, June 1, 1970.

47. Gary Alinder: "Gay Liberation Meets the Shrinks," *Come Out!*, April–May 1970.

48. "GLF and Women's Lib Zap Shrinks."

49. Step May: "Offing the Shrinks," *Come Out!*, September–October 1970.

50. "Mattachine Vice-Pres. Addresses Nurses," GAY, August 17, 1970.

51. "Milne on Panel," *Mattachine Times* (New York), August 1970

52. "Mattachine Vice-Pres. Addresses Nurses."

53. "Psychologists Get Gay Lib 'Therapy,'" *The Advocate*, November 11–24, 1970.

54. Tony DeRosa: "Los Angeles Gays Invade Psychologists Conference: 'Guinea Pigs' Rise Up in Protest," GAY, December 7, 1970.

CHAPTER 14

1. Donovan Bess: "Homosexual Call for Militancy," *San Francisco Chronicle*, August 12, 1970.

2. "No Support for Thorp 'Violence' Speech, Kight Says," *The Advocate*, September 16–29, 1970.

3. Dennis Altman: "A Young Australian Speaks His Mind About Gay Liberation," *Vector*, October 1970, p. 38.

4. From Charles Thorp's "Keynote Speech for the National Student Gay Liberation Front Conference."

5. Altman: "A Young Australian Speaks His Mind About Gay Liberation."

6. Jonathan Black: "A Happy Birthday for Gay Liberation," *Village Voice*, July 2, 1970.

7. Larry Powell: "The Declining Family: The New Morality and the Homophile," *Concern* (published by PURSUIT for the Southern California Council on Religion and the Homophile, L.A.), February 1967.

8. Edmund White, in an unpublished essay, "The Gay Philosopher."

9. Nick Benton: "Gay Is the Most," *Gay Sunshine*, October 1970.

10. Sue Katz: "Some Thought After a Gay Woman's Lib Meeting," *Come Out!*, December 1970–January 1971.

11. Craig Schoonmaker, in a letter to the author, November 4, 1970.

12. Suzannah Lessard: "Gay Is Good for Us All," *The Washington Monthly*, December 1970, p. 49.

13. Jim Kepner: "Angles on the News: NACHO in Future-Shock," *The Advocate*, September 30–October 13, 1970.

14. Dick Leitsch: "N.A.C.H.O. '70—San Francisco," *Mattachine Times* (New York), September 1970.

15. Jim Rankin: "NACHO Upside Down," *Gay Sunshine*, October 1970.

16. "Brown Urges Gays Join with Other Minorities," *The Advocate*, September 30–October 13, 1970.

17. Lessard: "Gay Is Good for Us All," p. 47.

18. From a leaflet sent out by *HI!* to various gay organizations (1970).

19. From a leaflet distributed to recruit members for *HI!* (1970).

20. William McAllister: "A California County Fumes as Homosexuals Talk of a Take-over," *Wall Street Journal*, October 27, 1970.

21. Jim Kepner, in a memo to the author, November 23, 1970.

22. "A Gay 'Nation' in the Sierras?", *The Advocate*, November 11–24, 1970.

23. "The Great Gay Conspiracy," *San Francisco Examiner*, October 18, 1970.

24. Don Collins: "Topic of the Day in Alpine: Homosexuals," *The Advocate*, November 25–December 8, 1970.

25. Don Collins: " 'Gay Nationalism' in the High Sierras," GAY, December 7, 1970.

26. "California, Gay Mecca No. 1," TIME, November 2, 1970.

27. George Draper: "Minister's Challenge to Gay Takeover," *San Francisco Chronicle*, October 27, 1970.

28. "Preacher Out to Stop Alpine," *The Advocate*, November 25–December 8, 1970.

29. Collins: "Topic of the Day in Alpine: Homosexuals."

30. "Boodle of the Queen Bobbles a Drive for County Takeover," *Alpine Beacon*, November 1970.

31. Jack Welter: "Alpine Freeze May Upset Gay Lib Plan," *San Francisco Examiner*, October 22, 1970.

32. "Committees Formed in Alpine County to Deal with Gays," *The Advocate*, December 9–22, 1970.

33. "Bear Valley Hoping It Can Outvote Gays," *The Advocate*, December 9–22, 1970.

34. Antony Grey: "Sex, Morality & Happiness," *Concern* (published by PURSUIT for the Southern California Council on Religion and the Homophile, L.A.), June 1968.

35. "Stonewall," *Gay Flames*, No. 7.

36. "A Gay 'Nation' in the Sierras?"

37. "Berkeley GLF Opts Out," *The Advocate*, November 25–December 8, 1970; "San Francisco GLF Affirms Alpine Support," *The Advocate*, December 9–22, 1970.

38. Jim Kepner, in a memo to the author, November 24, 1970.

39. " 'Circle the Wagons!' " (editorial), *The Advocate*, November 11–24, 1970.

40. "California, Gay Mecca No. 1."

CHAPTER 15

1. Leo Skir: "The Road That Is Known," *Evergreen*, September 1970, p. 16.

2. Ibid.

3. "Gay Holiday," *New York Hymnal* (Homophile Youth Movement), January 1970.

4. Jonathan Black: "A Happy Birthday for Gay Liberation," *Village Voice*, July 2, 1970.

5. Ibid.

6. Angelo d'Arcangelo: "The Limp Arm of the Law," GAY, August 24, 1970.

7. Black: "A Happy Birthday for Gay Liberation."

8. Bob Kohler: "Clap Your Hands Miss Thing! Clap for Us All!", *Gay Power*, No. 20.

9. "After Gay Pride Day," *Mattachine Times* (New York), August 1970.

10. Nora Sayre: "New York's Gay-in," *New Statesman* (London), July 17, 1970, p. 53.

11. Black: "A Happy Birthday for Gay Liberation."

12. "Parade," *The New Yorker*, July 11, 1970, p. 40.

13. Jason Gould: "Out of the Closets and into the Streets," GAY, July 20, 1970.

14. Sayre: "New York's Gay-in," p. 53.

15. "Parade," p. 20.

16. Robert Liechti: "Of the Day That Was and the Glory of It," *Gay Scene*, No. 3.

17. "Love's Coming of Age: June 28, 1970" (editorial), GAY, July 20, 1970.

18. "Parade," p. 20.

19. Gould: "Out of the Closets and into the Streets."

20. Two lesbians: "Christopher Street Liberation Day," *Come Out!*, September–October 1970.

21. Perry Brass: "We Did It!", *Come Out!*, September–October 1970.

22. Gould: "Out of the Closets and into the Streets."

23. Cary Yurman: "We Broke the World's Kissing Record!", GAY, August 3, 1970.

24. "Love's Coming of Age: June 28, 1970."

25. John LeRoy: "Toward a New Morality: The Challenge of Gay Liberation," GAY, July 27, 1970.

26. Liechti: "Of the Day That Was and the Glory of It."

27. Sayre: "New York's Gay-in," p. 54.

28. "Gay Pride," TIME, July 13, 1970.

29. Charles Costa: "Latin Americans Celebrate Gay Liberation," GAY, August 17, 1970.

30. Michael Holm, in a letter to the author, August 1970.

31. Lee Heflin: "The Great Parade: Christopher Street West," gay lib supplement of the *Los Angeles Free Press*, August 14, 1970.

32. "Christopher West Pin Brings Lewdness Bust," *The Advocate*, July 22–August 4, 1970.

33. "Gay Pride."